This major new addition to Cambridge Studies in Modern Economic History analyses the economic policies of the Attlee government, both international and domestic, in the light of Labour's ideas and doctrines about the economy.

Jim Tomlinson highlights the concern of the government with issues of industrial efficiency, and how this concern pervaded all areas of economic policy. He focuses on the economic aspects of the creation of the welfare state, and how efficiency concerns led to a great deal of austerity in the design of welfare provision. In addition, Tomlinson offers detailed discussion of the labour market in this period, both the attempts to 'plan' that market and the tensions in the policies created by attempts to attract more women into paid work.

Students, professional historians and even politicians will greatly benefit from this broad-based reappraisal of a crucial era.

Cambridge Studies in Modern Economic History 3

Democratic socialism and economic policy
The Attlee years, 1945–1951

Cambridge Studies in Modern Economic History

Cambridge Studies in Modern Economic History is a major new initiative in economic history publishing, and a flagship series for Cambridge University Press in an area of scholarly activity in which it has long been active. Books in this series will primarily be concerned with the history of economic performance, output and productivity, assessing the characteristics, causes and consequences of economic growth (and stagnation) in the western world. This range of enquiry, rather than any one methodological or analytic approach, will be the defining characteristic of volumes in the series.

The first titles in the series are:

Democratic socialism and economic policy

The Attlee years, 1945–1951

Jim Tomlinson

CAMBRIDGE
UNIVERSITY PRESS

Published by the Press Syndicate of the University of Cambridge
The Pitt Building, Trumpington Street, Cambridge CB2 IRP
40 West 20th Street, New York, NY 10011-4211, USA
10 Stamford Road, Oakleigh, Melbourne 3166, Australia

First published 1997

Printed in Great Britain at the University Press, Cambridge

A catalogue record for this book is available from the British Library

Library of Congress cataloguing in publication data
Tomlinson, Jim.
  Democratic socialism and economic policy: the Attlee years,
1945–51 / Jim Tomlinson.
      p.   cm. – (Cambridge Studies in Modern Economic History; 3)
  Includes bibliographical references and index.
  ISBN 0 521 55095 5 (hbk)
    1. Great Britain – Economic policy – 1945– 2. Great Britain –
Economic conditions – 1945–1993. 3. Labour Party (Great Britain) –
History – 20th century. 4. Socialism – Great Britain – History – 20th
century. I. Title. II. Series.
HC256.5.T66 1997
338.941 – dc20   96–14040   CIP

ISBN 0 521 55095 5 hardback

wv

To my mother and father

Contents

Tables

Acknowledgements

This book was written without the benefit of research funding from external resources, but has been much helped by the recognition by Brunel University's Economics Department that historical research cannot be conducted sitting in front of a computer screen in Uxbridge.

Over the years many people have offered helpful comments on aspects of the Attlee government's policies, including Martin Francis, Lewis Johnman, John Kent, Helen Mercer, Neil Rollings, Rodney Lowe, Noel Whiteside and Ina Zweiniger-Bargielowska.

Two people have been especially important. I have worked with Nick Tiratsoo over a number of years and his knowledge of sources and his sceptical enthusiasm for understanding the Attlee government have both been invaluable. Last but not least, Sir Alex Cairncross, whose own *Years of Recovery* is the foundation of serious scholarly studies of the period, has been a key figure. In a serious sense this is a 'post-Cairncross' work, building on and attempting to go beyond what he wrote.

Thanks are due to the following archivists for permission to quote from sources in their charge: Stephen Bird for Labour Party records, Henry Gillett for the records of the Bank of England, and the Copyright Officer at the PRO for the Public Records. I am grateful to J. W. Piercy for permission to cite the papers of the first Baron Piercy. I am pleased to acknowledge permission from the University of Chicago Press to use material which first appeared in *The Journal of British Studies*, and to Oxford University Press for material which first appeared in *Twentieth Century British History*. Some of the material in chapter 4 first appeared in *The Economic History Review*.

Abbreviations

AACP	Anglo-American Council on Productivity
BEC	British Employers Confederation
BIM	British Institute of Management
BLPS	British Library of Political and Economic Science
CEPS	Central Economic Planning Staff
CIC	Capital Issues Committee
DSIR	Department of Scientific and Industrial Research
EPB	Economic Planning Board
ETU	Electrical Trades Union
FBI	Federation of British Industries
FCI	Finance Corporation for Industry
FSP	For Socialism and Peace
GDFCF	Gross Domestic Fixed Capital Formation
GDP	Gross Domestic Product
GNP	Gross National Product
ICFC	Industrial and Commercial Finance Corporation
ILO	International Labour Organisation
IMF	International Monetary Fund
ITO	International Trade Organisation
JPC	Joint Production Committee
LNSO	Labour and the New Social Order
LPA	Labour Party Archive
LPACR	*Labour Party Annual Conference Report*
LRC	Labour Representation Committee
NCB	National Coal Board
NEC	National Executive Committee
NIB	National Investment Board
NIC	National Investment Council
NIH	National Institute of Houseworkers
NJAC	National Joint Advisory Council
NPACI	National Production Advisory Council for Industry
NUM	National Union of Mineworkers

OEEC	Organisation for European Economic Co-operation
OR	Operational Research
PEP	Political and Economic Planning
PP	Parliamentary Papers
PRO	Public Records Office
SDF	Social Democratic Federation
SRU	Special Research Unit
TA	Trade Association
TWI	Training Within Industry
UNRRA	United Nations Relief and Rehabilitation Administration
WCC	Women's Consultative Committee

1 Introduction: Labour and the economy 1900–1945

Introduction

The Labour government of 1945–51 had to confront unprecedented economic problems, especially problems of the balance of payments, whilst at the same time attempting major reforms of the economy. How this task was managed, and the political and economic tensions it created, is the major theme of this book. Much recent writing has focused on the extent of consensus (benign or malignant according to taste) underlying policy in the 1940s.[1] In contrast, this book concentrates on the relation between policy in this period and specifically Labour (or democratic socialist) ideas. The key concern is the interaction between such ideas and the constraints of actual policy-making.

The purpose of this introductory chapter is to put Labour's approach to the economy in 1945–51 into a longer-term perspective, by looking at the broad developments of its economic policy from the party's foundation (as the Labour Representation Committee) in 1900. The concluding chapter will, in similar vein, look at the *political* assumptions involved in economic policy-making in 1945–51 in the light of Labour's approach to politics.

A recent author has described the Labour leadership of the late 1920s as assuming 'evolutionary change and the Webbian "inevitability of gradualness"': socialism would not murder capitalism but emerge from it. For them social justice and economic efficiency through organisation,

---

[1] Proponents of the benign consensus include P. Addison, *The Road to 1945* (1975) and P. Hennessy, *Never Again: Britain 1945–51* (1992). The 'malignant' approach is most evident in two books by C. Barnett, *The Audit of War* (1986) and *The Lost Victory* (1995), though these books are explicitly driven by a desire to shape current events rather than by normal scholarly standards. For discussion of the extent of consensus see, for example, K. Jefferys, 'British Politics and Social Policy during the Second World War', *Historical Journal* 30 (1987), pp. 123–44; N. Tiratsoo (ed.), *The Attlee Years* (1991). For a survey R. Lowe, 'The Second World War, Consensus, and the Foundation of the Welfare State', *Twentieth Century British History* 1 (1990), pp. 152–82. On the importance of ideology, M. Francis, 'Economics and Ethics: The Nature of Labour's Socialism, 1945–51', *Twentieth Century British History* 6 (1995), pp. 220–43.

co-ordination, and application of science were the hallmarks of the modern world'.[2] This quotation aptly summarises much of Labour's approach to the economy, extending both before and after the 1920s. On the one hand, 'social justice and economic efficiency' is probably the best one-line description of Labour's general approach to policy-making through most of its history;[3] on the other hand, the idea that socialism would emerge, in evolutionary fashion, from capitalism equally helps us understand much of Labour thinking, though this evolutionism was, to an extent discussed further below, challenged in the 1930s by the evident failure of capitalism to continue 'evolving' in the expected direction.

In looking at the development of Labour's approach to the economy in this light, I have divided the period 1900–45, in conventional fashion, into three: from 1900 to 1918; from 1918 to 1931; and from 1931 to 1945.

From 1900 to 1918

From its foundation in 1900 until 1918 the Labour Party was a body whose programmatic and policy-making side was extremely underdeveloped. As is well known, the basis for the foundation of a distinct Labour Party was the desire to represent the interests of the working class better, where that representation was seen as being a process of giving voice to a distinct social group, rather than as involving a distinct policy programme.[4] In its early years, most adherents to the party recognised that too large an effort to forge a programme would only emphasise differences and create dissension. As one union leader put it at the 1903 conference of the LRC, 'wherever parties trusted to programmes they were very hard up. Programmes wrecked parties. Let this conference stick to principles.'[5]

With the founding of the Labour Party in 1906 this stance shifted only a little. In 1907 the annual conference rejected the idea of writing a socialist 'objective' into its constitution, but the following year this decision was reversed (albeit by only 514,000 votes to 469,000), but at

---

[2] P. Williamson, *National Crisis and National Government: British Politics, the Economy and Empire, 1926–1932* (Cambridge, 1992), p. 37.

[3] In order to emphasise the priorities of the 1945–51 period we might want to reverse this to 'economic efficiency and social justice'. See, especially, chs. 4, 11 and 12 below.

[4] K. D. Brown (ed.), *The First Labour Party 1906–14* (1985), Introduction; D. Howell, *British Workers and the Independent Labour Party 1885–1906* (Manchester, 1983), chs. 15, 16.

[5] *3rd Conference of the LRC*, Feb. 1903, p. 36.

the same time the conference rejected common ownership as a *programme*.[6]

The point is not that Labour at this time had no policies, but that by and large these were *ad hoc* responses to current events. For example, at what appears to be the first ever conference of MPs and candidates to discuss policy, in 1904, a whole range of areas was identified: trade union legislation (i.e. reversal of the Taff Vale decision); opposition to indentured labour in the Transvaal; taxation of the 'unearned increment', especially on urban land; opposition to tariffs; support for universal suffrage; opposition to sectarian education; calls for expansion of workers' compensation; support for temperance; nationalisation of the railways; and support for the general use of the referendum.[7]

To stress the *ad hoc* nature of these policy decisions is not to dispute that behind them lay some general ideals and ideas. Above all, the defeat of poverty by the introduction of the 'national minimum' was central. The idea here was that by political action Labour would raise the standards of all to those they hoped would be achieved by the well-organised workers by means of collective bargaining.[8] But the primary aim of Labour was not to draw on this general purpose to provide 'a programme so much as a propaganda of ideas and principles, setting the various items in a conception of social necessity and human justice'.[9]

All this seems to highlight the great difference between the pre-1918 Labour Party and its later forms. It was highly self-consciously not a socialist but a Labour Party. Partly because of this, and partly because it did not anticipate forming a parliamentary majority in the near future, it did not have a 'programme', i.e. a comprehensive platform of related policy measures, or the administrative structure to generate and sustain such a programme. It did have policies, but these were primarily formulated as tactical responses to particular situations, or as general principles for propaganda purposes.

Despite the lack of a programme, Labour in this period developed certain attitudes and approaches to the economy which were to have long-term consequences. In summary terms, we may say that in this early period Labour drew heavily on the ILP for its 'ethical socialism',

---

[6] *LPACR* (1907), pp. 51–3, 60; *LPACR* (1908), pp. 57–9, 64, 76–7.

[7] BLPES R (COLL) MISC 196, *Infancy of the Labour Party*, vol. I, *Conference of Members and Candidates, April 1904* (1904).

[8] J. Harris, 'Political Values and the Debate on State Welfare, 1940–45' in H. L. Smith (ed.), *War and Social Change* (Manchester, 1986), pp. 250–4.

[9] BLPES (COLL) MISC 196, *Infancy of the Labour Party*, vol. II, *The Labour Party, Report of a Sub-Committee on Policy* (n.d., but 1906).

on the SDF for a mechanistic Marxism, but predominantly on the Fabians for most of its policy thinking.[10]

Labour and Fabian approaches to economic policy in this period can only be understood in the context of the pre-eminence of the 'social question', focused on the interrelationship of the issues of poverty and unemployment. The domestic politics of Britain from the 1880s down to 1914 can plausibly be characterised as dominated by the emergence, consolidation and mutation of this question.[11]

As already noted, discussion of policy in the Labour Party asserted the reduction of poverty as the central goal. The remedies suggested for this were threefold: (i) support from 'palliatives', for example infant feeding; (ii) anti-sweating measures, for example, Trade Boards in industries where unions were absent; and (iii) nationalisation, as a means of depriving monopolies of their capacity for raising prices.[12]

A number of points may be made about this agenda. It does link poverty with what today would be called economic and industrial issues, but in its own peculiar way. The agenda was not one of 'managing' the economy, but of establishing a national minimum of income levels plus an anti-monopoly policy. The former would force private firms to pay higher wages. A key assumption here is that low wages are the result of inefficiency, but also that low wages *cause* inefficiency. The poorly-fed worker, in ill health and ill-educated, provides a poor basis for industrial efficiency, as much, in a wider context, as a poor basis for military defence of the empire. In this view 'social policy' had a quite particular relation to the economy – not a burden on economic performance, but a positive contribution to that performance.[13]

Also important in this general approach was the idea that nationalisation would be aimed neither at superseding competition nor at conquering the economy's commanding heights. Rather, the aim was

---

[10] This undoubtedly is to oversimplify a complex story of convergences and divergences of these different groups, and to neglect the role of the unions and the TUC in influencing Labour's positions. On these issues see J. Callaghan, *Socialism in Britain since 1884* (Oxford, 1990), chs. 4, 5; R. E. Dowse, *Left in the Centre: The ILP 1893–1940* (1966), ch. 1; K. O. Morgan, *Keir Hardie: Radical and Socialist* (1975), esp. ch. 16; H. Collins, 'The Marxism of the S.D.P.' in A. Briggs and J. Saville (eds.), *Essays in Labour History* (Oxford, 1971), pp. 47–69; A. M. McBriar, *Fabian Socialism and English Politics 1884–1918* (Cambridge, 1962), esp. chs. 10–13.

[11] J. Harris, *Unemployment and Politics: A Study in English Social Policy 1886–1914* (Oxford, 1972).

[12] *Labour Party, Report of a Sub-Committee on Policy.*

[13] This was, of course the great theme of the 'Efficients', to whom key Fabian figures attached themselves. See A. Friedberg, *The Weary Titan: Britain and the Experience of Relative Decline, 1895–1905* (Princeton, 1988), pp. 86–8; G. R. Searle, *The Quest for National Efficiency* (Oxford, 1971); S. Webb, *Twentieth Century Politics: A Policy of National Efficiency*, Fabian Tract 108 (1901).

to redress a maldistribution of income and a source of inefficiency brought about by monopoly and the rise of the 'trusts'. This growth of monopoly was generally regarded in Labour circles (and here Marxist influences converged with Fabian) as an evolutionary trend which *in principle* reflected the growth of efficiency.

This position is put forcibly in the first collection of *Fabian Essays* (1889). Clarke, author of the major piece on industry in that collection, wrote: 'The combination can be shown to be the most economical and efficient methods of organising production and exchange. They check waste, encourage machinery, dismiss useless labour, facilitate transport, steady prices and raise profits – i.e. they best effect the objects of trade from a capitalist's point of view.' The aim of socialists, then, should not be to break up these combinations but to 'absorb and administer them'. The owners of these monopolies had become functionless parasites, extracting a rent, which could be abolished by nationalisation, which would simultaneously allow the full flowering of the productive potential of these enterprises.[14]

This position was common on the left in this period, gaining support from many Liberals as well as socialists.[15] It was powerfully argued by the Webbs in their *Problems of Modern Industry*. Like Clarke and so many others, the Webbs had no doubt that the trusts represented an evolutionary triumph of the efficient over the inefficient: 'the advent of the Trust almost necessarily implies an improvement in industrial organisation, measured that is to say, by the diminution of the efforts and sacrifices involved in production'. What is needed, therefore, is the public regulation or ownership of the trusts, combined with the national minimum. In this way efficiency in all senses will be secured.[16]

This approach involved no critique of industrial organisation. This was not a problem, due to the evolution of the trust. Collectivism involves embracing the outcome of the survival of the fittest. This attitude also underpinned Fabian enthusiasm for the industrial *manager* (as opposed to owner) and the lack of enthusiasm for worker management. Freed from the encumbrance of the parasite capitalist, the expert manager would be freed of any interest but that of efficiency and the public good. The problem of efficiency would then be solved by capitalism; the tides of history in this area, as in others, were on Labour's side.

[14] W. Clarke, 'The Basis of Socialism: Industrial' in B. Shaw et al., *Fabian Essays in Socialism 1889* (1948 edition), pp. 87, 92, 95.
[15] e.g. J. A. Hobson, *The Evolution of Modern Capitalism* (1894); H. W. Macrosty, *Trusts and the State* (1901) and *The Trust Movement in Great Britain* (1907).
[16] S. and B. Webb, *Problems of Modern Industry* (1902), pp. xxi–xxvii.

As suggested, this position entailed 'social welfare' in the sense of the national minimum as part of that evolutionary trend towards increased efficiency. At the same time it was envisaged that this greater efficiency would make available the revenues for other measures for the relief of poverty. This is a point that needs to be handled with some care. The question of the state's role in social welfare was a controversial one in Labour circles at this time. Many trade unionists and Labour supporters saw such provision as undermining collective bargaining and involving undemocratic state control. But gradually support for reform as legislated for by the Liberals after 1906 increased, though many regarded these reforms as both inadequate in scope and undemocratic in administration.[17]

Finally, on this pre-war period, it is important to note Labour's attitude to the unemployment issue. Labour focused on three aspects of this problem. First, partly because of a strong belief in technological unemployment, there were proposals for restrictions on child labour and a reduction in working hours. Second, there was advocacy of public relief works as a *palliative*, not fundamental, measure. Third, and usually linked to such works, was the call for the Right to Work. The last of these was Labour's main concern, based on the idea that the claim for such a right would expose a basic weakness of capitalism – its inability to provide jobs for all. The Right to Work was much more a principle to be propagandised than the basis of a programme of action. When it was embodied in draft legislation it was aptly described as 'a peroration put into the language of a statute'.[18]

Labour before 1914 had an agenda of 'social justice and economic efficiency' of a very specific kind, as outlined above. The war was to lead to a fundamental reshaping of Labour's political strategy, but to have a much more ambiguous impact on the broad thrust of its economic and social thinking.

The roots of the shift in Labour's political strategy have been explored in detail by authors such as Winter and McKibbin, and led to the major reform of party structure embodied in the 1918 constitution.[19] Here the

---

[17] On Labour's pre-1914 attitude to the budget and taxation, see P. Snowden, *A Few Hints to Lloyd George: Where is the Money to Come From?* (1909); P. Thane, 'The Working Class and State "Welfare" in Britain, 1880–1914', *Historical Journal* 27 (1984), pp. 877–900.

[18] K. D. Brown, *Labour and Unemployment 1900–1914* (Newton Abbott, 1971). The quotation is from p. 117.

[19] J. M. Winter, 'Arthur Henderson, the Russian Revolution, and the Reconstruction of the Labour Party', *Historical Journal* 15 (1973), pp. 753–73; J. M. Winter, *Socialism and the Challenge of War* (1974); R. McKibbin, *The Evolution of the Labour Party 1910–1924* (Oxford, 1974), pp. 91–106.

concern is not with these structural changes but the accompanying programmatic changes, embodied in the document, largely written by Sidney Webb, and accepted by the 1918 conference, called *Labour and the New Social Order*.

LNSO began by stating that Labour aimed not at tinkering but at a reconstruction of 'society itself'. This new society would be built on the basis of four pillars – universal enforcement of the national minimum; democratic control of industry; a revolution in national finance; and surplus wealth for the common good. The national minimum proposal reasserted the pre-war elements of minima of leisure, health, education and subsistence, but linked them to the problem of demobilisation and the threat to employment as the war ended.

Similarly, the sectors on national finance and surplus wealth basically adapted old pre-war themes into new post-war circumstances. Together, these sections emphasised that the costs of the war should be borne by the rich, and that in the longer run this revenue would be added to by the programme of municipalisation and nationalisation. In line with pre-war views, private ownership was attacked as involving 'a perpetual private mortgage upon the annual product of the nation'.[20] But nationalisation was not just a redistributive issue, and this is where the shift in Labour's thinking is of most interest.

The demand for democratic control of industry was singled out as Labour's most distinctive proposal – the gradual elimination of private ownership. The embodiment of public ownership in Clause IV of Labour's new constitution is the best known consequence of the new strategy of 1918, but in the current context what is of interest is the reasons given for advocating public ownership. As noted above, this principle went back almost to the beginnings of the Labour Party, but *LNSO* struck a new note in making the case:

And the Labour Party refuses absolutely to believe that the British people will permanently tolerate any reconstruction or perpetuation of the disorganisation, waste and inefficiency involved in the abandonment of British industry to a jostling around of separate private employers ... What the nation needs is undoubtedly a great bound onwards in its aggregate productivity. But this cannot be secured merely by pressing the manual workers to more strenuous toil, or even by encouraging the Captains of Industry to a less wasteful organisation of their several enterprises on a profit-making basis. What the Labour Party looks to is a genuinely scientific re-organisation of the nation's industry no longer deflected by individual profiteering, on the basis of Common Ownership of the Means of Production.[21]

[20] *Labour and the New Social Order* (1918), p. 19.
[21] Ibid., pp. 11–12.

This emphasis on the *inefficiency* of private ownership was reaffirmed in the discussion of the more immediate sectors to be taken over by the state. In the case of electricity, for example, this was underpinned by an argument to become very typical in Labour's case for nationalisation: that only public ownership could ensure that potential economies of scale were properly exploited: 'Even in the largest cities we still "peddle" our electricity on a contemptibly small scale. What is called for, immediately after the war, is the erection of a score of gigantic "super power stations" which could generate, at incredibly cheap rates, enough electricity for the use of every industrial establishment and every private household in Great Britain.'[22]

The shift in Labour's perceptions suggested by *LNSO* should not be exaggerated. Its 'productionist' orientation was not universally admired, as shown by, for example, the divided response to a speech by Ramsay MacDonald at the 1918 Labour Party conference proposing a resolution on 'the need for increased production'. In part, no doubt, this 'productionism' was a war-induced, short-term posture. But equally it was not just that. There was a sense in which the war was revelatory about British industry and this did bring an important change of perception, especially, perhaps, amongst Labour's theorists. As the Webbs argued in 1920:

it was one of the unexpected discoveries of government during the Great War that the system of capitalist profit-making, as a method of producing commodities and services, habitually fell so enormously short of the maximum efficiency of which it was capable . . . We had, most of us, not realised that this competitive rivalry, where it existed uninformed and unrestrained, involved incidentally an extraordinary wasteful organisation, or rather lack of organisation of the means of production, distribution and exchange on which the community depends.[23]

This recognition of inefficiency led them to propose a 'Standing Committee on Productivity' as part of the reorganisation of government, to aid all industries to conduct themselves more efficiently.[24]

However, this recognition of industrial inefficiency was largely restricted to *competitive* private industry. Trusts and amalgamations were still regarded as productively-efficient, though with a rather more qualified tone than in pre-war eulogies.

---

[22] Ibid., p. 15.
[23] *LPACR* (June 1918), pp. 44–6.
[24] S. and B. Webb, *A Constitution for the Socialist Commonwealth of Great Britain* (1920), pp. 324, 328–30.

We need not ignore the industrial advantages of these successive concentrations, with their production of standardised articles on the most gigantic scale, and their progressive elimination of unnecessary costs. But in them it is clear, the world loses a great deal of the industrial initiative, the personal risk, and the freedom of enterprise with which the capitalist system started, and by which it achieved its greatest triumphs. What is more serious is that the consumer loses that security against excess of price over cost; that guarantee of variety and quality; and even that assurance of abundance which free competition was assumed to afford him.[25]

Although there remained ambiguities in the Webbs' view of the relationship between ownership and industrial efficiency, what is important is that they now opened up a 'second front' of attack on private ownership. It could now be condemned as inefficient as well as exploitative: 'All the facts of modern industry prove conclusively that the competitive management of property invested in industrial enterprise, and its management in detail by individual owners, leads to hopeless inefficiency.'[26]

This critique of private sector inefficiency brought the Webbs, and to a degree Labour in general, closer to notions of industrial efficiency commonplace in the later twentieth century – involving issues of scale economies, technical development, managerial competence, etc. – and away from the 'national efficiency' framework of the pre-war years. It also linked to other parts of their analysis, notably the question of technical and managerial roles. This had two facets. On the one hand the Webbs saw the rise of the salaried 'brain worker' in the industrial enterprise as exposing the purely rentier, parasitic character of most private owners. On the other hand, these brain workers, this *nouvelle couche sociale*, are the basis for an alternative system of industrial organisation. These industrial brain workers would make possible a more efficient industry, because they were professionals, on a par with the doctor, the architect or the engineer.[27]

In sum, for the Webbs and many in the Labour movement, the First World War had exposed unexpected weaknesses in industrial organisation and efficiency, which grated with the evolutionism so evident in pre-war discussions. It no longer seemed so clear that socialism could be built on top of a technically efficient capitalism. The programmatic results of this exposure of the weakness of capitalism were a new boldness behind claims for public ownership, now necessary for efficiency

[25] S. and B. Webb, *The Decay of Capitalist Civilisation* (1923), p. 18.
[26] Ibid., p. 117.
[27] Ibid., p. 124; S. Webb, *The Works Manager Today* (1917), pp. 2–6.

as well as to end exploitation. There was also talk of the supersession of private competition by 'planning', though that registered more an accelerated loss of faith in the benefits of competition rather than a coherent alternative and positive approach to regulating the economy.[28]

1918 to 1931

In the 1920s Labour made its first tentative moves from a party of propaganda and protest to one of programmes and power. But a feature of the party in this decade was the insulation of those who gained some measure of power for Labour, the leadership of the party, from the theorists and producers of programmes. Despite the proliferation of policy advisory committees under the 1918 constitution, many of these quickly faded away and economic policy-making soon became highly concentrated in the hands of the leadership. This meant, above all, in the hands of Philip Snowden, not only Labour's Chancellor in 1924 and 1929–31, but also its chief economic 'theorist' throughout this period.

Snowden's position on the economy can be seen in a number of lights. Partly, it reflected a profound anti-intellectualism in much of Labour's hierarchy, perhaps especially in Snowden himself, which made them all suspicious of 'theorists' of any kind, but especially those with innovative ideas.[29] This attitude in turn partly reflected Labour's overall strategy in the 1920s – 'MacDonaldism' focused on gaining Labour legitimacy precisely by the presentation of a respectable, orthodox line which assumed that Labour would be judged by an electorate distrustful of radical change and innovation, but equally that what change was occurring was moving in Labour's direction. Williamson notes of the 1929 government that it 'had innocent notions about progress and of an imminent, emerging consensus on social justice and state regulation' and this is broadly true of the approach of the leadership to politics right through the 1920s.[30]

The continuing hold of evolutionism amongst the leadership was reflected in the approach to the economy. Whilst the 1918 programme had been based on the assumption of a restoration of prewar prosperity, this proved not to be the case after the collapse of the short-lived 1919–20 boom. This raised a major dilemma for Snowden. The assumption had been that as capitalism evolved it would generate both the revenues

---

[28] A. Oldfield, 'The Labour Party and Planning – 1934, or 1918?', *Bulletin of the Society for the Study of Labour History* 25 (1972), pp. 41–55.

[29] D. Tanner, *Political Change and the Labour Party 1900–18* (Cambridge, 1990), pp. 436, 439–40.

[30] Williamson, *National Crisis*, p. 536.

for financing social reform at the same time as the evident parasitism of the capitalist would increase the political possibility of raising that revenue by high taxation of the rich. But in the 1920s British capitalism proved inefficient, and it seemed logical therefore to restrict reforms until prosperity was restored.[31]

Most obviously this attitude led to a high degree of budgetary orthodoxy in Labour thinking. The context of this in the 1920s was, of course, the huge budget deficits of the war and the consequent multiplication of the national debt. At first Snowden supported the idea of a capital levy to reduce the debt. This fitted in with general support for budgetary orthodoxy and balanced budgets, because government borrowing meant transferring income from the poor to the rich bond holder. Before 1914 this had led to budget proposals for shifting the tax burden from indirect taxes paid by the poor to direct taxes paid by the better-off, whilst avoiding deficits. This *redistributive* case for budgetary orthodoxy became all the more powerful when the national debt was so large after 1918. But at the same time Labour was vulnerable to the argument that if it wanted to restore prosperity *direct* taxation needed to be reduced not increased. If you adopt a 'goose that lays the golden eggs' approach to financing reform you are obviously vulnerable to the charge that the goose is being strangled if the economy is evidently depressed, as it was in the 1920s. Eventually Labour retreated from the commitment to the capital levy and high direct taxation of the early 1920s to an even more orthodox budgetary stance.[32]

Labour's budgetary orthodoxy in the period down to 1931 is one of the most frequently noted and criticised features of its policy stance.[33] Some of that criticism retains its force, but its context needs to be emphasised. First, opposition to budgetary unorthodoxy was not a new feature of the 1920s but grounded in a long-standing argument about the redistributive aspects of public debt. It was summed up by Snowden: 'Government borrowing creates a *rentier* class who can live in idleness on the productive work of others.'[34] For socialists, this was the ground of debate about the fiscal system as much as any 'macro-economic' aspect, right down to the 1940s. Second, budgetary orthodoxy, as suggested above, flowed from the evolutionism of Labour's thought, the assumption that a technically efficient capitalism would yield greater and greater tax revenue for social reform without any need

[31] A. Thorpe, *The British General Election of 1931* (Oxford, 1991), p. 13.
[32] Tanner, *Political Change*, pp. 435–7.
[33] R. Skidelsky, *Politicians and the Slump: The Labour Government of 1929–31* (1970).
[34] P. Snowden, *Labour and National Finance* (1920), p. 55. This approach is crucial to Labour's cheap money policy of the 1940s. See ch. 8 below.

for borrowing. Finally, in the specific context of the 1920s, budgetary orthodoxy made sense if the depression was seen as a temporary deviation, caused by war, from the long-run upward trend of the economy, a trend which could be returned to if pre-war conditions were restored. This was the perspective that dominated Labour's policy approach in the 1920s.[35]

Much of the focus on Labour's budgetary policy in the 1920s derives from a framework which sees the party's failure to adopt Keynesianism in this period as the sign of its political and intellectual weakness.[36] This approach assumes that Keynesian solutions to the problems of the period were both available and workable, neither of which assumptions is obviously the case.[37] In addition, this framework exaggerates the conservatism of Labour in the area most usually criticised in discussion of budgetary positions – its attitude to public works. These works figured famously in the Liberals' programme for the 1929 general election *We Can Conquer Unemployment*, and received the endorsement of Keynes in his *Can Lloyd George Do It?*[38] *Labour and the Nation*, the party's position statement of 1928, was strikingly vague on such issues, and this has been commonly compared unfavourably with the detailed programme of works put forward by the Liberals.

But the approach of *Labour and the Nation* was the result of particular short-term political calculations, not the sum total of Labour's approach to economic management. In fact, as Williamson has shown, alongside this manifesto Labour prepared a detailed programme of public works which, whilst not as large as that proposed by Lloyd George, envisaged significant state borrowing to pay for a 'great emergency programme' to combat unemployment. As Williamson summarises, this programme

> was not quite so ambitious as *We Can Conquer Unemployment*, its work-schemes and finance not so detailed, and it lacked the *imprimatur* of an eminent economist. But its authors expected to enter into possession of departmental and local authority plans, and as they were not engaged in election propaganda, their stated objectives were arguably more realistic. In principle, these Labour proposals were very similar to these subsequently published by Lloyd George.[39]

If the Labour leadership's budgetary orthodoxy can be exaggerated, especially as it had developed by the end of the 1920s, there is no doubt

[35] A. Booth and M. Pack, *Employment, Capital and Economic Policy: Great Britain 1918–31* (Oxford, 1985), ch. 1.
[36] Skidelsky, *Politicians*, Conclusion.
[37] R. McKibbin, 'The Economic Policy of the Second Labour Government 1929–31', *Past and Present* 68 (1975), pp. 95–123.
[38] D. Winch, *Economics and Policy* (1972), ch. 7; J. Tomlinson, *Problems of British Economic Policy 1870–1945* (1981), ch. 5; Booth and Pack, *Employment*, pp. 48–52.
[39] Williamson, *National Crisis*, p. 40.

that for most of that decade it based its hopes for the revival of the economy on the pre-war pillars of Britain's economic policy – the gold standard, free trade and a balanced budget. The assumption was that the restoration of 'normalcy' by these means would revive the international economy and in doing so revive the features of Britain's staple export industries. Given the scale of dependence of these industries on export markets, this was an understandable if optimistic approach to adopt.[40] Only very late in the 1920s is there much sign in the leadership of either the Labour Party or the Conservatives of an appreciation that this approach was not working.[41] But in the wider arena of Labour Party politics criticism of this approach grew quickly from mid-decade.

The most important of the challenges to the Snowden–MacDonald orthodoxy came from the Independent Labour Party. The most detailed of them was the 1925 *Revolution by Reason*, which embodied neo-Keynesian proposals for an expansion of demand via a nationalised banking system coupled to a floating exchange rate. The following year another group of ILP members published *The Living Wage*, which drew much from J. A. Hobson's underconsumptionist theories to argue for a minimum wage and large-scale redistribution of income by steeply progressive taxation. Such approaches made little impact on the leadership, and the same is true of the most famous critique of Labour's policies, embodied in Oswald Mosley's unpublished Memorandum of 1930.[42]

These programmes from the ILP were, as Booth and Pack have argued, 'incisive coherent programmes with much greater realism than anything produced by contemporary academic economists'.[43] Unfortunately, they remained 'position statements', being neither subjected to close scrutiny and refinement by a wide range of expert commentators, nor providing the basis for Labour's policy formulation. Whilst the 'orthodoxy' of Snowden and MacDonald may have been subject to some exaggeration, their determination to hang on to their dominance of policy-making never wavered, so the ILP programmes were condemned perhaps even more for their implication of criticism of the leadership than for their precise content.[44]

[40] R. D. Boyce, *British Capitalism at the Crossroads* (Cambridge, 1987), chs. 1–4.
[41] On the Conservatives, see P. Williamson, ' "Safety First": Baldwin, the Conservative Party, and the 1929 General Election', *Historical Journal* 25 (1982), pp. 385–409.
[42] J. Strachey, *Revolution by Reason* (1925); these proposals were largely the work of Oswald Mosley: H. N. Brailsford et al., *The Living Wage* (1926). On Mosley's memorandum see Skidelsky, *Politicians*, ch. 8, and Skidelsky, *Oswald Mosley* (1975), chs. 9, 10.
[43] Booth and Pack, *Employment*, p. 26.
[44] Tanner, *Political Change*, p. 439.

Economic policy debate in the Labour Party in the 1920s focused upon unemployment. Because of the predominance of Keynesian attitudes in the historiography of the period, this concern has been looked at mostly in terms of the development (or lack of development) of Labour's macroeconomic policy. But unemployment also influenced Labour's attitude to industry.

In line with its general caution, Labour eschewed any strong commitment to nationalisation in its 1923 election manifesto, though in government in 1924 it did revive the idea of much greater expenditure on aiding standardisation of electricity generation, with many arguing that this could only be secured by nationalisation. Nothing directly came of this whilst Labour was in office, though it gave impetus to the pressures which eventually led to the creation of the Central Electricity Board in 1926. Here was a classic case, in Labour's view, where private enterprise seemed incapable of achieving the potential economies of scale, and where a technical and non-political case for nationalisation could have wide appeal.[45]

Nationalisation of electricity could readily be incorporated into a view which saw cheap electricity as a source of competitive strength in a revived international economy. Politically much more problematic was the question of 'rationalisation'. This was a vague term from the late 1920s, imported from Germany, with an imprecise set of meanings, but usually assumed to mean industrial concentration into larger units and the closure of obsolete capacity. The obvious difficulty for Labour was that such changes almost inevitably increased unemployment, at least in the short run.

A growing interest in rationalisation is evident in Labour (and other) circles in the late 1920s as part of the declining faith that international economic reconstruction could rebuild Britain's staple exports to their previous levels. In *Labour and the Nation* in 1928, rationalisation was urged as a solution to the 'waste and inefficiency of private ownership in industries which, whether called private or not, are essentially public in character'.[46] But, as with so much in that document, little was offered beyond vague generalisations.

The following year, in the explicit response to the Liberals' *We Can Conquer Unemployment*, the party argued that unemployment necessitated 'drastic reorganisation' of the staple export sector, but also recognised that unemployment was being caused by rationalisation of other industries. Rather than face this dilemma directly, however, the docu-

---

[45] L. Hannah, *Electricity before Nationalisation* (1979), pp. 88–9.
[46] *Labour and the Nation*, pp. 23–4.

ment offered just a broad statement emphasising the need for the state to be involved in reform of the staples, 'not by uniform measures applied to them all, but by a variety of steps designed to eliminate waste and wasteful competition, to improve and co-ordinate methods of marketing, purchase of materials, and production, and to adapt business structure to the changed economic conditions of the postwar world'.[47]

In office after 1929, Labour did pursue policies of 'rationalisation', most notably in the coal industry. The Coal Mines Reorganisation Act of 1930 embodied proposals for amalgamation of pits, alongside protection of coal market by cartels. However, it is right to say that it was the latter part of the Act which owed most to Labour thinking.[48] Perhaps more symbolic of Labour's attitudes was the initiation of the London Passenger Transport Board, a publicly owned body based on the idea that private competition in public transport was inefficient and that amalgamation under public ownership could achieve substantial economies of scale.[49] The LPTB also inaugurated the 'Morrisonian' corporation, returned to in the next section.

Rationalisation figured quite largely in the rhetoric of the 1929–31 government, but the obvious difficulty with such an approach, given the escalating unemployment of the period, was that it had to be an essentially long-run measure. In the short run rationalisation could only exacerbate the problem, and this probably explains why, despite the rhetoric, little action followed. By and large Labour in this period handed over its role in this policy to the Bank of England, whose priorities remained essentially financial rather than directly with industrial modernisation.[50]

The concern of this chapter is with the development of Labour's attitudes and approaches to the economy, not the details of its performance in office. In any event, that performance in the 1929–31 period is extensively covered in the literature.[51] Two points to be emphasised here are, first, the extent to which the Snowden–MacDonald leadership kept a tight lid on the bubbling up of opposition to their positions from within the Labour Party. The removal of this duo from the leadership, and the debacle of 1931 itself, opened up the space for a policy debate similar to that of 1918 but with rather more long-term consequences. Also to be noted is the ambivalence of Labour towards the development of capi-

---

[47] Labour Party, *Labour's Reply to Lloyd George: How to Conquer Unemployment* (1929), pp. 13, 14.
[48] M. W. Kirby, *The British Coal-Mining Industry 1870–1946* (1977), ch. 6.
[49] H. Morrison, *Socialisation and Transport* (1933).
[50] e.g. S. Tolliday, 'Steel and Rationalisation Policies, 1918–50' in B. Elbaum and W. Lazonick (eds.), *The Decline of the British Economy* (Oxford, 1987), pp. 82–108.
[51] Most recently in Thorpe, *British General Election* and Williamson, *National Crisis*.

talism. The evolutionist perspective, so strong before 1914, which saw Labour as the legatee of a dynamic if exploitative capitalism, was slowly being displaced by an acceptance that British capitalism at least had lost its dynamism, and that the socialist task was to rebuild that dynamism as a necessary precondition for achieving other goals.

1931–1945

The 1931 debacle led to a 'riot of research, policy-making and propaganda'. Policy research, in particular, was seen as a precondition for avoiding the recurrence of such events.[52] The most important document produced as a result of this bout of policy design was *For Socialism and Peace* in 1934. Whilst this document was wide-ranging, covering all Labour's main concerns from foreign policy through to the preservation of political democracy, the area which excited most interest and debate, at least down to 1935, was economic policy.[53]

The central theme of *FSP* was the need for 'a policy of full and rapid Socialist economic planning under central direction'. Crucial to this planning would be a National Investment Board, alongside the nationalisation of the Bank of England and the clearing banks. The NIB was intended to play a macroeconomic role in the determination of total investment, and a microeconomic role in determining its allocation.[54]

If reform of the financial system was central to Labour's proposals for planning in the 1930s, so planning was at the centre of Labour's programme as a whole. As Brooke points out, in the 1930s planning became 'the *lingua franca* of Labour's resurgent socialism'.[55] Planning, it should be emphasised, was about the creation of wealth not just its distribution. As Dalton wrote, in the book which summarised much of Labour's thinking in this period, planning aimed to 'release those forces which are today impoverished and frustrated by the institutions of capitalism; to abolish poverty, social inequality and the fear of war; to make our society prosperous, classless and free'.[56]

This central role for planning in Labour's programme was not just a matter of enthusiasm for a particular instrument of policy. In many ways planning symbolised the whole meaning of socialism – a conscious direction of effort aimed at communal needs, founded on a profound distrust of both competition and the market. Planning also suggested

---

[52] Thorpe, *British General Election*, p. 275; Williamson, *National Crisis*, p. 462.
[53] Booth and Pack, *Employment*, pp. 125–33; Oldfield, 'Planning'.
[54] Chapter 9 below.
[55] S. Brooke, *Labour's War* (Oxford, 1992), p. 21.
[56] H. Dalton, *Practical Socialism for Britain* (1935), p. 26.

the dominance of economic motives in Labour's socialism – the ethical socialism of the 1920s, with its evident failure to come to grips with economic realities, was displaced by planning as a practical device for reviving Britain's economic fortunes prior to the achievement of any other socialist goals.[57]

Alongside planning in Labour's programme of 1934 was nationalisation. The striking feature of the case for nationalisation argued there was its derivation from a case for industrial reorganisation (what in the 1920s would have been called rationalisation).[58] It was argued that 're-organisation from the point of view of productive efficiency' had six objectives:

(i)   the introduction of efficient methods of production;
(ii) the organised purchase of raw materials;
(iii) the establishment of collective selling agencies;
(iv) the elimination of unnecessary changes;
(v)   reasonable wages and conditions for the producers;
(vi) reasonable prices for the consumers.

In most cases, it was said, such reorganisation would require nationalisation, and the priority sectors would be, alongside banking and credit, transport, water, coal, electricity, gas, agriculture, iron and steel, shipping, shipbuilding, engineering, textiles, chemicals and insurance.

Booth and Pack are critical of this focus on nationalisation for efficiency, as inappropriate for the immediate need for reducing unemployment.[59] But in longer term perspective it does emphasise the extent to which nationalisation was by this time seen as a pragmatic, quasi-technical device to correct the failings of industry, rather than an 'ideological' objective linked to control over industry. Finally, on this issue of industrial modernisation, *FSP* accepted that the need for reorganisation went beyond those industries that were likely to come quickly into the public sector, and there was some vague talk of the need to 'enforce' such a policy. But no details of what this might involve were given.[60] Here, perhaps, we can see the development of an attitude that the private sector need not be seriously addressed as in need of reform because nationalisation would *eventually* be appropriate for almost all industries – though this view remained implicit rather than explicit in Labour's discussions in the 1930s.

---

[57] Brooke, *Labour's War*, pp. 19–20.
[58] *For Socialism and Peace* (1934), pp. 14–20.
[59] *Employment*, p. 127.
[60] *For Socialism and Peace*, p. 16.

For Socialism and Peace embodied the results of heated debate in the early 1930s on the form of nationalisation. At the end of this debate a majority of the Labour Party accepted the case for a 'Morrisonian' corporation, largely autonomous of government, run by experts, and without any direct role for workers in its management. This was a model grounded in the technocratic belief in the efficiency of large-scale organisations run by expert managers motivated by a desire for public service. In economic terms it represented a belief that efficiency springs largely from combining economies of scale and technical expertise, though Morrison himself also strongly held that public ownership would unleash an enthusiasm for production from the workers.[61]

Though the precise list of industries for nationalisation was to vary through the late 1930s and down to 1945, the emphasis on efficiency goals pursued via the public corporation as the preferred form of nationalisation was to remain the basis of the case for nationalisation down to the Attlee government. A direct line can quite readily be traced from *For Socialism and Peace* and Labour's attitude to economic policy in 1945 in respect of the commitment to planning as well as nationalisation, even if the meaning of that planning and the mechanisms of its operation remained obscure. But in respect of macroeconomic policy the strands of thinking are much more difficult to identify.

In her major work on the economic thinking of a few of Labour's intellectuals in the 1930s, Elizabeth Durbin has shown in great and fascinating detail how this group, with strong links to Labour's future Chancellor of the Exchequer, Dalton, responded to the revolution in economic thinking in the 1930s. She covers the impact of the 'imperfect competition', socialist planning, and national income revolutions, but above all the manner in which Keynesianism was incorporated into Labour's approaches to economic policy. Her conclusion is that by the outbreak of war Labour

had travelled light years in the depth and sophistication of its knowledge of British financial institutions and economic policy options since the dark days of 1931 . . . a practical programme of institutional reform had been officially adopted, which would ensure central control over the forces determining money supply, exchange rates and investment . . . Furthermore, the education of its leaders and the establishment of an informed and professional group of financial and economic experts had greatly increased the Party's competence to handle overall economic policy and its flexibility to meet new situations.[62]

---

[61] Nationalisation is discussed in detail in chapter 5.
[62] E. Durbin, *New Jerusalems: The Labour Party and the Economics of Democratic Socialism* (1985), pp. 261–2.

Whilst noting the continuing resistance to budgetary and monetary orthodoxy in *Labour's Immediate Programme* in 1937, she sees the fruition of all this effort in the statement on *Full Employment and Financial Policy* of 1944, a document seen to embody an essentially Keynesian approach to economic management.[63]

Whilst Durbin's analysis of the economic arguments of the 1930s is a model of the history of economic thought, there are problems with the generality of the conclusions which have been drawn from her work. First there is the obvious point that Keynesianism is the grid through which economic analysis and policy is assessed, so that the question at stake is certainly seen to be 'How far did Labour accept the Keynesian approach?' Yet, as Durbin's own book demonstrates, there were many other strands of economic debate in the 1930s, and some of them, e.g. on pricing policy in nationalised industries, in many ways had potentially more direct relevance to Labour's policies after 1945 than, say, the case for budget deficits.

Second, whilst Keynesian (and other) ideas undoubtedly permeated the thinking of Labour's experts in the 1930s, it is less clear how far this affected policy-making. Thus, whilst the 1944 *Full Employment and Financial Policy* did reflect the role of Keynesians in Labour's policy-making apparatus, it was widely regarded as excessively revisionist in Labour Party circles[64] and its impact on budgetary policy is much less clear, as discussed at length in chapter 10. Budgetary policy, like other economic policy, is rarely decided directly by issues of economic theory.

Third, whilst undoubtedly Keynesianism impacted on Labour's approach in the 1930s and 1940s, there remained a very strong commitment to 'planning', which, whatever its precise meaning, for most of its proponents did *not* mean Keynesian-style national income planning but something more interventionist. This was therefore something quite antithetical to the basic Keynesian idea that if appropriate macroeconomic management could ensure the full use of resources, the market could be left to ensure the efficient production and distribution of the fruits of the use of those resources. The battle between these views was to be fought in the years of the Attlee government.[65]

To put Keynesianism into perspective it is worth looking at Dalton's *Practical Socialism for Britain* of 1935, which accurately conveys the major concerns of Labour's economic policy thinking in the 1930s. In

---

[63] Ibid., pp. 262–3.
[64] Brooke, *Labour's War*, p. 263.
[65] Winch, *Economics and Policy*, Appendix: 'Keynes and the British Left in the Interwar Period', p. 358; chapters 6 and 10 below.

this book 90 pages are devoted to the socialisation of industry, 70 pages to planning, 60 pages to finance and the reform of financial institutions. Keynesian-style macro policy is little in evidence. In Douglas Jay's *The Socialist Case* two years later there is much more of an embracing of the Keynesian message, and much scepticism about the weight given in Labour's programmes to planning and nationalisation. But this remained an unorthodox and largely unheeded position before 1945. 'In general, Keynesian policies of demand management and fiscal policy were not completely accepted by socialist economists by the time the war broke out. At best Keynesian demand management would complement the planning of supply through institutional controls and public ownership', and despite further shifts by 1945 'demand management had certainly not replaced socialist planning as the dominant strain in this programme'.[66]

Labour programmatic endeavours in the 1930s and early 1940s embraced social as well as economic policy. In line with the technocratic and centralising tendencies of economic policy were similar tendencies in discussion of social security and health services. Social insurance seems to have gained support among the working class in the 1930s, partly because of the rigours of the alternatives, like means-tested benefits.[67] This household means test had been the focus of Labour's social policy arguments in the 1930s, its alternative being a national minimum guaranteed by the state. Proposals for pensions on a contributory social insurance basis were adopted in 1937 and the general principle that this form of social security was preferable to direct state finance seems to have aroused little controversy. Before the war Labour's approach to social security was rather piecemeal, but in 1942, eight months before the Beveridge plan was published, the party put forward a proposal for a comprehensive system of social security based on contributory insurance principles.[68] A major Fabian Report in 1943 stressed 'how large a measure of agreement exists between the Beveridge Report and the Fabian Plan', but this was a matter of convergence of broad principles, not Labour and the left simply adopting Beveridge.[69]

Similarly in health care: Labour had a long history of proposals to reform this area, and had, for example, been calling for the nationalis-

---

[66] Dalton, *Practical Socialism*, pp. 257–66, defends loan-financed public works against the 'Treasury view', but the budgetary implications are dealt with extremely cursorily; D. Jay, *The Socialist Case* (1937); Brooke, *Labour's War*, pp. 22, 239, 251.

[67] Harris, 'Political Values', p. 251.

[68] Brooke, *Labour's War*, pp. 146, 156–60. Note that the issue of family allowances was much more contentious for Labour, and not resolved until 1942 (ibid., pp. 149–55, 159–60).

[69] W. A. Robson (ed.), *Social Security*, 2nd edn (1943), p. 4.

ation of hospitals since before the First World War. Pressed by the Socialist Medical Association, in the 1930s the party progressively adopted many of the SMA's approaches, though again it took the war for a party policy for a comprehensive, free and universal health service to emerge.[70]

On education the party was far more divided than on the question of social security or health. Similarly, the division was between those who wanted free secondary, and especially grammar school education to be available to all, and those who wanted a single structure of 'multilateral' or comprehensive schools. In the inter-war period the former view had dominated the Labour Party, though a minority pressed the case for more radical reform. This difference was to continue right through the 1940s, with the leadership favouring retention of the grammar school but increasing numbers of Labour's educational experts favouring a comprehensive solution.[71]

In sum, as Brooke has persuasively argued, it has too commonly been accepted by historians and commentators that Labour simply embraced a consensus on social reform, largely developed elsewhere in the war years. However, whilst there was a consensus on the need for some reform of social security, health and education, the content of this reform was far from consensual: 'In health, education and social insurance, for instance, the Labour Party maintained a distinctive edge to its social policy. The party's planners viewed the reports and White Paper emanating from the coalition not as blueprints for easy appropriation, but as platforms on which to build more radical reforms.'[72]

Conclusions

It would plainly be wrong to deny that the Second World War had a significant impact on Labour Party thinking on economic and social policy. But that impact in many cases was to crystallise existing tendencies rather than bring about an abrupt change of line. The emphasis on nationalisation as a necessary condition for efficiency, on planning as vital to the maintenance of full employment, on social welfare to be provided by radical reform and the building of *national* systems of provision were all clearly established before the war. In many ways the war provided a political opportunity to assert what was already believed in by the party. This was perhaps especially the case for economic plan-

---

[70] Brooke, *Labour's War*, pp. 134–45.
[71] Ibid., pp. 112–33; R. Barker, *Education and Politics* (Oxford, 1972).
[72] Brooke, *Labour's War*, p. 110.

ning. Even an earlier sceptic like Jay argued at the end of the war that the war had shown the efficacy of such planning.[73]

The debates of the 1930s had led to a clear if broad consensus in the party, in which 'the problem of inequality was not taken any less seriously than in the past, but it was thought that it could be overcome through a planned economy rationally distributing the productive wealth'.[74] Social reform was to be built upon a healthy economy, but this prosperity was still to be achieved when Labour won its majority in 1945.

[73] D. Jay, *Change and Fortune* (1980).
[74] Brooke, *Labour's War*, p. 20.

2   Labour and the international economy I
Overall strategy

The domestic economic policies of the Attlee government can only be understood in the context of the international economic issues which the government faced, and the means by which it chose to try and resolve these. Those issues cannot be reduced simply to the immediate problem of balancing the international accounts, serious as that undoubtedly was (it is dealt with in detail in the next chapter). The government had also to deal with questions about the kind of trade and payments regime they wanted to see, a problem high on the agenda because of the very strong US commitment to a multilateral, non-discriminatory trade regime and a 'liberal' exchange regime under the auspices of the IMF. This US commitment was one that plainly could not be ignored because of the dependence of the UK on financial resources from the USA in these years of chronic 'dollar shortage'. Equally, the government had to deal with the question of the sterling area, which during the war had grown willy-nilly into a regional economic bloc, with Britain at the centre. Though not totally coterminous, the sterling area was in turn clearly linked with the empire, so policies on this issue were affected by broad considerations about the future of that empire. Finally, but not least, the existence of the sterling area raised questions about the role of sterling as an international currency, which again was not just a simple 'economic' issue but one with profound implications for Britain's actual or perceived role in the world.

This chapter focuses upon the broad strategic issues of international economic policy, whilst chapter 3 discusses more directly the macroeconomic problem of the balance of payments. This distinction is in a sense artificial as the balance of payments problem was the consequence of certain strategic constraints and choices. But given this it makes sense to look at those strategic issues before moving on to the balance of payments policies for which they provided the framework.

The American challenge

Labour's attitude to international economic relations was formed by a number of forces, some ideological, some more pragmatic.

Ideologically, the party in 1945 was strongly committed to some notion of national economic planning, even if the strength of the commitment was not always matched by the clarity of discussion of this concept (chapter 6 below). This commitment was ambiguous in relation to the international economy. It was generally accepted in wartime discussions that 'Britain has depended in the past more upon foreign trade than any other great nation' and 'We must exchange part of our products with those of other lands. Full employment and a full standard of life require full trade'.[1] These observations led to a stress on the need to *reverse* the autarkic policies of the 1930s: 'it is obvious that the barriers to trade had grown too high in the capitalist world before the war. The channels of exchange were choked and congested.' The need postwar was, therefore, to find agreement on the 'progressive and mutual reduction of tariffs and other impediments, such as import quotas, to the exchange of products between the nations joining in the Agreement'. This document also stressed the need to make 'sensible international arrangements for the management of the exchanges' and called for 'careful study' of the proposals emerging from Bretton Woods.[2]

This view flowed in part from the influence of Labour economists like Meade, Gaitskell, Durbin and Dalton. Meade, for example, was active from early in the war in promoting policies for trade liberalisation in the form of a commercial union, and in supporting Keynesian proposals for a 'Clearing Union'. In this he gained wartime support from Dalton and Gaitskell.[3] On the other hand, these views were coupled to a clear declaration that 'Socialists believe in the planning of imports and exports and the present apparatus of control – foreign exchange control, import programmes, allocation of scarce materials for the export trade – should remain in existence'. These pronouncements, replete with ideological tension about how far the international economy could be 'planned', did not amount to a clear policy. As Brooke[4] rightly remarks of the war period, 'Labour's policy was often vague and uncertain in this field (no more so, however, than that of either the government or other groups)'.

[1] Labour Party, *Full Employment and Financial Policy* (1944), p. 7.
[2] Ibid., pp. 7, 6.
[3] PRO T230/125, J. Meade, 'A Proposal for an International Commercial Union'; S. Howson, *British Monetary Policy 1945–51* (Oxford 1993), pp. 80–3, 91–4.
[4] Labour Party, *Full Employment*, p. 7; Brooke, *Labour's War*, p. 247.

Let Us Face the Future, Labour's manifesto of 1945, was almost entirely bereft of any position on international economic policy. Apart from the statement that 'The economic well-being of each nation largely depends on world-wide prosperity', the manifesto focused on domestic means for maintaining employment, coupled to mainly political declarations about the need for Britain to play a leading role in international affairs, especially through the UN.[5]

Of course, the manifesto didn't represent the sum of Labour's understanding of the international economic situation, and above all there was undoubtedly a growing recognition in the period before Labour came into power that the immediate legacy it would inherit would be dependence on US financial help.[6] It was this issue that was to bring the need for Labour to make major policy decisions on the international economy soon after its accession to office. The initial stimulus to the dollar problem was the cessation of Lend-Lease immediately on the defeat of Japan. Lend-Lease had covered over 60 per cent of Britain's £10bn. cumulative trade deficit during the war period. When this aid ended in August 1945 the new government was faced with an immediate problem of how to pay for dollar imports with a seriously depleted capacity to produce and sell goods of any kind.[7] In fact, discussions were already going on in Washington on how Britain was to deal with its post-war financial problems, including the issue of a loan to Britain. But the issue of a loan could not be isolated from the other big issues of international economic policy. First, in Article VII of the Lend-Lease agreement Britain had given an undertaking to reduce trade discrimination in the post-war period, an undertaking to be the cause of much dispute between Britain and the USA over the succeeding years. From the US point of view discussions of a loan also required a settlement of policy on post-war trade. Negotiations on this issue, and the idea of an International Trade Organisation to oversee the liberalisation of trade, were, like discussions on finance, already in train in Washington when Labour came to power. Second, Britain had already published proposals agreed with the USA for an International Monetary Fund, arising from the Bretton Woods Conference in 1944. Neither the British nor the US government had in August 1945 yet committed itself to these proposals, and they too were to be mixed up with the loan bargaining.[8]

---

[5] Labour Party, *Let Us Face the Future* in F. W. S. Craig (ed)., *British General Election Manifestos 1900–1974* (1974), pp. 123–31.

[6] Brooke, *Labour's War*, p. 247.

[7] A. Cairncross, *Years of Recovery: British Economic Policy 1945–51* (1986), pp. 4–6; on Lend-Lease see R. S. Sayers, *Financial Policy 1939–45* (1956), ch. 13.

[8] On Article VII, see Sayers, *Financial Policy*, pp. 405–13; L. Pressnell, *External Economic Policy since the War*, vol. 3, *The Post-War Financial Settlement* (1986), ch. 4.

These discussions in Washington eventually led to agreement on a US loan to Britain of $3.75bn., repayable over fifty years at 2 per cent interest, repayment to begin five years after the loan was made. A waiver of repayment could be made if the British dollar balance of payments position was so weak as to make that repayment unsustainable. In addition, Britain was granted $650m. in final settlement of Lend-Lease.

The loan was tied to a British commitment to reverse the wartime policy of strict control over the convertibility of pounds into dollars one year after the loan was ratified. This was the most explicit policy concession made by Britain in return for the loan. But the loan agreement was accompanied by a separate agreement on commercial policy which was capable of differing interpretation, but which seemed to commit Britain (and the USA) to an effort at trade liberalisation, though without any firm commitments or timetable.[9]

The period of international economic negotiation between the USA and Britain, extending from the Lend-Lease agreement of 1942 to the loan agreement of 1945, and its ratification the following year, is probably the most intensively studied topic in modern economic history. Apart from the *Collected Writings* of Keynes, who was Britain's main negotiator throughout, the matter has been analysed in great depth by a range of scholars, and no attempt will be made here to replicate that discussion.[10] Rather the concern here is to analyse the Labour government's response to the situation presented by the loan negotiations and other major issues bound up in those negotiations.

The issue came to the Cabinet in November 1945. In proposing support for the agreements Dalton, the Chancellor of the Exchequer, stressed that the loan, Bretton Woods and the ITO formed a package which would have to be accepted or rejected as a whole. He made clear his unhappiness with some of the proposals – both the terms of the loan itself, and some aspects of the Bretton Woods and financial proposals. In particular, whilst accepting the case for more stable (but not fixed) exchange rates under the IMF, Dalton was worried about the movement towards rapid convertibility. But he comforted the Cabinet with the point that convertibility was not to come immediately, and the idea of linking acceptance of Bretton Woods to a declaration that countries would not be obliged to deflate to support financial goals if this involved

[9] Pressnell, *External Economic Policy*, pp. 320–30.
[10] J. M. Keynes, *Collected Writings*, vols. XXIII–XXVII; Pressnell, *External Economic Policy*; Cairncross, *Years of Recovery*, chs. 4, 5; D. E. Moggridge, *Maynard Keynes: An Economist's Biography* (1992), chs. 26, 28–30; J. K. Horsefield, *The International Monetary Fund 1946–1965*, 3 vols. (Washington, 1969); A. van Dormel, *Bretton Woods: Birth of a Monetary System* (1978); R. N. Gardner, *Sterling–Dollar Diplomacy* (Oxford, 1956).

creating unemployment. He supported a further conference on the proposed ITO as involving no definite commitments from Britain.

Dalton's Cabinet document and the discussion which followed his statement embodied most of the economic issues raised by the agreements for the Labour Party.[11] On the specific issue of convertibility he seems to have been quite cynical, accepting that the loan was conditional on that clause, but doubtful whether Britain would be able to sustain such a policy.[12] On the broader issues he also reflected the doubts about the agreements held in the Labour Party – especially on the issue of compatibility of full employment with the liberal international regime proposed by the USA. British perceptions were consistently that the USA did not have the same commitment on the employment issue as Britain and other Commonwealth and European countries. This perception seems to have been to a degree accurate, as US negotiators in all the discussions of the 1940s tended to see the liberalisation of the world economy as primary, though believing this would maximise employment, whilst the British saw creating domestic full employment as primary, and indeed as a precondition for acceptance of liberalisation.[13]

This attitude strongly coloured attitudes to international economic policy in the late 1940s. Concern about an American slump, and a likely weak response of the US authorities to such a slump, persisted into the 1950s. But in practice the threat to full employment in this period came not from an absence of international (or indeed, domestic) demand, but from problems of supply. Given that dollar shortage was a key aspect of that problem of supply, the major threat to full employment could plausibly be said to be non-acceptance of the US conditions for a loan, and hence the danger of a drying up of the supply of dollars.[14]

Those in Cabinet opposed to the 1945 agreement emphasised the threat posed to the sterling area. Shinwell, Minister of Fuel and Power, argued that the US policy was to 'break up the Sterling Group'. This point was reiterated by the other vocal opponent, Aneurin Bevan, the Minister of Health, who went on to denounce the general policy of favouring free trade 'based on a nineteenth century attitude towards international trade, which was unlikely to find acceptance by such states as the Soviet Union'.

---

[11] PRO CAB128/4, 6 Nov. 1945, 29 Nov. 1945; CAB129/5, 'Financial Agreement with the USA', 28 Nov. 1945.

[12] Pressnell, *External Economic Policy*, p. 329.

[13] Gardner, *Sterling–Dollar Diplomacy*, esp. pp. 104–6.

[14] J. Tomlinson, *Employment Policy: The Crucial Years 1939–55* (Oxford 1987), chs. 5, 8; this was a point made by Dalton in the House of Commons debate on the loan; see discussion below.

In response, both the Chancellor and the President of the Board of Trade (Cripps) stressed that the sterling area was not a united, stable bloc and that already some of its members wanted to move away from the close wartime links with Britain. In addition, they pointed out that any concessions on imperial preference would only come about if the USA also cut tariffs and so helped British exports. They also stressed that the declared policy of the Labour Party was to make 'a sincere attempt at securing, in co-operation with other countries, a multilateral basis for world trade'. [15]

This discussion again indicated a key issue for Labour in international economic relations in this period. On the left especially, a general enthusiasm for 'planned' trade, and a dislike of being dictated to by capitalist America, was coupled to a more explicit enthusiasm for resisting US multilateralism in the name of building up the sterling area as a separate economic bloc.

This was arguably a paradoxical position for the left, with its traditional anti-imperial attitudes, as well as hostility to the idea of sterling as a world currency. But attitudes to the empire and the sterling area had been strongly affected by the war period: first, because the sterling area had emerged as a dollar-discriminating zone whose continuation was plainly vital for Britain's postwar balance of payments, at least in the short run; second, because the empire seemed to offer an alternative sphere of influence to weigh against overweening American power; and finally because of the significant contribution made by the empire to the war effort.[16] Shinwell in 1944 voiced typical sentiments from the left about the new view of the empire encouraged by the war: 'the UK should do its utmost by close co-operation and regard for the different points of view of the nations of the Commonwealth to preserve in the peace the unity of purpose and sentiment which has held them together in time of war'.[17]

This enthusiasm for empire was to have major and paradoxical results for the Labour government's policies, both in the approach to defence and directly in economic relations with empire countries. Because it was so closely related to balance of payments issues, it is taken up in detail in the next chapter.

---

[15] PRO CAB128/4, 6 Nov. 1945.
[16] Gardner, *Sterling–Dollar Diplomacy*, pp. 154–5.
[17] Cited ibid., p. 155. The impact of imperial preferences on trade were much exaggerated at the time (I. Drummond, *Imperial Economic Policy 1917–39* (1974), chs. 6, 7). Discrimination via the operation of sterling area exchange controls were much more important – see below, chapter 3.

Imperial sentiment tended to unite left and right opponents of the 1945 agreement. The government also recognised the importance of the sterling area to the immediate balance of payments of the UK, but this problem, like all others, was in their view outweighed by the immediate economic consequences of having severely to curtail dollar imports. In Cabinet Bevin, the Foreign Secretary, spoke of his unhappiness with the agreement, but opposed rejection because that would mean 'asking the British people to endure, for perhaps another three years, standards of living even lower than those to which we had been reduced at the end of the six years of war'.[18]

At the end of the Cabinet debate only two ministers – Shinwell and Bevan – voted against the agreements. The size of the Cabinet majority reflected no great enthusiasm for the deal, and concealed, as already suggested, doubts whether it could be fully realised. Nevertheless, its acceptance was guaranteed by the absence of any plausible alternative. There was some talk of asking instead for a purely commercial loan from the US, an option already in fact explored in the Washington talks. But ultimately there was no *political* alternative. Britain was part architect of the Bretton Woods agreement and the proposed ITO, and was committed to close co-operation with the USA. Rejecting the agreements would have meant a break in political relationships with the country with whom Britain had been closely co-operating for four years and with whom she wished to continue to co-operate, and this, even more than the possible economic consequences, compelled the government into acceptance.[19]

The parliamentary debate on the agreements followed in December 1945.[20] Again, as Moggridge suggests, the government offered only a weak defence of the agreements: 'It stressed Britain's need for the Loan and the importance of maintaining good Anglo-American relations, rather than the positive aspects of the Fund and the commercial policy proposals.'[21] This perhaps exaggerates a little – Dalton, for example, did offer a defence of the IMF proposals on exchange rates, stressing

---

[18] PRO CAB128/4, 6 Nov. 1945. On the accuracy of such calculations, see below, chapter 3.

[19] As P. Burnham (*The Political Economy of Postwar Reconstruction* (1990), p. 35) notes, Cabinet ministers such as Cripps and Dalton did in these discussions support the broad idea of multilateralism, but this was not the central issue in deciding the debate. A *de jure* commitment to multilateralism was unavoidable to maintain good relationships with the USA, though this was combined with a *de facto* bilateralism.

[20] *Hansard* (Commons) 1945: vol. 417, cols. 421–558, 12 Dec. 1945; cols. 641–736, 13 Dec. 1945.

[21] Moggridge, *Maynard Keynes*, pp. 815–16.

the desirability of agreed rules to govern exchange rate changes, to allow such changes under specified conditions whilst outlawing competitive devaluations as in the 1930s.[22] Nevertheless the general point remains true that the basic government line was 'there is no alternative', no alternative source of dollars, and above all no alternative political posture than alliance with the USA. It was appropriate that it was Bevin as Foreign Secretary who wound up the debate for the government, stressing the *political* issue of the American alliance as the ultimately decisive concern.[23]

This debate did not help define a clear Labour philosophy on the international economy any more than that in the Cabinet had done. Boothby from the Opposition benches taunted Labour with its attachment to a planned economy at home but 'laissez-faire' abroad.[24] Apart from Dalton's defence of the IMF rules on exchange rates, Cripps linked a broad defence of liberalism in trade with the need to eliminate 'financial, commercial and industrial practices and methods which have in the past proved themselves so fertile a seedbed for war'. If, he declared, we are internationalists, we should show it in policy. But he himself summed up the combination of internationalist rhetoric and calculated, pragmatic policy that characterised events at this time: 'We agree to the initiation of a process of bargaining, the ultimate objective of which may be looked upon as the elimination of discriminatory methods of preferences and the reduction of tariffs, but we are absolute masters as to whether we get to that objective or not.'[25]

The parliamentary debate was characterised by opposition from the left to this concession to American pressure, but an absence of a plausible alternative. Much play was made of the sterling area as an alternative trading and financial zone, but, as Keynes was to argue persuasively in the parallel debate in the House of Lords, the sterling area was no real alternative as it too was hungry for dollar goods and could not be plausibly built up into a self-sufficient entity.[26]

In the end the agreements passed the Commons, with most of the Opposition abstaining but 23 Labour MPs (and 77 others) voting against. On this basis the loan was secured. In the short run the only unambiguous commitment given in exchange for the loan was the return to convertibility, due in the summer of 1947 (one year after the loan

---

[22] *Hansard* (Commons), vol. 417, cols. 432–5, 12 Dec. 1945.
[23] Ibid.; see also speech by Evan Durbin, cols. 646–52, who stressed at the end that the key issue of the debate was maintaining the alliance with the US.
[24] Ibid., col. 465.
[25] Ibid., cols. 492–3.
[26] Moggridge, *Maynard Keynes*, p. 817.

was ratified by the US Congress). But by then the political context of debate about international economic relations had undergone a major shift.

Marshall Aid to Korean rearmament

In June 1947 with his address at Harvard, Marshall publicly signalled a shift in US perceptions of the post-war situation in Europe. On the one hand there was the consolidation of Soviet control over much of Central and Eastern Europe and a growing perception, realistic or not, of a threat of communism spreading to Western Europe.[27] Roughly in parallel with this shift of perception about the likely political settlement in Western Europe was the evident failure of the idea of a rapid movement towards a liberal economic regime in Western Europe. Whilst contemporary notions of an imminent 'collapse' of the Western European economies may have been greatly overstated, there is no doubt that a chronic dollar shortage made a rapid freeing of foreign payments wholly implausible.[28]

This latter point was graphically illustrated in the British case in the summer of 1947. The implementation of the commitment under the loan agreement to sterling convertibility led to a five-week period of accelerating reserve losses in Britain, before convertibility was suspended in August 1947. Cairncross has argued persuasively that convertibility itself only added to an underlying problem of the weak current account position of the whole sterling area, exacerbated by the flow of capital from Britain to other parts of that area.[29] The suspension of convertibility symbolised the fact that whatever might have been said or hoped by the Americans or the British previously, there was to be no rapid movement towards the Bretton Woods ideal of a liberal payments regime. The pound was to remain *de facto* inconvertible down to 1954. Fortunately from the British point of view, the changes in US strategic perceptions noted above meant that Britain's reneging on the loan agreement did not bring a crisis in US/UK relationships, as might have occurred in 1945/6 if Britain had resisted signing the agreement.

[27] Certainly the *military* threat by the Soviet Union on Western Europe seems to have been greatly exaggerated.

[28] There is now a substantial literature on the state of the Western European economies at the initiation of Marshall Aid. The key 'revisionist' text, arguing that Europe was suffering primarily from the balance of payments consequence of rapid growth is A. S. Milward, *The Reconstruction of Western Europe 1945–51* (1984); C. P. Kindleberger, *Marshall Plan Days* (Boston, 1987), ch. 14, criticises this position.

[29] Cairncross, *Years of Recovery*, ch. 6; the impact of this capital flow is discussed more fully in chapter 3 below.

The Labour government's response to the new era of US policy inaugurated by Marshall's speech was complex. On the one hand, there was recognition of the need for US aid to deal with the dollar problem, which by no means disappeared with the suspension of convertibility. On the other hand, there was strong hostility to the US emphasis on economic and political integration within the Marshall Aid proposals. The response of the government was to embrace enthusiastically the idea of Marshall Aid, whilst seeking to orchestrate a Western European response which would maintain the dominance of national governments in policy-making and limit any integrationist moves.[30]

This hostility to economic integration in Western Europe has often been pictured as a *folie de grandeur*, as Britain resisting its 'natural' home in Western Europe in the name of being a world power, especially by trying to preserve the sterling area. No doubt all sorts of illusions about Britain's role in the world were rife at this time – symbolised above all by Bevin's Middle Eastern and African obsessions[31] – but the sterling area cannot simply be reduced to such a *folie*. In a context of almost worldwide dollar shortage, coupled with large accumulations of sterling, the role of sterling looked at purely as an instrument of economic transactions was bound to be a large one. Sterling was simply available to many who had no access to dollars. In this context Britain had to balance the need to obtain US dollars under Marshall Aid, the accompanying pressure for closer co-operation with Europe, with the need to preserve the sterling area as a multinational trading zone.[32]

The idea of a customs union in Western Europe, encouraged by the Americans, and taken up especially keenly by the French, was strongly resisted by almost all Labour figures. Bevin, it is true, wavered on the issue and talked vaguely of a 'Western Union' as a desirable policy

---

[30] Burnham, *Reconstruction*, pp. 92–6; A. Danchev, *Oliver Franks, Founding Father* (Oxford, 1993), ch. 4; H. Pelling, *The Labour Governments 1945–51* (1984), ch. 10. Barnett (*Lost Victory*, pp. 378–9) argues that Britain 'wasted' the Marshall Aid counterpart funds (the sterling equivalent to Marshall Aid dollars) by spending them on debt retirement rather than investment. This is based on a simple economic misunderstanding. As counterpart was by definition in sterling, it could not be used to increase investment, which was constrained by the supply of physical (not financial) resources and dollars.

[31] J. Kent, *British Imperial Strategy and the Origins of the Cold War* (Leicester, 1994), esp. ch. 5.

[32] C. Newton, 'The Sterling Crisis of 1947 and the British Response to the Marshall Plan', *Economic History Review* 37 (1984), pp. 391–408; C. Newton, 'Britain, the Sterling Area and European Integration, 1945–50', *Journal of Imperial and Commonwealth History* 14 (1985), pp. 163–82. Curiously, Barnett (*Lost Victory*, p. 369) quotes from the Treasury paper pointing out the crucial role of the sterling area in maintaining international trade, but ignores this point in his sweeping condemnation of Britain's support for the Area; PRO T133/49 'The Sterling Area', 7 July 1948.

Table 2.1   *Geographical distribution of British trade in 1947*

(% values in 3rd quarter, 1947)

	Imports	Exports
Hard currency areas		
USA	19.5	5.6
Canada and Newfoundland	13.3	3.8
Argentina	7.9	3.3
Other Latin American countries	2.7	2.7
Sweden, Switzerland and Portugal	3.5	5.4
Total	46.9	20.8
Soft currency areas		
Sterling area	30.4	49.9
Europe, other than above	19.7	23.4
Rest of world	3.1	5.8
Total	53.1	79.1

Source: Board of Trade Journal 154 (21 Jan. 1948), p. 171.

goal.[33] But the economic departments were unanimous in their hostility to such a union.

This hostility was partly founded on the belief that economic links with Western Europe were relatively small in comparison with those of other continents. For example, it was calculated in 1947 that under 25 per cent of British exports went to European countries and their colonies, and under 20 per cent of British exports came from them (table 2.1). In this view Europe was only one of Britain's concerns, and by no means the pre-eminent one. Oliver Franks, Britain's ambassador to the US, was told to convey the British view of the customs union idea to the Americans in the following terms:

In Summary, the principal objective of our policy is to reconcile our position as a world power, as a member of the British Commonwealth, and as a member of the European Community. We believe that we can effect this reconciliation, but that if we are to do so, we cannot accept obligations in relation to Western Europe which would prevent or restrict the implementation of our responsibilities elsewhere.[34]

[33] G. Warner, 'The Labour Governments and the Unity of Western Europe, 1945–51' in R. Ovendale (ed.), *The Foreign Policy of the British Labour Governments 1945–51* (Leicester, 1984), pp. 61–82; see also PRO FO371/62552, Hall Patch to Bevin, 7 Aug. 1947. For a highly critical view of Labour's policies on European integration, see E. Dell, *The Schuman Plan and the Abdication of British Leadership in Europe* (Oxford, 1995).

[34] PRO CAB129/37, 'Proposals for the Unification of Europe', 25 Oct. 1949, Annex.

The judgement on the customs union was, then, fundamentally a political one, though bolstered by economic argument. However, this distinction, as always, was messier than a simple dichotomy. Several of the briefing documents on this issue *accepted* the standard economic case for a customs union, that in the long run it would bring about a more competitive and hence more productive environment.[35] However they also stressed the short-term disruptions and difficulties of any movement in this direction. It would also seem to be the case that many officials and politicians saw the logic of international trade as suggesting union with areas of complementary rather than competitive forms of economic activity. This attitude was neatly summed up by Cripps when he argued that 'The principal value of any arrangement we might enter into with Western Europe lay in the Colonial resources which this might make available to us'.[36] The idea that Western Europe would be the dynamic source of growth of *markets* for British goods, perhaps not surprisingly, occurred to few people at this time.

Also central to the rejection of the idea of the customs union was the idea of 'economic sovereignty' – that Britain should retain control of the levers of economic policy. Hence in the major position paper on the customs union in this period, it was laid down that Britain would accept no proposals which involved:

(a) loss of governmental responsibility for credit and budgetary policy or loss of reserves;
(b) hindrance to British attempts to earn dollars;
(c) any European influence on the size of British dollar-earning or dollar-saving industries;
(d) any undermining of the system of imperial preference.[37]

With these positions in mind, Britain's attitude to the Customs Union proposals was to regard them as an example of US ill-informed enthusiasm for abstractions, coupled with French opportunism. But given the need to get dollars, the public position was generally one of 'talks without commitment', though by 1949 it was decided to make clear many of the points of objection discussed above, which had previously only been made in private.[38]

The policies which eventually emerged from this conundrum of wanting the dollars whilst resisting a key policy aim of the USA were by

---

[35] e.g. PRO PREM8/1146 European Economic Co-operation Committee 'European Customs Union', 7 Sept. 1948; ibid., 'Customs Union, Interim Report of Interdepartmental Study Group', 6 Nov. 1947.

[36] PRO PREM8/1146, Economic Policy Committee, Minutes, 7 Nov. 1947.

[37] PRO CAB129/37 'Proposals for the Unification of Europe', 25 Oct. 1949.

[38] See generally PRO PREM8/1146, 'Customs Union' Pts I and II, 1947–50; FO371/62552, 'Customs Union with Western Europe', 1947.

no means clear-cut. The government conceded to US pressure for a liberalisation of OEEC trade in 1949, partly as a counter-proposal to the US pressure for greater convertibility of European currencies. Policy thus edged towards liberalisation within Western Europe (as well as the sterling area) whilst continuing to hold on to discrimination against the dollar.[39]

This was not an easy policy to pursue. The USA still regarded movement towards non-discrimination in trade as an important policy goal, and stressed that the agreement to restore non-convertibility of the pound in 1947 had not changed this stance. This pressure was very evident at the Geneva trade negotiations of 1947, where there was talk of the UK's attachment to discrimination, especially in the sterling area, threatening receipt of Marshall Aid.[40]

Whilst in private both civil servants and politicians expressed serious doubts about US policy objectives, in public the overriding aim to maintain the US alliance led to verbal commitments to multilateralism. However, the USA became increasingly frustrated by the gap between British liberal rhetoric and the continued use of tight controls and discrimination. The British stance was shifted in relation to Western Europe, as noted above, when the alternative seemed to threaten even worse. But it was here, as elsewhere, a story of Britain responding to US pressures on the basis of an overriding commitment to the Atlantic Alliance, but never giving more than was deemed politically inescapable to maintain that alliance. This is not to say that the British rhetorical commitment to multilateralism was cynical, only that Cabinet ministers were adamant that whilst the imbalance of trade with the US continued 'non-discrimination is nonsense'.[41]

Discussion of these issues usually remained at a fairly pragmatic level – commonly a calculation of what the USA could be persuaded to put up with as British response to its initiatives. But the continuing dollar problems in 1949, even when Marshall Aid started to be received, seem to have provoked some broader speculations.

In July 1949 Cripps (by then Chancellor of the Exchequer) set out two ways of dealing with the continuing dollar problem. One was the 'two-world' option of accepting and strengthening two currency blocs around the dollar and the pound. This was rejected as 'I do not believe that we have at present the resources or reserves to forge a third inde-

---

[39] e.g. PRO CAB128/15, 30 May 1949; PREM8/1412, S.E.V. Luke to Attlee, 18 Jan. 1950; Burnham, *Reconstruction*, pp. 106–7.

[40] PRO CAB129/21, S. Cripps, 'The Tariff Negotiations in Geneva', 24 Sept. 1947.

[41] PRO CAB129/36, H. Wilson, 'The Future of Multinational Economic Co-operation', 12 Sept. 1949.

pendent economic area, let alone any strategic area between the Russians and the Americans'. The only alternative, he opined, was 'one-
world', with concessions on domestic policy to make this viable. This
choice, he suggested, had effectively been made earlier in the postwar
period 'and we must follow that choice while yet trying to guard our
own policies against the effect of our close association with a powerful
and partly free capitalist economy in the USA'. Cripps made this choice
more palatable by suggesting that the philosophy of a post-New-Deal
USA was not as divergent from that of Britain as often alleged by critics
of the USA.[42]

The issue of what economic concessions could be wrung out of the
USA without threatening the Atlantic Alliance was very important in the
discussion surrounding devaluation of the pound from \$4.03 to \$2.80 in
September 1949. Politically it was deemed important *not* to be seen
'offering' devaluation to the USA as a bargaining counter for concessions on their part. This would expose the government to domestic
criticism for bowing to the USA. On the other hand, by telling the US
of the decision to devalue at the Washington talks just prior to the
devaluation, the British created the climate for quite substantial US concessions on tariffs around the American economy and on increasing US
investment abroad – both important in trying to make dollars more
freely available to the rest of the world.[43] This devaluation may also
have helped to reduce US criticism of the 'restrictivist' aspects of British
policy as it showed a willingness to let the price mechanism be used to
try and correct the payments position.

The devaluation of 1949 cannot be seen only in terms of Anglo-
American relations.[44] Whilst there had been persistent encouragement
by the Americans of such a change in the parity of the pound from the
end of the war, this had been resisted on the British side because of a
belief that with a basically supply-constrained economy, the early
devaluation of the pound would simply turn the terms of trade in an
adverse direction without significant correction of the balance of payments. When the crisis blew up in the summer of 1949 this argument
was undercut by growing evidence of the uncompetitiveness of British
goods in US markets. The US recession of 1949 also shifted the economic context of the debate, by exposing the fragility of the British (and

---

[42] PRO CAB134/222, S. Cripps, 'The Dollar Situation', 4 July 1949.
[43] Cairncross, *Years of Recovery*, p. 186.
[44] Devaluation is dealt with in detail in Cairncross, *Years of Recovery*, ch. 7; B. Eichengreen
and A. Cairncross, *Sterling in Decline* (Oxford, 1983), ch. 4. There is a very full set of
PRO papers on this issue in T269/1–5.

other European economies') dollar-earning position. Eventually there occurred a loss of confidence in the pound which made devaluation inescapable.

However, devaluation was not, of course, just a matter of changing economic circumstances. It was linked to arguments about 'confidence', which, as in 1931 (or 1967), were to fuse the economic issues with the highly political. Much opposition to devaluation came from those advisers to the government who wanted to present the evident loss of confidence in the pound as a judgement on the whole conduct of economic policy, and therefore argued that a major change in domestic policy and not devaluation was the real answer. Above all, this meant, in the view of such critics, a tougher anti-inflationary stance pursued by tighter fiscal and monetary policy. As it was generally agreed in these same circles that taxation was already too high, the tightening of fiscal policy implied significant cuts in public expenditure (see the discussion in chapter 12).[45]

Cobbold, the Governor of the Bank of England, took a similar if more extreme line: 'the two things which would really change the atmosphere in North America and make it more possible for the USA and Canada to help in dealing with fundamental problems, as they are anxious to do, would be a real attack on Government expenditure and a deferment of further nationalisation plans'. Cobbold went as far as to say that he would 'refuse to make any attempts to restrict credit or raise interest rates if there was going to be no reduction in Government expenditure'.[46]

However, unlike in 1931, specific cuts in public expenditure were not accepted by the government as necessary to restore confidence. A general exhortation to economy was made, but an attempt by officials to write explicit commitments on cuts into the ministerial brief for the Washington conference was rejected by ministers.[47]

Some limited cuts in public spending were made after the devaluation, and this fed into the whole debate about welfare spending that troubled the government's last years in office (chapter 11). But the devaluation did not result in a wholesale shift in domestic economic policy; the bogy of 'confidence' did not have the force of earlier or later

---

[45] PRO T269/1, E. Bridges to Chancellor of the Exchequer, 18 June 1949; ibid., E. Bridges to Attlee, 23 July 1949; T269/2, B. Gilbert, 'The Burden of Government Expenditure', 25 June 1949.

[46] PRO T269/1, Cobbold to Bridges, 14 July 1949; W. Eady to Bridges, 24 July 1949.

[47] PRO T269/3, 'Draft Brief for Ministerial Talks in Washington' para. 13 was deleted from the final version at CAB129/36.

crises of the pound under Labour governments, partly because of the tightness of exchange control, and partly because of the unity and determination of the government.

The crisis surrounding devaluation in 1949 was succeeded in 1951 by the crisis following from the scale of rearmament Britain committed herself to in response to the Korean War which began in June 1950, especially as that process of rearmament involved large increases in imports of raw materials at rapidly rising prices. Britain hoped to offset the balance of payments costs of rearmament in significant part from American military aid, but this did not prove forthcoming.[48]

The scale of Britain's rearmament effort represented in large part a political posture. Britain shared the US perception that the Korean invasion was part of a Soviet-inspired expansionist programme. The government was therefore anxious to demonstrate Britain's capacity to act as a great power in its own right, though accepting the indispensable role of the USA as the West's greatest military power.[49]

The scale of the rearmament programme envisaged in 1950/1 was unsustainable in an economy already close to full employment. The attempt to squeeze more out of the economy led to battles over public expenditure, notably on the NHS, although the actual sums involved (£13m. in health spending of about £400m.) suggest the battle was highly symbolic of the political tensions in the Cabinet rather than in itself terribly significant.[50] Unusually in this period, the Left in the Cabinet proved perceptive about the economic situation, when they argued that the rearmament programme was not only unwise but infeasible, because of shortages of raw materials and machine tools.[51] So it proved.

Paradoxically, however, the flow of dollars into Europe begun under Marshall Aid, but continuing thereafter on a much larger scale, did what the Labour government had always argued was a precondition of international economic liberalisation – made dollars freely available in the rest of the world. Hence as the dollar shortage evaporated in the 1950s, so the process of liberalisation accelerated.[52]

The willingness to make concessions to US policy apparent in the late 1940s was not evidence of a wholesale subordination of British policy to US designs. The concessions which were made fell far short of a wholesale 'liberalisation' of the economy, with exchange control and trade

[48] Cairncross, *Years of Recovery*, pp. 214–25.
[49] Burnham, *Reconstruction*, pp. 151, 160–1. Compare Cairncross, *Years of Recovery*, pp. 232–3.
[50] On the public expenditure aspect see chs. 11 and 12 below.
[51] PRO CAB128/18, 25 July 1950; CAB128/19, 15 Jan. 1951, 9 April 1951.
[52] The other key precondition of acceptance of liberalisation especially in Britain was, of course, continuing full employment.

controls still widely used, even prior to the tightening of controls evident at the time of Korea. At that date only 18 per cent of non-dollar imports were subject to no controls ('Open General Licences') and all dollar-goods were subject to restriction.[53]

The clear limits on Britain's willingness to concede to US pressure where this resistance fell short of leading to an open breach is particularly evident in the Marshall Aid context. As already noted, Britain enthusiastically embraced the notion of such dollar aid, whilst resisting the integrationist aspects which the USA wished to make part of the deal. Britain quite successfully pursued its policy of 'more cash and less strings'.[54]

A similar story can be told about other aspects of policy which the USA wished to exert constraints over in return for its help. For example, the USA wanted to have a clause in the Marshall Aid agreements giving the American authorities a say in whether aid recipients had a 'valid rate of exchange'. This was strongly resisted by the Labour government, so that the final agreement said only that Britain would 'use its best endeavours . . . to stabilise its currency, establish or maintain a valid rate of exchange, create or maintain internal financial stability and generally restore or maintain confidence in its monetary system'.[55]

Similarly, the US pressure for a policy of balanced budgets was offset by an interpretative minute in the agreement saying that this pronouncement did not preclude short-run deficits as part of a planned policy of balance over a number of years.[56] What can be said for economic policy was true on the political and strategic front. Frank Allaun at the 1950 Labour conference suggested that the price paid for Marshall Aid included Britain's involvement in the Korean War: 'I have no objection to Marshall Aid, but I object to the price we are being asked to pay for it, which is to fight America's wars for her.'[57] In fact, as noted above, the decision to commit recklessly large amounts of resources to that war was an attempt to demonstrate Britain's independent strength, not a bowing to US pressure.

Principles and policies

The complexity of the international economic (and political) environment in the late 1940s makes it perhaps unsurprising that the government found it difficult to come to a coherent view of appropriate

[53] J. C. R. Dow, *The Management of the British Economy 1945–60* (Cambridge 1965), pp. 154–5.
[54] Foreign Office to Oliver Franks, cited Danchev, *Oliver Franks*, p. 59.
[55] PRO T236/812, 'Marshall Plan: Bilateral Negotiations', 1948.
[56] Ibid.; fiscal policy is discussed in chapter 10.
[57] *LPACR* (1950), p. 101.

policies. Gardner[58] argued that 'National policy is rarely influenced as much by impressive blueprints for future action as by daily expedients contrived to cope with current problems'. Perhaps this point is worth re-emphasising, when so much discussion of the period is framed by the 'impressive blueprint' of Bretton Woods and the parallel US ideas for trade liberalisation.

Labour had an ambiguous relationship to those blueprints. As already discussed, their attraction to many on the left lay in their commitment to end economic restrictiveness, which most people on the British left, like many in the USA, saw as the underlying cause of the rise of expansionist right-wing regimes in the 1930s. On the other hand, the commitment to domestic economic planning, plus the realisation of Britain's immediate economic weaknesses, led to a general belief that progress on the road to liberalisation would be slow if Labour's whole domestic programme was not to be threatened.

The liberalisation programme was essentially a liberal rather than a socialist policy, in the sense of relying on a belief in the capacity of (properly regulated) market mechanisms to deliver the best possible economic outcomes. This point should not be exaggerated. For example, Bretton Woods was based on the idea of fixed, not floating, exchange rates so should not be seen as on a par with the *laissez-faire* enthusiasm for market rates of exchange of the 1960s and 1970s. Similarly the ITO was designed to establish 'rules of the game' for international trade, not to allow a complete free-for-all.[59] Nevertheless it was a regime designed to maximise international transactions and to minimise physical controls of such economic transactions.

Against this essentially liberal vision there was little opposition which carried with it a worked-out alternative picture of how the international economy might work. The most consistent opponent of this type of liberalism was Thomas Balogh, an economist allied to the Labour Party, but with no official position under the 1945 Labour government. Both at the time and subsequently he argued that the commitments made by Britain to Bretton Woods and to multilateralism reflected the attachment of its advisers to outdated economic precepts which in the conditions of the 1940s had become 'a silly anachronism'.[60]

Balogh was commonly accused of proposing as an alternative to multilateralism a restrictive bilateralism which would aim to balance

---

[58] *Sterling–Dollar Diplomacy*, p. 165.
[59] G. D. A. Macdougall, 'Britain's Foreign Trade Problem: A Reply', *Economic Journal* 58 (1948), pp. 86–98; J. Meade, 'Bretton Woods, Havana, and the UK Balance of Payments', *Lloyds Bank Review* 7 (1948), pp. 1–18.
[60] T. Balogh, *Unequal Partners*, vol. 2, *Historical Episodes* (Oxford, 1963), p. 6.

trade between every pair of countries, and which in the case of a country with Britain's trading patterns would be bound to lead to an enormous fall in total trade. In fact, Balogh explicitly repudiated this view of the choices available. Although certainly an enthusiast for controls in general (one of Meade's 'Gosplanners' – see below), Balogh's key argument was based on what he saw as the need to restore a broad economic equilibrium between Europe and the USA which, if it was to be secured on an expansionist basis, would require 'a *permanent* rechannelling of trade by discriminatory methods and complex preference arrangements' (emphasis added).[61] Britain, in his view, should in the 1940s have 'reorganised Europe under British leadership'. The meaning of this is not quite clear, but it would seem to involve the idea of expanding the sterling area to embrace Western Europe, to provide a dollar-discriminating bloc. 'The Sterling Area, though it was potentially an anomaly, could with patience and care have been used to strengthen Britain as the centre of the system, while promoting growth all round.'[62]

In some ways Balogh stated publicly evident truths that others feared to say. He was quite right that Bretton Woods was unworkable whilst the massive and almost universal dollar shortage persisted. He was right to say that multilateralism of the American type was impossible in the short run, and that, given the repudiation of deflation as a policy, trade discrimination was inescapable for the foreseeable future.

But Balogh's alternative vision of an expanded sterling area, embracing much of Western Europe, was surely unworkable in the strong sense in which he envisaged it. Eventually of course Western Europe and the sterling area did become a dollar-discriminating bloc, after the change in US policy in 1947. But Balogh seemed to suggest not only that this should be a semi-permanent arrangement, but also that it could and should be close to self-sufficiency. This latter idea was unworkable, given the great dependence of many overseas sterling area producers on the US market.[63]

Against Balogh's position it may be argued that an explicit repudiation of Bretton Woods and the liberal trade arrangements by the Labour government would have caused enormous political problems without achieving much more than was actually done, to some degree by a combination of rhetorical commitments to such arrangements and practical foot-dragging and backsliding.

Amongst the economists, Balogh found few supporters. Hubert Henderson from the right was also a sceptic about the internationalist

[61] Ibid., p. 191.
[62] Ibid., pp. 20–1; Balogh, *The Dollar Crisis: Causes and Cure* (Oxford, 1949), ch. 1.
[63] Macdougall, 'Britain's Foreign Trade', p. 90.

line, and his argument has something in common with that of Balogh. Essentially, he shared the perception that the postwar dollar balance of payments problem would be long term, and that whilst it persisted balance of payments disequilibria would render a multilateral trade regime a dead-letter. He argued that such disequilibria were not readily amenable to changes in relative prices: 'The forces of the price system are strong enough to effect small adjustments smoothly; but when the work they have to do is large, they are apt to prove clumsy, wasteful and ineffective.' The conclusion was that quantitative controls must remain a weapon of balance of payments adjustment for the foreseeable future.[64]

But such views were not typical amongst economists in the 1940s. More common were views close to those of James Meade, who was the government's chief economic adviser (as head of the Economic Section) until late 1946. Meade had been one of the originators of the idea of some institution like the ITO in the war years, and a supporter of Keynes' advocacy of an International Clearing Union, the British version of the IMF, which was displaced by the less expansionary but not wholly dissimilar 'White Plan' largely adopted at Bretton Woods. His view of international economic relations was clearly spelt out in his Diary when he first learnt of Labour's victory in 1945:

The effect of the Labour Government upon the external economic settlement will depend very largely upon whether the Liberal-Socialists or the Gosplanites win the internal struggle. If the Liberal-Socialists win out an economic settlement with the USA a la Article VII would not be impossible ... if the Gosplanites won it would seem difficult to attach much meaning to Article VII discussions, since there would be no internal system of prices and costs on which degrees of protection or discrimination could be measured.[65]

This notion of a struggle between liberal-socialists and Gosplanners was one employed by Meade in other contexts.[66] However, it is a dichotomy which tends to exaggerate the importance of economic principles to the determination of government policy in this period. If we look at the Labour discussions of international economic policy issues, it is apparent that general economic concepts played rather a limited role in decision-making.

It has already been noted that, at the time of the decision on whether to accept the US loan in 1945, the key issue was the combination of a

[64] H. Henderson, 'A Criticism of the Havana Charter', *American Economic Review* 39 (1949), pp. 605–17.
[65] J. Meade, *Collected Papers*, vol. VI, *Cabinet Office Diary 1944–46* (1990), Aug. 1945, p. 118.
[66] Below, ch. 6.

dire need for dollars and the need above all to preserve the political alliance with the USA. Little discussion involved issues of fundamental economic principle.

A further illustration of the kind of discussion which seems to have shaped policy comes from the advice given by Douglas Jay to Attlee in 1945/6. Jay consistently argued that the danger to Britain's economic position arose more from the trade agreements under the proposed ITO than from the convertibility aspect of the loan agreement. For him the key issue was the preservation of full employment, and free trade he assumed would be incompatible with that full employment. The key component of any international economic arrangement should be the acceptability of any measures necessary for a country to defend itself against deflation from elsewhere. To defend the balance of payments against such threats took precedence over any other consideration. In defending the use of trade controls Jay suggested that 'I think our experts are inclined to give too little weight to this [need for physical controls] and too much to doctrinaire inferences from free trade ideas'. This is perhaps an especially interesting comment coming from some-one very much on the right of the Labour Party, author of a seminal prewar 'revisionist' text.[67]

This absence of a clear left/right division in political discussions of international economic policy is apparent throughout the period. In 1949 a general debate on the issue of policy in this area was stimulated by a paper from Cripps which asserted that 'It should be recognised that in the management of our general balance of payments indirect measures of control must play an increasing part, primarily by anti-inflationary internal policies and a strict external financial policy'.[68]

This assertion was responded to strongly by Gaitskell (at that time Minister of Fuel and Power, soon to be Chancellor of the Exchequer). He disputed the case for further trade liberalisation in the near future, but also criticised the whole approach of Cripps' paper. He argued that physical controls were necessary as an alternative to unemployment or inflation.[69] His Cabinet statement in support of his paper is worth quoting at some length.

Monetary and budgetary weapons were not enough. He considered that the retention of quantitative import controls, exchange controls, building controls and controls in respect of certain raw materials were essential. He feared that

[67] PRO PREM8/195, Jay to Attlee, 17 Dec. 1945; Jay to Attlee, 6 Feb. 1946; Jay, *The Socialist Case*.
[68] PRO CAB134/223, S. Cripps, 'Balance of Payments 1950', 7 Dec. 1949.
[69] PRO CAB134/225, H. Gaitskell, 'Economic Planning and the Liberalisation of Trade', 7 Jan. 1950.

the liberalisation of trade, if pursued in order to ensure Marshall Aid and to secure the co-operation of various European countries might lead to the whole system of controls becoming undermined. The US administration might be urging the liberalisation of trade in order to reconcile the grant of Marshall Aid with the needs of US industries, but this should not be allowed to prejudice the planned economy of this country. The aim should be to bring OEEC back to the fundamental problem of securing a balance with the $ area and the maintenance of full employment in Europe.[70]

This position was quite consistent with Gaitskell's strong defence of the indefinite continuation of some controls over the domestic economy.[71] It also provoked a very interesting response from Cripps. He argued that one had to be on one's guard against those who thought in terms of a free rather than a planned economy. At the same time, an element of compromise was necessary from time to time if this country was to secure the benefits of Marshall Aid and the co-operation of other countries in Western Europe. He went on to spell out the advantages which had been gained from the liberalisation of trade: 'It had secured a continuance of Marshall Aid and had enabled this country to avoid an inter-European payments scheme which had been full of dangers. It had also enabled us to escape from the obligations in respect of non-discrimination which had to be accepted when the dollar loan was negotiated.'

The closest Cripps came to linking his position to any economic analysis was to suggest that the problem was how to 'retain the necessary physical controls and at the same time favour the progressive firm and stimulate efficiency'.[72] (This comment, of course, fitted well with Cripps' role as the key promoter of industrial efficiency in the Attlee government.)[73]

Gaitskell's position statement reflected a fear that the government's pragmatic policy of incremental changes to policy would lead unintentionally to the abolition of physical controls.[74] This was an accurate reflection of how policy developed: step by step rather than in response to any overall perspective.

---

[70] PRO CAB134/226, Economic Policy Committee Minutes 19 Jan. 1950.
[71] N. Rollings, 'The Reichstag System of Governing? The Attlee Government and Economic Controls' in H. Mercer et al. (eds.) *Labour Governments and Private Enterprise: The Experience of 1945–51* (Edinburgh, 1992), pp. 15–36; Rollings, 'Poor Mr. Butskell: A Short Life, Wrecked by Schizophrenia?' *Twentieth Century British History* 5 (1994) pp. 190–5.
[72] PRO CAB134/226, Economic Policy Committee Minutes, 19 Jan. 1950.
[73] See chapter 8 below.
[74] PRO CAB134/225 Gaitskell, 'Economic Planning and the Liberalisation of Trade', 7 Jan. 1950. Gaitskell disagreed with Cripps' view that competition was crucial for the efficiency of domestic producers, arguing that the problems for those producers was not so much costs as the availability of materials.

To say that there was no grand plan is not of course to say there were no consistent themes in Labour policies on the international economy. As already noted, full employment was always an issue in Labour minds, though in practice no serious threat emerged to the buoyant labour market. Secondly, there was the concern to appear to be clearly in control of policy rather than subject to foreign (US) pressure. This was an issue in relation to Marshall Aid, as previously noted. It also came up on the occasion of the Washington talks of 1949, when Bevan objected to the idea that Britain's policy on public expenditure should be a subject of international discussion. In response, Attlee stressed that 'our internal economy is a matter for ourselves alone and is not to be a factor in any bargaining'.[75]

One theme which is *not* strongly evident in all these discussions is the idea of the defence of the pound as an international currency, other than in a wholly pragmatic sense. In other words, the idea that the status of the pound as an international currency should itself be an objective of policy does not seem to have significantly informed Labour's approach. This is not to say that the point was wholly absent. In 1950 a Cripps Cabinet paper emphasised the world role of the pound, financing 36 per cent of all world visible trade, and perhaps 50 per cent of total trade, and also a major reserve currency. Cripps said he was committed to maintaining this role for the pound.[76] This position was certainly shared by the Treasury, which in a paper in 1950 asserted that, 'Regardless of the extent to which our current and future external problems may spring from the international position of sterling, it can be taken for granted that we shall not adopt abandonment of sterling as an international currency'.[77]

It would seem that this idea of the role of the pound as important in its own right survived in the 1940s, though not as central to policy debate, at least as far as the politicians were concerned. On the other hand, there is little evidence of opposition to this position, such as was to emerge in the 1950s.[78] Indeed, as already stressed, left critics of the Attlee government's policies tended to want to build up the role of the pound to provide a counter-bloc to that of the dollar. Indeed, this position tended to be supported even by members of the government once they had left office. For example Gaitskell in 1952 argued that the ster-

[75] PRO PREM8/1178 Pt I, Attlee to Bevan, 2 Sept. 1949.
[76] PRO CAB134/225, Cripps, 'EPU', 3 March 1950.
[77] PRO T232/199, Treasury Overseas Finance Division, 'Summary of Fundamentals of External Financial Policy', 10 March 1950.
[78] e.g. A. Shonfield, *British Economic Policy since the War* (1959). For a critical view of these arguments see C. R. Schenk, *Britain and the Sterling Area: From Devaluation to Convertibility in the 1950s* (1994).

ling area should be strengthened, and its activities more fully co-ordinated. This was a common position across the Labour Party in the early 1950s.[79]

Under Labour the conditions remained in place for the revival of the pound as a major reserve as well as a transactions currency in the 1950s. Sterling balances, despite all the US pressure, were not reduced, essentially so as not to offend members of the sterling area, and to encourage holding of the currency.[80] From 1951 an unintended legacy to the Conservative government was thus the ability to 're-establish sterling as a general international currency and of London as an open financial market place'.[81]

Overall, Labour's international economic policies in the 1945–51 period were formed by a combination of changing economic circumstances and pragmatic response, rather than following a coherent, predetermined path. Perhaps no such path could have been plotted, given the rapid shifts in circumstances which occurred in the period. Certainly there was little evidence of a consistent alternative being put forward, including from the Labour left. The major idea of this grouping on international economic policy was to look for a 'third way' between American capitalism and Soviet communism. But there was little economic or political basis for such a way. The economic dominance of the USA was such that, even if a political break had been made with that country, the possibility of finding satisfactory alternative partners was extremely bleak. Reflecting this, most of the left-wing opposition to the leadership's policies faded away after Marshall Aid was accepted.[82] Ideas of developing trade with the Soviet Union and Eastern Europe were put forward, but could never have substituted for the dependence on US dollars which Britain's balance of payments position involved, and in any event many on the Left quickly came to see the dangers of extensive economic reliance on the USSR.[83] The left was reduced to 'well-intentioned generalisations' which could make little headway in the crisis-ridden climate of the late 1940s.

[79] H. Gaitskell, 'The Sterling Area', *International Affairs* 28 (1952), pp. 170–6; H. Cole and M. Shanks, *Policy for the Sterling Area*, Fabian Tract 293 (1953).

[80] Pressnell, *Economic Policy*, pp. 363–6; PRO CAB21/1868, 'Sterling Area Negotiations', 1949/50.

[81] S. Strange, *Sterling and British Policy* (Oxford, 1971), p. 64; S. Blank, 'Britain: The Politics of Foreign Economic Policy, the Domestic Economy, and the Problem of Pluralistic Stagnation', *International Organization* 31 (1977), pp. 673–721. Blank would seem to exaggerate the extent to which such a position was consciously supported by the Labour government – or at least its Cabinet as opposed to officials.

[82] J. Saville, *The Politics of Continuity* (1993), p. 174.

[83] Ibid., p. 174; J. Schneer, *Labour's Conscience: The Labour Left 1945–51* (1988), pp. 87–93.

3   Labour and the international economy II
The balance of payments

Much of the economic history of the Attlee period could be written around the biennial balance of payments crises of the period. Few governments have devoted so much energy to this one policy area.[1] But the balance of payments in this period cannot be treated as a simple economic constraint, imposing inescapable policy responses. On the one hand, the balance of payments problem was not simply a matter of exporting enough to pay for necessary imports, as contemporary economic propaganda often suggested.[2] It also involved very substantial outflows for both overseas government expenditure and foreign investment. Equally, the responses to the payments problem were not preordained by the state of the economy, and the choice of those responses had a number of highly significant political as well as economic ramifications.

Given the broad context of international economic policy set out in chapter 2, the purposes of this chapter are threefold: to outline some of the complexities of the payments situation in the 1945–51 period; to discuss some of the military expenditure and foreign policy aspects of that situation, and how these were debated at this time; finally, the third section discusses one of the most politically problematic aspects of balance of payments policy in this period – its impact on the sterling area in general and the colonies in particular.

The scale of the problem

What was the balance of payments problem in this period? Clearly the legacy of the war was a huge current account deficit, with exports in 1945 at only 30 per cent of their pre-war level (imports 60 per cent), and shipping earnings substantially diminished. On capital account, around a quarter of pre-war foreign investments had been sold, and very

[1] Approximately half of Cairncross, *Years of Recovery*, is taken up with external issues, a proportion which reflects the problems of the period as seen by the government.
[2] For example, *Economic Survey for 1947*, Cmd. 7046, Parl. Papers 1946/7, paras. 66–74.

Table 3.1   *British trade and payments, 1946–50*

(£m. current prices)

	1938	1946	1947	1948	1949	1950
Exports	564	960	1,180	1,639	1,863	2,261
Imports	849	1,063	1,541	1,790	2,000	2,312
Visible trade	−285	−103	−361	−151	−137	−51
Current account	−55	−230	−381	26	−1	307
Government						
current transactions	−19	−363	−230	−87	−140	−125
Capital exports	+5	−643	−432	−447	+1	

Sources: CMD 8201 – UK Balance of Payments 1946 to 1950; *Economic Trends: Annual Supplement* 1989; 1938 from C. H. Feinstein, *National Income, Expenditure and Output of the UK, 1855–1965* (Cambridge, 1972).

large debts accumulated in the form of sterling balances. No wonder then, that at the cessation of Lend-Lease, which had until VJ day bridged the gap in the British accounts, Keynes could talk of a 'financial Dunkirk'.[3]

Whilst the problems of the overall balance of payments hardly came as a surprise (though the speed with which Lend-Lease ended did come as a shock), the dollar problem was less anticipated. For most of the 1940s the main problem from the British point of view was the dollar shortage, which was the key to the reserve position.[4]

Plainly the wartime legacy mightily constrained the policy options of the Attlee government. Any government would have been likely in such a situation to control imports, promote exports and borrow in the meantime.[5] Nevertheless, there was still considerable scope for policy to affect the situation. This is suggested clearly in table 3.1. The balance of payments problem plainly cannot be reduced to one of 'how to pay for essential imports'. A significant part of the problem was related on the one hand to the scale of government overseas expenditure (government current transactions), and on the other hand to the scale of capital

[3] A phrase first used by Keynes in July 1945, and repeated in a key paper on 'Our Overseas Financial Prospects' used in preparation for the US loan negotiations (*Collected Writings*, vol. XXIV (1979), pp. 374, 410).

[4] Pressnell, *External Economic Policy*; Cairncross, *Years of Recovery*, pp. 43–6. Recent work has emphasised the European-wide dimensions of this dollar problem, e.g. Milward, *Reconstruction*.

[5] Keynes' 'starvation corner' (as an alternative to the US loan), in his sense of radical reductions in consumption levels, was hardly a possibility on political grounds.

Table 3.2 . *Trade and payments with the dollar area*

(in £m.)

	1946	1947	1948	1949	1950
UK balance on current account	−301	−510	−252	−296	−88
Rest of sterling area balance on current account	−73	−306	−65	−54	170
Gold sales to UK by sterling area	82	84	55	68	100
Other transactions with non-dollar countries and organisations	46	−260	−95	−89	−12
Capital transactions	21	−32	−49	23	137
Gold and dollar balance	−225	−1,024	−406	−348	308

Source: Cairncross, *Years of Recovery*, p. 202.

exports. Both of these (though in different ways) were strongly connected to policy decisions taken by the Labour government, discussed in the next section.

Table 3.2 gives some details of the dollar balance. It shows that whilst the UK was in large deficit in trade with the dollar area, in most years this was added to significantly by the deficit of the rest of the sterling area. (Broadly speaking the dominions minus Canada, plus the colonies, plus a few other countries like Iraq.) Gold, which was, of course, substitutable for dollars, was obtainable on a limited scale from South Africa by trade within the sterling area. The huge loss of dollars under 'other transactions' in 1947 reflects the short-lived abolition of controls over access to dollars in that year.

Political and military spending

The scale of Britain's overseas government expenditure was a source of intense debate at the time, and has remained a source of criticism of that government's policies. Was this a case of *folie de grandeur,* in which Britain's economic recovery was sacrificed to anachronistic (and unsocialist?) attempts to retain a great power stance in the world?[6]

This was certainly how Keynes saw it, in one of his last memos in February 1946.[7] In this paper Keynes argued that imports were being

[6] For this debate see, for example, A. Bullock, *Ernest Bevin, Foreign Secretary* (Oxford, 1983); E. Barker, *The British between the Superpowers* (1984), ch. 4; R. N. Rosencrance, *Defence of the Realm: British Strategy in a Nuclear Epoch* (1968), chs. 2, 3.

[7] J. M. Keynes, 'Political and Military Expenditure Overseas' in *Collected Writings* vol. xxvii (1980).

efficiently controlled and close to the minimum for essentials. The problem lay elsewhere:

the current and prospective demands upon us for political and military expenditure overseas have already gone far beyond the figure which can, on any hypothesis, be sustained ... It would not be a source of comfort to the hard-pressed British public if they were to become aware that (reckoning our overseas statistics globally) not a single bean of subsistence for themselves or of capital equipment for British manufacturers is likely to be left over from the American credit; and that we shall require, on balance, the whole of it, and, unless we change our ways, much more to feed and sustain Allies, liberated territories and ex-enemies, to maintain our military prestige overseas, and, generally speaking to cut a dash in the world considerably above our means.

The 'extremely shocking' figures suggested that the foreign exchange costs of these commitments could amount to £1,500m. in the period 1946–8.[8]

Keynes was by no means a lone voice in criticising the extent of government overseas commitments. The (unpublished) Economic Survey for 1946, the Balance of Payments Working Party, and the Bank of England all expressed grave doubts on this score.[9] The figures in table 3.3 show how many of these responsibilities were eventually reduced, prior to the Korean War, but much more slowly than Keynes and others called for. The table makes it clear that the bulk of overseas government expenditure was incurred within the rest of the sterling area (RSA), and did not therefore add directly to the dollar problem. But this is misleading in the sense that much of this expenditure did generate purchasing power in recipient countries, which led to demand for dollar goods, demands which were not effectively curtailed by the exchange controls (a point returned to below).

The debate on overseas government expenditure in the crucial period up to the sterling crisis of 1947 can be characterised, in broad terms, as a battle between Dalton and Attlee on the one side, Bevin and the service chiefs on the other. However, Attlee's position was a complex one. On the one hand, he was more ready than anyone to criticise strategic arguments used to justify such expenditure. On the other hand, Bevin was perhaps the key minister in the government after Attlee, and Attlee was never willing to push the arguments to the extent of causing a serious rift with Bevin.

When Keynes' memo was discussed at the Cabinet in February 1946, defence expenditure for 1946/7 had already been cut by 14 per cent.[10] But there was a marked reluctance to take on board the seriousness of

[8] Ibid., pp. 465–6.
[9] Pressnell, *External Economic Policy*, pp. 358–60.
[10] PRO CAB131/1, Defence Committee Minutes, 15 Feb. 1946.

Table 3.3   *Government transactions, 1946–50*

(£m.)

	1946	1947	1948	1949	1950
Sources of debits					
Military	374	209	113	110	94
Administration and diplomacy	20	25	29	30	36
Relief and rehabilitation	83	37	15	11	11
Germany (net)	40	81	16	9	2
Colonial grants	10	7	10	16	19
War disposals, etc.	−164	−129	−96	−36	−25
Total	363	230	87	140	137
(Total current debits)	1,691	2,171	2,263	2,507	2,903
Area/currency of debits on government transactions					
Dollar area	25	60	−2	1	−2
Other W. Hemisphere	6	2	2	1	—
OEEC	32	23	25	9	4
Other non-sterling	72	40	22	29	13
RSA	169	66	23	89	47
Non-territorial	59	39	17	11	8
Total	363	230	87	140	70
Total deficits in gold and dollars (UK only)	316	662	326	291	−2

Source: Cmd. 8201, UK Balance of Payments 1946 to 1950 (PP 1950/1, 21).

the situation sketched by Keynes (which was broadly supported by a paper from the Balance of Payments Working Party).[11] Whilst there was a general recognition that the matter must be discussed further, only Dalton urged support for the general thrust of Keynes' paper. Bevin said little directly on the issue, except to stress the political problems of a rapid withdrawal from the Netherland East Indies and the need to consult the Chiefs of Staff. Attlee proposed further discussion at the Defence Committee, whilst stressing the impossibility of any immediate withdrawal of British forces from India, Indonesia or Palestine.[12]

Most of the key decisions on military and political expenditure overseas seem to have been taken in the Defence Committee, and simply endorsed by the Cabinet. Here the line-up was normally Dalton plus Attlee (plus occasionally Morrison) versus Bevin and the Chiefs of Staff,

[11] PRO CAB129/7, Balance of Payments Working Party, '1946 Import Programme', 8 Feb. 1947.
[12] PRO CAB128/5, 11 Feb. 1946.

supported by Alexander, the Minister of Defence. This line-up was apparent from the Defence Committee's first meeting on 11 January 1946, when Dalton and Attlee queried the level of British forces around the world, and Bevin and the defence chiefs defended them. In this and succeeding meetings the focus of attention was primarily on the manpower involved in the armed forces, with some discussion of the public expenditure costs. There was, at this stage and in this forum, no discussion of the direct foreign exchange costs of those overseas commitments.[13]

Attlee was not content simply to urge the need for economies. He also challenged the centrepiece of the overseas stance of the Chiefs of Staff and Bevin – the belief that the Mediterranean was absolutely crucial to Britain's international position. He 'hoped that the strategic assumption that it was vital to us to keep open the Mediterranean and that in fact we could, should be re-examined. He did not see how we could possibly do so under modern conditions.'[14] The ensuing debate encapsulates much of importance in the evolution of overseas expenditure in the early years of the Attlee government.

Bevin, in response to Attlee's scepticism on Britain's Mediterranean posture, argued that the stability of the area was enormously important to prevent war. At the same time, he tried to make an economic case for expenditure in that area: 'Moreover, from the trade point of view, this area was probably worth between one and one and a half million employed men to this country. If we lost our political influence in this area we should suffer a great economic setback.'[15]

The debate was later joined at greater length, following circulation of memorandums by Attlee, Bevin and the Chiefs of Staff. The paper by Attlee has been described by Bullock as 'amongst the most radical produced by a British Prime Minister in Office'.[16] Attlee attacked the whole basis of seeing the Mediterranean as crucial to Britain in time of war, arguing that with the development of air power the resources needed to protect sea-routes from Gibraltar to Suez would be impossible to find. He further argued that no conceivable military strength in the area could defend access to oil resources against attack from the north (i.e. the USSR). The Suez route to Australia could be replaced by the Cape route or via the Panama Canal. He saw the attachment to the Middle

---

[13] PRO CAB131/1, Defence Committee Minutes, 1 Jan. to 15 Feb. 1946.
[14] Ibid., 15 Feb. 1946.
[15] Ibid., 15 March 1946.
[16] Bullock, *Ernest Bevin*, p. 242. See also R. Smith and J. Zametica, 'The Cold Warrior: Clement Attlee Reconsidered', *International Affairs* 61 (1985), pp. 237–52. The Attlee paper is 'Future of the Italian Colonies', PRO CAB 131/2, 2 March 1946.

East by Britain as 'sentimental', and wanted to redefine Britain as the easterly extension of a strategic area based in the USA, rather than a power looking eastwards through the Mediterranean to India and the East.

Bevin's response was implicitly to accept the strategic vulnerability of the Middle East in wartime, but to argue that Britain's presence in that area was crucial to Britain as a great political power. Bevin did not accept Attlee's idea of re-siting Britain's main base in Africa, but he did share in a developing view that Africa should play a much greater role in Britain's imperial policy, especially because of its (alleged) economic potential.[17]

The Chiefs of Staff focused on the strategic arguments for the British presence in the Middle East. The basic idea of their paper was that if Britain didn't dominate an area, the Russians would. This general doctrine applied particularly to the Middle East because: (i) it lay on the route of any Soviet expansion into Africa; (ii) it could provide bases for a Soviet role in Africa; (iii) it formed a forward position for defending South Africa and India; (iv) it was a base for bombing the Soviet Union; and (v) Middle Eastern oil supplies could be defended.[18]

These papers were debated inconclusively at the Defence Committee meeting on 5 April 1946. Further inconclusive discussion followed on 27 May 1946 and again on 19 July. At the second of these meetings Attlee stressed that the strategic arguments about the Middle East would not work because no country would be willing to grant bases for military action, and we would therefore needlessly and pointlessly threaten the Russians. He argued that access to oil resources could be secured by negotiation with the Soviets. Against this the Chiefs of Staff reiterated their view of the strategic importance of the Middle East and the belief that the area must be dominated by either Britain or the Soviets.[19] These arguments rumbled on into 1947. But by March 1947 the Chiefs of Staff were recording a victory for their view of the Middle East, and were arguing that this implied that Britain must hang on to the right to return to bases in Egypt, even in the absence of agreement.[20] Montgomery claimed that the basis of Attlee's climbdown on this central issue for Britain's post-war overseas policy stance was a threat from

[17] J. Kent, 'Bevin's Imperialism and the Idea of Euro-Africa, 1945–49' in M. Dockrill and J. W. Young (eds.), *British Foreign Policy, 1945–56* (1989), pp. 47–75; Kent, 'The British Empire and the Origins of the Cold War, 1944–49' in A. Deighton (ed.), *Britain and the First Cold War* (1990), pp. 165–83; Kent, *British Imperial Strategy*, ch. 5.

[18] PRO CAB131/2, 'Strategic Position of the British Commonwealth', 2 April 1946.

[19] PRO CAB131/1, Defence Committee Minutes, 19 July 1946; CAB131/3, 'British Strategic Requirements in the Middle East', 18 June 1946.

[20] PRO CAB131/4, 'The Defences of the Commonwealth', 7 March 1947.

the Chiefs of Staff to resign if Attlee persisted in his criticisms. However, there is no evidence for this, although their opposition no doubt weighed with Attlee. The more likely explanation for his climbdown was the Soviet acquisition of nuclear weapons, and the belief that British deterrence to this new threat required bases in the Middle East.[21]

A number of points may be made about this argument. First, it is apparent how little the Foreign Office and Chiefs of Staff took on board the problems of the British economy. As far as the Foreign Office was concerned, post-war economic problems were transient. This view is summarised in a memorandum sent to embassies abroad by the Foreign Office early in 1945. This argued for a necessary linkage of diplomatic commitments to economic strength, but then went on to argue that Britain's looming economic problems were likely to be temporary: 'It must, however, be stressed that, given skill and good fortune, our financial difficulties will be acute only during the immediate post-war years. There are sound reasons for hoping that they will be a temporary phenomenon, for this country possesses all the skill and resources required to recover a dominating place in the economic world.'[22] There is little to suggest this view changed, at least until the sterling crisis of 1947.

Similarly the Chiefs of Staff showed little appreciation of the economic context. Attlee chided them for ignoring any notion of what the country could afford in suggesting armed forces levels, and for suggesting that cutting spending on the armed forces to £700m. could virtually immobilise them.[23] Amongst ministers, Alexander seems to have represented this insouciant attitude to the economic problem, arguing at one stage that there should not be a problem of competition for manpower between civilian and military uses as 'a slight increase in productivity' would solve the manpower gap.[24]

The Chiefs of Staff also seem to have been strikingly narrow in their strategic vision, in being willing to ignore the political and diplomatic problems arising from Britain's role in the Middle East. For them, if strategic necessity were established, local sentiment could ultimately be set aside. Bevin and the Foreign Office were on occasion more sensitive on the issue of hanging on in areas where Britain was unwanted – but in Bevin's case this produced the bizarre proposal to hang on in the

[21] B. Montgomery, *Memoirs* (1956), pp. 435–6; C. J. Bartlett, *British Foreign Policy in the Twentieth Century* (1989), p. 74.
[22] PRO FO371/45694, 'Effect of Britain's External Financial Position on Foreign Policy', 9 Feb. 1945. For the Foreign Office see A. Adamthwaite, 'Britain and the World 1945–9: The View from the Foreign Office', *International Affairs* 61 (1985), pp. 223–35.
[23] PRO CAB131/5, Defence Committee Minutes, 18 Sept. 1947.
[24] Ibid., 14 Jan. 1947.

Middle East from a base in inhospitable (if British) territory 2,000 miles from the Suez Canal. Even Bullock is forced to concede that Bevin was 'obsessed' with the Middle East, an obsession he seems never to have lost.[25]

If we make the economic issue central, the justification for a continued British presence in the Middle East was access to oil. It follows that the key issue is the extent to which there was (or was believed to be) a significant Soviet threat to those supplies, especially in southern Iran.

Yet at the time of the great debates over defence and the Middle East in 1946 the evidence suggests that Britain had a realistic view of Soviet intentions in this area – that these intentions fundamentally consisted in a determination to secure access to oil concessions in northern Persia. This view, which had been accepted by Britain at an earlier date, was reiterated by the Ministry of Fuel and Power to the Defence Committee in 1946.[26]

If the foreign and defence policy-makers may be accused of insufficient attention to the economic aspects of their policies, it is far from clear that the economic arguments were pressed in a manner most likely to cause a reassessment of overseas commitments. Despite Keynes' memo, the foreign exchange aspect of overseas government expenditure was strikingly absent from the debate in the Defence Committee from its beginnings in 1946 right through to August 1947, by which time it may be argued that damage had largely already been done. In a memo in that (crisis) month the Ministry of Defence seemingly for the first time addressed the issue of the foreign exchange costs of existing policy. The ministry was responding to the claim by the Chancellor of the Exchequer at the end of July that Britain's overseas military expenditure was running at £140m.[27]

In response, the Ministry of Defence argued that of the 2 million British troops overseas, 200,000 were in areas that did not create a foreign currency liability, and of the rest few were in areas requiring direct dollar expenditure: 'it follows that the contribution to be made to the balance of payments problem by the withdrawal of troops in overseas

[25] Bullock, *Ernest Bevin*, pp. 113, 215–16.

[26] PRO CAB131/2, 'Petroleum Resources in the Middle East', 1 April 1946. On Soviet intentions in Iran, see B. R. Kuniholm, *The Origins of the Cold War in the Near East* (1980), esp. pp. 34–50. On British policy, L. L'Estrange Fawcett, 'Invitation to the Cold War: British Policy in Iran, 1941–47' in A. Deighton (ed.), *Britain and the First Cold War* (1990), pp. 184–200.

[27] PRO CAB129/20, 'Balance of Payments', 30 July 1947. Within the Treasury the issue of the foreign exchange cost of overseas military expenditure was a live one from Keynes' memorandum onwards, but did not surface at Cabinet level.

theatres will be strictly limited, will apply only to those areas when there is at present a currency obligation, and will produce little or no direct dollar saving'.[28] This argument seems to have had some effect, for whilst the Chancellor of the Exchequer was asked to look more closely at the dollar costs of overseas forces, the Ministry of Defence view that no further cuts in forces should be found was accepted.[29]

At one level the Ministry of Defence argument about the dollar costs of overseas expenditure was not absurd. Most of the expenditure was outside the dollar area, and didn't give rise to immediate dollar payments. But, other things being equal, such financial transfers would ultimately lead to a real resource transfer to the recipients of expenditure. If the consequence were a rise in imports of dollar goods, then a significant impact on the sterling area's reserves of dollars and gold would be felt. In conditions of general 'dollar shortage' the effects were likely to be significant.[30] In addition, the effects of overseas political and military expenditure were not exhausted by the more or less direct effects on the balance of payments but obviously involved tying up substantial numbers of men in the armed forces and the supply industries.

In fact, most of the debate about Britain's military expenditure (home and overseas) in this period was conducted in terms of manpower targets, a legacy of the war which was continued by the Labour government as an important 'planning' device. Hence most of the pressure on the military to reduce their activities took the form of persistent downward revision of the numbers of men (and the rather limited number of women) allocated to them. The reduction in numbers was still startlingly low – for example, even after the convertibility crisis of 1947 had led to a further downward revision of the targets for 31 March 1948, there were still 937,000 in uniform, supported by 350,000 in supplying industries. (At 1 July 1947 there were approximately 2 million troops overseas).[31] Dalton was fond of contrasting these numbers with the half a million total troops thought likely to be necessary in peacetime by the wartime coalition.[32] The other way in which the economic aspects of military expenditure were presented was in the form of the public expenditure costs. However, this was definitely secondary to the manpower approach, though again Dalton liked to contrast actual levels of expenditure with the £500 million which the coalition thought likely to be

[28] PRO CAB131/4, 'Strength of the Armed Forces', 2 Aug. 1947.
[29] PRO CAB131/5, Defence Committee Minutes, 18 Sept. 1947 and 29 Sept. 1947.
[30] Cairncross, *Years of Recovery*, pp. 156, 162.
[31] PRO CAB128/10, 2 Oct. 1947; CAB129/20, 'Balance of Payments', 30 July 1947.
[32] e.g. PRO CAB131/1, Defence Committee Minutes, 11 Jan. 1946.

necessary in peacetime, pointing out in early 1947 that the current level of expenditure at over £800m. meant 2s in the pound extra on the income tax in comparison with the coalition figure.[33]

The debate about overseas government expenditure may be seen in one sense as straightforward – an unsurprising clash of departmental interests which, given the political weight of the participants, led only to a gradual but cumulative reduction in commitments. Until the 1947 crisis drove home the extent of Britain's overseas payments difficulties, Bevin and the Chiefs of Staff were able to defend their programmes quite successfully. The protagonists of a more rapid rundown were hampered by the domination of the debate by manpower figures, which led the issue away from the balance of payments. Protagonists of more rapid reductions in overseas expenditure also tended to fall into the trap of contrasting such expenditure with expenditure on imported consumption goods. The problem was commonly posed as guns versus butter, or in the case of Keynes' original memorandum, overseas troops versus the bacon ration. Defenders of the scale of British commitments, then and more recently, have thus been able to ignore the extent to which not only consumption but also production and productive efficiency were inhibited by the dollar shortage – both directly by restricting currency available for imported capital equipment, and indirectly by diverting domestic output of such equipment into dollar markets.[34]

Finally on this aspect of the problem, there is the question of Germany.[35] In the immediate post-war period Germany was the single most important source of dollar drain. This outcome was an unintended consequence of Britain's successful attempt to occupy the most industrialised and populous part of Germany. In other words, to a degree the burden of Germany on the balance of payments was in part the result of Britain's 'great power' posture, and not just the consequence of the military pattern that emerged during the conquest of Germany. Unfortunately for the British government, this occupation zone was unexpectedly severed from its traditional sources of food in the East, and being unable to feed itself became reliant on supplies of food from dollar areas.

[33] For example, in PRO CAB129/21, 'Defence Requirements' 30 Sept. 1947 by the Ministry of Defence, the focus is manpower, with the public expenditure aspects taken up only in an annex: CAB131/4, 'Defence Estimates for 1947/8', 9 Jan. 1947.

[34] J. M. Keynes, Collected Writings, vol. XXVII, p. 467. Thus, for example, Bullock (Ernest Bevin, p. 363) poses the problem as foreign policy versus domestic social reform. See the Foreign Office reply to Keynes 1946 (Memorandum T236/406, 'Overseas Deficit', 26 Feb. 1946), in which the problem is posed as 'easements for the civilian population' versus 'remaining a Great Power'.

[35] On the division of Germany see T. Sharp, The Wartime Alliance and the Zonal Division of Germany (1975).

The position was rectified only slowly, by getting the USA to take on part and then the whole of the burden by the end of 1947.

Foreign Investment

Very different was the issue of foreign investment. Whilst the scale of British overseas military commitments was widely debated in Parliament, in the Labour Party, as well as within the government, the scale of foreign investment and its key role in the overall balance of payments position was little known and therefore largely unremarked. Whilst an earlier generation of writers had noted this feature of the period,[36] it was not until the recent work of Cairncross that the significance of this outflow was realised. Partly this was because the current account deficit appears much smaller in current (1990s) data than it was thought to be by contemporaries, mainly it would seem because the invisible position was actually much better than was then realised. Retrospectively we know that capital outflow took place on a massive scale, amounting to £1500m. in 1947–9, well in excess of the receipts from the US loan. In 1947 alone the figure was £643m.:

Given the straits to which the British economy was reduced in 1947, when it was necessary to ration even bread and potatoes, an outflow of capital equal to about 8 per cent of national income and nearly equal to total net domestic capital formation (including stock-building) is a very extraordinary event. It was certainly not the purpose for which the American and Canadian loans were procured.[37]

How did this bizarre situation come about? The brief answer might be that it was an unintended consequence of a largely implicit and undebated policy decision. The policy decision was to maintain the sterling area, above all in its 1940 form as a zone of exchange control. This meant no controls on foreign investment within that zone, and the unintended consequence of this was a huge capital outflow from Britain to the sterling area as London rediscovered its traditional predilection for investing in the 'White Commonwealth'. As with military expenditure, the effects of this were not, however, limited to the sterling area – capital inflows allowed much larger demands on the dollar pool by recipient countries (and this is to ignore the possibility of 'leakage' into dollars or sterling via weaknesses in the control mechanisms – a point returned to below).

[36] P. W. Bell, *The Sterling Area in the Post-War World* (Oxford, 1956), pp. 367–81; A. R. Conan, *The Sterling Area* (Oxford, 1952).
[37] Cairncross, *Years of Recovery*, pp. 80–1, 153.

When it is said that the continuation of the sterling area was an 'implicit' decision (and sharply contrasting with the debates on overseas expenditure), the point being made is that this continuation was not the result, it would seem, of any debate within the Attlee government. Aspects of sterling's position as an international currency, notably the sterling balances, were, of course, vigorously discussed in the war period, above all as the result of US pressure to reduce them. And this did raise the whole issue of the future of the sterling area. But what is striking about the debates on this was the shared assumption that the area was a 'good thing' for Britain. The issue discussed was how best to secure its future.[38] But I have found no evidence that at any stage anyone said, 'What is this sterling area, and is it obviously a good thing for Britain?' Typically the sterling area was assumed to be a 'good thing', the justification of it needing only to be made to foreigners (especially Americans). The major economic argument for the area was as a way of expanding the zone of multilateral trade in the short run, and as a source of 'highly beneficial trading and banking relations'.[39] Whilst such a view is not absurd, it hardly touches on the issues which would have to be addressed for any overall assessment.

Whilst the authorities do not seem to have been aware of the scale and significance of capital flows within the sterling area, they were aware that the exchange controls in that area were not all that London hoped. For example, a major recipient of capital from the UK in this period, Australia, had notoriously 'leaky' controls – in 1947–8 it was supposed to spend $80m. and spent $200m.[40] Some of the reasons for the over-spending were technical, i.e. the lack of an effective administrative apparatus, but in addition there was a clear political hostility in several countries to London's control of decision-making on the allocation of gold and dollars. There were some attempts on consultation, notably with commonwealth finance ministers in 1947 and 1949, but the relationship is perhaps symbolised by the fact that the sterling area

---

[38] On the sterling balances, Pressnell, *External Economic Policy*, pp. 215–27, 289–92; R. W. B. Clarke, *Anglo-American Co-operation in War and Peace, 1942–49*, ed. A. Cairncross (Oxford, 1982), pp. 56–7. On the wartime debate over the sterling area see Keynes, *Collected Writings*, vol. xxiv, pp. 19–22, 66–9; Pressnell, *External Economic Policy*, pp. 140–4, 225, 233–4. Broadly, Keynes resisted the Bank of England's proposal to expand the sterling area as an alternative to Bretton Woods. Keynes argued that such an area, unavoidably discriminating against the dollar on a semi-permanent basis, would have few attractions and would require extension of controls within the area. In this view, sterling could not survive as an international currency in a context of non-cooperation with the USA.

[39] PRO T236/822, 'The Sterling Area', 7 July 1948.

[40] Conan, *Sterling Area*, p. 156.

Table 3.4 *Dollar drawings/contributions to gold and dollar pool, 1946–50*
(drawings = –, contributions = +) ($m.)

	1946	1947	1948	1949	1950
Ireland	–2	–120	–33	–8	–17
Australia	–30	–200	–48	–60	+32
New Zealand	–31	–80	–41	–52	+19
South Africa	–30	–80	+289	+36	+187
India	+44	–249	–96	–69	+79
Pakistan	—	—	–9	–46	–23
Ceylon	+13	–1	+38	+17	+58
Burma	n.a.	–5	–20	–3	n.a.
Iraq	–1	–35	–20	–10	n.a.
Iceland	n.a.	n.a.	n.a.	n.a.	n.a.
Southern Rhodesia	+ 7	–7	+2	+6	+22
Total independent countries	–59	–777	+62	–191	+257
Malaya	+122	+162	+140	+150	+360
British West Africa	+49	+38	+87	+ 82	+108
British East Africa	–5	–28	–7	n.a.	+13
Other dependants	–8	–110	+13	–3	–45
Total dependants	+158	+62	+233	+135	+436

Source: P. W. Bell, *The Sterling Area in the Post-War World* (Oxford, 1956), pp. 56–7.

countries were not consulted on devaluation in 1949, just informed of the decision a day or two before it took place.[41]

The precise distribution of this outflow of foreign investment is shrouded in mystery. Conan suggests that Australia may have received £550m. from Britain in the period 1945–51, South Africa perhaps £400m. over the same period.[42] Cairncross, citing other figures from the 1950s, suggests a comparable figure for South Africa, but a much lower figure for Australia.[43] Whatever the details, it seems clear that (a) except in the case of India, little of the capital flows took the form of a rundown of sterling balances; (b) most of the investment flow was to the 'white commonwealth', especially South Africa; (c) the colonies saw net disinvestment. Each of these points requires some comment.

On sterling balances, the pattern was one where some countries ran down their balances significantly, whilst others accumulated more (table 3.4). The aggregate of outstanding balances fluctuated quite violently,

[41] Ibid., pp. 155–62.
[42] Ibid., pp. 125–6.
[43] Cairncross, *Years of Recovery*, p. 158.

falling sharply especially in 1947, but for 1945–51 as a whole it fell by
only £70m.[44] The major country to draw down its balances was India;
the main countries to accumulate balances were the colonies, with the
white commonwealth falling in between.[45] In the event, the sterling balances were much less of a problem from London's point of view than
was commonly anticipated when the scale of their wartime accumulation was first discussed in the mid-1940s.

Secondly, the huge flow of UK investment into South Africa was
especially into gold-mining expansion.[46] The consequences of this
investment for the sterling area were complex, as South Africa was, of
course, the world's major gold producer. But in the early post-war years
her import surplus was so large that despite expanded gold exports she
was a net drawer on the sterling pool, until she left the pool at the end
of 1947.[47] In 1947 the Treasury did raise the question of excluding South
Africa (and India) from the sterling area because of the effect of their
behaviour on the reserve position, but this was ultimately rejected. In
1947 it was agreed to impose exchange control on exports of capital to
South Africa, but this idea was not pursued when these flows ceased in
1948.[48] Despite the costs of South Africa to the sterling area in this
period, Labour was determined to hang on to good relations with that
country, so as neither to break up the commonwealth nor to disrupt the
perceived strategic centrality of South Africa to military policy.[49] This
friendly stance was little affected by the Nationalist victory in 1948.[50]

Whilst London did not much consult with the dominions on financial
matters (though it made a public ploy of doing so), it lacked the political
will or administrative means to make the rigorous control of dollar
imports practised in the UK effective in those countries. As on other
occasions, imperial sentiment was a weak basis for a key part of British
policy.

Perhaps the oddest consequence of the evolution of the sterling area
as a zone for British balance of payments policy was the relationship

---

[44] Ibid., p. 80.

[45] Detailed estimates are in H. A. Shannon, 'The Sterling Balances of the Sterling Area',
Economic Journal 60 (1950), pp. 531–51; for India see B. R. Tomlinson, 'Indo-British
Relations in the Post-Colonial Era: The Sterling Balance Negotiations 1947–49', *Jour-
nal of Imperial and Commonwealth History* 13 (1985), pp. 142–62.

[46] N. N. Franklin, 'South Africa's Balance of Payments and the Sterling Area', *Economic
Journal* 61 (1951), pp. 290–309.

[47] Ibid., pp. 306–7.

[48] Cairncross, *Years of Recovery*, pp. 133–4; PRO T236/1570, 'Sterling Area: Preparation
of Briefs for the Commonwealth P.M.s', Oct. 1948.

[49] R. Hyam, 'Africa and the Labour Government 1945–51', *Journal of Imperial and Commonwealth History* 16 (1988), pp. 148–52.

[50] R. Ovendale, 'Introduction' in Ovendale (ed.), *Foreign Policy*, pp. 14–16.

which developed with the colonies. Treating the sterling area as a single bloc meant, logically, maximising dollar receipts for the area as a whole and minimising dollar debits. Such a policy could be much more effectively applied to colonial territories, where British control of trade and payments was well entrenched. The colonies as a group quickly emerged as a key part of British strategy because they were net dollar earners (basically because of exports of Malayan rubber and West African products such as cocoa) and could be made so on a bigger scale by a number of policy devices. The result of this was that net disinvestment took place in the colonies in the Labour government period, as inflows of funds were about £40m., whilst sterling balances grew by £160m.[51]

This outcome was not the consequence of any direct intention to exploit the colonies. Rather it followed from the notion that the economic development of Britain and the colonies was interdependent and complementary, and from the assumption that what was good for Britain was good for the colonies.[52] This implied a division of labour between manufacturing activity in the UK and raw material and food production in the colonies, a doctrine which the Colonial Office broadly accepted, and which was in line with its lack of sympathy with colonial industrialisation as likely to be socially and politically disruptive.[53] Thus the Treasury faced little opposition to its policies on the basis that the sterling area was in any way harmful to the interests of the colonies.[54]

More controversial was the manner in which Britain turned the terms of trade in its favour and directly squeezed the incomes of colonial producers by bulk purchasing of colonial products at below world prices.[55] This caused disquiet amongst colonial officials and led Creech Jones, the Colonial Secretary in the later years of the Labour government, to circulate a memorandum to the Cabinet in early 1947 which said:

I know full well how important it is that our overseas payments should be kept as low as they possibly can be, but I cannot believe that this justifies a course which is contrary to our declared policy in regard both to Colonial and to com-

---

[51] D. J. Morgan, *Official History of Colonial Development*, vol. II: *Developing Colonial Resources 1945–51* (1980), ch. 1; A. Hinds, 'Imperial Policy and the Colonial Sterling Balances 1943–56', *Journal of Imperial and Commonwealth History* 19 (1991), pp. 24–44.

[52] PRO CAB134/65, 'Report of Colonial Development Working Party', 11 Oct. 1948; Cripps' speech to African Governors Conference, 12 Nov. 1947, in A. N. Porter and A. J. Stockwell, *British Imperial Policy and Decolonisation 1938–64*, vol. I, *1938–51* (1987), Document 44.

[53] Porter and Stockwell, *British Imperial Policy*, p. 49.

[54] PRO CAB134/65, 'Conference of Colonial Supply Officers', 28 June 1949.

[55] P. Bauer, 'Statistics of Statutory Marketing in West Africa, 1939–51', *Journal of the Royal Statistical Society* 117 (1954), pp. 1–20; Bauer, *West African Trade* (1963), chs. 20–3.

mercial matters and contrary also to the policy which has long been pursued by the Labour Party.

But in the face of Treasury and Ministry of Food objections, nothing came of this.[56] The Treasury policy, especially from late 1947, was to badger the colonies to provide data on which a rigorous system of dollar exchange control could be imposed, a system which was imposed from December 1947.[57] This was coupled to a policy of discouraging as far as possible even UK imports into the colonies on the grounds that this would divert UK exports from dollar to soft currency areas like the colonies,[58] and hence the accumulation of colonial sterling balances. This policy, which was very much stimulated by the crisis around convertibility in 1947, was tightened up even further at the time of the next sterling crisis in 1949.[59] Colonial dollar imports fell from $376m. in 1947, to $355m. the following year, and to $260m. in 1949. By early 1950, following renewed cuts, the annual rate was down to around $170m.[60]

The balance of payments crisis, in combination with fears of Russian expansionism created a growing Labour interest in the empire in general and Africa in particular. The possibility of increased dollar receipts was coupled with a belief that Africa could be a strategic centre for British power, untainted by the nationalism which had eroded British power in Asia.[61] The search for dollars led to grandiose plans for African economic development, most famously the groundnuts scheme, though that was not the only madcap project to surface in this period.[62] The contribution of such schemes to either dollar receipts or colonial development was more or less zero. But the ruthless pursuit of dollars in the colonies exacerbated political tensions, and probably sped the rise of African nationalism.

Fieldhouse has summarised British colonial policy in this period:

The ironical and fundamental point is that during these post-war years, when international demand for tropical commodities for the first time since 1921 really

[56] Reprinted in Porter and Stockwell, *British Imperial Policy*, Document 42; also PRO CAB134/64, 'Dollar Situation and the Colonies', 1 July 1949.

[57] PRO T236/689–693, Dollar Drain (Colonies) Committee, 1946–7.

[58] PRO T236/693, Telegram from Secretary of State for Colonies to Colonial Governors, 6 Aug. 1947; PRO T236/1814, O. Williams, 'Colonial Import Policy', 16 Oct. 1947.

[59] PRO CAB134/65, 'The Colonies and the Dollar Standstill', 27 July 1949.

[60] PRO T236/2480, 'Colonies: Import Policy 1949/50'.

[61] Hyam, 'Africa', pp. 148–57; P. J. Cain and W. G. Hopkins, *British Imperialism: Crisis and Deconstruction* (1993), pp. 278–81.

[62] Morgan, *Official History*, chs. 5 and 6. On the general role of Africa in British policy see Kent, 'Bevin's Imperialism'; P. S. Gupta, 'Imperialism and the Labour Governments, 1945–51' in J. M. Winter (ed.), *The Working Class in Modern British History* (Cambridge, 1983), pp. 98–120.

justified vast investments in the Colonies; when the Colonies had a huge back-
log of demand for essential equipment; when at last the British government was
equipped with power to give or lend considerable sums to top up what the
Colonies could afford to invest from their own accumulating surplus; and when,
finally, a new political awareness was making Colonial populations more than
ever critical of their relationship with the metropolis, Britain, for the first time
in her modern Imperial history, was literally unable to deliver the goods.[63]

But as a result of the sterling area policy, Britain not only failed to
deliver the goods but actively exploited colonial producers in a fairly
blatant manner.

An ambiguous legacy

In 1952 A. R. Conan wrote: 'When all factors are taken into account,
there seems some evidence to support the view that the balance of payments of the UK after the war might be considered fundamentally more
satisfactory than in 1939.'[64] This may be a little exaggerated, but it
makes the point quite nicely that the commodity position of British
trade recovered strikingly well after 1945 – essential imports could readily be paid for by exports plus the American loan remarkably quickly
after the end of the war. The underlying balance of payments problems
stemmed essentially from the scale of government overseas expenditure
and foreign investment that was allowed, amounting to more than 8
times the aggregate current account deficit for 1946–50 (table 3.1).

On overseas government expenditure Attlee fought a campaign with
what has been called an 'impressive "Little Englander" pragmatism'
which, however, ran against the rocks of Bevin and the Chiefs of Staff.[65]
Nevertheless, and no doubt too slowly, illusions of grandeur were slowly
given up and Britain's incapacity to live with the superpowers to a
degree accepted. And in the light of simplistic attacks on this government's policies in this regard from critics on both the left and right, it
is worth noting some qualifications to the common critiques of its 'great
power' pretensions.[66]

First, Britain's 'overstretch' was significantly reduced in this period
by the retreat from both India and Palestine. Britain did not show the

[63] R. Fieldhouse, Review of Morgan, *Official History*, *English Historical Review* 97 (1982),
pp. 386–94.
[64] Conan, *Sterling Area*, p. 165.
[65] Hyam, 'Africa', p. 158.
[66] Barnett, *Lost Victory* Pt 1 gives a crude and highly tendentious account of this issue,
which – except rhetorically – adds little to criticisms made since the 1950s. For brief
critiques from the Left which say similar things, see J. Callaghan, 'In Search of Eldorado: Labour's Colonial Economic Policy' and F. Carr, 'Cold War: The Economy and
Foreign Policy' in J. Fyrth, ed., *Labour's High Noon: The Government and the Economy
1945–51* (1993), pp. 115–34 and 135–47 respectively.

willingness to 'hang on at all costs' that the French were to manifest so disastrously in South-East Asia and North Africa. Second, if economically overstretched by overseas commitments in some areas, Britain was also of course highly dependent on US aid, and these issues were interlinked. For all the anti-British imperialism to be heard in Congress in this period, the US government was keen to see Britain maintain its overseas commitments as part of the fight against communism. Too rapid a retreat from such commitments would have threatened the alliance with the USA and the dollar aid.

Third, the maintenance of the sterling area in the late 1940s cannot be accounted simply a case of ambition overburdening the British purse. As stressed in chapter 2, the preservation of the area was economically rational in this period. Sterling remained a major world currency, and the sterling area a zone for maximising trade in the face of world-wide dollar shortage.

Of course the area had its price. For Britain this was the avenue it created for massive capital outflow. For the colonies it facilitated a major squeeze on their standard of living. The second of these aspects has only relatively recently emerged in the published literature on the Labour government, but it is now a commonplace, certainly amongst imperial and colonial historians.[67] As noted above, in the 1940s it aroused some concern in the Colonial Office, but little elsewhere, though the nature of the squeeze was very clearly spelt out by the economist Arthur Lewis in 1952.[68] It is generally accepted that this arose from a strange but perhaps explicable mixture of compelling desire to rescue the British economy with a Fabian paternalism which saw a 'natural' path to colonial development in the expansion of traditional (dollar-earning) commodity production. Fieldhouse drives the point home when he argues that 'between 1945 and 1951 Britain exploited those dependencies that were politically unable to defend their own interests in more ways and with more serious consequences than at any time since overseas colonies were established'. This was, he argues, 'social imperialism in an extreme form'.[69]

But 'social imperialism' suggests the main beneficiaries of this policy were British consumers, and one writer has gone as far as to argue a

---

[67] Hyam, 'Africa'; A. E. Hinds, 'Sterling and Imperial Policy, 1945–51', *Journal of Imperial and Commonwealth History* 15 (1987), pp. 148–69; R. F. Holland, 'The Imperial Factor in British Strategies from Attlee to Macmillan', *Journal of Imperial and Commonwealth History* 12 (1984), pp. 165–86; D. K. Fieldhouse, 'The Labour Governments and the Empire Commonwealth 1945–51' in Ovendale, *Foreign Policy*. Compare Pelling, *Labour Governments*, ch. 8.

[68] Saville, *Politics of Continuity*, pp. 158–9.

[69] Newton, 'Britain, the Sterling Area, and European Integration', p. 178; Fieldhouse, 'The Labour Governments', pp. 95, 99.

direct link to the Attlee government's social reforms: 'The nationalisations, medical provision and expansion of education so magnanimously
legislated by the Labour Minister were largely achieved because the
Bank of England kept the sterling area show on the road.'[70] But plainly
this is to ignore the extent to which the immediate beneficiaries of the
sterling area were the dominions rather than British citizens, a point
neatly summarised by table 3.4.

But in the longer run the accentuation of the sterling area policy, and
its apparent success, especially in the explosion of colonial dollar-
earning from the time of the Korean War commodity boom,[71] re-
established the pound as a major currency, a role which seemed unlikely
in 1945. Thus what Strange calls sterling's role as a 'negotiated' currency – a top currency on the slide, which has to be constantly
defended – emerged strengthened enormously from the Attlee period,[72]
and this must be seen as a major part of the legacy of that government.

The Attlee governments were faced with a complexity of economic
and political problems that mean it, perhaps above all modern British
governments, should be spared the condescension of posterity. Nevertheless, given that those governments left such an enduring legacy, the
limits of their policy appraisal need to be stressed. There is little sign
that the government was able to find the time or the inclination to look
up from short-term crisis management in order to assess sceptically the
framework within which balance of payments policy was conducted.
Reductions in overseas government expenditure took place, albeit reluctantly and more gradually than now seems desirable. But the more fundamental issue (in the long run) of sterling and the associated question
of the role of the City of London seems to have been little discussed.
In other words, Labour's 'pragmatic' response to the recurrent payments crisis tended to enhance the taken-for-granted desirability of sterling's role as a world currency. When policy was seen to be hurting the
colonies, some protested. But even the many who accepted that British
relations within her colonies were unsatisfactory, saw this as a relatively
minor blemish on an otherwise desirable system.

In this Crosland was typical. In his book *Britain's Economic Problem*,
which was almost all about the balance of payments, he accurately outlined the broad trends in the balance of payments described above, and
the extent to which the sterling area relied on the colonies. But his
response was merely to press for a greater supply of British goods to

---

[70] Holland, 'Imperial Factor', p. 168.
[71] Cairncross, *Years of Recovery*, p. 86.
[72] Strange, chs. 1, 2.

those colonies to reduce their sterling balances.[73] The broader questions of Britain's role as a capital exporter, the role (economic and political) of the City linked to the status of the pound are all neglected. In this neglect Crosland reflected the generality of Labour opinion. Despite its important success in managing the balance of payments in the short run, this indifference must count as a significant failure of policy for a democratic socialist government.

[73] C. A. R. Crosland, *Britain's Economic Problem* (1953), pp. 149–53, 165.

4   Industrial modernisation

The historiography of the 1945–51 Labour governments' economic policies is dominated by three interconnected themes. First, the preeminence of macroeconomic issues: Cairncross' magisterial work, for example, omits 'any extended discussion of regional, commercial and industrial policy', and he 'recoiled from giving to microeconomic policy . . . the extended treatment that I have given to macroeconomic policy'.[1] Second, this focus on macro policy, whilst coupled to a recognition of the importance of planning and controls in early post-war policy, emphasises the movement away from such methods towards the dominance of the fiscal policies of the 1950s and 1960s.[2] Third, the effect of all this is to concentrate attention on economic policies concerned with stabilisation rather than modernisation.[3]

Against the picture sketched above, this chapter emphasises the centrality of microeconomic or supply-side policy to the government's programme. Second, and linked to this first point, is the place of planning

---

[1] Cairncross, *Years of Recovery*, pp. xi, xiii; Dow (*Management*) also focuses on management of the economy in a macroeconomic sense (pp. 2–3), though he has one chapter on controls. G. D. N. Worswick and P. H. Ady (eds.), *The British Economy 1945–50* (Oxford, 1952), give a much broader picture of the government's policies, but obviously suffer from the lack of access to the public records. A. Robinson ('The Economic Problems of the Transition from War to Peace, 1945–9', *Cambridge Journal of Economics* 10 (1986), pp. 165–85) has criticised this focus.

[2] Cairncross, *Years of Recovery*: 'Macroeconomic policy was born in the years after the war and survived more or less unchanged for at least two more decades' (p. 19); 'Economic planning was increasingly seen in terms of measures to maintain full employment, check inflation and maintain external balance. Demand management, rather than intervention to control the use of resources directly or improve their efficiency, was the order of the day' (p. 328). He suggested that '*From one point of view* the history of those years is the writing of the emergence of demand management' (p. 501). This point of view has become the prevalent one, e.g. G. Foote, *The Labour Party's Political Thought: A History* (Beckenham, 1985), p. 191: 'After 1947, Labour economic policy shifted away from the direct intervention of controls to the Keynesian techniques of "fine-tuning" the economy through fiscal and monetary policy.'

[3] Cairncross' treatment highlights the balance of payments problem and the crises which flowed from this problem (p. xii). He notes the emphasis on raising productivity (pp. 499–500), but does not set out to discuss the policies that flowed from this.

and tripartism as integral to those policies.[4] Third, it is argued that these policies, whilst certainly affected by the compelling needs of economic stabilisation, embodied a significant project of modernisation. The argument is not that this project wholly succeeded, but it is important to know that it was tried and what limited its achievements.

Overall, the chapter argues that there was a much more distinctive and significant notion of democratic socialist economic policy than the existing literature implies. More generally, the argument is that Labour's policies are radically misunderstood unless we recognise that the old adage that historically Labour has been a party concerned with redistribution not production is quite misplaced. The important issue is why it was so difficult to make that concern with modernisation of production fully effective.[5]

Production and modernisation

The pre-eminence of concern with the balance of payments under the Attlee government has been discussed in previous chapters. A key policy response to this concern was a campaign to increase output, given that the immediate problem was seen to be a supply constraint, not the uncompetitiveness of British goods. This led to a government 'prosperity' campaign, launched at the beginning of 1946. The initial focus of this was on how to 'man-up' certain industries to expand their output, but it quickly became apparent that with an almost fixed supply of labour, and constraints on the expansion of the capital stock (returned to below), most of the expansion could only come from increased productivity. By late 1946 this was explicitly recognised, Herbert Morrison proclaiming in October that he 'would put this problem of increased productivity first among the current problems to which planning must help to find the answer'. From then on raising productivity was to be at the centre of Labour's policies, as shown, for example, in the *Economic Surveys* of 1947 to 1950.[6]

This immediate macroeconomic crisis undoubtedly gave a weight to the concern with productivity which it would have otherwise lacked. But it was far from being the origin point. Ministers like Dalton and Cripps had acquired from their wartime experience as ministers (at the Board of Trade and Aircraft Production respectively) a good insight

---

[4] The more general issue of the meaning and significance of planning under Labour is taken up in chapter 6.

[5] This point would also apply to the 1964–70 Labour government.

[6] PRO CAB134/189, H. Morrison, 'Address to Institute of Public Administration', 17 Oct. 1946.

into the shortcomings of British industry and a desire to seek remedies for those shortcomings.[7]

Some of the remedies they tried to apply drew directly on their wartime ministerial experience. Cripps recreated in the Board of Trade the Production Efficiency Service with almost exactly the same personnel as the Production Efficiency Board in the MAP, though its focus seems to have widened from 'motion study' to broader management issues. The PES aimed at providing a free consultancy service, especially to small firms. The stated aims of the PES were both short and long-term: 'In the short-term it endeavours to bring about an increase in the productivity of the individual firm or group of firms which seek its end. In the long term: it aims at making industry aware of the possibility of increasing its efficiency by the study and application of up-to-date methods.'[8]

Similarly, Cripps created the Special Research Unit in the Board of Trade to deploy the OR techniques which were perceived to have been so successful in the wartime RAF. The SRU focused most of its attention on the issue of standardisation of production, and the relationship between standardisation, productivity and consumer needs.[9]

Cripps and Dalton, worried about the quality of British management, together pushed for public money for the creation of the British Institute of Management, an issue on which they had been defeated in the coalition government. Despite tussles with the Treasury over the scale of finance the BIM became a body whose existence is owed to the Labour government.[10]

Management education was also a subject of concern, and the government set up a committee (chaired by L. F. Urwick) on Education for Management.[11] However, this initiative was largely lost in the complexities of the politics of higher education in Britain, and a similar fate befell the attempts to expand higher technical education, as pressed by

---

[7] On the wartime debate on British industrial efficiency in which they both participated, see especially PRO CAB87/63, 'General Support of Trade', 15 Oct. 1948; K. Middlemas, *Power, Competition and the State*, vol. 1, *1940–61: Britain in Search of Balance* (1986), pp. 53–7.

[8] PRO BT64/2324, Board of Trade, 'The Production Efficiency Service', 30 Nov. 1945.

[9] PRO BT64/2314–20, Board of Trade SRU, 'Standardisation and Productivity Research Projects 1946–8'; J. Rosenhead, 'Operational Research at the Crossroads: Cecil Gordon and the Development of Postwar OR', *Journal of the Operational Research Society* 40 (1989), pp. 9–15.

[10] PRO T228/624, Treasury, 'Advisory Bureau of Industrial Management'.

[11] On the approach to management education in this Report see P. Armstrong, *The Abandonment of Productive Intervention in Management Teaching Syllabi: An Historical Analysis* (Coventry, 1987).

the Percy and Barlow Committees.[12] However, lower level part-time technical education continued its rapid wartime expansion, the numbers involved rising from about 40,000 pre-war to 200,000 by 1948/9. The emphasis on technical education is illustrated by the high priority it was given in the claims made by the Ministry of Education for building resources – claims resisted by the Treasury on the somewhat ironic grounds that education spending was considered part of social services which had to be cut to free resources for fuel, transport and industry.[13] Parallel to this was the perceived success of Training Within Industry (TWI), aimed at foremen and expanded significantly in the late 1940s to cover 270,000 workers and 2,724 firms by 1950.[14]

On the quality of capital inputs, Labour expanded the Department of Scientific and Industrial Research and its sponsorship of the Research Associations. Total government expenditure on civil R & D rose by around 5 times in real terms between 1945/6 and 1950/1,[15] though much more was spent on atomic and other defence research. A specific initiative of Labour was the creation in 1948 of the National Research and Development Council to provide aid for the exploitation of inventions.[16]

One theme which unified a lot of Labour's effort to improve efficiency in British industry was that of standardisation, the belief that substantial economies of scale could be attained by reducing the variety and number of goods produced. Such concern with standardisation is evident in the work of the SRU and the PES. It was a major concern of the Ministry of Supply, which established a committee on Standardisation in the Engineering Industry and pursued the issue with some vigour with employers in the industry generally, and with car producers, who also fell under its aegis.[17]

[12] R. Locke, *Management and Higher Education since 1940* (Cambridge, 1989), pp. 155–6; M. Sanderson, *The Universities and British Industry, 1850–1970* (1972), ch. 7; *Report of Percy Committee on Higher Technological Education* (1945); *Report of Barlow Committee on Scientific Manpower* (1946).

[13] G. Lowndes, *The Silent Social Revolution* (2nd edn, 1969), pp. 326–7; PEP, *Technological Education* (1952), pp. 61–80; PRO T229/492, Investment Programmes Committee, 1947–9: Ministry of Education, esp. Vinter to Strath, 20 Oct. 1949.

[14] Ministry of Labour, *Report for the Year 1950* (1950), pp. 86–7; PEP, *Manpower* (1951), pp. 20–5. Foremen were commonly seen as a key group in the enterprise in this period.

[15] N. J. Vig, *Science and Technology in British Politics* (Oxford, 1968), pp. 14–17; P. Gummett, *Scientists in Whitehall* (Manchester, 1980), p. 39; D. Edgerton, 'Whatever Happened to the British Warfare State? The Ministry of Supply, 1945–51' in Mercer et al., *Labour Governments*, pp. 91–116.

[16] PRO CAB134/648, 1st Report of NRDC, 8 Nov. 1950.

[17] PRO CAB134/639, Ministry of Supply, 'Standardising and Simplifying Engineering Products', 8 Sept. 1948; PRO SUPP14/333 Standardisation of Engineering Products – Publication and Consideration 1950/51; PRO SUPP14/151, National Advisory Council

Standardisation and the idea of unexploited economies of scale is also evident in the proposals for Development Councils. In many ways these councils were Labour's most distinctive policy proposal, drawing on the inter-war rationalisation movement and wartime Industrial Board proposals, but including a trade union as well as an expert element. The government saw them as sponsoring amalgamations and technical change, especially in fragmented consumer goods industries. Government hopes for their success rested in part on the support of many of the Board of Trade working parties, which seemed in many cases a possible tripartite route to industrial reorganisation. Eventually only four Development Councils were established, and only one of these – in cotton – in a significant industry, largely because of employer resistance.[18] Standardisation was also a theme of many of the reports of the Anglo-American Council on Productivity, probably Labour's best known activity on the supply-side. However, the message of these reports was highly ambiguous. Much space was taken up with vague and dubious extolling of the American Way of Life, often based on a narrow range of experience in the USA. Serious discussion of the relevance of US technologies to British circumstances was usually absent. In addition many of the reports were clear that the prime responsibility for Britain's lag in productivity lay with management, which did not encourage the FBI in particular to make more than a minimalist response to the reports.[19]

In Labour's 1945 manifesto, *Let Us Face the Future*, a great deal of weight was put upon anti-monopoly policy. This concern eventually led to the 1948 Monopolies and Mergers Act, but this Act was very much a damp squib, above all because of the way in which the Board of Trade was 'nobbled' by industry, both in its referrals to the Monopolies Commission and action upon the commission's reports. There was also undoubtedly an ambiguity in Labour's thinking about competition – many saw nationalisation rather than a revival of competition as the appropriate solution to monopoly.[20]

for Motor Manufacturing Industry, 1946–54. The ministry pursued a general policy of using its purchasing power to encourage standardisation. PRO CAB134/591, Productivity (Official) Committee, 17 Nov. 1948. On the role of the Ministry of Supply in this period see Edgerton, 'Whatever Happened'.

[18] H. Mercer, 'The Labour Governments and Private Industry, 1945–51' in Tiratsoo, *The Attlee Years*.

[19] J. Tomlinson, 'The Failure of the Anglo-American Council on Productivity', *Business History* 33 (1991), pp. 82–92. For a rather different view see A. Carew, *Labour under the Marshall Plan* (Manchester, 1987).

[20] H. Mercer, *Constructing a Competitive Order: The Hidden History of British Anti-Trust* (Cambridge, 1995); Mercer, 'Anti-Monopoly Policy' in Mercer et al., *Labour Governments*, pp. 55–73.

An even more prominent theme in Labour's approach to the supply-side of the economy was that of 'human relations'. This approach started from the assumption that the key element in enterprise efficiency was the co-operation of labour, and this co-operation was to be secured by recognising the social significance of work to the individual. Whilst not a unified field, the approach drew a great deal on the psychological and especially psychoanalytic approach to work of the Tavistock Centre, work about which Cripps was well informed.[21] The centrality of human relations to Labour's approach to the enterprise is evident in the central role given to 'human factors' in the setting up of the Committee on Industrial Productivity.[22] It is also evident in the campaign by the Labour government to revive workplace Joint Production Committees on the model of those widespread during the war. The JPC campaign was seen by the government not as a drive for 'industrial democracy' in the sense of, say, the guild socialism of the early twentieth century or the Bullock Report thirty years later, but as part of a programme to encourage workers' co-operation and involvement without infringing managerial prerogatives. Whilst this campaign was not entirely unsuccessful, it was constrained both by a large measure of employer hostility and by a lack of enthusiasm amongst many rank-and-file trade unionists, though union leaderships were almost unanimously supportive.[23] Human relations ideology is perhaps most obviously apparent in the drive by the Ministry of Labour, continued from the war period, to encourage the extension of factory welfare, with particular emphasis on personnel management.[24]

Human relations gained pre-eminence in part from the widespread perception that the coming of full employment had fundamentally shifted the balance of power in the workplace, and that work discipline could no longer be maintained by the threat of the sack. This is a major theme of ministerial speeches, TUC resolutions and managerial writings

---

[21] PRO CAB124/1093, Committee on Industrial Productivity, 1947.

[22] PRO CAB132/31–5, Committee on Industrial Productivity, Human Factors Panel, 1948–50. A classic spin-off from the Human Factors Panel's work is E. Jaques, *The Changing Culture of a Factory* (1951).

[23] J. Tomlinson, 'Productivity, Joint Consultation and Human Relations: The Attlee Government and the Workplace' in A. McKinlay and J. Melling (eds.), *Management, Labour and Production in Twentieth Century Europe* (1996), pp. 25–43; J. Hinton, *Shop Floor Citizens: Engineering Democracy in 1940s Britain* (1995); H. A. Clegg and T. E. Chester, 'Joint Consultation' in A. Flanders and H. A. Clegg (eds.), *The System of Industrial Relations in Great Britain* (Oxford, 1964), pp. 338–46; National Institute of Industrial Psychology, *Joint Consultation* (1952); W. A. Brown and N. Howell-Everson, *Industrial Democracy at Work* (1950); W. H. Scott, *Industrial Leadership and Joint Consultation* (Liverpool, 1952).

[24] Ministry of Labour, *Handbook of Industrial Relations* (1953 edn), ch. 7.

in this period.[25] Plainly such a humanistic approach to the workplace had its appeal to social democrats, though in other ways it was highly problematic from the point of view of traditional socialist views. It rested on belief in the enterprise as a unitary entity in which there was no fundamental conflict of interest, and in which therefore trade unions would seem to have no clear role.[26]

All the above efforts give the lie to any crude notion that Labour was solely concerned with welfare and neglected production.[27] As Douglas Jay put the point in his memoirs: 'A myth has grown up since then that the Attlee Government after 1945 plunged into vast expensive welfare schemes and ignored the hard economic base of production and exports which could alone support them. This is almost the reverse of the truth.'[28]

At the macroeconomic level this priority for production is clearly shown in Cairncross' account of the allocation of output in this period.

Few governments also have held back consumption more assiduously so as to let the pace be set by exports and investment, as recommended by a later generation of experts on growth. They were successful in a fast growth in exports, eliminating in turn the external deficit and then the dollar deficit and sustaining a high level of industrial investment in spite of the virtual cessation of personal savings.

Between 1946 and 1952, whilst GNP expanded by 15.3 per cent, consumption rose by 5.9 per cent, exports by 77.3 per cent and investment (GDFCF) by 57.9 per cent.[29]

Within this overall picture of priorities,[30] there is a range of issues about the microeconomic aspect of resource allocation, especially of investment. The best known is the question of housing – how far did the undoubted political emphasis on the housing programme inhibit industrial investment?[31] First, it must be said that whilst housing investment was high relative to other European belligerents as a share of GNP it was no higher than 1925–37, and the relative costs of housing had

---

[25] e.g. PRO LAB10/655, TUC, 'Production under Full Employment', 5 Nov. 1946.

[26] J. Child, *British Management Thought* (1969), pp. 117–36.

[27] Barnett, *Audit of War*, chs. 1, 12–14.

[28] Jay, *Change and Fortune*, p. 152.

[29] Cairncross, *Years of Recovery*, pp. 24, 500.

[30] This chapter ignores the external dimension covered in chapters 2 and 3.

[31] Barnett, *Audit of War* pp. 242–7; M. Chick, 'Economic Planning, Managerial Decision-Making and the Role of Fixed Capital Investment in the Economic Recovery of the UK 1945–55' (Ph.D. thesis, London School of Economics, 1986), pp. 38–43; S. Gilliat, 'The Management of Reconstruction with Special Reference to the Housebuilding Programme' (Ph.D. thesis, University of Sussex, 1982), chs. 7, 8. For a very useful discussion of this in one key region, see N. Tiratsoo, *Reconstruction, Affluence and Labour Politics: Coventry 1945–60* (1990).

Table 4.1 *Distribution of steel in 1948*

(000 tons)

Home investment	
Coal	568
Coke ovens	12
Electricity	530
Gas	155
Petrol	427
Railways	876
Other transport	96
Agriculture and fish	73
Iron and steel	209
Shipbuilding	537
Industrial building	292
Housing	106
Education and health	115
Defence, public administration	94
Other	
Building and civil engineering	304
Plant, machinery and vehicles	1,920
Total investment	6,314
Home, non-investment	785
Exports	3,200
Nuts, bolts, etc.	1,028
	11,327

Source: PRO CAB134/191, 'Capital Investment in 1949: Report by Investment Programmes Committee', 20 July 1948, para. 30.

risen sharply.[32] Second, the trend in housing investment both in absolute terms and relative to other investment was clearly downwards from 1947.[33] In so far as there was crowding out of industrial investment in this period this primarily operated through the allocation of steel, but housing was not a major consumer of steel – the crowding out which undoubtedly did take place was in favour of exports (see table 4.1).[34]

Housing was undoubtedly a significant consumer of timber, though this is often exaggerated (see table 4.2). It was also a big user of labour (table 4.3) at a time when labour shortages were endemic. However, whilst timber and labour resources were clearly significant, it is far from

[32] Milward, *Reconstruction*, pp. 479–80; R. C. O. Matthews, C. H. Feinstein and J. Odling-Smee, *British Economic Growth 1856–1973* (Oxford, 1982), pp. 332, 413–14.
[33] Cairncross, *Years of Recovery*, p. 456.
[34] Ibid.

Table 4.2   *Timber allocations for 1947*

	Total supply	Housing allocations	Proportion (%)
Softwood	192,500 standards	43,665 standards	22.7
Hardwood	249,000 cu. ft.	11,000,000 cu. ft.	2.2
Plywood	80,000,000 sq. ft.	7,360,000 cu. ft.	9.2

Source: PRO CAB134/478, Material Allocations Committee, 'Timber Allocations in 1947', 13 Nov. 1947.

Table 4.3   *Distribution of industrial population, 1947*

(000s)

Coal	758
Public utilities	270
Transport and ships	1,438
Agriculture	1,055
Building and civil engineering	1,364[1]
Engineering	2,876
Clothing and textiles	1,483
Distribution	2,351
Consumer services	2,120
Civil service	692
Local government	1,105
Total	18,887

[1] Of whom approximately 600,000 in housing.
Source: Economic Survey for 1947, Table XXI.

obvious that they could have been readily transferred into the shortage areas. While they could no doubt have been transferred fairly readily into industrial building, the scale of this was much more limited by steel than anything else. Secondly, it is not at all clear that the investment that was required at this time was primarily in buildings; it was rather in plant and machinery, where labour or timber from housing could have done little to help. As Plowden wrote to Cripps:

It is still true that we do not have enough factory space for all our workers. One of the problems is that the workers are in the wrong places. This is because the housing shortage means a considerable immobility of labour. So it can be argued with some truth that more houses will ease our industrial problems appreciably in 1948.[35]

[35] PRO T229/66, Plowden to Cripps, 10 Dec. 1947.

Finally, it is worth noting at least the possibility that the government's commitment to housing (by stressing its commitment to expansion at a time when a slump was widely feared), 'crowded in' industrial investment.[36]

Arguably more important than the debate about housing is the issue of how far the pattern of investment reflected too great a priority for immediate, macroeconomic concerns at the expense of long-run efficiency gains for the economy. Did the priorities established, however compelling at the time, distort the economy from a path that would have yielded greater returns in the long run?

This is a very difficult question to answer. We can begin with the stated priorities of the government. The 1947 *Economic Survey* set out six priority sectors – agriculture, building, coal, electricity, textiles, and iron and steel.[37]

One question to be asked is whether a benign dictator, with the knowledge available at the time, and concerned to maximise the long-run growth of the British economy would have accorded these industries priority. Coal, iron and steel and electricity perhaps yes – at that time these three industries looked crucial to any industrial expansion. Building also would appear sensible, as this was increasingly the building of infrastructure and factories rather than housing. Agriculture is much more problematic – here the compelling desire to save dollars is apparent, and whatever the technical efficiency of British agriculture, its overall efficiency was low.[38] Textiles presents more of a conundrum. Again, the emphasis derived very much from the industry's capacity to sell exports, but what was its long-term potential? Plainly, all European textile producers had before the war come under increasing pressure from Asian producers, and this was bound to re-emerge post-war. But was the collapse of the British industry in the 1950s inescapable? Many have argued so, on the basis of a product-cycle form of analysis in which textiles could not be profitably produced in high-wage European countries.[39] However, it may be argued that certainly the extreme scale of collapse in the 1950s was avoidable, if the opportunity of high profits, government incentives and little competition of the late 1940s had been grasped.[40]

---

[36] Milward, *Reconstruction*, p. 484.

[37] *Economic Survey* for 1947, pp. 82–117.

[38] B. Holderness, *British Agriculture since 1945* (1985), ch. 6.

[39] J. Singleton, 'Planning for Cotton 1945–51', *Economic History Review* 43 (1990), pp. 62–78; J. Singleton, 'Showing the White Flag: The Lancashire Cotton Industry 1945–65', *Business History* 32 (1990), pp. 129–49.

[40] J. Tomlinson, 'Planning for Cotton 1945–51: A Comment', *Economic History Review* 44 (1991), pp. 522–5; J. Singleton, 'Planning for Cotton: A Reply', *Economic History Review* 44 (1991), pp. 526–30.

If the priorities in the desired direction of investment appear on the whole not unreasonable, what of the quality of investment? Was too much spent on 'patch and mend' to maximise immediate output at the expense of long-run efficiency?

For coal the answer would seem to be clearly a negative – mechanisation was slow, but this does not seem primarily a consequence of a 'patch and mend' investment policy.[41]

For electricity the picture is a mixed one. Tight controls on investment may have contributed to the sub-optimal scale of generating sets, but this outcome was also powerfully affected by the engineering conservatism of the industry and that of the generator producers, although some progress was made towards standardisation under Ministry of Supply pressure.[42] Technical development in railways was slowed in this period, but this also reflected as much engineering conservatism as investment constraints.[43]

Iron and steel remains a highly controversial sector, in this as in other regards. The plan for the industry produced in 1946 did envisage a much more ambitious investment strategy, including more plant closures and development on greenfield sites than did eventually take place. But it is far from clear that this strategy was viable in view of the shortage of the new plant it would have required. In any event many firms in the industry were resistant to such a strategy, given the strong demand for steel in the period: 'What happened resembled the normal pattern of boom development, which made it desirable to keep all existing plant in use and tempting to expand it all' and 'the proposals in 1947/8 to concentrate for a short time on relatively minor but quickly rewarding jobs at the expense of radical change were essentially wise'.[44]

In the non-nationalised industries there seems little evidence of modernising investment strategies being crucially undermined by governmental 'short-termism'. In the case of Courtaulds the main constraints seem to have been inadequate R & D and shifts in market demand.[45] At ICI investment constraints did not prevent the construction of the new plant at Wilton or significantly impede other expansion plans.[46] In

[41] W. Ashworth, *The History of the British Coal Industry*, vol. v: *The Nationalized Industry* (Oxford, 1986), ch. 3.

[42] L. Hannah, *Engineers, Managers and Politicians: The First Fifteen Years of Nationalised Electricity Supply in Britain* (1982), chs. 3, 4, 8.

[43] T. Gourvish, *British Railways 1948–1973: A Business History* (Cambridge, 1986), ch. 3, esp. pp. 85–90.

[44] D. Burn, *The Steel Industry 1939–1959* (Cambridge, 1961), pp. 252, 267; cf. M. Chick, 'Economic Planning', ch. 6; P. Payne, *Colvilles and the Scottish Steel Industry* (Oxford, 1979), ch. 11.

[45] D. Coleman, *Courtaulds: An Economic and Social History* (Oxford, 1980), vol. II, ch. 3.

[46] W. J. Reader, *ICI: A History* (1975), vol. II, pp. 407–8, 461–2.

textiles we have a clear picture of the industry resisting the blandishments of government to go for a more radical reconstruction of the industry.[47]

Planning and production

The pattern of investment which did emerge has to be seen in the context of Labour's whole approach to economic management, and especially planning.[48] The general issue of Labour and planning is dealt with in detail in chapter 6. The key point for the current discussion is that all the debates on this concept in the 1930s and 1940s failed to produce a clearly articulated doctrine of planning tied to the range of objectives that socialists might want to pursue. Too often it was grounded in little more than an instinctive dislike of the 'anarchy' of the market and a subordination of all economic issues to questions of ownership, with nationalisation thus emerging as the key economic policy.[49]

Labour's inheritance in 1945 was, of course, much more than an ideology of planning. The wartime coalition had erected a comprehensive set of controls over the economy, over investment, consumption and prices, manpower, trade and foreign exchange, which meant that the market mechanism had been supplanted over large parts of the economy, and that the economy was already substantially planned or at least controlled. It was widely agreed that most of these controls would have to be retained in the period of transition to a peacetime economy.[50] For Labour the issue was how far these controls were what should be meant by plans, and what their role should therefore be beyond the transition period.

In *Let Us Face the Future* the emphasis was on controls as a means of securing an egalitarian distribution of limited supplies of goods, and as an instrument to help offset the expected slump. The implication was that the controls would be maintained for a long time, but this extended time horizon was most explicit in relation to investment, where a National Investment Board was to be established for both microecon-

---

[47] R. Streat, *Lancashire and Whitehall: The Diary of Sir Raymond Streat*, ed. M. Duprée (1987), e.g. pp. 383–5.

[48] Planning was not, of course, just an 'economic issue', but related to the characteristic Labour world view in which rational organisation was seen as the central feature of the desirable society.

[49] Durbin, *New Jerusalems*.

[50] Cairncross, *Years of Recovery*; Addison, *Road to 1945*, ch. 9; the need to retain controls was the basis of a famous article by R. H. Tawney, 'The Abolition of Economic Controls 1918–21', *Economic History Review* 13 (1943), pp. 1–13.

Table 4.4   *Controls, 1946–51*

(%)

	1946	1948	1951
Proportion of consumers' expenditure subject to rationing	28	31	10
Proportion of imports controlled	96	91	54
Proportion of industrial raw material controlled	94	81	41
Price-controlled goods as proportion of consumer expenditure	48	49[1]	40

[1] = 1949
Source: Dow, *Management*, tables 6.3, 6.4, 6.5, 6.6.

omic and macroeconomic purposes 'to determine social priorities and promote better timing in private investment'.[51]

The logic of controls intended to deal with a supply-constrained economy was that they would disappear as the supply constraint lessened. To a significant degree this happened after 1945 (table 4.4). The picture is complicated by the Korean War, which reversed the trend towards decontrol in some areas. This trend, even if uninterrupted, would still have left a significant part of the economy subject to control by the time Labour left office. Partly it reflected the continuing constraint of the balance of payments, but it also reflected a profound ambiguity in Labour's thinking about the role of controls in economic policy.

Wilson's 'bonfire of controls' of 1948 fitted in with the belief, general in the government, that many of the controls had outlived their purpose and were an unnecessary electoral liability. However, this was by no means the same as a general commitment to abolish all controls. The long-term future of controls was very much a live issue in the later years of the Labour government. The dominant line which emerged from these debates was that of Gaitskell, who argued that some of the controls, previously based on wartime emergency powers, should be put on a permanent basis for reasons which were largely macroeconomic. He argued that to combine full employment (including in the Development Areas) and balance of payments equilibrium, and to avoid inflation a variety of controls would be required – controls over prices, building activity, imports and exports, over consumer goods and materials.[52]

[51] Labour Party, *Let Us Face the Future*.
[52] Rollings, 'The Reichstag Method of Governing?', pp. 15–36, Cairncross, *Years of Recovery*, pp. 329–32, 352–3.

It is important, therefore, not to exaggerate either the scale of decontrol under Labour or the extent to which the idea of controls as part of economic policy had been given up. On the other hand, the permanent controls envisaged by Gaitskell were for purposes of economic stabilisation rather than modernisation, and were consequently negative rather than positive – aimed at stopping certain kinds of economic activity, not making things happen. This conflict between a view of controls as negative instruments, essentially concerned with macroeconomic objectives, and planning as a modernising, microeconomic instrument, can be seen clearly in Labour's policies on investment.

As will be discussed in detail in chapter 7, the most explicit commitment to planning in 1945 was to the planning of investment via the National Investment Board. The proposal for a NIB presupposed that effective control of investment could be secured by financial mechanisms, yet the conditions for such control to be effective were entirely absent. On the one hand, the government was committed to cheap money, so control via interest rates was ruled out. On the other hand, companies generally were cash-rich in 1945 (for example, Courtaulds had £40m., Vickers £12.5m. in liquid assets)[53] and also saw a very rapid profit revival after 1945, so they were generally little constrained in their investment behaviour by finance.[54] This situation also meant that the wartime Capital Issues Committee, whilst it continued in peace, had little impact on investment. The burden of controlling investment fell, then, almost entirely on physical controls.

In wartime controls over investment had operated via a combination of building licensing, machinery licensing and raw material allocations. The second of these largely ended in early 1946, and from then on the other two were the main instruments used.[55] In the initial post-war period investment boomed with seemingly little control, the level in 1946 being 150 per cent above the previous year (table 4.5), encouraged by high levels of consumer demand, wartime backlogs, and the encouragement of increased investment allowances.[56] Only in 1947 did a serious attempt get under way to control this tide of investment, which was

[53] Coleman, *Courtaulds*, vol. II, p. 11; J. D. Scott, *Vickers: A History* (1962), p. 301.
[54] T. Barna, 'Those "Frightfully High" Profits', *Oxford University Bulletin of Statistics* 11 (1949), pp. 213–26. On the whole physical versus financial control of investment, N. Rollings, 'The Control of Inflation in the Managed Economy: Britain 1945–58' (1990).
[55] PRO CAB134/63, Committee on Control of Investment, Report, 23 July 1949.
[56] PRO CAB134/63. Initial allowances were introduced in 1932 at 12%, and increased to 20% in 1945, and for plant and machinery 40% in 1949 (20% for buildings). Committee on Control of Investment, Report, 23 July 1949, para. 6; Dow, *Management*, pp. 205–6.

Table 4.5 *Investment and its distribution at 1958 prices*

(£m.)

	1946	1947	1948	1949	1950	1951
Dwellings		523	486	476	465	456
Other new buildings and works	930	446	480	588	661	640
Plant and machinery	452	626	765	845	942	1,026
Vehicles, ships, aircraft	331	404	404	424	397	347
Total	1,713	2,000	2,135	2,333	2,459	2,469
Manufacturing and construction	n.a.	n.a.	554	626	714	768
Gas, water and electricity			206	252	282	284
Transport and communication			344	355	334	292
Distribution, road haulage			187	231	251	250
Social and public services			123	151	182	201
Agriculture and mining			181	189	179	164
Total	1,713	2,000	2,135	2,333	2,459	2,469

Source: Cairncross, *Years of Recovery*, p. 456.

much beyond the capacity of the economy to complete. The key body in this attempt was the Investment Programmes Committee, a subcommittee of the Steering Committee on Economic Development, the main economic committee of officials, which worked in close collaboration in the Central Economic Planning Staff, also created in the middle of 1947. This committee quickly produced a report which was widely welcomed in government circles, and a slightly amended version appeared as a White Paper.[57]

The year 1947 is commonly seen as one in which the Labour government turned decisively towards Keynesian economic policies, and certainly the second budget of that year did introduce a much tougher and more explicit fiscal policy (see chapter 10). But the events of 1947 can be given a different colour. As Cairncross notes, Dalton responded to the Investment Programmes Committee Report by welcoming it as 'a real start to central planning'.[58] Cripps saw it in a similar light – rather than fiscal policy replacing planning, a tighter fiscal policy was perceived as necessary to make planning effective.[59] But effective at what? Here it would seem the advisers of government were largely consistent – the

[57] PRO T229/66, 'White Paper on Investment Programmes 1948', 16 Oct. 1947; *Capital Investment in 1948*, Parliamentary Papers 1947, vol. IX.

[58] Cairncross, *Years of Recovery*, p. 452.

[59] Cripps, 'almost appeared to regard budgetary policy as no more than the background to planning proper' (Dow, *Management*, p. 36).

aim was to get as quickly as possible back to a 'normal' economy where planning (including of investment) would be unnecessary. This was the view of Plowden, the Chief Planning Officer, who agreed with Austen Robinson that 'the main aim of planning should be to make planning unnecessary'.[60] This view has recently been reiterated by Robinson.[61] It also seems to have been the view of the key advisers in the Economic Section, which acted as a major source of anti-microeconomic planning views in the late 1940s (see chapter 6).

Parallel to this was a lack of interest and concern with issues of industrial modernisation. Economists in general knew little and had little helpful to say on such issues – for example, the Economic Section's role in the productivity debate seems to have been largely restricted to advocacy of anti-monopoly policy and the need for more incentives. Whilst some members of the Central Economic Planning Staff tended more towards dirigistic planning ideas, these were not taken up at the highest levels.[62]

Cairncross thus rightly points to a conflict in notions of planning between 'a liberal, Keynesian, approach which saw planning as a corrective to the operation of market force and dwelt particularly on the need for a level of effective demand adequate to maintain full employment' and socialist planning. However his characterisation of that socialist planning as an 'egalitarian approach which saw planning as a purely organisational activity akin to the planning that goes on within a productive enterprise', whilst accurate as far as it goes, leaves out the modernising aspect of planning as perceived by people like Cripps.[63] Undoubtedly planning in that sense was ill thought out and not the dominant approach (especially amongst the economists) but it clearly links to Cripps' and to a degree Dalton's modernising cast of mind. Planning was not just about restoring an economic equilibrium but also about giving investment and other kinds of priority to sectors considered vital for the foreseeable future.

This duality in the role of investment controls is reflected in the work of the committee set up to look at the long-term aspects of investment

---

[60] E. Plowden, *An Industrialist in the Treasury* (1989), p. 46; this phrase comes from PRO T229/47, 'Comments on Economic Section's Survey for 1948–51' by E. A. G. Robinson, 23 June 1947. Also PRO T229/29, 'Note by CEPS on Economic Survey 1948–51', 1 Aug. 1947.

[61] A. Robinson, 'Economic Problems', pp. 177–80: 'We consciously used controls and more generally the resources of government in many cases not to change a destination but to save time in reaching the same destination' (p. 177).

[62] Cairncross and Watts, *Economic Section*; for example, PRO T229/166, 'Level of Industry Planning', undated, but 1948.

[63] Cairncross' distinction perhaps reflects the traditional economists' analysis of planning versus the price mechanism as essentially an issue of allocative efficiency.

control. The two objectives of control were argued to be to 'ensure that important investment was not swamped by less essential work, secondly, to lessen the danger that an excessive concentration of resources on investment would damage other sections of the economy, particularly exports, or render the inflation problems insoluble'.[64]

The draft report spelt out that the only effective control over investment in plant and machinery was the steel allocation, and assumed that as steel supplies increased this would disappear. It went on to argue that the only effective control would then be via depreciation allowances, which it accepted would be used to control the volume but not the direction of investment. This view was based partly on discussions with the Inland Revenue, who had opposed any 'discriminatory' aspect being given to the tax system. Finally, the draft report looked forward to the continuation of building licences for the foreseeable future, but made clear its conclusion that 'So far as the investment by private firms and individuals is concerned, the methods of influence will inevitably be through general fiscal and financial measures'.[65]

The final version of the report tried to be more optimistic on the effects of government, invoking hopes of continued consultation with big firms even as controls were being reduced, and similarly hopes that financial institutions would conform to government policy on investment. But there was a clear acceptance that at best government could only 'influence' not 'control' investment.[66] This report probably reflected the predominant view of senior civil servants, advisers and ministers by this time. Clearly, with highly liquid companies on the one hand, and a largely uncontrolled financial sector on the other, control of investment decisions by financial mechanisms would have required radical policy initiatives which never surfaced in this period. Discontent with Labour's incapacity to influence, let alone control, the decisions of private sector industrial firms is certainly evident, most especially in a widely discussed paper by Harold Wilson.[67] But he did not link his discussion to financial mechanisms or to the wider aspects of the possible reforms of Britain's financial system (see chapter 7). Overall, Labour failed to evolve any mechanisms of long-term investment planning in the private sector. Financial mechanisms able to discriminate between sectors were not developed, and direct controls, in this area at least, came to be seen as purely transitional. Manpower planning, which

[64] PRO CAB134/63, Committee on Control of Investment, Draft Report, 23 July 1949, para. 2.
[65] Ibid., para. 18.
[66] Final version of Report, 5 Sept. 1949.
[67] PRO, PREM8/1183, H. Wilson, 'The State and Private Industry', 4 May 1950.

also figured highly in Labour's discussions, also came to very little (see chapter 8).

In sum, Labour's concept of planning was underdeveloped, and thus became easily conflated with the issue of controls seen as being basically about macroeconomic stabilisation. Concern with industrial modernisation was widespread in the government but ways of making this the prime objective of economic planning were difficult to develop, especially as it became apparent that the newly nationalised industries would be very difficult to control and could not therefore act as spearheads of economic policy, as many had envisaged before 1945.[68] In all this the economists were of little help – even the broadly sympathetic figures like Meade and Hall were to some extent like generals fighting the last war, concerned with macroeconomic stabilisation rather than economic modernisation.

Tripartism

The story of planning under Labour is not just one of the failure to find mechanisms to make industrial modernisation the centrepiece of economic planning. Labour was strongly committed to what was called democratic as opposed to totalitarian planning, 'planning from the ground up'.[69] This emphasis led to two kinds of policy responses. On the one hand, it led to great campaigns of propaganda and exhortation as a way of trying to persuade people to fall in with the economic policy priorities of the government – campaigns with variable levels of success.[70] On the other hand, it led to the revival or creation of a whole range of tripartite bodies – bodies with trade union and employer representatives sitting alongside government representatives. Much has been made, especially by Middlemas, of the significance of the higher level of such bodies, like the National Joint Advisory Council (covering broadly wages and conditions), the National Production Advisory Council on Industry (covering production issues) and the Economic

[68] TUC, *Interim Report on Postwar Reconstruction* (1944).
[69] *Economic Survey* for 1947, para. 8; *Let Us Face the Future.*
[70] W. Crofts, *Coercion or Persuasion? Economic Propaganda 1945–51* (1989); S. Carruthers, 'Manning the Factories: Propaganda and Policy on the Employment of Women', *History* 75 (1990), pp. 232–56. On the populace's understanding of economic issues stressed by the government, see, for example, PRO RG23/103, *Survey of Knowledge and Opinion about the Economic Situation*, Nov. 1948. This found that, despite intense publicity on the topic in recent weeks, only 18 per cent of respondents understood the notion of productivity, 22 per cent confused it with production, 10 per cent gave totally wrong answers, 50 per cent said they did not know and didn't try to define it.

Planning Board (covering the broad issues of economic policy). For Middlemas such bodies represent a significant corporatist element in British politics.[71]

However, a number of points can be made to qualify any picture of a drawing in of the main interest groups into a consensual policy-making framework. First, any reading of the above records suggests they were not arenas where crucial economic policy issues were hammered out. Rather they acted as sounding boards for government ideas or places for transmitting information to the non-governmental participants. Rarely did key issues get resolved in such arenas. The Labour government was very strongly committed to notions of parliamentary sovereignty, which plainly militated against any real power-sharing, though the government certainly listened to what the FBI and TUC had to say.[72] Secondly, whilst employers went along with such tripartism in national bodies, at lower levels they were much more resistant. They strongly and largely successfully resisted Development Councils, perhaps Labour's most central proposal for new institutions in industry.[73] They also resisted strong trade union representation on other industrial bodies, like the Advisory Councils in engineering and cars.[74] More generally, whilst reluctantly accepting the government's idea of promoting the revival of factory-level Joint Production Committees, the employers made sure these remained purely consultative in character, and in particular resisted any idea that they should have any inter-factory role, for example by links to the Regional Industrial Boards. Any such links were rejected by employers on both the NJAC and NPACI, despite the support of Cripps.[75] As so often, the employers' resistance was abetted by the conservatism of the Ministry of Labour, and its notion that JPCs should be seen as just good industrial relations policies, not as part of any experiment in involving workers and unions in production issues.[76]

Popular involvement in production could never substitute for adequate economic mechanisms for giving priority in resources to certain industrial sectors. Nevertheless, this 'democratic planning' was an important and unduly neglected part of Labour's policies, especially at

---

[71] Middlemas, *Power*.
[72] NJAC records are at PRO LAB10/652, 655–8; NPACI at BT190/2, 4–7; EPB at T229/28–42 and CAB124/210–14. This point is taken up in chapter 13, below.
[73] Mercer, 'Labour Governments'.
[74] PRO SUPP14/137, 'Ministry of Supply: Proposals for an Engineering Industries Advisory Board', 1946; SUPP14/151, 'National Advisory Council for the Motor Manufacturing Industry', 1946.
[75] PRO BT190/2, NPACI Minutes, 8 Aug. 1947; CAB124/351, 'Investigation by Postmaster General of Regional Boards and District Committees', Sept. 1947; CAB124/349. Minutes of Midlands Regional Board for Industry, 15 Oct. 1947.
[76] PRO LAB10/721 'Ministry of Labour, JPCs: Report to NJAC', 26 Jan. 1949.

the factory and regional levels as opposed to central government. Labour was strongly committed to a consensual industrial policy, aimed at engaging the support of employers and unions for its policy goals. How did this approach help or hinder its concern to modernise British industry?

On the union side the government was strikingly successful in engaging the support of trade union leaderships for its productivity drive. How far this leadership enthusiasm was translated into support at shop-floor level is much less clear. James Hinton argues for a widespread 'productionist' enthusiasm amongst workers and especially shop stewards in the 1940s, though he accepts this was at its peak in 1941/2, rather than in the post-war period.[77] Employers, as they always do, sounded off about union restrictive practices, but hard evidence on their prevalence, let alone their effects, is difficult to come by. In cotton, for example, long-standing 'restrictionist' union policies were changed when the Weavers' Amalgamation accepted more looms per worker, but the spinning unions were more resistant to change.[78]

Even in the 'notorious' home of restrictive practices, shipbuilding, an official report of 1950 said that 'In general, although the unions in the shipbuilding and ship-repairing industry maintain that workers displaced should have preference and that machines should not be operated by "cheap labour" they have not resisted the introduction of new machines or processes'. Overall, it is difficult to accept the recently expressed view that restrictive practices were the major obstacle to productivity increase in this period.[79]

On the employers' side the picture is somewhat clearer, at least as regards the FBI. Contrary to the assertions of writers like Blank, the federation seems to have encouraged and co-ordinated a fairly hostile response to many government initiatives, including those which might be seen as part of the modernisation programme. For example, it co-ordinated opposition to Development Councils and made only a mini-

[77] Hinton, *Shop Floor Citizens*; J. Tomlinson, 'The 1945 Labour Government and the Trade Unions' in Tiratsoo, *The Attlee Years*. On TUC official acceptance of the centrality of increased productivity see TUC, 'Productivity: Report of the General Council to the Special Conference of TU Executive Committees', 14 Nov. 1948.

[78] H. A. Turner, *Trade Union Growth, Structure and Policy: A Comparative Study of the Cotton Unions* (1962) pp. 5–6, 332; PRO BT195/4, 'Notes from P.M.s Meeting with Cotton Industry', 22 March 1948; F. Zweig, *Productivity and the Trade Unions* (Oxford, 1952), p. 157; compare Crofts, *Coercion*, pp. 150–2.

[79] PRO LAB10/932, 'Restrictive Practices in Shipbuilding and Ship-repairing', 16 Jan. 1950; S. Broadberry and N. Crafts, 'Explaining Anglo-American Productivity Differences in the Mid-Twentieth Century', *Bulletin of the Oxford University Institute of Statistics* 52 (1990), pp. 375–402.

malist response to the government's productivity drive on such bodies as the AACP and the Committee on Industrial Productivity.[80]

At a lower level, trade associations seem to have played a more equivocal role. As already noted, engineering and car employer associations wanted very much to limit the role of trade unions, which were taking an aggressively 'productionist' line on the role of industrial advisory bodies. On the other hand, some TAs, in engineering for example, do seem to have been active to a degree in encouraging standardisation, an important part of the modernisation process.[81] Overall, however, it is likely that the TAs remained predominantly restrictionist bodies, involved primarily in price-fixing and other defensive procedures rather than being agencies of economic change.[82]

The general picture would seem to be that the government found trade unions much more corrigible than employers in their attempts to reform British industry. The problem was that, of course, employers for most purposes mattered much more – they held the major levers of power. The issue that remains is whether a different strategy towards private sector employers could have yielded richer dividends. This is a vast and complex issue, but one possibility it does raise is whether Labour could have pushed much harder the role of industrial managers at the expense of owners of private industry.

Management of industry was not traditionally an area of great concern to the Labour Party. The commitment to free collective bargaining on the one hand, and on the other to changes in the ownership of industry, tended to squeeze out any serious discussion of management either as a social category or as a functional entity in the economy. To a degree this attitude was shifted by the experience of the wartime ministers like Dalton and Cripps (himself an industrial manager in the First World War) who were drawn willy-nilly into issues of management. At roughly the same time Labour backbenchers like Albu and Mikardo tried to get the left to take a more positive view on both the social and political role and economic functions of management.

This movement in Labour views was not entirely without its effects. There is evidence that some sectors of management (along with other sections of the middle class) became more sympathetic to Labour during the war period. Cripps, for example, seems to have been a popu-

---

[80] S. Blank, *Government and Industry in Britain: The FBI in Politics 1945–65* (Farnborough, 1973), ch. 4; Mercer, 'Labour Governments'; Tomlinson, 'Failure'.

[81] PRO SUPP14/333, 'Standardisation of Engineering Products', 2nd Review, Dec. 1950; PRO BT195/1, 'Standardisation in Industry', Engineering Advisory Council (49) 14th, 3 March 1949.

[82] Mercer, *Constructing a Competitive Order*, pp. 23–7.

lar figure, at least amongst some managerial echelons. Attlee and other ministers had established links with sympathetic businessmen through the 1944 Association, which acted not only as a 'dining club' but provided memoranda to the government on major policy issues.[83]

However, one of the obstacles to a more 'managerialist' stance by Labour was its commitment to tripartism. Management lacked the representational institutions to challenge the political role of the 'peak associations' of the FBI and BEC. These bodies in turn used their representation on the advisory bodies to resist a larger role for management and other professional bodies.[84]

This problem was discussed in the civil service when the issue of the structure of various advisory bodies was raised. For example, in the formation of the Committee on Industrial Productivity there was resistance by civil servants to giving the British Institute of Management a place alongside the TUC and FBI, a representation itself regarded as 'one of the unfortunate political necessities of the day'.[85] This particular issue raised the general problem of management wanting to be a 'third estate'. It was argued that if the BIM claim to be on this committee were accepted it would open the door to others. In fact, every two-sided body might well become triangular in future, and the role of the independent or government member to ensure that the work got done with the maximum reconciliation of the employers and trade unionists would tend to disappear in the claims of the non-elected manager to speak in effect for the public interest in efficiency. This would be the 'managerial revolution' with a vengeance'.[86] Ministers seem to have followed this line of thinking, and the FBI, BEC and the TUC were unchallenged in their domination of the various 'representative' bodies established by Labour. This led to a loss of faith by some management opinion in the Labour government.[87]

---

[83] For example, editorial in *Industry*, 21 April 1948, where the creation of the BIM is credited to the 'indomitable resolve' of Cripps. Records of (some of) the meetings of the 1944 Association are in the Labour Party archives.

[84] e.g. the attempt by the Institute of Production Engineers to play a larger role as, effectively, management consultants. PRO SUPP14/140, 'Engineering Advisory Council, Memo by Institute of Production Engineers for Increased Productivity', Feb. 1949.

[85] PRO BT64/2360, Committee on Industrial Productivity, S. A. Dakin to B. M. Nowell, 16 April 1948.

[86] Ibid., Dakin to Nowell, 6 May 1948. Reference to the managerial revolution reflects the wide impact of the book of that title by James Burnham, first published in 1941. The Board of Trade resisted pressures from Ian Mikardo to get management represented on various bodies, (PRO BT64/2360 Minutes of Meeting with BIM, 6 May 1948).

[87] *Industry Illustrated*, Editorials, October 1945, December 1945. The latter lamented that 'One would have thought this government would have been the most ready to listen, to recognise and appreciate Industry's *tiers état*' (p. 11). Management is, of course, an ambiguous category. The BIM probably came to represent middle management, whilst

Of course, this representation problem was not the only obstacle to Labour becoming much more of a party of industrial management. Management presumably was also affected by the general shift of middle-class opinion back to the Tories in the late 1940s.[88] Nevertheless, for a government which put such weight on formal mechanisms of interest representation it was a serious blow to (some) management hopes when the FBI/BEC and TUC retained their stronghold on representative bodies. Equally, that management did not become a political 'player' and possible ally is a not insignificant part of the limits of the government's 'modernising' role.

Production: the bridge to socialism

Strategy is an overused word today, and to suggest Labour had a strategy of modernisation is to exaggerate the coherence and strength of its policies in that regard. Nevertheless, it did pursue a number of policy initiatives which were aimed at improvement in the long-term efficiency as well as the short-term output of British industry, and these needed rescuing from their neglect by most historians of the Attlee government. These initiatives, in summary, included the encouragement and financing of higher investment, the establishing of the BIM, a much expanded DSIR and other means of support for R & D, and encouragement of the processes of standardisation of products and rationalisation of industrial structure.

In all this the constraints were formidable. Primary, perhaps, was the necessity for more output now rather than competitiveness in the future, which post-war macroeconomic and political circumstances made unavoidable. Second, whilst enthusiasm for increased efficiency embraced most of the major Labour figures in this period, it is clear that Cripps, followed perhaps by Morrison, were particularly important in this issue. One of the problems that flowed from this was that much of the efficiency effort was initiated by Cripps when he was at the Board of Trade in 1945–7, and continued by Harold Wilson at the Board thereafter. But the Board of Trade's direct responsibilities were largely limited to consumer goods industries, and in particular it had little direct role in the key area of engineering, which was the responsibility of the Ministry of Supply. This ministry had much weaker ministers than the

the FBI mainly represented the executive groups who might or might not also be major shareholders. These were also the kind of people ministers met informally at such bodies as the 1944 Association.

[88] H. G. Nicholas, *The British General Election of 1950* (Oxford, 1951), p. 296.

Board of Trade, seems to have had much less drive to change the industries with which it was involved, and generally seems to have been characterised by a rather 'cosy' relationship with those industries. Certainly it lacked the high-profile emphasis on productivity and efficiency of the Board of Trade.[89]

It may also be noted that the Ministry of Supply successfully resisted the pressures for tripartism so strongly pursued by Cripps, so that, for example, there was never a realistic likelihood of a Development Council in the car industry, despite union and political pressure. Here the hostility of the employers to a strong union role led to the establishment of an Advisory Council with a very limited union role. Arguably, the absence of such tripartite structures could have facilitated a more discriminatory industrial policy, as tripartism may inhibit policies which favour some firms or sectors at the expense of others because of the desire to maintain consensus.[90] But what was also important in the case of the Ministry of Supply was the greater reliance of its industries on government purchasing than most British industries, and though the use of this power to change the practices of the firms concerned seems to have been limited, as has already been noted, the policy of standardisation was pursued by this route.[91]

Another major problem for the government was the difficulty of dealing with a suspicious and largely hostile private sector which at the same time lacked the incentive for radical change in a world of easy markets and high profits. But the problem also stemmed in part from Labour's own weaknesses. Without help from the economists, Labour's conception of economic policy was often fragmented, usually unified by reference to 'planning', which was a rhetorical device as often as a coherent programme of action. A negative capacity for preventing things from happening too often substituted for more positive instruments that would shape events. A rather unreflective *dirigisme* too often stood in place of a more subtle understanding of state capacities in the emergent 'mixed economy'.

The success of the Labour government's drive to raise production and efficiency is the source of some controversy. Partly this relates to differing views about what generates efficiency – for example, it is clear that few in Labour circles at this time believed that competition was

[89] Edgerton, 'Whatever Happened?'

[90] L. Kenworthy, 'Are Industrial Policy and Corporatism Compatible?' *Journal of Public Policy* 10 (1990), pp. 233–65.

[91] T. Balogh, 'Britain's Economic Problem', *Quarterly Journal of Economics* 58 (1949), pp. 32–67.

crucial to efficiency, so those who do believe in the importance of this factor tend to look sceptically on Labour's claims in this area.[92] Judgement is also difficult because of the impossibility of ascribing any proportion of whatever productivity performance did occur to the role of government. Plainly, in the late 1940s the economy was undergoing a 'natural' recovery from the war period which would presumably have occurred whatever was done by government.

With these problems in mind, what do quantitative studies suggest about productivity at the time of the Attlee governments? Cairncross, the author of the most authoritative macroeconomic survey of the period, accepts Feinstein's conclusion that GDP per head rose 1.6 per cent per annum between 1945 and 1951, and 2.5 per cent per annum in the three years 1948–51. Labour productivity in manufacturing apparently followed a similar pattern, rising at an average rate of 2.6 per cent per annum across the six years, but accelerating to 3.5 per cent per annum between 1948 and 1951.[93]

These recent calculations may be compared to those made at earlier dates. Rostas, writing in 1952, focused on labour productivity and measured output in physical terms. Using 1948 as a base year with value 100, he demonstrated that performance in large industries had been very variable, so that the index of output per head in 1951 ranged from 99 for cotton to 129 for steel tubes, with the (unweighted) average being 118.[94] Such estimates are broadly in line with those calculated by Nicholson and Gupta, who focused on the period 1948–54.[95] Finally, there is the pioneering study of what would later be called total factory productivity, published by Reddaway and Smith in 1960. These authors suggest that (allowing for increased labour and capital inputs) the rate of productivity increase changed positively between 1948 and 1951, allowing an average of 3.3 per cent per annum. This performance compared well with that achieved over the following four years, when the comparative figure was only 1.1 per cent per annum.[96]

Taken together, therefore, the figures do at least imply that productivity was tending to improve appreciably in the late 1940s. Indeed,

---

[92] N. Crafts, 'Adjusting from War to Peace in 1940s' Britain', *The Economic and Social Review* 25 (1993), pp. 1–20.

[93] Cairncross, *Years of Recovery*, pp. 18–19, based on C. H. Feinstein, *National Income, Expenditure and Output of the UK, 1855–1965* (Cambridge, 1972).

[94] L. Rostas, 'Changes in the Productivity of British Industry, 1945–50', *Economic Journal* 62 (1952), pp. 15–24.

[95] R. J. Nicholson and S. Gupta, 'Output and Productivity Changes in British Manufacturing 1948–52' *Journal of the Royal Statistical Society* 23 (1960), pp. 427–59.

[96] W. B. Reddaway and A. B. Smith, 'Progress in British Manufacturing Industries 1948–54', *Economic Journal* 70 (1960), pp. 17–31.

Rostas referred to a 'general favourable development' during this period, while Reddaway and Smith noted that their data might appear 'too good to be true'. But had this pattern been shaped in any way by government policies? The latter authors felt that the acceleration of 1948–51 had reflected 'recovery from wartime organisation' and would prove unsustainable.[97] Rostas accepted there was some force in this point, but argued that an enhanced 'productivity consciousness' had also been important: 'This meant that the large potentialities for an immediate improvement of productivity were realised, that ways and means to improve productivity were expected and that positive measures were adopted in many factories and workshops for this purpose.'[98]

This material is sufficient, at least, to suggest that the Attlee governments' efforts in this direction deserve rather more positive assessments than they have often been given, though no one would suggest they resulted in extraordinary success. The constraints they faced are put in a broader context in the concluding chapter.

Production: The Bridge to Socialism was the title of a pamphlet produced by the Labour Party in 1948. It called on all 'active public-spirited citizens' to make every effort to raise production. And in particular it urged Labour Party members to give a lead in campaigning for more output and increased efficiency.[99] Party political rhetoric is, to say the least, to be treated with some caution when its significance is being considered. But the idea that raising output and efficiency provided the route out of the dilemmas of economic policy in the late 1940s is too prevalent to be dismissed as a passing propaganda stunt. As this chapter has demonstrated, increased output and increased productivity both followed 'logically' from the focus on the balance of payments as the key issue for economic policy; in a supply-constrained economy more output, from an almost static labour force, led simply into an emphasis on (labour) productivity. Equally, the desire for increased efficiency shaped Labour's attitude to a range of policy areas, not least that of equality (see chapter 12). For both these reasons, this policy concern deserves to have a central place in our understanding of the Attlee government.

---

[97] Rostas, 'Changes', p. 20; Reddaway and Smith, 'Progress', pp. 29–30.
[98] Rostas, 'Changes', pp. 24–5.
[99] Labour Party, *Production: The Bridge to Socialism* (1948), p. 11.

5   Nationalisation

Nationalisation was at the heart of Labour's economic policies in 1945. It was central to Labour's programmatic statements of the 1930s (see chapter 1), and the commitment was strengthened by the war. Nationalisation was 'out of bounds' under the wartime coalition; whilst Labour's commitment to controls over the economy matched both the demands and political possibilities of war, the Conservatives would not stomach public ownership. Hence the war contrived to 'make public ownership a cherished icon. Labour's distinctive vision of economic change centred more and more on what was being denied it during the war.'[1]

Nationalisation – before, during or after the war – never had a simple justification. In the 1930s the emphasis tended to be on the monopolistic and inefficient character of the specific industries concerned; in the war period the view that the role of nationalisation was part of a more general picture of a hierarchy of economic controls, aimed especially at securing full employment, gained ground.[2] After 1945 both these objectives were central to the argument, though they were coupled to broader aims of depriving private capital of power and enhancing democracy. Nationalising was a means of increasing efficiency, a means of planning the economy, but for some an end in itself, as representing the appropriate form of ownership for a socialist economy.

In the context of the late 1940s' desire for output and efficiency (see chapter 4), along with the existence of other instruments of economic control (both physical and fiscal), and the lack of any immediate threat of mass unemployment, the debate on nationalisation tended to shift towards 'efficiency' issues. The other aspects of nationalisation did not go away, and indeed the important debate about *future* nationalisation

---

[1] Brooke, *Labour's War*, p. 241.
[2] These different arguments are well illustrated in the TUC *Interim Report on Post-War Reconstruction* (1944), though it also makes clear we should note the continuity between the approaches of the 1930s and 1940s as well as the differences. See also J. Tomlinson, *Government and the Enterprise since 1900: The Changing Problem of Efficiency* (Oxford, 1994), ch. 8.

which began in Labour circles as early as 1947 was not just about how much to nationalise, but also about its purposes. Nevertheless, it was the efficiency aspect which tended to dominate the governmental agenda.[3]

Nationalisation and efficiency

In 1945 *Let Us Face the Future* set out the nationalisation programme in terms of 'service to the nation', and argued for priority to be accorded to the nationalisation of fuel and power industries, inland transport and iron and steel. The efficiency case for nationalisation of coal was spelt out in typical fashion:

For a quarter of a century the coal industry, producing Britain's most precious national raw material, has been floundering chaotically under the ownership of many hundreds of independent companies. Amalgamation under public owner-ship will bring great economies in operation and make it possible to modernise production methods and to raise safety standards in every colliery in the country.[4]

If efficiency derived from scale, from co-ordination rather than com-petition, it was hardly surprising that the entities nationalised were industries rather than companies. These industries were in some cases 'natural monopolies', in which case their nationalisation would fit with an orthodox economist's views of how such non-competitive industries might be dealt with.[5] But it should be said that a key target of nationalis-ation, coal, was quite clearly not a natural monopoly and that generally the role of economists' arguments in the nationalisation programme should not be exaggerated. Note that the conception of efficiency behind discussion of nationalisation was that of technical or productive efficiency, *not* allocative efficiency, which is where overwhelmingly econ-omists have focused their attention. Equally, of course, for most econ-omists competition is the royal road to efficiency – and in many ways nationalisation reflected a direct repudiation of that view.

Nowhere in this period was there such a direct relationship between programmatic intent and policy outcome as in nationalisation. By 1951, all the sectors proposed for public ownership in 1945 had indeed been nationalised. The scale of that massive transfer in ownership is sug-gested by table 5.1.

[3] The debate about the nationalisation of the Bank of England was quite separate from that of industrial nationalisation, and is dealt with in chapter 7. For the debate on which industries should be nationalised, see R. Millward and J. Singleton (eds.), *The Political Economy of Nationalisation in Britain 1920–50* (Cambridge, 1994).
[4] *Let Us Face the Future*, p. 5.
[5] e.g. PRO CAB124/915, 'Socialisation of Industries: Note by the Economic Section', 6 Nov. 1945.

Table 5.1   *Major state-owned enterprises in 1951*

	Turnover (£m.)	Employment (000s)
Inland transport	617	888
(of which, railways)	385	600
Coal	541	780
Iron and steel	502	292
Electricity	269	182
Gas	241	148
Airways	44	25
Total	2,214	2,315

Source: T. Gourvish, 'The Rise (and Fall?) of State-Owned Enterprise' in T. Gourvish and A. O'Day (eds.), *Britain since 1945*, p. 113.

Debate about the organisation of nationalisation before the war had largely focused on the desirability of control of the industries by interest groups or by boards appointed for their competence and expertise. This debate went back to the origins of the Labour Party before the First World War, but was formally resolved in the early 1930s by Labour's agreement to what was to become known as the Morrisonian corporation. This name derived from the role of Herbert Morrison in designing what was deemed to be one of most successful of the inter-war nationalisations, the London Passenger Transport Board. In Morrison's view this body combined 'public ownership, public accountability, and business management for public ends'.[6] The board would be appointed by the relevant ministry as an autonomous body, made up of experts, not of representatives of the industry. It would be subject to only general control by the government, explicitly different from the direct control embodied in the Postmaster General's control of the Post Office.

This public corporation model drew wide support across the political spectrum in the 1930s, the Conservatives and the Liberals welcoming it as 'taking business out of politics' and allowing space for private sector-style management prerogatives. For Labour the model was more problematic because, whilst involving a clear repudiation of 'workers' control' approaches to nationalisation, it left vague the extent to which the role of workers would be enhanced and changed under public ownership.

[6] Morrison, *Socialisation and Transport*, p. 149.

The repudiation of workers' control came only after passionate debates at Labour Party and TUC conferences in the early 1930s.[7] The reasons have been well summarised as follows:

Two features of the Fabian conception of the state and government led inevitably to the rejection of workers' control. The first was the acceptance of parliamentary supremacy as an expression of the majority will . . . all attempts to impinge on the Supremacy of Parliament or to weaken Parliament as a majoritarian institution were consistently opposed by the Fabians . . . To have any public official ultimately responsible to some agency other than Parliament was a denial of the whole meaning of the British constitution . . . The other determining feature of the Fabian conception of government was an uncommon respect for the expert.[8]

The official resolution of the debate about workers' control determined that after 1945 public ownership meant the public corporation. This did not end the debate. There remained many on the left who still believed in some form of workers' control, and who persistently raised the issue, albeit without success, in the late 1940s.[9]

The repudiation of workers' control still left the question of the workers' role in the new public enterprises unresolved. One aspect of Labour's enthusiasm for the public corporation model was undoubtedly a growing view in influential Labour circles that management was a technical expertise, which public ownership would free from the shackles of restrictive and nepotistic private ownership, thus allowing modern managerial methods to be applied. This attitude is evident in, for example, the interest in ICI or General Motors as having developed models of management in the private sector which could be applied to the newly nationalised enterprises.[10] But alongside such 'technocratic' approaches was a strong commitment, even by the most enthusiastic supporters of the Morrisonian corporation (including Morrison himself), to a greater role for workers in the nationalised sector.

Whilst Fabian conceptions of democracy as equivalent to parliamentary sovereignty were very important in gaining support for the Morrisonian corporation, Labour was also committed to the idea that

[7] R. Dahl, 'Workers' Control of Industry and the British Labour Party', *American Political Science Review* 41 (1947), pp. 875–900; G. N. Ostergaard, 'Labour and the Development of the Public Corporation', *Manchester School* 22 (1954), pp. 192–216; J. Tomlinson, *The Unequal Struggle?: British Socialism and the Capitalist Enterprise* (1982), ch. 4.

[8] Dahl, 'Workers' Control', pp. 877–8.

[9] For example, the Union of Post Office Workers consistently supported joint (government/union) management of the Post Office.

[10] PR CAB134/688, H. Morrison, 'Taking Stock', 18 July 1947; and ibid., 'Decentralised Administration in an American Business', 15 Dec. 1947.

democracy required a greater day-to-day role for the worker in the enterprise. A major policy statement in 1950 argued that 'Democracy is developing in the publicly owned enterprises. The task in the next few years is to aid and train workers to take their place as full partners, so that the public industries become models of industrial democracy.'[11]

Alongside this notion of democracy was a very strong belief that human relationships thrive in the nationalised industries better than in the private sector. The emphasis on human relations was, as already suggested in chapter 4, a striking feature of Labour's ideology of the late 1940s. Partly it flowed from the perception that the arrival of full employment made it not only undesirable but impossible to use the 'stick' of the sack as a major way of maintaining work effort and discipline. Partly also it came from the belief that social science research, such as the Hawthorne experiments, had shown the capacity of good human relations to raise productivity. In addition, human relations ideology, for some at least, embodied the idea that as a political principle the worker could and should have a positive input into the production process.

Other aspects of the same design in the nationalised sector were the appointment of trade unionists to many posts of labour director or similar jobs responsible for industrial relations, an emphasis on personnel management as a function to be expanded in the new corporations, and the need for properly trained supervisory and managerial staff, fitted to treat labour with proper respect and not just as 'hands'.[12]

Also important was the idea that nationalised industries would offer a ladder of opportunity, whereby even those in the humblest of jobs would have the chance, if they merited it, of advancing up the hierarchy of public corporations, including to the board level. This idea of a 'career open to talents' was pursued via the provision of training facilities by the nationalised corporations, so that those already in their employment would be able to acquire the skills needed for such advancement.

The precise impact of all this is returned to below when the experience of coal nationalisation is looked at in some detail, but two general points may be emphasised at this stage. First, the rejection of 'workers' control' by the Labour leadership did not mean that the workers' role was settled. Opinion amongst Labour figures was divided, but none espoused a simple philosophy of letting the nationalised boards do as they wanted in relation to the role of workers. Views on the capacity of

[11] Labour Party, *Labour and the New Society* (1950), p. 36.
[12] D. N. Chester, *The Nationalisation of British Industry, 1945–51* (1975), pp. 786–96 (pp. 844–64 give an overview of this issue).

workers, and hence the scope of the role they could play in the enterprises, varied, but for no one was managerialism so strong as to preclude some hope of an increased involvement by workers.

Second, the commitment to this involvement was the product of intertwined concerns. On the one hand, it was linked with what may be called social democratic aims of the 'humanisation' of work and the enhancement of the status of the worker. On the other, there was the striking contemporary concern with efficiency and productivity. Many in the Labour ranks implicitly believed in a happy coincidence between the desired character of the organisation of work and the type of organisation which would yield most output. The happy worker would also be a productive worker.

The happiness of the workforce provided one link between nationalisation and efficiency. Set alongside this link was the idea that nationalisation would make possible a rationalisation of industry in order to yield economies of scale and opportunities for greatly enhanced investment, which together would greatly increase productivity. Labour in this regard shared the common view of informed opinion in inter-war Britain. Industrial efficiency in this period was seen as having been blocked by the fragmented, small-scale structure of British industry, which market forces had failed to change significantly. Equally, attempts by the 1930s Conservative government to promote, if only implicitly, cartels and monopolies to give a breathing space for industrial reorganisation, were seen as having failed.[13] Hence Labour's policies on nationalisation could be seen as aimed at rationalisation by new means, giving a 'socialist' twist to a well-established consensual agenda.

This interpretation of Labour's position serves to emphasise the conception of efficiency that underlay most of the nationalisation debate. Leaving aside the human relations aspect, this conception depended upon what may be called an 'engineering' approach, where efficiency is a function of the scale of activity and the extent of mechanisation of its various parts. Economies of scale are assumed to be generally available once the impediments of private ownership are removed, and the state makes available the necessary funds for mechanisation. This kind of approach, it may be noted, was parallel to that of the dominant conception of productive efficiency amongst economists at this time, with their notion of downward-sloping long-run supply curves, with the division of labour and capital accumulation as the key routes to enhanced efficiency.[14] Whether espoused by politicians or economists, this was

---

[13] Tomlinson, *Government and the Enterprise*, ch. 5.
[14] M. Chick, 'Competition, Competitiveness and Nationalisation, 1945–51' in G. Jones and M. Kirby (eds.), *Competitiveness and the State* (Manchester, 1991), pp. 62–3.

rapidly to prove an excessively simple view of the sources of industrial efficiency in the nationalised industries.

Nationalisation and the national economy

If the efficiency aspect of nationalisation dominated much of Labour's agenda in the 1945–51 period, the idea of using nationalisation as a tool to plan or manage the economy had by no means disappeared. In some respects this aspect was diminished compared with the 1930s by the availability of other instruments – physical and fiscal – but nevertheless it remained important.

The relationship between the nationalised industries and the rest of the economy was partly an issue of full employment. In the 1930s it had been assumed that these industries could and should play a significant role in contra-cyclical investment policies, and this remained the view in the 1940s, though one which, because of the pressure of full employment, did not require much action by the government.[15]

The nationalised industries were important microeconomically because of their large role as purchasers of private sector outputs. When the government was trying to change the practices of many private sector companies in the name of efficiency, the leverage provided by this purchaser role was potentially powerful. For example, in the pursuit of standardisation, nationalised industries did affect the output and hence production processes in some private sector companies – e.g. the producers of electricity generator sets.[16] In this case the policy was pursued because of perceived benefits to the Electricity Generating Board rather than because of government persuasion, so there was an unproblematic coincidence of governmental and nationalised board interests here, not always evident in other policy areas.

But, given the nature of the industries nationalised in 1945–51, their most important link with the rest of the economy was as suppliers of inputs – inputs of fuel, power and transport to the private industrial (as well as consumer) sector. As suppliers of such inputs to most of the rest of the economy, at a time when excess demand characterised the economy, the nationalised industries were at the forefront of the drive to increase output. Indeed, it would be a reasonable generalisation to say

---

[15] Though even planning for the eventuality of unemployment caused problems for government/nationalised industry relations, as will be detailed in the final section of this chapter.

[16] Hannah, *Engineers, Managers and Politicians*, pp. 23–8, 101–10. More generally on this issue N. Tiratsoo and J. Tomlinson, *Industrial Efficiency and State Intervention: Labour 1939–51* (1993).

that in this period at least that was what government above all wanted from the nationalised industries – more of whatever it was that they produced. This meant that the concern with 'efficiency' was of a particular kind – it meant getting more total output in a supply-constrained economy. Expansion took precedence over nicely weighted issues of comparative costs. To put the point slightly differently, the long-standing economists' debate about the appropriate pricing policy for nationalised enterprises, an issue of allocative efficiency, whilst continuing to be a live issue amongst economists,[17] had rather little impact on nationalised industries policies. In the case of electricity, for example, the public corporation did its best to sabotage the policy of marginal cost-pricing imposed upon it.[18]

This 'output maximisation' approach was not greatly constrained by the well-known injunction to the industries to balance costs and revenues over a series of years. Within a general context of excess demand, cost increases could usually be passed on into prices. The rise in nationalised industry prices worried the government, especially when they were trying to check increases in the cost of living to lever down wage inflation, but they didn't stop the industries from raising prices faster than the general rate of inflation over the period.[19] Hopes that the efficiency gains in the nationalised industries would be such that the output would continually increase and prices at the same time decrease appear in retrospect naive, though of course the price inflation reflected macro- as well as microeconomic forces.

The lack of much concern with the allocative role of prices was compatible with the belief in planning and co-ordination of economic activity rather than competition. Thus in the discussion of transport, where different nationalised modes competed for traffic, ministers generally saw the proper method of allocation between modes as one of administrative decision rather than response to market demand. This was just another part of the view that nationalisation was a (superior) alternative to competition in generating efficiency.[20]

Questions about the use of the nationalised sector to plan or manage the economy raised broad questions about the respective responsibilities of the ministries and the nationalised boards. The Morrisonian corporation clearly embodied the idea of day-to-day autonomy for the boards,

[17] e.g. T. Wilson, 'Price and Outlay of State Enterprise', *Economic Journal* 55 (1945), pp. 454–61.
[18] M. Chick, 'Marginal Cost Pricing and the Post-War Demand for Electricity 1945–51' in M. Chick (ed.), *Governments, Industries and Markets* (Aldershot, 1991), pp. 110–26.
[19] PRO CAB21/2327, A. Johnston to H. Morrison, 8 July 1949.
[20] Chick, 'Competition'.

whilst giving ministries power of general direction. Such formulations left enormous scope for interpretation and disagreement, which in turn raised questions about the Morrisonian corporation. By the end of the 1940s its status as the preferred form of nationalisation was being increasingly questioned.

Coal nationalisation

The industries nationalised in the 1945–51 period were in many respects extremely diverse, with widely varying histories, structures and market positions. Nevertheless, to focus on coal as an example of some of the issues raised by nationalisation in its early stages is helpful. Most of those issues were discussed and addressed in relation to coal, and much of the general debate on nationalisation treated coal as a primary reference point. Coal was the first 'big' nationalisation (after the Bank of England and Cable and Wireless) and thus reflected both its economic and political centrality for the government. As a strong supporter of nationalisation wrote in 1948: 'Thus the coal problem is, in every sense, a test case for Britain. Economically, because without a strong coal industry we cannot stand on our own feet as a prosperous nation. Politically, because the success of nationalisation would speed up and strengthen the nationalisation of other key industries, such as iron and steel.'[21]

The nationalisation of the industry had, of course, long been part of Labour's programme, but by the end of the war it appealed to many outside the traditional public ownership camp, if only because no other means seemed to have any chance of encouraging improved industrial relations and technical reorganisation.[22] This sense of the lack of alternative to nationalisation was enhanced by the combination of growing state involvement in the industry, evident since 1916 but greatly expanded in the war, and recognition that its productive performance could only be improved by the support of workers, which meant only in conditions of public ownership.[23] The extensive state intervention in the war had been far from a success story. Coal output fell in every year of the war and productivity continued its long-run decline. Net investment in the wartime industry was negative, its conditions of work unattractive. In the words of the historian of the wartime industry: 'the

[21] M. Heinemann, *Coal Must Come First* (1948), p. 16.
[22] B. Supple, *The History of the British Coal Industry*, vol. IV, *1913–1946: The Political Economy of Decline* (Oxford, 1987); D. Greasley, 'The Coal Industry: Images and Realities on the Road to Nationalisation' in Millward and Singleton, *Political Economy*, pp. 37–64.
[23] Supple, *History*, ch. 13, pp. 667–8, 624–7.

war aggravated rather than improved the condition of the industry. No other major industry carried so many unsolved problems into the war; none brought more out.'[24]

In the second reading debate on the Bill to nationalise coal in early 1946 the Labour spokesmen based their case around three major points: first, that the quantity and price of coal was a vital national interest, given coal's role as a 'common service' industry supplying others; second, that this requirement necessitated a thoroughgoing modernisation of the industry which could not be secured under private ownership: 'Lack of planning, the use of out-of-date technical equipment, and the fratricidal competition amongst the owners themselves has brought the industry to its present position'; third, only public ownership could secure both the means of such technical modernisation and the necessary reform of human relations in the industry: 'The Board must conform to the standard of a model employer, and interpret this obligation in a fashion that will speedily remove the strained atmosphere that has surrounded the industry.'[25]

The argument that only nationalisation could provide the means to ensure the technical modernisation of the industry drew heavily on the Reid Report, published early in 1945.[26] Reid did not advocate public ownership, but it did advocate 'nationalisation' in the sense of the imperative need for the industry to be run on a national basis, with a powerful central authority to drive through the mechanisation and investment needed. The Reid Committee clearly regarded the existing pattern of dispersed ownership and localised management as obstacles to modernisation. Unsurprisingly, Labour regarded the report as an endorsement of its proposals for public ownership: 'Without public ownership and state control it is not possible to put the Reid Report into effect.'[27]

In many ways Reid made a powerful case in support of a 'technocratic' argument for public ownership of the mines. Most compelling, it stressed the links between the structure and organisation of the industry and the possibilities of technical modernisation. Radical restructuring of the former was a precondition for the achievement of the latter.

However, Reid was not a simplistic endorsement of economies of scale in mining. For example, it emphasised that the poor output per

[24] W. H. B. Court, *Coal* (1951), p. 391.

[25] *Hansard* (Commons) vol. 418, 30 Jan. 1946, H. Morrison, cols. 960–72; W. Foster, col. 894; 29 Jan. 1946, E. Shinwell, col. 706.

[26] *Coal Mining. Report of the Technical Advisory Committee* (1945). It is summarised in Supple, *Coal Industry*, pp. 615–19.

[27] *Hansard* (Commons), vol. 418 (30 Jan. 1946), col. 885.

man shift (OMS) in the industry was not just a problem of the low level of mechanised coal-cutting, but above all a problem of underground haulage (both of coal and miners) where complex layouts and antiquated methods were major constraints. The implication of this was that raising productivity was going to be a long job, requiring both large investment and good management to co-ordinate changes in the different aspects of coal mining. This prospect of change taking a long time was, in the event, also accurate because of the compelling need to get coal from almost any source in the immediate post-war years, which obviously militated against concentration and rapid closure of low-productivity pits. This focus on immediate output was strengthened by the 1947 coal crisis, when the vulnerability of Britain to coal shortage was so starkly demonstrated.[28] Here there was an obvious conflict between output maximisation and modernisation of production.

The 'technocratic' case for coal nationalisation usually assumed that private owners would be unable to finance the level of investment necessary for the industry's modernisation – especially given the run-down state of the mines at the end of the war. The 1950 *Plan for Coal* put the capital costs of needed development at £635m. (at 1949 prices), where the private owners in 1945 had thought £100m. would suffice.[29] In practice, in the early years of the nationalised industry finance was not the constraint on investment, but, as with all other capital projects, the problem was the availability of physical resources. The pattern seems to have been that the NCB had almost complete autonomy in drawing up investment proposals, the Ministry of Fuel and Power checking only the conformity of these proposals with the Investment Programmes Committee allocation of physical resources.[30]

This non-interventionist attitude of the ministry towards the NCB's investment plans was not complete. For example, the ministry wanted the board to press ahead with a large coke oven programme to supply the steel industry, but this was resisted. The NCB emphasised its duty to break even and therefore not to engage in projects it didn't think would pay.[31] Whilst not a major issue at the time, this disagreement

---

[28] Ashworth, *Coal*, pp. 13–16, 159–62, 138. When the miners' leaders met Attlee in 1947 they attacked reorganisation in the mines as 'too leisurely' and argued that the 500 uneconomic pits were pulling down the OMS to an unacceptable degree. They pressed for faster reorganisation (PRO POWE37/77, 'Note on NUM Meeting with Attlee', 18 April 1947).

[29] Ashworth, *Coal*, p. 16.

[30] PRO CAB21/2327, ' Socialisation of Industries: Relations of Boards with Ministers and Government Departments', 1949–51; CAB134/642, Investment Programmes Committee, 'Report on Capital Investment in 1950–52', 24 May 1949.

[31] Chester, *Nationalisation*, pp. 982–3; PRO CAB134/690, Ministry of Fuel and Power, 'Comment on Ministers' Powers to Direct Capital Investment', 30 May 1949.

illustrated the general problem of the extent to which the government could and should regulate investment by the nationalised industries organised on a 'Morrisonian' basis. Whilst the source of considerable debate (see further below) in coal, as elsewhere, this issue was effectively shelved because in conditions of macroeconomic excess demand, the major controls over investment through the Attlee period were physical and part of a national 'plan', rather than specifically related to the nationalised industries.

In other areas ministers did use the compelling macroeconomic circumstances to justify small interventions in the commercial policies of the industries. For example, the NCB was persuaded to export coal to Canada to gain dollar receipts, despite the price being 25s per ton lower than in European markets.[32] But again, the sense of compelling short-term economic problems being used to justify an *ad hoc* measure was evident.

The price of coal

In terms of the commercial aspects of the NCB's operations, nowhere was this issue of the extent of government control more problematic than in the case of prices. There were two pricing issues. One concerned the relative prices of different types of coal and how these should be determined. The second was the question of the overall, average price to be charged for coal.

The first issue was notable mainly for the debate between the NCB and the ministry on the one hand and the economists of the Economic Section on the other. The latter, true to their calling, proposed marginal cost pricing, to be used not only for current pricing but also as the basis for investment decisions. In contrast, the ministry and NCB wanted a system of prices reflecting the heat output of the coal when burnt. This debate dominated the proceedings of the Working Party on Prices Policy of Nationalised Industries, which met from 1948 to 1951 but failed to submit a report.[33] The NCB views seem to have been dominated by the idea of (a) covering average costs, and (b) fixing relative prices by reference to the technical characteristics of the coal, not the demand and supply situation at the margin. It is clear that the economists' views were regarded as naive, because of the problem of information about marginal costs, but also because the clear implication of that approach would be extremely decentralised pricing and investment

[32] PRO CAB134/690.
[33] PRO CAB130/39, 'Working Party on Pricing Policy of Socialised Industries', 1948–51.

decisions against the *national* policy pursued by the board and supported by the ministry.[34]

Whilst the civil service debate on relative prices meandered on without resolution, the NCB got on and adjusted its prices broadly in line with calculations of the relative calorific value of different coals. In conditions of general shortage and compulsion to produce more, the economists' advocacy of the nice adjustment of prices to marginal cost appeared as 'unworldly innocence' to be bypassed rather than heeded.[35]

If the matter of principle involved in the relative price debate – the relevance of marginal cost pricing – remained unresolved in this period, the same can also be said about the principles governing control of the general price level. The board levied prices which covered operating costs, in that sense pursuing 'average cost' pricing. On the other hand, the extent to which prices should finance investment was not resolved. As already noted, the major constraint on investment in this period was physical, and finance from the Treasury was readily available (at low interest rates) to pay for more projects than the Coal Board could actually undertake.

Whilst the Coal Board was undoubtedly charging less for coal than the market would have borne in the late 1940s, the rise in price of coal (as well as the outputs of other nationalised industries) led to much consumer discontent, exploited by the political Opposition. One response by the government was to set up a committee on the control of nationalised industries prices.[36] This committee brought out the extent to which, except in the case of transport tribunals, the prices of the industries were out of the formal control of the government, and conformity with government wishes relied on the goodwill of the boards. No decision was taken to alter this state of affairs. The NCB undertook to consult with its ministry on the issue, but was under no legal necessity to do so.[37]

All this meant that a key issue for nationalised industries of later years, the extent to which their pricing policies should be subordinated to national macroeconomic considerations, was not resolved in this period.

---

[34] Ibid., 2nd Meeting, 29 Sept. 1948; PRO POWE37/29, 37/31, 'Working Party on Pricing Policy of Socialised Industries', 1948–51.

[35] Ashworth, *Coal*, p. 177; for a contemporary statement of the economists' argument see S. R. Dennison, 'The Price Policy of the NCB', *Lloyds Bank Review* 26 (1952), pp. 17–34.

[36] PRO CAB134/692, 'Report by Official Committee on Control of Prices and Charges of Nationalised Industries', 12 July 1951; see also CAB130/39, 'Working Party', 1948–51; Chester, *Nationalisation*, pp. 738–43.

[37] PRO CAB124/945, H. Morrison, 'Some Current Problems in Socialised Industries', 9 April 1948.

It was agreed that their prices must be set so as not to lead to operating losses, and this meant an explicit rejection of marginal cost pricing if this involved such losses.[38] But in this period of excess demand operating losses were not an issue for most of the nationalised industries. The major exception was transport, but here the government did have a clear statutory role via the transport tribunals, and was able to influence that agency in the regulation of rail fares. This set up a lengthy debate about the extent to which the threat of financial losses by the railways should be accepted in order to keep charges down, especially given the knock-on effects on other sectors of the economy. No resolution of this general problem had been found by the time the Attlee government lost office.[39]

In the case of coal, the board made an operating loss in 1947 but offset this by surpluses in succeeding years, though the paying off of the deficit created in 1947 was slower than the board wanted because of government pressure to limit price increases in 1948 and 1949. The operating loss in 1947 was £9.2m., with surpluses of £1.7m., £9.5m. and £8.3m. respectively in the following three years.[40]

Human relations and coal

The claim that nationalisation was necessary to improve the efficiency of the industries involved rested as much on the idea that public ownership would revolutionise human relations in the industry as on the argument that it was a precondition for radical reform of the techniques of production. Nowhere was this truer than in coal. The lamentable state of industrial relations in coal had of course been widely felt in the previous decades, not least in the general strike of 1926. But more narrowly, coal was a labour-intensive industry where output was still heavily dependent on the number of workers and the amount of worker effort.

---

[38] PRO CAB134/687, Ministerial Committee on Socialisation of Industries Minutes, 14 May 1946. This decision involved a rejection of the view put forward by the Economic Section that 'covering costs' should involve only marginal costs, and not include depreciation and debt changes. This position was strongly advocated by Meade, but rejected on the grounds that any legitimising loss making by a nationalised industry (not covering *average* costs) would fatally weaken managerial discipline (Chester, *Nationalisation*, pp. 564–9).

Meade anticipated that *on average* nationalised industries would have a surplus including capital charges, but marginal cost rules would mean some would have losses. He had proposed to Keynes a 'new rule of financial orthodoxy', that revenues of nationalised industries should be paid into an extra-budgetary fund and that this fund should be for socialised industries *as a whole*, and must on an average of years be self-supporting (PRO CAB124/916, J. E. Meade to J. M. Keynes, 17 Jan. 1946).

[39] Chester, *Nationalisation*, pp. 735–7.

[40] NCB, *Annual Reports and Statements of Account* 1947, 1948, 1949, 1950.

Poor human relations would be likely to reduce both recruitment to the industry and the productivity of the existing workforce. This was likely to be especially so when full employment offered alternative job opportunities to potential miners, opportunities obviously not nearly so prevalent in the pre-war years.

In this context, the Coal Board, like other nationalised corporations, was expected to be a model employer, an expectation embedded, albeit in general terms, in the nationalisation statutes. To act as a model employer nationalised industries were obliged to participate in and encourage collective bargaining with trade unions. By and large, in coal this involved no obvious problems, not least because the NUM was one of Britain's few industrial unions, representing an overwhelming proportion of the industry's manual workers. Much more problematic for the coal industry, and broadly for the nationalisation programme as a whole, was the issue of joint consultation. All the nationalised industries (except the Bank of England) had a statutory requirement to set up consultative structures, though the form such structures were to take was left to the individual boards. In fact, from the beginning the form of consultation was regarded as a matter of high policy not to be left entirely to the boards. The Ministerial Socialisation of Industries Committee discussed the issue at length, especially in relation to coal. Eventually a structure was devised in which (against the preferences of the Ministry of Labour) the machinery of joint consultation would be clearly separate from that used for collective bargaining, and would broadly mirror the structure of the Coal Board. In coal, unlike other nationalised industries, nominees for miners' representatives on the consultative committees would have to be NUM members, but initially all miners would have the right to nomination and voting. This pattern reflected the clear ministerial view that, whilst joint consultation should build on union structures, it should try not to reproduce the adversarial positions intrinsic to collective bargaining.[41]

Ministers took joint consultation extremely seriously. Its scale and results were to be a persistent issue for discussion at the highest level throughout the Attlee government. It is important to emphasise this, as it might be imagined that, given the acceptance of the Morrisonian model of nationalisation, worker involvement in the management of the industries was to be minimised. But this was definitely not the case. Ministers like Morrison emphasised that the boards were to retain ultimate responsibility for the management of the industries, but they were

---

[41] PRO CAB134/687, Ministerial Committee on Socialisation of Industries, esp. Minutes, 29 March 1946, 14 May 1946, 8 July 1946. There were consultative committees at national, divisional, area and colliery levels.

adamant that consultation should be pursued seriously. Indeed, ministers seem to have been quite Utopian in their hopes of nationalisation coupled to joint consultation, expecting them to engender a rapid improvement in industrial and human relations, and a consequent significant improvement in productivity.[42]

In addition to formal structures of consultation, improvement in human relations was pursued by the appointment of trade unionists to board level in the nationalised industries. Two trade unionists – the General Secretaries of the NUM and TUC – were appointed to the NCB, along with others at lower levels in the organisation, with a remit to cover industrial relations issues whilst not 'representing' the workers in the industry.

Another important parallel initiative was to try and build up a managerial cadre from within the industry. Shinwell had emphasised this point in the debate on the coal nationalisation Bill, and it was a continuing theme of statements on coal and other industries. Internal promotion was seen as the way of squaring the need for expertise with the desire to be seen as not drawing management entirely from the old privately owned industry.[43]

Finally, as well as shifting the social base of management, the Coal Board was pressed to alter management practices. In line with the emphasis on human relations, the government was keen on training managers in personnel issues, and pressed for the appointment of specialist personnel managers.[44]

What was desired by ministers was not necessarily delivered by the nationalised boards. But in this broad area of human relations there seems little doubt that the top echelons of the boards, at least, did take the issue seriously.

On joint consultation, the principle seems to have been accepted without question by the NCB. The precise form of such machinery was much debated by the board, and issues such as the amount of information to be supplied to union representatives were the subject of disagreement, but the structures were quickly established.[45]

---

[42] These views on nationalisation should be seen as part of a broader attempt by Labour to 'build communities', as persuasively argued by S. Fielding, S. Thompson and N. Tiratsoo, *England Arise! The Labour Party and Popular Politics in the 1940s* (Manchester, 1995), ch. 5.

[43] Chester, *Nationalisation*, pp. 539–47; *Hansard* (Commons), vol. 418 (29 Jan. 1946), col. 708; PRO CAB134/691, 'Speech by Ernest Davies MP', Nov. 1950.

[44] PRO POWE37/81, NCB Personnel Management, Meeting of Minister of Labour and NCB, 26 Jan. 1951.

[45] PRO COAL26/68, 26/69, 'NCB Industrial Relations Dept.: Consultative Machinery', 1946–8. The arrangements were spelt out in NCB, National Consultative Committee, *Joint Consultation in Coal* (1948).

Equally elaborate mechanisms for training of Coal Board personnel, from face workers upwards, were established. Scholarships, apprenticeships, part-time release, weekend and summer schools proliferated. Typical of the approach was the 'Ladder Plan' presented by the NCB in 1950, which aimed to give every recruit a chance of systematic training for a career whilst improving the standard of technical knowledge and skill in the industry. Whilst it was accepted the process would take a long time, the idea that eventually most management in the coal industry would be recruited internally was accepted as both desirable and plausible by the board.[46]

The appointment of personnel managers was more problematic for the NCB. Whilst the need for radical improvements in human relations in the industry was acknowledged, the obvious place for personnel managers was at colliery level. But colliery managers were appointed for their certificated technical competence (unlike managers in most of British industry) and so the imposition of a separate management functionary would cut across the tradition of pit management. The Coal Board's response was to appoint personnel managers at divisional and area level to advise colliery managers, and to encourage technically qualified colliery managers to broaden their competence.[47]

Quite quickly the attempt at radical reform of human relations in coal by this range of methods was regarded as having failed. It was registered in a number of ways. With coal production and productivity crucial to Britain's overall industrial prospects, performance in these areas was soon regarded by ministers as falling well short of what had been hoped. Numbers of workers in the mines rose in 1947 and 1948, then fell back. Output per man shift rose consistently, but only from 1.09 tons in 1947 to 1.24 tons in 1951. Total output in consequence rose, but only slowly, from 187.5m. tons in 1947 to 212.9m. tons in 1951.[48]

The evidence that better human relations failed to manifest themselves in increased production needs to be treated with some care. The nationalised coal industry inherited an ageing and in many respects demoralised workforce, working worn-out capital equipment. Similar conditions elsewhere in Europe produced similar problems in raising productivity.[49] Equally, buoyant general employment offered job oppor-

[46] NCB, *Annual Report* 1948; Acton Society Trust, *Training and Promotion in Nationalised Industry* (1951), ch. 3.
[47] PRO POWE37/81, 'Ministry of Power: Relations between Management and Men', 1948–51.
[48] Ashworth, *Coal*, appendix tables A1, A2.
[49] Heinemann, *Coal*, pp. 14–15; D. Burn ('The National Coal Board', *Lloyds Bank Review* 19 (1951), p. 37) shows OMS in coal in Britain in 1950 much higher relative to 1937 than other European countries, though rising generally more slowly over the period 1946–50.

tunities which short-run improvements in 'human relations' in coal were unlikely to counteract quickly. The negative attitudes of the miners were greatly exaggerated at the time, as illustrated in, for example, the figures of absenteeism. Nationalisation did coincide with a cut in absenteeism, though this proved a once-and-for-all change.[50] Overall, as contemporary commentators noted, the performances of coal and other nationalised industries in this period 'justify the view that no very obvious Stakhanovite movement seems to have swept the nationalised enterprises', but perhaps it was Utopian to expect it would.[51]

Disillusion was not just restricted to those concerned with the hoped-for economic benefits from improved human relations. That improvement itself was often alleged to have proved largely a mirage. At the most basic level, industrial relations did not show the expected improvement after nationalisation. Unofficial strikes still took place with some frequency, most famously at Grimethorpe in 1947, where the miners did not accept the NCB's view about what could be expected from them in terms of increased output in return for the establishment of the five-day week. However, it has been persuasively argued that industrial relations in coal are determined largely by local colliery conditions, and therefore are generally little affected by nationalisation.[52]

Unrest in the late 1940s partly reflected the complexities of some radical changes in the pattern of wage determination in the pits, where an effort was made to rationalise the extremely diverse patterns inherited from private ownership. But there seems little doubt that it also reflected a continuing distrust of management and its motives by many miners, even after the abolition of private ownership. As a report by the Action Society Trust argued of the nationalised boards in general, 'they have not succeeded to any marked extent in dispelling the traditional suspicion of employees and in opening up that new era of harmonious co-operation for which some had hoped'.[53]

As the same report noted, one reason for this continued suspicion was the belief that nationalisation had not changed the managerial per-

[50] Ashworth, *Coal*, pp. 165–6; on the unattractive perception of coal mining as a job see PRO RG23/129A, 'Men and Mining', 1948, pp. 9–13; RG23/85, 'The Recruitment of Boys to the Mining Industry', 1947. Most of the boys surveyed thought mining 'unhealthy, dangerous and that the work is too hard and the prospects poor' (p. 9).

[51] S. Florence and G. Walker, 'Efficiency under Nationalisation and its Measurement', *Political Quarterly* 21 (1950), p. 201.

[52] Ashworth, *Coal*, pp. 166–70; PRO POWE20/115, 'Strikes and Disputes: Grimethorpe 1947'. This file brings out the extent to which the Grimethorpe episode was a failure of NCB management, an aspect glossed over entirely in the NCB, *Annual Report* (1947), paras. 74–8. I. M. Zweiniger-Bargielowska, 'Miners' Militancy: A Study of Four South Wales Collieries during the Middle of the Twentieth Century', *Welsh History Review* 16 (1993), pp. 356–89.

[53] Acton Society Trust, *The Men on the Board* (1951), pp. 14–15.

sonnel of the industries significantly, that the 'old gang' was still in power. This attitude had a grounding in the facts. Most of the board members in nationalised industries (about 80 per cent of full-timers) were inherited from its private predecessors. And in coal in particular, a large degree of continuity was evident at the managerial level the typical miner had most contact with – the colliery manager. In both cases the reason lay not so much in a 'jobs for the boys' approach, but was simply a problem of competence, especially in the case of colliery managers, where technical certification was a necessary qualification for the job.[54]

As had been pointed out in the second reading of the Coal Nationalisation Bill such lack of change in the short run was largely inescapable. After nationalisation the miner 'will go to the same pit and get the same lamp from the same man; he will go into the same cage and will probably be lowered by the same man . . . he will see the same manager, the same deputy, the old roadway, the same coalface and, on Friday, he will probably be paid by the same man'.[55]

This problem was addressed by the policies on internal promotion, about which the Coal Board were particularly keen. However, their efforts, in any event medium- and long-term in character, faced substantial constraints. On the one hand, the idea of a 'career open to talent' conflicted with the idea of promotion by seniority, a principle strongly supported by many managers and workers, though perhaps particularly prevalent on the railways, rather than in coal. Second, undoubtedly, was the ingrained suspicion of the miners in particular about anyone, regardless of background, who achieved managerial status. Survey evidence at the time found 'a deep suspicion of all those in authority, who are thought to be idle or venal, when not cruel or malicious'.[56] Although it was understandable, given the history of the industry, such an attitude meant that any attempt to promote social mobility in the industry faced great obstacles. As a result, training opportunities and scholarships seem to have faced serious problems of lack of interest on the part of miners.[57]

Attempts to promote effective joint consultation also faced considerable problems. Partly they related to the kind of information available

---

[54] Ibid., p. 11. Precise figures on the level of continuity among colliery managers do not seem to have been calculated. PRO CAB134/691, 'Speech by Ernest Davies MP', Dec. 1950.

[55] Major Lloyd George, *Hansard* (Commons) vol. 418, col. 879, 30 Jan. 1946.

[56] Acton Society Trust, *Problems of Promotions Policy* (1951); Acton Society Trust, *The Workers' Point of View* (1952), p. 11.

[57] Acton Society Trust, *Training and Promotion*, p. 31.

at the individual colliery level. For example, neither managers nor workers were given information about the performance of individual pits, yet for most miners this was the crucial unit they were concerned with. Survey evidence found that, unsurprisingly, joint consultation was dominated by local issues, and yet managers themselves often lacked information about important factors affecting such local concerns.[58]

In this respect undoubtedly the NCB was at fault. But equally, joint consultation had to be conducted in the general climate of suspicion already noted. As the Action Society survey insisted, the difficulties for effective joint consultation were not just lack of information, but the framework ('prejudices') within which information was interpreted. In that context it was naive to believe more information would have a magical effect in inspiring more co-operative attitudes at pit level.[59]

This is not to say joint consultation was an entire failure. It plainly was very uneven in the extent to which it was taken seriously and how it performed. The NCB pointed proudly to examples where such consultation had smoothed the path to changes in the organisation of pits.[60] It certainly wasn't generally true that joint consultation was ignored by the miners: one survey, for example, found a 62 per cent turn out in elections to a colliery consultative committee, hardly suggestive of apathy. But the same study also identified major problems in maintaining interest, partly because of the poor levels of reporting back from the committees to their electorate. Interestingly, however, output issues did dominate the agendas of the committees – they did not get bogged down in the 'tea and toilets' welfare issues which seem to have often dominated joint production committees in the private sector.[61]

The NUM seems to have had ambiguous feelings about pit consultative committees. The initial acceptance that the elected members should not require union nomination was later reversed, because of fears of the 'irresponsibility' of some of the worker representatives, and this kind of emphasis on a 'single channel' of representation was strongly supported by the Ministry of Labour.[62] The problem was, as G. D. H. Cole put it: 'The miners in many cases do not know what to do with Joint Consultation now that they have got it, and know still less how to solve the

---

[58] Acton Society Trust, *Workers' Point of View*, p. 8; PRO COAL26/69, NCB Minutes, 9 Dec. 1946.
[59] Acton Society Trust, *Workers' Point of View*, p. 21; M. Benney, *Charity Main* (1948).
[60] NCB, *Annual Report* (1949), paras. 341–3.
[61] Acton Society Trust, *Workers' Point of View*, pp. 16–18.
[62] PRO BT64/2416, 'Socialisation of Industries: Workers' Role in Management', 1946–51; CAB124/928, 'Wing Commander Cooper: Workers' Assistance in the Management of Socialised Industries', 1946.

problem of adjusting the respective responsibilities of the pit or colliery consultative committee and the miners lodge.'[63]

But not all the problems were on the miners' side. One contemporary analysis noted the continuation of adversarial attitudes amongst both management and workers, and the apprehension shown by many managers in discussing issues traditionally their prerogative. In addition, the failings of consultation at colliery level often seem to have been linked to a desire to maintain national standards and procedures, and so the unions in particular tended to push issues up the consultative hierarchy, rather than settling them at the local level.[64]

Coal and centralisation

The question of what levels of decisions were to be taken in the Coal Board had wider ramifications than the workings of the consultative machinery. Partly because of perceived failures in the coal industry to bring about the climate in human relations that had been hoped for and anticipated prior to nationalisation, 'decentralisation' was put forward as a means of reversing this failure. Decentralisation therefore came to be seen as almost a panacea for the industry's ills. Apart from the belief that over-centralisation was inhibiting the improvement in human relations, it was widely alleged that the industry was 'top-heavy' with too many 'non-productive' personnel in offices away from the pit. Such allegations of excessive 'bureaucracy' seem to have gained support from a number of points of view. For the Conservative opposition, it fitted in with a general focus on criticising the government for over-centralising power in monolithic bureaucracies.[65]

Second, it probably reflected the colliery manager's (correct) perception that under nationalisation he was losing some of his powers to the area and divisional level, where many specialists were concentrated. However, this trend had begun before nationalisation, and in part reflected the desire of the NCB to economise on scarce trained manpower. Colliery managers were also losing authority vis-à-vis the miners because of the tight labour market of the 1940s.[66]

Finally, the miners themselves tended to reinforce this attitude of scepticism about the role of white-collar workers because of a wide-

---

[63] G. D. H. Cole, 'Labour and Staff Problems under Nationalisation', *Political Quarterly* 21 (1950), p. 164.

[64] Acton Society Trust, *The Framework of Joint Consultation* (1952), pp. 16–21, 26; PRO POWE37/77, 'NCB: Relations between Management and Men', 1948–9.

[65] Acton Society Trust, *The Extent of Centralisation* (1951), pp. 33–6.

[66] Ibid., pp. 25–6; I. M. Zweiniger-Bargielowska, 'Colliery Managers and Nationalisation: The Experience in South Wales', *Business History* 34 (1992), pp. 59–78.

spread suspicion of managers *per se*, as well as the feeling that away from the pit the NCB was providing 'jobs for the boys'.[67]

The idea of decentralisation as a solution to coal's problems was taken seriously in ministerial circles.[68] However, it was in many ways a simplistic approach. It ignored the fact that the logic of the nationalisation of coal lay in the need to correct its excessive fragmentation, and to drive through as rapidly as possible an increase in output with a shortage of competent technical staff. This meant that a considerable degree of centralisation was unavoidable.[69] Equally, to propose decentralisation as a response to problems in human relations did not necessarily make sense. As Michael Young (then Research Officer for the Labour Party) pointed out, if decentralisation meant delegating more from national to area levels without increasing democracy, this would risk putting more authority 'in the hands of area general managers which would vest power in the hands of irresponsible despots of a particularly reactionary type'. As Young suggested, decentralisation was not necessarily the road to improved human relations. And arguably, the easy slogan of decentralisation may have inhibited the development of an adequate central management, so that, for example, inadequate control was exercised over investment projects.[70]

The issue of centralisation and decentralisation was not just about the best internal form of organisation for nationalised industries, but was also linked to the wider political status of nationalised corporations. The high degree of centralisation of the coal industry reflected views about the sovereign role of Parliament and these corporations:

The first consideration was, of course, to make these industries responsible to the public through Parliament. But there can be no responsibility without power; if the Coal Board (for instance) is to be held responsible for mistakes committed in the pits, it must have power to rectify these mistakes. As long as this is regarded as necessary, no exhaustive de-centralisation is possible. The Coal Board must have all-embracing powers, the only issue is how much restraint it should display in using them.[71]

---

[67] Eventually in 1953 an NUM inquiry accepted that these allegations were largely without foundation (PRO POWE37/7 NCB, 'Number of Non-Industrial Staff', 1953).

[68] e.g. PRO CAB134/688, Socialisation of Industries Committee, H. Morrison S1(M) (47) 11th, 19 Nov. 1947; ibid., Ministry of Labour, 'Taking Stock', 12 Nov. 1947.

[69] PRO CAB134/688, H. Gaitskell, 'Taking Stock', 13 Nov. 1947; CAB134/689, H. Gaitskell, 'Decentralisation in the Coal Industry', Jan. 1948; Acton Society Trust, *Extent of Centralisation*, p. 31.

[70] PRO CAB21/2759, M. Young to H. Morrison, 17 May 1950. It is of note that one of the problems at Grimethorpe in 1947 was the poor decisions made by local managers in the human relations field (PRO POWE20/115, 'Inquest on Grimethorpe', 16 Dec. 1947); NCB Advisory Committee on Organisation (Fleck) (1955) paras. 306–11, 341.

[71] Acton Society Trust, *Extent of Centralisation*, pp. 3–4.

In all the intensive debate about the coal nationalisation in the earliest days after the formation of the NCB, the question of the respective powers of the board and the minister, and the related one of the extent of parliamentary accountability of the boards, were always contentious. As already noted, Shinwell, the first Minister of Fuel and Power under Attlee, did persuade the industry to go against its perceived interests on the question of exports, but failed to do so on the issue of building more coke ovens. What gradually emerged from this kind of tension was that, whilst ministers in law had substantial power to direct the corporations, in practice they were heavily dependent on informal channels of influence. A legal dispute between ministers and their boards was almost unthinkable, so much depended on the relations between specific ministers and their boards. Shinwell was succeeded by Gaitskell at the end of 1947, and the latter seems to have been less willing to try and interfere in the NCB than his predecessor, whilst attempting to cultivate good personal relationships.[72] Apart from this evolution from formal to more informal interaction between the politicians and the boards, the precise limits of the responsibilities of each party were not clearly defined by discussions about the coal industry.

The same may be said about the issue of parliamentary accountability. Again, the notion that ministers had a general responsibility for policy, leaving the boards to day-to-day management left many disputed areas, and this became an issue of great political importance in the coal crisis of early 1947, when the degree of responsibility of the minister, Shinwell, was much disputed, not least by Shinwell himself.[73]

Overall, the experience of coal nationalisation in the late 1940s raised a host of problems for the whole idea of nationalisation. Partly this was to do with the crucial role of coal in the expansion of the economy in this period, and the evident failure of public ownership to bring an expansion at the desired rate. However, it may be doubted whether *any* reorganisation of the coal industry could have produced the coal so desperately desired, at least in the time span of the Attlee government. The legacy of geological problems, low investment, and poor industrial and 'human' relations was too great for any short-term policies to overcome.

Because so much emphasis was put on nationalisation of coal as a route to better human relations, the evident failure of the industry to produce all that was asked of it has been commonly ascribed to miners' disillusionment with the nationalised industry. The miner, it is argued,

---

[72] Ashworth, *Coal*, pp. 128–9.
[73] Ibid., pp. 130–8.

was not made a happy worker, and so also failed to become a productive worker.[74]

Yet this argument relies much too heavily on the attitudes and views of the politically active and vocal amongst miners. Ina Zweiniger-Bargielowska has persuasively argued that for the bulk of miners nationalisation did deliver what they most wanted, which was better pay and conditions, greater security, and entrenched trade union rights. In consequence there was 'generally speaking, surprisingly little disenchantment and the majority of rank and file mine workers were either never disillusioned with nationalisation or disillusioned only after the run down of the industry and colliery closures from the late 1950s or early 1960s onwards'.[75] It was mainly the miners' leaders, who had entertained such high hopes of nationalisation, who quickly became disillusioned by its results.[76] However, they were probably more influential than the rank-and-file miner in forming the attitudes of Labour leaders in this period, and helped to create a general climate of disappointment with the results of nationalisation which is evident even before the end of the 1940s.

Debate and disillusion

Nationalisation had a number of purposes – to help in the planning of the national economy, to raise the efficiency of the industries concerned, and to shift the balance of power in the economy. After 1945 the last of these was more explicitly linked to the notion of promoting 'industrial democracy', a term increasingly popular in Labour circles.[77]

In general it may be argued that these were too many purposes for one policy. In part the debate and degree of disillusion over nationalisation in both ministerial and Labour Party circles in the late 1940s may be seen as resulting from this overburden of objectives. Problems also arose from the chosen instrument of nationalisation, the public corporation. There was an obvious problem in, on the one hand, intending to use the nationalised corporations in planning the economy and, on the other, conceding the autonomy of the Morrisonian public board. But this was not just a problem in relation to government macroeconomic

[74] M. Cole, *Miners and the Board*, Fabian Research Series (1949) is a classic statement of the disillusion thesis.
[75] Ina Zweiniger-Bargielowska, 'Industrial Relationships and Nationalisation in the South Wales Coal Mining Industry' (Ph.D. thesis, Cambridge 1990), pp. 312–13.
[76] Ibid., ch. 5.
[77] Labour Party, Research Department Paper RD38, *Public Ownership: The Next Step* (by Michael Young), 20 Jan. 1947; Labour Party, *Labour Believes in Britain* (1949), p. 7.

objectives; it extended also to the question of efficiency. If the government, as it did, put a great deal of emphasis on increasing efficiency in the economy as central to its policies, how was it to react if the boards did not seem to be pursuing this objective with sufficient enthusiasm? The same issue arose if the boards did not seem to be pursuing improved human relations to the extent desired by the government.

The Morrisonian corporation form also left open for debate the nature and extent of parliamentary accountability of the boards, which again was partly a question of how far ministers as politicians could force them to pursue objectives which they might not otherwise have done.

The final section of this chapter looks at the debates on these and related issues in both ministerial and Labour Party circles in the late 1940s, and tries to assess how the experience of 1945–51 changed Labour's approach to nationalisation by the time it left office.

With respect to the issue of using nationalised industries to help 'plan' the economy, a crucial point about the 1940s is that the government (and many others outside its ranks) expected an imminent return of a threat of mass unemployment. Planning to counteract such a threat was a major issue on which government tried to shape the behaviour of nationalised industry.

In 1946 a report to the Investment Working Party argued that the government's 'direct influence over board investment decisions' would be increased from 29 per cent in 1938 to 50 per cent by 1947 because of the extension of nationalisation. This influence should be used for employment policy: 'we recommend that socialised industries be plainly instructed to frame their programmes with employment policy in mind'.[78] The strength of this recommendation was substantially reduced in subsequent discussion, but one proposal did emerge from such approaches to the role of nationalised industries. This was for the industries to be invited to draw up a 'reserve of works', a shelf of investment projects to be activated when a slump threatened. But the industries proved reluctant to go down that path. They felt that their staff and resources for investment planning were already overstretched, and that it was no part of their job to undertake the unremunerative work involved in preparing such a 'shelf'.[79]

Such attitudes were resented by ministers, and Morrison, for example, stressed that the 1944 *Employment Policy* White Paper had envisaged that public sector investment would play a key role in regulat-

---

[78] PRO T161/1297/S53555/06, 'Draft Report on Preparation of Investment Projects in the Public Sector', Oct. 1946.
[79] Tomlinson, *Employment Policy* (Oxford, 1987), ch. 5.

ing demand in the economy in pursuit of full employment. It was particularly in relation to the investment issue that he remarked that 'the Government has a wider viewpoint of the public interest than the Boards, and I am far from happy that we are in a position to exercise the control on wide issues of policy which the national economy requires'.

But important as it was, investment was not the only issue in the question of the use of the nationalised industries for national economic policy ends. During the ministerial debate on this issue in 1949 Morrison listed four areas of concern as (1) control of investment; (2) 'social' questions, such as location of industry; (3) efficiency; and (4) training, education and research.[80] It was on the third of these that, apart from investment, most conflict developed in the 1940s.

Morrison proposed in 1947 that greater efficiency in the nationalised industries might be achieved by the creation of an 'efficiency unit' covering all the nationalised industries. The motives for this proposal seem to have been a combination of genuine concern over the efficiency of nationalised industries, perhaps particularly coal, where by 1947 the problems discussed in the previous sections were beginning to appear, and worries about the need to be seen to be 'doing something' in the face of criticisms of the industries.[81]

But the chairmen of the boards were strongly resistant to this idea, as derogating from their responsibilities for the individual industries. They stuck to this opposition despite Morrison strongly suggesting that if this unit did not go ahead, Parliament would press for some other form of reassurance about the industries' efficiency, which might be even less congenial to the chairmen.[82]

This dispute rumbled on for several years and, with no progress made, in March 1950 Morrison proclaimed that 'there was a strong and growing feeling in Parliament and among the public that the Government had not exercised the degree of control which was desirable over the socialised industries, and that more effective checks upon the efficiency of their management was requested'. But such views evoked little enthusiasm in the chairmen, some of whom would have accepted *ad hoc* external inquiries at the request of the industries themselves, but

[80] PRO CAB134/690, Socialisation of Industries Committee, 'Ministerial Powers to Direct Capital Investment', 28 July 1949; 'Government Control over Socialised Industries', 26 April 1949; 'Government Control over Socialised Industries', 3 Nov. 1949.

[81] PRO CAB134/688, Socialisation of Industries Committee, 'Taking Stock' 18 July 1947 and ibid., Minutes, 19 Nov. 1947.

[82] PRO CAB134/689, Socialisation of Industries Committee, Notes of Meeting of Committee with Chairmen of Nationalised Boards, 6 May 1948; CAB134/690, Minutes, 13 Jan. 1949; ibid., 'Taking Stock', 12 Jan. 1949.

none of whom would accept a common unit with responsibilities which undermined the role of the individual boards.[83]

Ministerial unhappiness with the behaviour of the nationalised boards is also apparent in another area which, at least in part, was concerned with efficiency – the improvement in human relations. As noted above in the discussion of coal, ministers had invested a great deal in such an improvement as a route to increased productivity. But increasingly evidence was presented to ministers suggesting how little improvement seemed to have taken place. For example, in 1950 ministers were presented with a report of a conference organised by the London Labour Party which told of widespread disillusion amongst employees of nationalised corporations, including those who supported public ownership:

> their experience from working within publicly-owned industry had caused doubts to arise in their mines as to its efficacy, and they were as ignorant as their opponents of the reasons for the difficulties encountered and for the explanation of actions taken by Boards and Management . . . Speaker after Speaker reiterated the fact that no attempt was made on the part of the management to inform the employees of what they were doing and why.[84]

A sub-committee set up to look at the evidence and reasons for such discontent accepted that unhappiness was widespread amongst employees in the industries. There was some active discontent 'but more often the attitude is more passive. It is rather that there is a widespread sense of frustration coupled with disappointment at the results of socialisation. Sometimes labour relations are good by any standards, but even where this is so there is rarely, if ever, any positive enthusiasm for the new order of things.' The conclusion was the need for ministers to press upon the boards the importance of the promotion of personnel management and joint consultation in improving human relations, a view very much in line with the arguments about the coal industry.[85]

By the end of Labour's period in office the conflict between the public corporation form of nationalisation, and its use as an instrument of economic policy, fears of which dated back to the 1930s, had become evident to many of those concerned. It was to be an issue that was to bedevil the whole history of nationalisation.[86]

---

[83] PRO CAB134/691, Socialisation of Industries Committee, Minutes, 21 March 1950; ibid., 1 Aug. 1950.

[84] Ibid., E. Davies MP to H. Morrison, 17 Nov. 1950.

[85] PRO CAB134/692, Socialisation of Industries Committee, 'Report of Sub-Committee on Relations with Workers in the Socialised Industries', 10 May 1951.

[86] Ostergaard, 'Labour', pp. 217–18; A. Albu, 'Ministerial and Parliamentary Control' in M. Shanks (ed.), *The Lessons of Public Enterprise* (1963), pp. 90–113; Tomlinson, *Govern-*

This issue of 'planning' was linked to another debate of importance in the 1940s, over the scope of parliamentary scrutiny of the nationalised industries. In part this was about how far the industries should be purely commercial concerns, and how far they should respond to other politically determined desiderata. In this debate the main ideologue of the public corporation, Morrison, tried to limit severely the extent of parliamentary scrutiny. He was opposed to a Select Committee on Nationalised Industries, and indeed used this as a 'threat' to try and get the chairmen to accept his proposal for an efficiency unit. Generally ministers acted to defend the boards against outside (including parliamentary) criticism, whilst trying to persuade the industries to be more responsive to such criticism. In practice, parliamentary scrutiny of the industries in this period was intermittent, poorly informed, and usually just an avenue for party-political point-scoring. A Select Committee was not established until after Labour left office.[87]

Probably realistically, the boards seem to have regarded the question of ministerial control of their activities as rather more compelling than Parliament's role. As already noted, this depended very much on informal contacts, but many drew the conclusion that whatever the sense of avoiding legal tangles in this area, the amount of ministerial control fell below what many on the left had anticipated would result from the process of nationalisation. Morrison himself, whilst defending the process of nationalisation, clearly felt by 1949/50 that the policy was in need of review, especially because of this issue of the division of responsibility between ministers and the boards: 'In some respects, however, the Boards have not fulfilled our hopes, and there is a good deal of disillusionment even among supporters of the principles of socialisation.'[88]

Morrison's position was very much informed by ministerial experience of the 'practicalities' of nationalisation. But the debate in Labour circles over nationalisation was wider than those 'practicalities', and eventually extended to the whole status of that policy in Labour's agenda. As early as 1946 the Labour Party NEC had called for a review of nationalisation policy. A Research Department document of that year laid down the criteria against which further public ownership, beyond that set out in *Let Us Face the Future* in 1945, was to be assessed. The

---

ment and the Enterprise, ch. 8; W. H. Ashworth, *The State in Business, 1945 to the Mid-1980s* (1991), pp. 173–81, 186–7.

[87] PRO CAB21/2322, Meetings with Chairmen of Boards, Summer 1950; Acton Society Trust, *Accountability to Parliament* (1950); H. Morrison, 'Evidence to Select Committee on Nationalised Industries', *Reports and Minutes*, HCP 235, PP 1952/3, vol. I, Qs. 381–507.

[88] PRO CAB21/2330, 'Efficiency and Public Accountability of Socialised Industries', 13 March 1950.

two key criteria were said to be aiding full employment, especially by regulating public investment, and raising production. The latter was to be achieved by a range of features of the nationalised bodies, from 'securing benefits of large scale organisation' to improving management.[89] This 'instrumental' attitude to nationalisation was *de facto* that largely involved in ministerial discussions, as outlined above. But by focusing on nationalisation as a means to an end, this approach tended to play down the idea of nationalisation as part of the socialist *goal*. Once this approach became established, the 'revisionist' argument about the efficacy of nationalisation as a means to Labour's goals would come to the centre of the debate on public ownership.[90]

This approach is clearly evident in a paper by Douglas Jay in 1948. He had before the war written a major 'revisionist' work, which supported nationalisation but as a secondary support to financial policy. In 1948, whilst accepting the case for the agenda of nationalisations pursued in 1945–51, he made a case for what he called 'competitive public enterprise':

We should move in the direction of establishing efficient public enterprise, competing, if necessary, with private enterprise, rather than the old pattern – to which we have perhaps given rather dogmatic adherence – of 100 per cent compulsory purchase by legislation, together with a ban on all outside competition with the public monopoly thus set up. It might assist if we stopped talk of 'nationalisation' of an 'industry' and thought in terms of public enterprise for higher production instead.[91]

This approach to nationalisation seems to have had wide appeal in Labour Party circles, extending well beyond the 'revisionists'. For example, at the 1950 Dorking conference to discuss future strategy, the Keeping Left group argued:

Now that the basic industries (when we have completed steel) are publicly-owned, we can dispense with nationalisation on the old pattern to the extent that we are prepared to develop, energetically and notwithstanding competition, such municipal trading, competitive public enterprise, co-operative trading, government bulk buying of manufactures, and the work of the Monopolies Commission and of Development Councils.[92]

[89] Labour Party Research Department Paper RD33, *Criteria for Nationalisation* (1946); RD38 *Public Ownership*.
[90] S. Brooke, 'Revisionists and Fundamentalists: The Labour Party and Economic Policy during the Second World War', *Historical Journal* 32 (1989), pp. 157–75.
[91] Labour Party Research Department Paper RD161, *Future Nationalisation Policy* (1948); Jay, *The Socialist Case*.
[92] Labour Party Archives, Morgan Phillips Papers, Box 24, Dorking Conference 1950, Keeping Left, 'Let Us Face the Facts', 18 May 1950.

By that time the policy had already been expounded upon and then publicly embodied in Labour's major policy statement in 1949, *Labour Believes in Britain*. This used a phrase about such nationalisation being appropriate where private enterprise was 'failing the nation', a term which was to become ubiquitous in Labour literature in the next few years.[93]

Whilst debate continued in the Labour Party about future nationalisation, this to some extent disguises the fact that by 1951 most people in the party accepted that the programme of 1945–51 completed at least a phase of public ownership, and that, at a minimum, in future the pattern of such ownership would be different from what had occurred in the 'heroic' period. By 1951 the outcomes of that programme were widely regarded as falling short of the high expectations entertained in 1945, and this view was common across the spectrum of Labour opinion, as Crosland stressed in 1956.[94]

Ultimately, Labour in 1945–51, for understandable reasons, linked to the compelling day-to-day economic necessities, failed to evolve a clear position on public ownership: 'it has failed to provide a coherent philosophy or code of conduct for nationalised industries, or think out what they should be expected to do in the present state of our society'.[95] This failure may be seen as reflecting in part the fact that the 1945–51 programme of nationalisation was in many ways a solution to the perceived problem of the 1930s – the need to plan industry for full employment, and the need to rationalise the basic industries. The former project proved difficult to realise with the public corporation; and the latter proved problematic both because 'rationalisation', and the implication of easily realisable 'economies of scale' proved a limited guide to the sources of efficiency in industry, and because of the imperatives of immediate output expansion after 1945. In addition, as discussed above, the idea that public ownership would prove a royal road to the improvement of human relations, with beneficial effects for industrial relations, productivity and happiness at work, proved optimistic.

[93] Labour Party Research Department Paper RD300, *Competitive Public Enterprise* (1949); Labour Party, *Labour Believes in Britain*, p. 12; Labour Party, *Labour and the New Society*, p. 24; Labour Party, *Let Us Win Through Together* (1950), p. 5.
[94] *The Future of Socialism*, pp. 474–82.
[95] Shanks, *Lessons of Public Enterprise*, p. 29.

6   Controls and planning

If there was one word that characterised Labour's approach to the economy in the 1940s that word would be 'planning'. In fact this was so from quite early in the previous decade. After 1931, as Stephen Brooke notes, 'the lingua franca of Labour's resurgent socialism in this regard was planning . . . Indeed to those within the Labour Party, planning and socialism became interchangeable terms.'[1] The broad development of Labour's policies in this direction have been outlined in the first chapter of this book, but this chapter focuses on planning both as a doctrine and as evolving policy in these decades. Whilst, of course, the main concern here is with the 1940s, the political and analytical context of the debates on planning in the 1930s is important.

Another feature of planning in the 1940s was that policy debates took place in the context of a much wider intellectual debate amongst economists. Disputes over economic planning were concerned with theoretical issues as well as policy in the 1940s, and whilst the primary concern of this book is policy, it is important to contextualise it with some account of the more theoretical debate.[2]

The general debate in the 1930s

One of the obvious difficulties in discussing the background to the planning arguments of the 1940s is the diverse meanings given to the term 'planning'. In this chapter it will normally be used to mean the allocation of resources by means other than markets. For academic economists, including those involved in the debates of the 1930s and 1940s, this definition is the usual one and uncontroversial. But it is clear that the

---

[1] Brooke, *Labour's War*, p. 19; S. Burgess, 'The Attlee Governments in Perspective: Commitment and Detachment in the Writing of Contemporary History' (Ph.D. thesis, London School of Economics, 1994), pp. 183–96.
[2] This debate surprisingly lacks a recent historical analysis, though see T. W. Hutchison, *Economics and Economic Policy in Britain 1946–66* (1968), pp. 55–67.

wider debate amongst politicians, political theorists and ideologues about planning beginning in the 1930s was around a much broader notion of the term, which was unified by little more than a rejection of *laissez-faire* and the perceived failings of the market economy in generating depression and mass unemployment. Thus in the 1930s there emerged a broad consensus from Harold Macmillan leftwards in favour of 'planning', where the term embraced almost any kind of government role in the economy, from the 'rationalisation' of individual industries to full-scale nationalisation, from monetary manipulation to Keynesian macroeconomic management. What Marwick long ago called 'middle opinion' became pro-planning without, however, agreeing what planning meant.[3] One obvious example is Keynes, whose advocacy of macro-planning went along with a life-long rejection of detailed intervention in the generality of market allocation of resources.[4] This consensus may be seen in the short run as rather unimportant in the sense that it largely excluded those in political power, though in the light of recent discussion this point should not be overstated.[5] But in the longer term, for the policies of the 1940s, this range of support for planning is of great importance, for in the 1940s it was to a considerable extent those who were 'out' in the 1930s who came to influence or to be in government.

What did the consensus of the 1930s contribute to the debate of the 1940s? First, a desire to distinguish clearly between democratic and totalitarian planning. Whilst the planning enthusiasm of the 1930s was given much impetus by the Soviet five-year plans, and most middle opinion was quite willing to learn from the Soviet experience, the desire to separate that kind of planning from what was advocated for Britain was almost universal.[6]

Second, the debate of the 1930s had little to say about the precise economic mechanisms by which planning in the narrow sense of resource allocation was to be conducted (see next section). This was partly because it was only one of the several aspects of the planning

---

[3] A. Marwick, 'Middle Opinion in the Thirties: Planning, Progress and Political "Agreement"', *English Historical Review* 79 (1964), pp. 285–98; D. Ritschel, 'A Corporatist Economy in Britain? Capitalist Planning for Industrial Self-Government in the 1930s', *English Historical Review* 106 (1991), pp. 57–64.

[4] Winch, *Economics and Policy*, p. 348; T. Cutler, J. Williams and K. Williams, *Keynes, Beveridge and Beyond* (1986), ch. 2.

[5] A. Booth, 'Britain in the 1930s: A Managed Economy?' *Economic History Review* 40 (1987), pp. 499–522.

[6] For example, Herbert Morrison, cited in T. Smith, *The Politics of the Corporate Economy* (1979).

debate. But it was also because there was so little practice on which to draw. It would seem that, despite the interest shown, little was actually known about how the Soviets conducted their planning.

Third, whilst there was no single reason for the popularity of planning in the 1930s, unemployment was crucial to it. It was the existence of mass unemployment in Britain from the 1920s onwards which, above all, led people to believe that the existing economic regime was unsustainable and/or undesirable and thus to embrace planning. This point should not be exaggerated. For example, there were important proponents of planning who advocated it because they believed the market system led to an inefficient distribution of resources, even if those resources were fully employed. Nevertheless, without widespread unemployment it is difficult to believe the vogue for planning would have been anything like as wide as it was. All these three elements were important legacies for the debates of the 1940s.

The calculation debate

Alongside the broad public policy debate of the 1930s there was a more specific debate amongst economists, especially between Austrian economists like Hayek and socialist economists. Its style and subject matter restricted its audience mainly to other economists – in the context of the wider discussion of planning, Smith is right to call the debate in the 1930s 'highly esoteric'.[7] This esoteric debate was nevertheless important, although clearly not for any immediate impact on economic policy. Its importance derived from two related factors. First, it was about a 'narrow' conception of planning, as a mechanism of resource allocation. It was thus at the heart of economics, a discourse founded on issues of resource allocation. So whilst it was esoteric in relation to the policy arguments of the 1930s, the debate was central to economics, which was in turn increasingly important for public policy. Second, the debate had a major impact on economists on the left in Britain, and thus on people who were to have a significant role when the political balance of forces shifted in the 1940s.

The economic planning debate amongst the economists in the 1930s is usually known as the calculation debate.[8] Its key starting point was an article by von Mises entitled 'Economic Calculation in a Socialist

---

[7] Ibid., p. 40. There were other writings by economists on planning in the 1930s which fall outside this debate. Probably most important in Britain was the work of G. D. H. Cole, *The Machinery of Socialist Planning* (1938), but his work seems to have had rather little impact on the public debate then or later.

[8] D. Lavoie, *The Calculation Debate Reconsidered* (Cambridge, 1985).

Community'. Von Mises argued that rational economic calculation in a centrally planned economy would be impossible because, even if a market existed in consumer goods, the planners would have no method of making proper decisions about what and how to produce because of the absence of valuations generated by a market for producer goods. Investment decisions could not be made rationally in the absence of the prices generated by such a market. The price system therefore provides the only plausible way in which rational production decisions can be made: 'The human mind cannot orientate itself properly among the bewildering mass of intermediate products and potentialities of production without such aid. It would simply stand perplexed before the problems of management and location.'[9]

The full complexities of the debate cannot be dealt with here, and there is an extensive literature on the issue.[10] But the quotation from von Mises raises the central issue. In the absence of markets can an efficient allocation of resources be achieved? Sometimes the debate is posed as one about the quantity of information which central planning would have to handle, covering millions of commodities and techniques. But Lavoie has persuasively argued that this is not the heart of the matter. For Hayek and the Austrians the point is not just that only a decentralised market system can handle the vast volume of information in a developed economy, but that this information is only *generated* in such an economy. It is not that there are millions of bits of objective data to be handled, but that knowledge of, for example, possible production techniques is inherently subjective. Economic knowledge (of costs and prices) is specific information available only to those who discover it, arising from their participation in particular markets and from engaging in competition with other producers. Economic knowledge therefore results from and is inseparable from the market process.

The importance of this distinction in the debate between 'objective' and 'subjective' knowledge was that it was used by Hayek against advocates of market socialism, i.e. those who proposed to combine public ownership of the means of production with decentralised management and a market system. He argued that such a system would generate unsustainable tensions between the managers of decentralised enterprises searching for new techniques, output patterns, etc. and the centre trying to plan. Crucial to this division is the fact that 'the method which under given conditions is the cheapest is a thing which has to be

[9] L. von Mises, 'Economic Calculation in a Socialist Community' in F. Hayek (ed.), *Collectivist Economic Planning* (1935), pp. 87–130.
[10] Lavoie, *Calculation Debate*; T. J. B. Hoff, *Economic Calculation in a Socialist State* (1949); for a summary J. Tomlinson, *Hayek and the Market* (1990), pp. 100–15.

discovered anew, sometimes almost from day to day, by the entrepreneur'.[11]

Hayek's debate in the 1930s was almost entirely with democratic socialist economists such as Lange, Dickinson and Durbin.[12] What must appear striking about this debate in retrospect is the extent to which the two sides shared common assumptions about the issues at stake. Broadly speaking, there was agreement about the pre-eminence of consumer sovereignty, about the centrality of freedom to the debate, and about resource allocation as a key issue. Above all, both sides accepted the undesirability of controls or planning in the sense of administrative allocation of resources as long-term mechanisms, believing them to be both inefficient and a threat to freedom.[13]

Keynes' impact on the left in the 1930s has been much discussed; that of Hayek less so. Both, I would argue, made a significant impact on democratic socialist notions of economic policy before 1939. By that date a synthesis could be seen emerging in the works of the authors already mentioned and of others like Meade, Hall and Jay.[14] Whilst there remained significant differences between individuals, this synthesis contained important common elements: first, a commitment to macro-stabilisation using both monetary and budgetary weapons, though one matter of dispute was how far it would require state control of investment decisions, and, second, agreement to use traditional microeconomics for analysing other economic issues. This agreement was largely on the tools of analysis, not the conclusions. Hence, for example, the debate between Durbin and Lerner on marginal cost pricing for socialised industries.[15] This was not a disagreement about the appropriate form of analysis to apply, but about the administrative and fiscal implications of an agreed analytical approach. Broader political differences, for example on the scale of nationalisation, could be accommodated within this consensus. Here there were arguments about how far, given the economists' criteria of monopoly, externalities, etc., such public ownership should extend. As Brooke has rightly argued, once these criteria were accepted, the traditional socialist arguments about public

---

[11] F. Hayek, *Individualism and Economic Order* (1948) p. 196.

[12] O. Lange and F. M. Taylor, *On the Economic Theory of Socialism* (New York, 1938); H. Dickinson, *Economics of Socialism* (Oxford, 1939); Evan Durbin, *Problems of Socialist Planning* (1949).

[13] Durbin, *New Jerusalems*. Evan Durbin was also influenced by Hayek's approach to macroeconomic fluctuations – the 'over-investment' theory of cycles (pp. 142–6).

[14] J. Meade, *An Introduction to Economic Analysis and Policy* (Oxford, 1936); R. Hall, *The Economic System in a Socialist State* (1937); Jay, *The Socialist Case*.

[15] Durbin, *New Jerusalems*, pp. 263–9.

ownership were effectively reorientated towards an agenda where the application of the economists' criteria put limits on the relevance of such ownership.[16]

Overall, the argument here is that before the outbreak of the Second World War socialist economics had been significantly affected by both Hayek and Keynes, and this had created a quite well-defined economic programme which embraced (like the Labour Party's 1937 *Labour's Immediate Programme*) a considerable amount of nationalisation as well as regulation of private investment on *macroeconomic* grounds and, therefore, considerable 'planning' in the broad sense of the term usually deployed in the 1930s. But this was quite compatible with a belief that markets should be the dominant means of resource allocation, in both the public and private sectors, and that they were necessary for reasons of economic efficiency and political freedom.

Policies in the 1940s

The actual economic policies pursued in the 1940s were not, of course, simple reflections of the debates of the 1930s. Not only does policy never follow theory in this way, but in between came the war, which had a major impact on both doctrine and the actual institutions within which Labour developed its policies in 1945, as suggested by the writings of Douglas Jay. In 1948 he stated his belief that wartime and early post-war experience had shown the effectiveness and desirability of more planning than he had suggested in his pre-war work.[17]

The extent to which this involved a reversal of his position since his pre-war *Socialist Case* should not be exaggerated. In 1948 planning was still seen largely in terms of the existence of 'conscious purpose' or 'purposive improvisation' rather than anything much more specific. Nevertheless, Jay's evolution is typical of the way in which the perceived success of wartime planning encouraged the view that planning was central to Labour's peacetime programme even amongst those usually thought of as on the right of the Labour Party. Not everyone shared this perception. Jewkes, who worked in the Economic Section and then in the Ministry of Aircraft Production, emerged a strong opponent of

[16] Brooke, 'Revisionists and Fundamentalists', pp. 157–75.
[17] Jay, *Road to Recovery*, pp. 9–10. See also Jay's response to Meade's views on economic planning whilst adviser to Attlee (PRO CAB124/891, Note by Jay, 14 Nov. 1945). Jay expressed general support for Meade's approach, but then attacked the idea that 'the great bulk of economic decisions should be left to the haphazard effects of competing consumer demands'.

planning. Devons, a wartime planner in the Ministry of Aircraft Production, pointed out the problems and administrative difficulties of wartime planning. But these views were exceptional.[18]

Again, the generality of the notion of planning predominant in the 1940s should be stressed. As in the 1930s, it covered almost all governmental action in the economy, and Jay's equation of 'conscious purpose' with planning was widely shared. But there is no doubt that Labour's notions of planning in 1945 did embrace the idea of substantial state allocation of resources, a position grounded not in economic theory but in the legacy of wartime controls.

The wartime coalition had instituted a comprehensive set of such controls over the economy, covering investment, consumption and prices, manpower, trade and foreign exchange, thus suspending market mechanisms over large parts of the economy. It was widely agreed that most of these controls would have to be retained in the period of transition to a peacetime economy. For Labour the issue was how far the controls were synonymous with planning mechanisms and what, therefore, their role should be beyond the transition period.

In *Let Us Face the Future* (1945) the emphasis was on controls as a means of securing an egalitarian distribution of limited supplies of goods, and as an instrument to help offset the expected slump. The assumption was that the controls would be maintained for a long time, but this assumption was most explicit in relation to investment, where a National Investment Board (NIB) was to be established for both microeconomic and macroeconomic purposes, 'to determine social priorities and promote better timing in private investment'.[19] For reasons analysed in the next chapter, the whole idea of the NIB and the use of financial mechanisms to control investment came to almost nothing in the 1940s. As table 6.1 demonstrates, one key reason for this absence was the unimportance of external sources of finance for investment in this period.

In the short run the absence of effective financial control over investment was at least partially offset by physical controls. In the war period these involved a combination of building licensing, machinery licensing and raw materials controls. The second was administratively very difficult to operate and was largely ended in early 1946, and from then on the other two were the main instruments used. Rosenberg's analysis of building controls shows the difficulty of regulating activity in an industry with thousands of separate enterprises and with an enormous demand

[18] J. Jewkes, *Ordeal by Planning* (1948); E. Devons, *Planning in Practice* (Cambridge, 1950); also Devons, *Essays in Economics* (1961), ch. 4.

[19] Labour Party, *Let Us Face the Future*, p. 5.

Table 6.1   *Sources of corporate investment finance, 1948*

(£m.)

New issues	300
Bank advances	125
Depreciation allowances	825
Undistributed profits	500
Reserves	250
Total gross investment	2,000

Source: PRO T230/143, 'Alternative Methods of Controlling Investment' by Mrs Hemming, 26 Feb. 1949.

for the diversion of building labour away from priority areas into house repair and maintenance.[20] In any case, controls operated via building licensing were, by definition, effective only in a shortage economy. Once building materials and labour became freely available, and similarly once raw materials were freely importable, then these controls would be undermined. Their use was in fact tightened up in 1947 to prevent a continuation of the excess demand for investment of the previous two years, but the longer term trend was for the easing of supply and balance of payments constraints on the economy to undermine physical controls over investment.

There is little evidence of a sustained attempt by the government or the Labour Party to search for methods of controlling private investment to support these wartime controls. There was some discussion of the use of the tax system, but whilst there was general support for (and use of) depreciation allowances, the Inland Revenue opposed any 'discriminatory' use of this instrument and so it was confined to a macroeconomic function.[21] Similarly, investment subsidies, apart from the unsuccessful case of the cotton industry, were not made into a significant instrument of planning.[22] Even in this case the policy's intellectual origins lay more with the inter-war rationalisation movement than with clear notions of socialist planning.

Of course, Labour's failure to control investment in the private sector is not surprising. In 1950 Harold Wilson called policies on the private sector 'almost a vacuum in socialist thought'.[23] The reason for the

[20] PRO CAB134/63, Committee on Control of Investment, Draft Report, 23 July 1949; N. Rosenberg, *Economic Planning in the British Building Industry, 1945–49* (Philadelphia, 1960).
[21] PRO CAB134/63, Draft Report.
[22] Singleton, 'Planning for Cotton 1945–51', pp. 62–78.
[23] PRO PREM8/1183, 'The State and Private Industry' by Harold Wilson, 4 May 1950.

vacuum was, of course, nationalisation, long seen as central to Labour's ideas about planning the economy by controlling the 'commanding heights'. For reasons outlined in the previous chapter, in practice the relation between nationalisation and investment planning was problematic. To a significant degree nationalisation as a means of planning the economy was a chimera, given the Morrisonian notion of public sector managerial independence.

Alongside investment planning, the other major strand in Labour's approach in 1945, was manpower planning. But again, despite the hopes of 1945, this form of planning rapidly declined after Labour's general election victory, for reasons returned to in chapter 8.

As we have seen in the case of investment controls, the general pattern under the Attlee governments was for controls to diminish, though with qualification. The Korean War saw a reversal of that trend, and the scope of controls was still very considerable in 1951. More importantly, despite Wilson's bonfire of controls, the Labour government had not decided to abolish all of them, and intended to retain some permanently, though largely for macroeconomic purposes.[24]

In practice, the most important form of planning under Labour was not any of those envisaged before 1945, but the planning of trade. The compelling problem of the trade (and especially dollar) deficit led to rigorous and eventually effective planning of imports and to some degree of exports too, though in the nature of things planning of the latter was restricted to the supply side and so necessarily weaker than control of the *demand* for imports. Cairncross sees this as the most successful part of Labour's planning effort in this period.[25]

Internally the diminishing role for controls was also a diminishing role for planning, because in many ways the two were effectively synonymous. Labour had largely failed to develop alternative mechanisms for allocating resources. As the logic of controls to allocate shortage resources worked itself out, and those controls fell into disuse, no alternative emerged. Planning, if not dead, was certainly in a weak state by 1951.

The great debate: (i) Hayek and Meade

How far did this evolution of policy follow the doctrinal debates over planning in this period? Before attempting to answer that question we need a more detailed picture of those debates. Cairncross sees

---

[24] Dow, *Management*, Table 4; Rollings, 'Reichstag Method of Governing?', pp. 15–36.
[25] Cairncross, *Years of Recovery*, (1985) p. 503.

a fundamental cleavage between two approaches to economic planning: a social-ist, egalitarian, approach which saw planning as a purely organisational activity akin to the planning that goes on within a productive enterprise, an army, or for that matter, a political party; and a liberal, Keynesian, approach which saw planning as a corrective to the operation of market forces and dwelt particularly on the need for a level of effective demand adequate to maintain full employment.[26]

To see how far such a fundamental divide underpinned the debates of the 1940s we can start with the response to a key text, Hayek's *Road to Serfdom* of 1944. In this, Hayek's most polemical work, he put forward two major and interconnected theses. One was that socialism was on a par with National Socialism and other forms of fascism; that the prevail-ing intellectual and political climate in Britain mirrored that in Germany during and after the First World War; and, furthermore, that this cli-mate was likely, if unchecked, to lead to the same disastrous conse-quences in Britain. Second, and more specifically on planning, Hayek argued that central direction of economic activity is incompatible with liberty, and that attempts to plan the allocation of resources centrally must either be given up or must lead inexorably down the road to serfdom.

Hayek's book was produced whilst the wartime coalition was still in power, and was explicitly aimed not just at the Labour Party and social-ists but 'the collectivists of all parties'. Indeed, the central message of Hayek's polemic was that there was no middle way between collectivism leading to serfdom and individualism leading to freedom. His argument was a variety of the 'slippery-slope' approach, in which it was suggested that Britain was already significantly down the road to perdition.[27]

The response to Hayek's work was, not surprisingly, extremely varied. But what seems so striking in retrospect is the limited extent to which the bases of his argument were attacked. Only Barbara Wootton really got to grips with Hayek's notion of freedom. She pointed out that what is meant by freedom is usually a conglomeration of freedoms and libert-ies rather than a single entity, and that there is no good reason to sup-pose these freedoms are strengthened or eroded together. Further, she said, one could sensibly support a positive notion of freedom (freedom *to* as opposed to Hayek's negative notion of freedom *from*) without equating it with omnipotence if that freedom was seen in this differen-tiated way. In other words, 'positive' freedom is an acceptable concept if it is freedom to attain specific ends rather than a singular and absolute state. Also, she argued, the compatibility of planning with different types

[26] Ibid., p. 308.
[27] F. Hayek, *The Road to Serfdom* (1944).

of social organisation was an empirical matter. She was able to show that although Britain was, according to Hayek, a long way down the road to serfdom because of planning, there was little evidence of significant erosion of liberties.[28]

Other responses were much less profound. Keynes was sympathetic to Hayek but rather beside the point. Keynes said of the *Road*: 'Morally and philosophically I find myself in agreement with virtually the whole of it.' His 'only serious criticism' was that Hayek gave no guidance on 'where to draw the line' and that he 'greatly underestimates the practicability of the middle course'. Keynes' view was that we want more planning, but under conditions where as many as possible of the planners share Hayek's moral position. This rather missed the point that Hayek denied the possibility of a sustainable middle course.[29]

Interestingly, Pigou's review of Hayek was both more critical and more to the point. Pigou pointed out that the consequences for freedom of one crucial kind of planning, that of manpower, depended entirely on how it was done. If it meant direction of individuals to specific jobs, plainly it was totally at variance with normal notions of individual freedom. If, however, it involved the government manipulating wages and conditions to attract/deter workers from particular sectors, could this be seen as an erosion of liberty?[30]

One of the most important commentators on Hayek was Durbin, a participant in the calculation debate of the 1930s and an important economic thinker in the Labour Party until his death in 1948. His article in response to Hayek's *Road* focused on the alleged misunderstanding of what socialists advocated. Durbin's central criticism of Hayek was that he misrepresented the notion of planning held by modern socialists. Durbin argued that socialists used planning to 'indicate a principle of administration and not an inflexible budget of production'. Reiterating some of his arguments from the 1930s, he maintained that 'the centrally directed economy can be, and should be, instructed to adapt its programme to the changing wishes of the consuming public and the changing conditions of technical efficiency' (p. 96). Durbin made it plain that what he meant by 'plans' were forecasts, for example bringing out the implications for inputs of future levels of output of particular commodities, where those outputs reflected the pattern of consumer preferences and could therefore be changed at any time (p. 98). Interestingly,

---

[28] B. Wootton, *Freedom under Planning* (1945).

[29] J. M. Keynes, Letter to Hayek in *Collected Writings*, vol. XXVII, *Activities 1940–46* (1980).

[30] A. C. Pigou, Review of *The Road to Serfdom*, *Economic Journal* 54 (1944), pp. 217–19. Pigou's views on planning are outlined in 'Central Planning and Professor Robbins', *Economica* 15 (1948), pp. 17–27.

Durbin chose as his example of the effects of economic planning the contentious industry of iron and steel. According to his definition, by subjecting iron and steel to economic planning 'we merely mean that the responsibility of the works' managers is changed from the Iron and Steel Federation, or even the representatives of small groups of share-holders in competing firms, to a Public Corporation, responsible in its turn to a Supreme Economic Authority representing the people'.[31] Durbin attacked Hayek primarily not because he disagreed with what he said about economic planning and its political implications, but because, according to Durbin, socialists did not intend to plan at all in Hayek's sense. How typical was this of left-wing economists in the 1940s?

The most important such economist in the early years of the Labour government was James Meade, head of the Economic Section in 1945 and 1946. Meade called himself a liberal-socialist, and already in 1936 had published a book which captured much of what he was to say in the 1940s (and indeed down to the 1970s).[32] In his 1936 textbook Meade had given overriding priority in economic policy to defeating unemploy-ment. This was to be achieved by measures affecting aggregate demand, especially the guidance of investment by a National Investment Board. Coupled to this were proposals for the public management of industries where competition was not prevalent, in accordance with the principles of marginal cost pricing. Finally, the fiscal system should be used to redress inequalities.

Meade was one of the participants in the great public debate about planning. In his *Planning and the Price Mechanism* (1948) he spelt out very clearly what he saw as the tasks of government in the economy in the 1940s. These tasks were to 'guide the economy from war to peace, to prevent inflationary and deflationary pressure, to ensure a tolerably equitable distribution of income and property, and to prevent or control the anti-social rigging of the market by private interest'. Adjusted for the changed times, this position was based on the same principles as the textbook of 1936. However, Meade went on to spell out his objections to centralised physical planning, which were threefold. Such planning, he argued, would be a major threat to freedom, partly because of the loss of consumer sovereignty, but above all because it would involve the allocation of labour. Second, such planning would breed spivvery and corruption. Third, it would require a large number of people to admin-ister the requisite controls: 'When one examines the possibilities of quantitative planning, one cannot but be appalled by the prospects of

---

[31] Durbin, *Problems*, pp. 95, 96, 98.
[32] Meade, *Economic Analysis and Policy*; Meade, *The Intelligent Radical's Guide to Economic Policy* (1975).

insidious threats to personal freedom and to public morality, of a swollen bureaucracy and of clumsy inefficiencies.'[33]

This public position was enthusiastically pursued in Meade's 'private' role as chief economic adviser to the government. His diary shows him in memoranda and verbal advice spelling out his conception of economic planning. In a memorandum under that title in September 1945 he made clear that planning should be largely macroeconomic in character, and explicitly repudiated the idea of planning by industrial sectors. Earlier, in May 1945, at the beginning of his period as head of the Economic Section, he had spelt out his view that the price mechanism should only be superseded where competition was not technically possible, such as in the case of natural monopolies.[34]

Meade had a clear view of the divisions in economic thought. For him there were three views – Hayek and the advocates of *laissez-faire*; his own liberal-socialist position, and the Gosplanners. Thus in reflecting on his review of Lerner's (1945) book in his diary, Meade commented:

what a breath of fresh air it is, after the dreadful arbitrary and authoritarian quantitative planning of a Balogh on the one hand and extreme *laissez-faire* attitudes of a Hayek on the other, to read an economist who starts out from the simple and fundamental economic proposition that the purpose of economic policy should be to make the economic calculus work'.[35]

How accurate was Meade's characterisation of the economic division of opinion? In relation to Hayek, it is interesting to note that, in response to queries from Morrison about the kind of advice likely to come from the Economic Section, Meade showed how much agreement there was between him and Robbins, Jewkes and Dennison. Robbins, of course, was a close collaborator with Hayek, especially in the 1930s; Jewkes was to write a Hayekian polemic against planning in 1948; Dennison was less well known but also a strong *laissez-faire* advocate.[36] Yet Meade was able to demonstrate large areas of agreement between these men and himself over issues of aggregate demand policy and international economic policy, with the differences limited to questions of 'industrial organisation'. By this he meant solely the issue of the extent of public ownership: 'all economists agree that at the one extreme there were

[33] Meade, *Planning and the Price Mechanism*, pp. vi, 6–7, 10.

[34] J. Meade, *Collected Papers*, vol. I, *Employment and Inflation* (1989), ch. 16; vol. IV, *The Cabinet Office Diary*, p. 79.

[35] *Cabinet Office Diary*, p. 37; Review of Lerner in 'Mr. Lerner on the Economics of Control', *Economic Journal* 55 (1945), pp. 47–69.

[36] Jewkes, *Ordeal by Planning*; Robbins also attacked peacetime planning in his *Economic Planning in Peace and War* (1947).

certain activities which should be publicly run and that at the other there were industries which should compete, but each drawing the dividing line at a different spot'.[37]

Meade was right to minimise the distance between his views and people like Robbins and Jewkes (and by extension Hayek). Whilst he may have disagreed with Hayek's macroeconomic views (as indeed did Robbins and Jewkes by this time), his view of the role of the state as regards industrial planning would not have been very different from the Austrian view.

On the other side of the argument Meade identified the 'enemy' as Balogh. Elsewhere he perceived others.

But I fear that Cripps (in this no doubt primed by Austen Robinson) wants a detailed Economic Plan in the sense of a statement of exactly how many shirts, how many pairs of boots and shoes etc. we should produce over each of the next five years. This, I believe, if taken seriously would lead to the sacrifice of all the flexibility which a proper use of the pricing and cost system demands.[38]

Meade's characterisation of Balogh is accurate up to a point. Balogh certainly saw himself as a planner. But his detailed discussions of what this might mean for policy were mainly limited to international economic issues, where he was a powerful proponent of maintaining physical controls, against the strong preferences of Meade, as noted in chapter 3. Whilst Balogh advocated more planning domestically, especially to address what he saw as the market mechanism's inability to generate enough savings and investment, he did not spell it out in detail. In addition, he held no official position in the policy-making or policy-advice apparatus.[39]

Meade's identification of Cripps as the chief advocate of planning in the government raises more complex issues. Cripps, like most ministers at this time, displayed a strong rhetoric in favour of planning. But beyond this he probably had the most developed notion of democratic planning and its implications for industry of anyone in the Attlee governments.

He wrote the introductory section of the 1947 *Economic Survey*, which gave a broad account of what economic planning involved in a democratic society. As Cairncross argues, this was a curious statement in that remarkably little was said about the mechanisms of planning. The emphasis was, first, on the essential difference between totalitarian and

---

[37] *Cabinet Office Diary*, pp. 115–16.
[38] Ibid., p. 202.
[39] Balogh, *Dollar Crisis*; 'Britain's Economic Problem', pp. 32–67; also *Unequal Partners*, vol. II, p. 269.

democratic planning, which ruled out in particular any direction of labour, and second, on the need to plan for the output of six basic industries, namely coal, power, steel, agriculture, transport and building. Beyond these sectors planning would consist of a set of budgets relating needs to resources. The budgets would be of manpower and of national income and expenditure, and would be supplemented by analyses of particular problems – foreign exchange, investment and basic materials.[40] The mechanisms available to government, Cripps argued, would be different from those available during wartime, because of the unacceptability of labour direction and the rapid decline in the role of government as purchaser of output. Many other wartime controls continued but, he argued, their effectiveness depended crucially upon consent: 'Events can be directed in the way that is desired in the national interest only if the Government, both sides of industry and the people accept the objectives and then work together to achieve the end.'

But whatever the political logic of this emphasis on co-operation, it could not be said that it provided a magic key to democratic planning, especially because, as Cairncross notes, the relation between planning and the price mechanism was entirely neglected in Cripps' discussion.[41] This is a crucial point about the debate on planning in the 1940s. Cripps in many ways represented a wide range of opinion, both within Labour and beyond, which on the basis of the experience of both the inter-war slump and wartime planning had come to have a deep, if often implicit, distrust of the price mechanism. This view was what Harrod denounced as 'This evil . . . distrust of the price mechanism and of the automatisms of the old economy'.[42]

Such distrust is perhaps best summed up in Franks' *Central Planning and Control in War and Peace*, which does not so much attack the workings of the price mechanism as assume its ineffectiveness and undesirability in dealing with contemporary economic problems, and consequently assume that the major issue is what kind of administrative mechanisms to put in its place.[43]

Meade offered a powerful critique of this view.[44] His key point was that the administrative issues of planning could not be separated from the issue of the role of the price mechanism. For example, in relation to the primary problem of the balance of payments, Meade argued that

[40] *Economic Survey* (1947), paras. 8, 12, 15–22; Cairncross, *Years of Recovery*, pp. 304–9.
[41] *Economic Survey*, para. 27; Cairncross, *Years of Recovery*, pp. 308–9.
[42] R. Harrod, Review of Jewkes, *Ordeal by Planning*, *Economica* 15 (1948), p. 223.
[43] O. Franks, *Central Planning and Control in War and Peace* (1947).
[44] J. E. Meade, 'Planning without Prices', *Economica* 15 (1948), pp. 28–35; see also D. H. Robertson, 'The Economic Outlook', *Economic Journal* 57 (1947), pp. 430–3.

Franks' discussion of the mechanism of control of exports and imports had to be linked to a discussion of the extent to which market mechanisms would fail to make the necessary adjustments, or would do so too slowly.

Whatever the undoubted omissions and confusions of Cripps' exposition or Franks' implicit defence of that position, it is doubtful whether Meade's picture of the minister as a Gosplanner is very accurate or helpful. Cripps did believe in planning of a sort, but his democratic planning owed much more to a tripartite style of industrial co-operation than to Soviet-style central planning. In his statement of aims when he was first appointed to the Board of Trade in 1945, Cripps spelt out this philosophy. The primary aim, he said, was to raise industrial efficiency, but central to its success was the mobilisation of consent in industry: 'We should avoid the impression that we wish to impose upon the industry a pre-conceived government plan. On the contrary, both sides of industry should feel that what the Government is trying to do is to help the industry help itself.' This ideology was the basis of Cripps' emphasis on working parties and later Development Councils as Labour's key policies for the non-nationalised sector.[45] If we want to understand Cripps' and to a large degree Labour's notion of democratic planning, it is this kind of proposal we need to focus on, not the economists' agenda of planning and the price mechanism as alternative means of allocating resources.

Meade identified Austen Robinson as the economic adviser behind Cripps' Gosplan approach. Again, this seems exaggerated. Robinson was certainly keener on government controls over resource allocation than Meade. But this needs to be qualified substantially. First, Robinson's enthusiasm for planning was primarily an enthusiasm for manpower planning – this was true in the 1940s and remained so into the 1960s. That, however, did not involve support for direction of labour, but of 'wage planning'.[46]

Second, and more importantly, Robinson saw the prime function of planning as speeding up the changes in the economy which the market mechanism was slow to make: 'the main aim of planning should be to make planning unnecessary'.[47] Hence he was not a Gosplanner any more than Cripps. Rather he was at one end of the spectrum of views

---

[45] PRO CAB71/21, 'The Government's Plans for Encouraging Industrial Organisation and Efficiency', 27 Aug. 1945; see also BT13/220, 'President's Morning Meeting', 29 Aug. 1945. On Development Councils see Mercer, 'Labour Governments', pp. 71–89.

[46] E. A. G. Robinson, *Economic Planning in the UK: Some Lessons* (Cambridge, 1967); 'Economic Problems', pp. 165–85.

[47] PRO T229/47, 'Comments on Economic Sections Survey for 1948–51' by E. A. G. Robinson, 23 June 1947; also 'Economic Problems', p. 177.

about how quickly wartime controls should be reduced as normality returned. He did not see a permanent role for those controls once the transition to that normality was made.

The general argument here is that Meade's view of the range of economic opinion amongst ministers and their advisers was distorted. There was no significant difference in basic economic views between him and people like Robbins and Jewkes. Similarly, there was no serious advocacy of Gosplan-style planning from ministers or economists in his period as head of the Economic Section. Meade's critique of the non-economist Franks had more relevance to the kind of ideas informing the planning proposals of people like Cripps than much of the 'great planning debate' amongst economists in this period.

The debate of the 1930s had focused on planning as a device for efficient resource allocation. In this debate Meade followed Keynes in believing that, given full employment of resources, the market (with qualifications) would deliver an efficient allocation of those resources. Hence both his enthusiasm for planning in the sense of national income planning, i.e. demand management, and his hostility to Gosplanners.

The use of this latter term raises a fundamental problem about what is meant by planning under the Labour government. The Soviet five-year plans were above all about *modernising* the Soviet economy, not reallocating an existing set of resources. One of the tensions not sufficiently recognised in Labour's economic policies was between what was essentially an economists' agenda of full use and efficient allocation of resources, and the modernisation aims of some ministers in the Labour government, such as Cripps and, to a lesser extent, Dalton. Thus the aims of planning were further complicated by this additional objective, which cut across the economists' agenda. But precisely what 'modernisation' meant never clearly emerged in this period, though it did involve a large number of initiatives by the government.[48]

The great debate: (ii) Hall and the events of 1947

In 1947 Meade was succeeded as head of the Economic Section by Robert Hall. Like Meade, Hall had been a pre-war advocate of 'liberal socialism', albeit of a much less clearly defined character. Like Meade, he kept a diary of his period in the Economic Section which has subsequently been published, but he is much less revealing about his policy views than Meade.[49] PRO material, however, makes clear that his pos-

[48] See chapter 4.
[49] Hall, *Economic System*; *The Robert Hall Diaries 1947–53*, ed. A. Cairncross (1989).

ition was very similar to that of Meade. In 1948 he wrote: 'In all of these you will see that my view is that a detailed plan is impracticable for an open economy, and that we should therefore plan for an adaptable system so that we could adjust ourselves to whatever fate has in store for us.' The following year he noted: 'my own view of the matter is that planning in the UK is primarily a matter of forecasting where we are going, making the best prediction we can of present trends and taking existing policies as given'.[50] Hall, then, maintained a great deal of continuity in policy advice with his predecessor. However, his period as head of the Economic Section coincided with the creation in 1947 of an Economic Planning Board (EPB) and a Central Economic Planning Staff (CEPS), which suggests that the government was increasing its commitment to notions of economic planning.

The significance of these events of 1947 is complex to unravel. Many analyses of the Labour government see 1947 as marking a decisive shift in policy away from planning and controls and towards the dominance of fiscal policy.[51] How does this view chime in with the creation of this new apparatus of planning? The central economic point is that prior to 1947 the government had not got to grips with the excess demand in the economy which resulted from the build-up of purchasing power in wartime and the limitations on supply. The changes of 1947 (especially the budget of November) were certainly 'Keynesian' in the sense that the budget was explicitly used to reduce the level of demand, but in other respects deeply ambiguous, a theme returned to in chapter 10.

Any idea of a simple move from planning to fiscal policy in 1947 therefore needs to be abandoned. On the other hand, was there a 'real start to central planning' in that year, as Dalton suggested?[52] As noted above, whilst investment was controlled more effectively after 1947, the controls (largely via raw material allocations, especially steel) were relevant only as long as shortages persisted. Alternative methods of allocating investment expenditure were not created.

Similarly, the importance of the EPB and CEPS for planning should not be exaggerated. The EPB, made up of employers and trade union representatives (plus civil servants), was largely a talking shop and of little significance in policy-making. The CEPS is of more interest because it created another, if limited, channel for expert economists to

---

[50] PRO T230/323, Hall to E. Plowden, 'Have We Got a Plan?', 21 April 1948; Hall to Wright, 4 March 1949.

[51] For discussion of this issue see Tomlinson, *Employment Policy*, ch. 5; Rollings, 'Reichstag Method of Governing'; A. Booth, *British Economic Policy 1931–49: A Keynesian Revolution?* (1989), ch. 6.

[52] Cited in Cairncross, *Years of Recovery*, p. 452.

influence policy-making. It was headed by Edwin Plowden, an industrialist/civil servant, but included among its staff Austen Robinson, who had figured in Meade's assessment of the state of opinion when he held a previous official appointment at the Board of Trade. Plowden himself seems to have shared the views of Robinson already noted, that 'the aim of planning should be to make planning unnecessary'.[53]

Amongst the adherents of this view of planning Robinson was certainly more sympathetic to quantitative targets than Meade was. Their difference in approach broadly speaking reflected a difference between the ethos of the whole Economic Section as opposed to that of the Planning Staff.[54] It is brought out quite explicitly in two documents produced by these departments. In one, entitled 'What Does the Economic Section Believe?', written in April 1949, David Butt of the section began with the question: 'Do we believe in economic planning?' Basically, his argument was that the section believed in 'mild' planning, planning in aggregate and some of the big investment programmes, but not in 'fierce' planning of specific resource allocations enforced by government.[55] This was really the Meade line continued.

On the other hand, a 1948 document by Robin Marris and Kenneth Berrill of the CEPS, produced in the previous year, began bluntly with the statement: 'Fundamentally the difference between the Economic Section and ourselves is that, as an act of faith, we believe in planning and they do not.' This was followed by a further statement of faith:

We believe that it is probable that the United Kingdom needs certain radical changes in the pattern of its economy and that on balance, the changes will come about more quickly if the economists use their judgement and advise on direction, quantities and methods than if all sit back and allow the machine to attempt to drive around the corner by itself.[56]

This was an important difference, and it was reflected in some of the work done in the different organisations. In the Economic Section, for example, any long-run forecasts were regarded sceptically. On the other hand, among the planning staff there was a clear interest in what was called 'level of industry' planning, and this led to work, at least of a preliminary kind, on input–output calculations of the structure of certain British industries. This work, however, seems quickly to have been abandoned.[57]

[53] Plowden, *Industrialist*, p. 46.
[54] See also Cairncross and Watts, *Economic Section*, esp. chs. 8, 9.
[55] PRO T230/143, 11 April 1949.
[56] PRO T229/166, 'Presentation of the Long Term Survey' by R. Marris and K. Berrill to A. Robinson, 15 June 1948.
[57] PRO T230/145, 'Questions for a Numerologist or Planner', R. Butt to R. Hall, 22 June 1948; T229/166, unsigned, undated memo, 'Level of Industry Planning'.

Thus the CEPS emerges as the closest to Gosplanners that Britain had within the official machine in the late 1940s. Some of its members certainly saw themselves as engaged in a battle with other economists: 'We have tried to argue a case not universally accepted by economists that detailed production planning is desirable on theoretical grounds to maximise output over time. Further, it is especially desirable where an economy needs rapidly to change its structure.'[58]

The result of all the discussion and debate within the CEPS was a fairly mild version of the planned economy:

> We believe that it is quite impracticable and far from desirable over the whole field of industry to set production targets for the whole range of final products . . . But we believe that, more particularly in the short period, it will be necessary both to set general targets for the basic industries . . . and in the case of the main manufacturing industries to establish the general levels of production which are necessary to meet the needs of the export market and the main needs of the home market.[59]

In any event, Robinson in the CEPS was not such an influential figure as Hall, the head of the Economic Section, and generally the Planning Staff seem not to have had very much impact on policy; much of what they did was to process the implementation of policy decisions unambiguously made elsewhere. Even their muted version of planning was thus rather marginal to the government machine.

Who was for planning

The previous sections have advanced the argument that, for all the rhetoric of planning in the late 1940s, influential advocates of planning in the narrow sense usually employed by economists were very thin on the ground. Economic advice to the government was overwhelmingly dominated by a 'liberal-socialist' view, which in Meade's later phrase, said 'two cheers for the market'.[60] This was not substantially altered by ministerial opinion. Cripps, who had the most developed concept of planning, was also totally committed to a consensual, co-operative view of government–industry relations which militated against any idea of Soviet-style planning. For him planning was mainly about the development of such good relations. When he committed himself on the issue of planning in the economists' resource allocation sense, he seems in fact to have shared the view that the aim of planning should be to restore the conditions for production to be guided by consumer demand: 'In a

[58] PRO T229/166, unsigned, undated memo, 'Long Term Economic Planning'.
[59] PRO T229/208, unsigned, undated memo, 'Economic Survey 1948–51', note by CEPS.
[60] Meade, *Intelligent Radical's Guide*, p. 162.

free society, planning should seek the satisfaction of consumer wants with the most economical use of our resources. In normal times production should be fitted to the pattern of market demand.'[61] This strong emphasis on consumer sovereignty was established in the debates of the 1930s, and was obviously central to economics as a discipline which regards consumption as the ultimate aim of economic activity. But this theoretical orientation also fitted with the political mood of an important part of public opinion in the 1940s, which saw rationing and consumer austerity as irksome, a view much emphasised by the Conservative opposition. Cairncross points out how sensitive economists were to the tide of public opinion, and Labour politicians were not immune.[62]

The most consistent advocates of planning in a radical sense in this period were probably the engineering unions. In a series of memoranda from 1945 to 1949 the National Engineering Joint Trades Movement and later the Confederation of Shipbuilding and Engineering Unions came out strongly for a system of targets for the sectors of the engineering industry to be turned into targets for individual factories. What is interesting about these proposals is not just that they were the most developed example of a case for planning made in this period, but also how little support they received. In particular what is of note is the resistance by the government even to having a Development Council in the industry. It agreed only reluctantly to the establishment of an Advisory Council with minority union representation and a purely advisory role.[63] The engineering unions do not seem to have gained TUC support for their position on planning: it is precisely their idiosyncrasy which makes them stand out in this period.

Conclusions

Socialist planning, a recent article observes, 'was a notable, if unlikely casualty of Labour government after the Second World War'.[64] Why did all the debates and discussions, intense since the 1930s, seem to come to so little in the 1940s? Stephen Brooke's argument is that the

[61] PRO T229/417, 'The Framework of Economic Planning' by Minister for Economic Affairs, 11 Nov. 1947.
[62] Letter to author, 1989; Ina Zweiniger-Bargielowska, 'Rationing, Austerity and the Conservative Party Recovery after 1945', *Historical Journal* 37 (1994), pp. 173–97.
[63] Modern Records Centre, Warwick University, MSS 292 615 2/5, 'The Engineering Worker and Economic Recovery', 5 Dec. 1949; MRC MSS44/TBN147, 'Plan for Engineering', 1949/50; PRO SUPP14/137, 'Proposals for an Engineering Advisory Board' 1946–52; Hinton, *Shop Floor Citizens*, ch. 8.
[64] S. Brooke, 'Problems of "Socialist Planning": Evan Durbin and the Labour Government of 1945', *Historical Journal* 34 (1991), pp. 687–702.

key problem in the 1940s was that such planning 'was untenable in practical terms given the intransigence of the unions'.[65] Whilst this view has a long pedigree, it seems to put too much emphasis on the unions *per se* as upholders of voluntarism and free collective bargaining. Support for such an attitude to wage bargaining was much broader and deeper than a 'government versus unions' analysis suggests.[66]

But whilst general support for free collective bargaining was an important political and ideological obstacle to a more thoroughgoing planning regime, it was by no means the only such obstacle. In addition, there was opposition from almost all private sector industrialists to the enhanced role of government in industry, and also opposition from those who took over the newly nationalised corporations. Relations with the first group were largely defined by a consensual, co-operative approach which in some ways generated the worst of both worlds. By focusing so much on the need for agreement it ruled out radical policy departures based on government leverage over private firms. On the other hand, by being coupled to such strong notions of parliamentary sovereignty it ruled out freeing the 'tripartite' bodies and allowing them to execute significant policy initiatives. The latter position ruled out, for example, any idea of a semi-autonomous *commissariat au plan* on the French model, let alone any Gosplan.[67] Similarly, the commitment to the Morrisonian corporation in the public sector ruled out the subordination of the newly nationalised industries to any national plan.

These features of Labour's position – consensual tripartism, the Morrisonian corporation, parliamentary sovereignty alongside free collective bargaining – provide what may be called the 'iron quadrilateral' of political positions which bound the government's economic and industrial policies. They are returned to in chapter 13. They militated strongly against any kind of planning in the narrow sense. Equally, Keynesianism eroded support for planning by seeming to present a solution to the unemployment problem without involving a compromise with these political principles. An alternative planning strategy, aimed at industrial modernisation, never cohered in this period. It didn't fit with the economists' approach to the issue, focused on resource allocation, which had become increasingly influential; and it threatened those political principles outlined above which bounded Labour's approach to industry. The (partial) triumph of demand management as an alternative to planning combined a doctrinal triumph for Keynesianism,

---

[65] Ibid., p. 700.

[66] See chapter 8.

[67] On British reactions to the Monnet Plan PRO CAB125/9242, 'Discussions on Monnet Plan', 5 Sept. 1945.

broadly defined; a (partial) triumph of a policy objective of stabilisation over modernisation; and a (partial) triumph of certain deep-seated aspects of Labour's political philosophy.

7   The financial system

The 1931 crisis and demise of the Labour government stimulated a radical reappraisal of Labour's whole approach to policy, especially economic policy. In the area of financial and monetary policy this concern to rework Labour's positions was driven not only by the general belief that the problems of 1929–31 had been in part a policy failure but also by the belief that the collapse of 1931 had flowed directly from a combination of the malevolence of financial institutions towards a Labour government ('the bankers' ramp') and weaknesses in Labour's understanding of those institutions. Hence, central to the Labour policy review of the 1930s was the reformulation of policy on money and finance, a review led by Hugh Dalton.[1]

This policy review ranged over most aspects of domestic monetary and financial policy – from how to secure price stability, the desirable exchange rate regime, through to specific proposals for institutional reform of the financial system. The focus of this chapter is the latter area, for two reasons. First, the problems of monetary policy have been exhaustively dealt with in recent work by Susan Howson.[2] Second, the striking feature of the 1940s is the extent to which all the debates of the 1930s seem to have had so little impact in the following decade. In an area where, arguably, Labour was as well prepared with detailed policy proposals as any, the actual experience of government after 1945 was that all these efforts yielded meagre results.

Between 1931 and 1945 most Labour and other progressive policy discussion assumed that radical reform of the financial system was required, and all Labour politicians assumed such reform would be cen-

---

[1] Durbin, *New Jerusalems*, ch. 10. Many of the Labour Party experts on these areas contributed to G. D. H. Cole, ed., *What Everybody Wants to Know about Money* (1936), which, whilst written in textbook form, represents much of Labour Party thinking by the mid-1930s. In this area Labour developed links with (a small number of) City experts via the XYZ Club, founded in 1932 (Durbin, *New Jerusalems*, pp. 81–3, 209–10).

[2] Howson, *Monetary Policy*.

tral to Labour's policies in office. As Brooke[3] stresses, 'the control of finance was perceived as the handmaiden to the socialisation of industry'. Three proposals for such reform were interwoven in Labour's statements in the 1930s and 1940s – nationalisation of the Bank of England, nationalisation of the joint-stock banks and a National Investment Board (NIB).

This chapter focuses on why so little came of these proposals, especially the NIB.[4] The NIB deserves this attention on a number of grounds. First, it was a proposal which had widespread support in the 1930s, well beyond Labour Party circles and into the wider fields of 'progressivism'. Second, such a board would seem to fit in with Labour's post-1945 concern to plan the economy, in which the planning of investment was generally accepted as crucial. Third, the failure to establish the NIB was the cause of dissension under Labour, and the debate over the failure to implement the proposal brings out some of the tensions in Labour's attempts to run the British economy in a new way after 1945.

Nationalisation of the Bank of England

The first of Labour's proposals from the 1930s may be dealt with briefly. By the 1920s Labour's leadership already supported the idea of nationalising the Bank of England. At various times in Labour's past this proposal had been put forward, and in 1928 it was embodied in the major policy statement, *Labour and the Nation*.[5] However, at this time, at least as far as the leadership of the party was concerned, this nationalisation would involve no significant policy departure. Given the Bank's central role in the financial system it was argued, it was right that it should be nationalised, but Snowden, Labour's spokesman on finance (and Chancellor of the Exchequer in the Labour governments of 1924 and 1929–31), stressed that nationalisation would have to be done by a means which secured the Bank from any political control. In this, as in so many other areas, Snowden was a vigorous supporter of financial orthodoxy. He explicitly repudiated using the nationalised Bank as a means either

---

[3] Brooke, 'Revisionists and Fundamentalists', p. 160.
[4] Howson's primary concern is with monetary policy, but she touches on the failure of Labour significantly to reform the financial system (*Monetary Policy*, chs. 2, 3).
[5] S. Pollard, 'The Nationalisation of the Banks: The Chequered History of a Socialist Proposal' in D. E. Martin and D. Rubinstein (eds.), *Ideology and the Labour Movement* (1990), p. 172.

of macroeconomic management or of microeconomic planning, as advocated especially by the Independent Labour Party in the 1920s.[6]

After the collapse of 1931 the desire to nationalise the Bank was strengthened by its alleged role in the so-called bankers' ramp which led to the collapse of the Labour government. In addition, the nationalisation appealed to a Labour Party searching for specific economic policy instruments to replace the windy rhetoric of socialism so prevalent in the 1920s. Nationalisation of the Bank became part of the agenda not only of the Labour Party but other 'progressive' forces as Keynesian-style macroeconomic management became an influential force under the impact of the mass unemployment of the 1930s. Keynes himself came to see nationalisation of the Bank as one condition for an active monetary policy.[7]

The nationalisation of the Bank gained support across the spectrum of views in the Labour Party, and was embodied in the major 1930s policy statement, *For Socialism and Peace*. In this case at least there was a unanimity of approach which ensured that the nationalisation of the Bank was one of Labour's earliest legislative acts after 1945. Symbolically important for Labour, it is doubtful whether this nationalisation made much practical difference, especially to the relations between a Labour government shorn of the hair-shirt financial orthodoxy of a Snowden, and the Bank without a dictatorial but guileful Montagu Norman. It was the combination of these two people and their approach to monetary policy which had made the Bank's activities seem so unacceptable to the vast majority of Labour and progressive opinion in the 1930s. But the post-1945 situation is well described by Lord Bridges, Cabinet Secretary under Attlee:

QUESTION: What practical difference in working between the Treasury and the Bank resulted from the Act of 1946?
BRIDGES: . . . I should have said very little . . . when the Government wanted to get on top they could always do so, but in the old days it might mean a good deal of fuss to get there. The Act merely meant that the Government could get on top more easily and *de jure* without having a fuss.[8]

Recent work has tended to be less complacent than earlier research about the relationship between the newly nationalised Bank and govern-

---

[6] Ibid., pp. 172–3.
[7] Durbin, *New Jerusalems*, p. 268.
[8] (Radcliffe) *Committee on the Workings of the Monetary System*, Minutes of Evidence Q.12558, HMSO 1959. Robin Marris records it being a popular joke in the 1950s that the key to changing the machinery of economic policy would be to nationalise the Bank of England (*The Machinery of Economic Policy* (1954), p. 25).

ment established by the 1946 Nationalisation Act. The precise measure of Treasury control over the Bank's decisions on monetary policy remained vague, and did not give the government the unambiguous powers that many proponents of nationalisation had anticipated.[9]

As Howson shows, the Governor of the Bank of England, Catto, fought an effective battle at the time of the framing of the nationalisation Act to limit the power of the Treasury to 'direct' the Bank, and to protect the Bank's informal relationship with the clearing banks. Despite what seems to have been the perception of ministers, including Dalton, at the time, the legislation put very tight constraints on the capacity of the government to influence clearing bank behaviour, though this did not clearly emerge until a legal opinion was taken in 1951.

The result of the nationalisation, as Fforde suggests, was to continue rather than resolve the ambiguous status of the Bank in relation to monetary policy, and to maintain the Bank's role as a spokesman for the City to government at least as much as an instrument of government policy *vis-à-vis* the City.[10] As so often, Labour seems to have been satisfied with a symbolic rather than substantive reform of a major institution.

Nationalisation of the clearing banks

The proposal to nationalise the clearing banks has been well analysed by Sidney Pollard. As he points out, the proposal has been periodically put forward as a Labour Party policy, and gained widespread support in the early 1930s as part of the Labour perception of the clearers' role in the 1931 debacle. At the 1932 Labour conference a motion to pursue such a nationalisation was embodied in Labour's policies, despite opposition from most of the party leadership. It was subsequently included in *For Socialism and Peace*, and was part of Labour's policy at the 1935 general election.

But after the general election defeat the proposal disappeared. In part this was an aspect of Labour's general reassertion of its 'moderation' in the face of continuing electoral unpopularity. But perhaps more significantly, it reflected the growing weight in Labour circles of those who emphasised the macroeconomic aspects of financial policy. For Labour intellectuals like Durbin, nationalisation of the clearers became

---

[9] Howson, *Monetary Policy*, pp. 113–17; J. Fforde, *The Bank of England and Public Policy 1941–1958* (1992), ch. 1.
[10] Fforde, *Bank of England*, pp. 12–13.

unnecessary if full employment could be secured by Bank of England regulation of general credit policy.[11]

As Pollard argues, support for nationalisation of the clearers had a range of objectives, and for many these included microeconomic as well as macroeconomic goals. For example, Radice argued that the nationalisation would make it possible for

> the distribution of credit to industry to be co-ordinated according to the general economic needs of the nation. Information could be pooled, industries could be dealt with as such and not as sets of isolated firms, and their reorganisation could be carried through in a way which would be impossible when the competing claims of firms on many different banking institutions have all to be taken into separate consideration.[12]

But despite such arguments, the nationalisation of the clearers had disappeared from official policy by the time of *Labour's Immediate Programme* in 1937, and reappeared in policy neither proposed nor carried out thereafter.

The National Investment Board

The third policy proposal prominent in the 1930s was that for a National Investment Board, though from the beginning there was little agreement on what exactly such a body might do or what other institutional changes might need to accompany it. The idea of an NIB seems to have been first explicitly put forward by the Liberals, in the Liberal *Industry Inquiry* of 1928, though similar proposals had been advanced by groups within the Labour Party, especially the Independent Labour Party earlier in the 1920s.[13]

Like the nationalisation of the Bank of England, an NIB became part of the 'progressive consensus' of the 1930s, rather than peculiarly a

[11] Pollard, 'Nationalisation', pp. 176–8; Durbin, *New Jerusalems*, pp. 155–6. See also E. A. Radice, 'Commercial Banks and Credit' in Cole, *What Everybody Wants to Know about Money*, esp. pp. 196–7.

[12] Radice, 'Commercial Banks', p. 197. This approach to the role of financial institutions reflected the widespread belief that these institutions should play a greater role in 'rationalising' staple industries. In fact, the main initiative in this came from the Bank of England, via the creation of the Bankers' Industrial Development Corporation and the Securities Management Trust (R. S. Sayers, *The Bank of England* (Cambridge, 1976), vol. I, ch. 14). The Bank was also active in help for the Special Areas, i.e. areas of high unemployment. But as so often with the Bank, its role was limited and often aimed at pre-empting more radical initiatives by others, usually government (Carol E. Heim, 'Limits to Intervention: The Bank of England and Industrial Diversification in the Depressed Areas', *Economic History Review* 37 (1984), pp. 533–50).

[13] Liberal Party, *Industrial Inquiry* ('Yellow Book') (1928; republished 1978), pp. 111–15, though this proposal is unclear on how far the Board would regulate *private* investment; Durbin, *New Jerusalems*, p. 51; Pollard, 'Nationalisation', pp. 170–3.

Labour proposal. However, whilst Keynes and the Liberals emphasised the macroeconomic aspect of the idea, most Labour supporters were also keen on the idea of its playing a microeconomic, allocative role. Labour's idea behind the NIB is well summarised by a proposal of 1931 which wanted such a body to 'control the amount and direction of home and foreign investment, to authorise new issues, to secure priority for enterprises of social importance and to assist in the work of National Planning'.[14]

At the 1932 Labour Party conference Hugh Dalton, by then the party's most important financial expert, moved the proposal to create the NIB: 'A National Investment Board is an essential instrument, in the opinion of the executive, in carrying out our policy of socialist planning. We must exercise control over the direction and over the character of new capital issues on the money market, and of new capital developments in different parts of the country, and in different industries.'[15]

In 1932, Labour published *Currency, Banking and Finance*, its most detailed discussion of the issues. This endorsed the NIB proposal, and spelt out how it would work. The document focused especially on control of new capital issues by the board: 'that with the object of preventing waste and misdirection in the use of long-term capital, the board should exercise control over all new public issues on the capital market, and its permission should be required before any such new issue could be made'. This was further spelt out in more specific terms: 'housing schemes should come before dog tracks, new plant for scientific treatment of coal before new plant for luxury trades'. The NIB, it was argued, 'should contribute, as it were, the general staff of the Government for planning and co-ordinating the mobilisation and allocation of that part of the national wealth which is destined for capital investment'.

Nicholas Davenport, who claimed to be the originator of the 1932 proposal, had actually called for *two* new bodies to be established. These were to be an NIB, which would focus on control of capital issues, and what he called an Industrial Finance Corporation which would *initiate* finance for both new and basic industries.[16] The latter part of the proposal might be seen as responding to the kind of concerns about the

---

[14] Durbin, *New Jerusalems*, pp. 207, 205. Keynes supported Labour's broad idea for the NIB, but wanted it to stick to 'quantitative' rather than 'qualitative' control of investment (J. M. Keynes, *Collected Writings*, vol. XXI (1982), pp. 133–7, 590–2). At the extreme right of the 'progressive consensus' Harold Macmillan, a future Conservative Prime Minister, supported the idea of an NIB in his *The Middle Way* (1938), pp. 260–4.

[15] Labour Party, *Annual Conference Report* 1932, p. 184.

[16] N. Davenport, *Memoirs of a City Radical* (1974), pp. 76–9, 246–9; H. Dalton, *Memoirs*, vol. I, *The Fateful Years* (1957), ch. 1.

British financial system articulated by the Macmillan Committee, which reported in 1931. It famously noted the existence of a 'gap' in the financial system in equity provision for small business. But in fact its criticisms of the system went much wider than that with the assertion that 'there is substance in the view that the British financial organisation concentrated in the City of London might with advantage be more closely co-ordinated with British industry'.[17]

However, this second aspect of financial reform tended thereafter to be neglected by Labour in the 1930s though *some* on the left continued to discuss the issue.[18] The creation of the Finance Corporation for Industry and the Industrial and Commercial Finance Corporation in the last period of the Second World War reflected the Bank of England's desire to pre-empt a more radical change in the financial system which a possible future Labour government might pursue.[19] Much later, in 1966, a Labour government created the Industrial Reorganisation Corporation, with a remit of encouraging mergers in British industry, in the hope that this would create large, efficient 'national champions'. Few would regard that policy as a notable success.[20]

The NIB proposal as spelt out in the 1932 document seems quite clear and straightforward, if rather general, until one also looks at what was explicitly exempted from the board's remit: 'The Board would not deal with the private investment of savings in private business, nor with the re-investment of undistributed profits by public companies in their own businesses, nor with the operations of municipal banks, building societies, co-operative societies or other bodies operating under the Industrial and Provident Societies Act.'[21] The limitation imposed on the NIB role in respect of investment of undistributed profits was to be a crucial problem after 1945, as discussed in the next section. The NIB approach to investment control implied that new issues would be crucial to the overall pattern of investment, an assumption already quite unjustified in the 1930s and to be further undermined by events in the 1940s.

The NIB proposal was embodied in *For Socialism and Peace* and became a staple of 1930s statements of policy by leading Labour figures, not least Dalton, who detailed its central role in Labour's plans for con-

---

[17] (Macmillan) *Committee on Finance and Industry* (1931), paras. 397–403.
[18] Howson, *Monetary Policy*, pp. 69–71.
[19] Fforde, *Bank of England*, pp. 704–26.
[20] D. C. Hague and G. Wilkinson, *The I.R.C.* (1983); Tomlinson, *Government and the Enterprise*, ch. 10.
[21] Labour Party, *Currency, Banking and Finance* (1932), pp. 2, 9, 10.

trolling 'long-term credit' in one of the major statements of Labour doctrine of the decade.[22] The proposal survived largely unaltered into the war period. It was embodied in *Full Employment and Financial Policy*, Labour's major wartime statement on economic policy; in the important TUC document 'Interim Report on Postwar Reconstruction' in 1944; and in the 1945 general election manifesto *Let Us Face the Future*, which said that under a Labour government 'planned investment in essential industries and on houses, schools, hospitals and civic centres will occupy a large field of capital expenditure. A National Investment Board will determine social priorities and promote better timing in private investment.'[23]

Yet despite all this background, the proposal came to almost nothing after 1945. A wartime Capital Issues Committee was continued under Labour (and, indeed, through most of the 1950s), but its impact was minimal. Dalton, Labour's first Chancellor, created a National Investment Council, but this was very limited in scope, focusing on such questions as bonus issues of shares, and faded away after a few meetings. Beyond this nothing was done.[24] In this area the 'progressive consensus' of the 1930s bore no fruit at all.

The NIB and the control of investment

Labour's failure to establish an NIB was a cause of considerable debate in the Labour Party after 1945. Most of this came at the time of Dalton's proposal for establishing a National Investment Council. From the beginning he was aware that this proposal fell far short of the idea of an NIB. The council was advisory in form. Its remit was supposed to include offering general advice on investment policy. At its first meeting Dalton spoke of its aim as being to see that 'the financial machinery is geared in with the general economic plan of campaign', but this agenda quickly narrowed to a focus on the minutiae of new issues.[25]

---

[22] Dalton, *Practical Socialism*, ch. 22; T. Burridge, *Clement Attlee: A Political Biography* (1985), p. 86.

[23] Labour Party, *Full Employment*; TUC, 'Interim Report on Postwar Reconstruction', in *Report of the Annual Congress of the TUC 1944*, esp. pp. 430–1; Craig, *General Election Manifestos*, p. 126.

[24] Cairncross, *Years of Recovery*, pp. 446–7. The *Financial Times* (29 July 1946) commented sardonically on the NIC: 'For all the Council's high-powered wisdom, however, we are now told that it is not worth summoning to Whitehall more than once a quarter.'

[25] PRO T233/61, National Investment Council; PRO T228/81–3, National Investment Council, Minutes and Memoranda. Curiously, in his memoirs, Dalton said the creation of the NIC stemmed from 'Tory requests when my Bank of England Bill was in Committee' (Dalton, *Memoirs*, vol. II, *High Tide and After* (1962), p. 96).

However, even this proposed broad advisory role was much less than many in the party had anticipated. In the Cabinet meeting discussing the proposed NIC, Dalton said:

Its function would be advisory and not executive. In this respect it would differ from the NIB which had long formed part of the Labour Party programme; but the position was different now that a Government was in power which was ready itself to take positive action to plan the use of the nation's economic resources. In present circumstances executive functions with regard to the control of investment should be exercised by the Government itself.[26]

At a prior ministerial discussion of the bill, Morrison in particular had stressed the limited scope of Dalton's proposals. He stressed that, 'while the Bill would provide an effective weapon for controlling borrowing, it did not touch the equally important problems of how to control the reinvestment by industry of reserve funds and undistributed profits'. In response, Dalton argued that the latter issue should be dealt with by the control of physical resources, a matter, he argued, primarily for the Board of Trade.[27] When the Bill came to the House of Commons debate, Dalton came under much stronger pressure, largely from his own side of the political divide.

In introducing the Investment (Control and Guarantee) Bill he spoke of it as 'a simple, short, modest measure . . . It will give the government a small but useful addition to their sets of tools for economic planning.' He emphasised that the financial controls (i.e. the Capital Issues Committee) envisaged in the Bill would *supplement* physical controls.[28] He went on to say why this was being introduced as an alternative to the NIB, which he noted had been advocated by the 'Yellow Book' and the Minority Report of the Macmillan Committee in 1931, and also, in a marvellous piece of selective memory given the historical background sketched above, he said: 'some members of the Labour Party have advocated it from time to time'. Now, he argued, the government had moved beyond that conception. The key point he argued was one of Cabinet responsibility: 'The Cabinet, subject always to the approval of the House of Commons, must be responsible, and is prepared to be held responsible, for economic and financial planning in this country. The Cabinet cannot delegate its Ministerial responsibility in these matters to any independent or semi-independent Board.'[29]

[26] PRO CAB128/2, Cabinet Conclusions CM55(45), 22 Nov. 1945.
[27] PRO CAB71/19, Lord President's Committee Minutes, 1 Nov. 1945.
[28] *Hansard* (Commons), vol. 418, cols. 1547, 1551, 5 Feb. 1946. During the Bill's progress it became the Borrowing (Control and Guarantee) Act, which more accurately summarised its purpose.
[29] Ibid., cols. 1556–7.

The most effective critic of Dalton's proposal was Christopher Mayhew. He argued that any attempt to control investment by controlling borrowing would be ineffectual. As he pointed out, only about one-eighth of investment was financed from borrowing, the rest from ploughed-back profits and other internal funds. The Bill, he said, 'controls the borrowing but not the spending of money. It is a different matter to control borrowing and to control investment.' Mayhew accepted that for the time being the other seven-eighths of investment was subject to physical controls. But he noted that everyone assumed these controls would be temporary, and the need was to develop comprehensive investment control for the period *after* those physical controls disappeared. His positive proposal was for capital budgets above a minimum level of £25,000 to be drawn up by all companies, and to be subject to control by an appropriate planning authority. Such controls would replace financial controls and provide a long-term basis for investment control.[30]

Mayhew's arguments went to the heart of the issue. The pre-war NIB had been proposed in a context in which government control over investment was extremely limited. By 1945 this had, of course, changed out of all recognition, with the imposition of controls on labour, machinery, building and materials allocations forming a comprehensive system by which government had an unprecedented capacity to determine the volume and direction of investment. Labour, strong advocates of 'planning' in the 1930s, now found themselves, thanks to the war, with systematic controls over investment (and other facets of the economy), which raised the key issue of how far these controls represented the permanent instruments of that desired planning regime.

There was no unanimous view on this issue in the Labour Party, and a complex and confused debate around it continued through the late 1940s. But, as Mayhew recognised as early as November 1945, there would be very strong pressures for many of these controls to be abolished as the supply shortages which underlay them disappeared. These supply constraints acted to give practical force to controls, but also gave them political legitimacy. Once the supply problem was reduced, however, the practical and political pressures to reduce controls were irresistible. That, broadly speaking, was what occurred.[31]

---

[30] Ibid., cols. 1606–12. Mayhew had been a major exponent of the idea of the NIB in the 1930s, and had recognised at that time that an effective board would have to go beyond control of new issues (C. Mayhew, *Planned Investment*, Fabian Research Series 45 (1939), esp. pp. 35–6).
[31] See chapter 6.

Table 7.1 *Composition of investment, 1948/9*

	%
Direct central and local government	25
Nationalised industries (including iron and steel)	25
Industries closely supervised by the government (agriculture, shipbuilding, petrol)	15
Manufacturing	20
Remainder (e.g. commercial)	15

Source: PRO T230/143, Economic Section, 'Alternative Methods of Controlling Investment'.

The erosion of physical controls still left the government with considerable powers in the investment field. Calculations for 1948/9 (table 7.1) suggested that one-quarter of investment was by central and local government, another quarter directly in the hands of nationalised industries, and another 15 per cent in areas where government had a very large influence. Nevertheless, this left 35 per cent of investment, and crucially most of manufacturing investment, increasingly unregulated as the physical controls were run down.

As Mayhew had indicated, the link between borrowing and investment was a small one. His estimate of one-eighth of company investment being financed from borrowing is not dissimilar to subsequent calculations which suggested that around 80 per cent of investment at the end of the 1940s was from internal funds (table 7.2).[32]

Table 7.2 *Sources of corporate investment finance, 1948*

(£m.)

New issues	300
Bank advances	125
Depreciation allowances	825
Undistributed profits	500
Reserves	250
Total gross investment	2,000

Source: PRO T230/143, Economic Section, 'Alternative Methods of Controlling Investment'.

[32] B. Tew and P. D. Henderson, *Studies in Company Finance* (Cambridge, 1959), suggest a figure close to that in Table 7.2, though differences of definition make a precise comparison difficult.

In fact, it is a long-standing feature of British companies that they finance their investment primarily from internal sources. But this was accentuated in the late 1940s by a number of factors. First, physical controls over investment in both the war and early post-war years left companies unable to invest as much as they wanted, so accumulating liquid reserves. Second, profits in the early post-war years were very healthy, reflecting the conditions of excess demand and easy markets. Finally, the tax regime at this time discriminated against distributed profits, so firms were given a substantial incentive to reduce dividend levels and retain profits in the business.[33]

This issue of the control of the use of ploughed-back profits was debated in the ministerial discussions prior to the 1946 Act establishing the National Investment Council. The Treasury was strongly hostile to any such controls, arguing that they would encourage higher dividends and be administratively very difficult to organise: 'it would require much more elaborate machinery to control than the Treasury has at present'.[34] These discussions do not suggest that ministers ever saw such controls as a serious possibility.

The actual pattern of investment control after 1945 was complex, with an excessive boom in 1945/6, more effectively curtailed from 1947, largely by physical controls. But as excess demand thereafter was reduced, those controls were relaxed. This led to a wide-ranging debate on the future control of investment within ministerial and civil service circles. A Committee on Control of Investment was established, which reported in 1949. This laid out the two aims of such control: 'to ensure that important investment was not swamped by less essential work, secondly, to lessen the danger that an excessive concentration of resources on investment would damage other sections of the economy, particularly exports, or render the inflationary problems insoluble'.[35]

It was recognised that physical controls had already been substantially run down, with the abolition of plant and machinery allocations in early 1946. Building controls, it was argued, were inappropriate for investment control because they had no direct relation to expenditure on plant

---

[33] Barna, ' "Frightfully High" Profits', pp. 213–26. This level of profitability seems to have been an unexpected feature of the post-war world. The Bank of England, for example, expected high taxation to reduce profits consistently as a source for investment after the war. Bank of England Archive, G14/155, 1968/2, *Financial Policy – Internal Committee on Post-War Domestic Finance*, 31 March 1943; Tew and Henderson, *Studies*, ch. 2.

[34] PRO T233/25, 'Borrowing (Control and Guarantees) Bill' 1946, Draft letter to President of Board of Trade, Nov. 1945.

[35] PRO CAB134/63, 'Committee on Control of Investment: Draft Reports', 1949, 23 July 1949, para. 1.

and machinery, so in effect the controls relied on steel allocations, which would be eroded by the growth of steel output. The result, the report argued, would be that in the long run, 'So far as the investment by private firms and individuals is concerned, the methods of influence will inevitably be through general fiscal and financial measures'.[36]

The final report of this committee tried to be more positive about what could be achieved in this area without the use of physical controls. It accepted most control would be by fiscal and financial measures, but went on to point out that big firms have become accustomed to discussing their investment programmes with the government and hoped this would continue. It 'hoped' that the banks, and institutions like ICFC and FCI would conform to government guidelines in their lending policies. In conclusion, the report emphasised a consensual approach to the issue: 'Indeed, it is discussion and practical collaboration rather than specific measures of formal control or financial leverage which should be the keynote in dealing with the investment programmes of all sectors of the economy, whether socialised industries, local authorities, or private industry.'[37]

These conclusions seem to have been in line with the general movement of opinion in the government. The reasons for this may be looked at separately in the area of macroeconomic and microeconomic issues. As noted above, it envisaged that the NIB would have a role in both of these aspects, regulating the total level of investment (what may be called its 'Keynesian' function) and the allocation of such investment (what may be called its 'planning' function).

The macroeconomic function of investment controls may be schematically described as moving away from physical means towards general fiscal measures through the late 1940s. Whilst there was no simple transition from controls to Keynesian fiscal policy in the late 1940s, the second budget of 1947 did mark a clear movement towards emphasising the function of the budget in determining the level of aggregate demand in the economy.[38] This new role for peacetime budgetary policy did not immediately displace the physical controls in their macroeconomic role, but paved the way for such a displacement as the general aim of controlling demand was added to by the ending of specific shortages, notably that of steel.

Under Labour this fiscal policy was not accompanied by the use of monetary policy. As is well known, the government was initially committed to a cheap money policy and under Dalton this became a cheaper

[36] Ibid., paras. 6, 18.
[37] Draft report, 5 Sept. 1949, paras. 37–42, 51.
[38] See chapter 10.

money policy, both to avoid raising the burden of the national debt and out of a general dislike of monetary stringency as a means of controlling the economy. In addition, Dalton saw cheaper money as a significant means of redistributing wealth by reducing *rentier* incomes. In addition, there were at the time many doubts about whether investment was very sensitive to small changes in interest rates.[39] But general budgetary policy was supplemented by investment allowances, revamped in 1945 in the form of initial allowances for plant and machinery of 20 per cent, later raised to 40 per cent.[40]

At the macroeconomic level it may be said there was a displacement of the proposed role of the NIB largely onto fiscal policy, or at least a clearly discernible trend in that direction under Labour. The government could reinforce that by its control or at least leverage over public sector investment, a leverage much greater than in the 1930s.[41] In that sense, the conditions of the 1940s may reasonably be said to have rendered an NIB redundant for control of the macroeconomy.

Much more problematic was the microeconomic, or 'planning' role envisaged for the board. It is important to note that almost all discussion in the 1940s assumed that government should have a role in the direction as well as the volume of investment. The question was, how was this role to be exercised. The Committee on the Control of Investment had raised the possibility of using the tax system in this investment allocation role. It held discussions with the Inland Revenue and Customs and Excise on this question, but was firmly rebuffed. These bodies argued, first, that the objective of the tax system was to raise revenue, not achieve other objectives. Second, they disliked any idea of discrimination in levying taxes between different firms, calling this a 'special case' approach, which would create all sorts of pressures from other taxpayers as well as threatening the revenue base. Finally, they pointed out that company taxation operated at the establishment level, which did not match any attempt to use the tax system to discriminate between industrial sectors. These views were accepted by the committee and by the government.[42]

---

[39] S. Howson, ' "Socialist Monetary Policy": Monetary Thought in the Labour Party in the 1940s', *History of Political Economy* 20 (1988), pp. 433–52 and more generally Howson, *Monetary Policy*. R. L. Hall and C. J. Hitch, 'Price Theory and Business Behaviour' (1937), reprinted in T. Wilson and P. W. S. Andrews (eds.), *Oxford Studies in the Price Mechanism* (Oxford, 1951), pp. 107–38.

[40] PRO CAB134/63, 'Report of Committee on Control of Investment', 5 Sept. 1949, para. 6.

[41] See chapters 5 and 13.

[42] PRO CAB134/63, Committee on Control of Investment, Minutes of 18 July 1949; ibid., 'Report' 5 Sept. 1949, para. 11. That it was so readily accepted by the government probably reflects the general unwillingness to operate a discriminatory industrial policy

With physical controls progressively reduced in scope and discriminating fiscal devices ruled out, the focus on consensus and persuasion becomes understandable. Yet more radical alternatives were proffered, as has been noted already: for example, Christopher Mayhew had suggested a 'national budget' of investment, with governments exercising control of investment by a direct say in firms' investment decisions. Such a proposal raises a number of problems, which are perhaps best looked at in the broader context of the debate over 'planning' in this period.[43]

Planning became the key concept in progressive and Labour discussions of the economy in the 1930s, but its generality of use cannot disguise its often limited content (see chapter 6). It could embrace a vast range of ideas, extending from those of people who saw it as concerned with national income planning in the classic Keynesian sense, with the plan being about matching aggregate demand and supply, to those who wanted to emulate Soviet-style central planning. Most of the British debate fell between these two extremes, but in the 1940s there was a debate about where the balance should lie between national income and more microeconomic planning. Most of the senior advisers to the government saw the latter form of planning as desirable only as a transitional method in the restoration of some sort of equilibrium in the economy, and regarded almost complete reliance on national income planning as the long-term goal. This may be seen as the classic Keynesian view, based on the belief that, given full employment of resources, and with a given income distribution, the market could be left to allocate resources efficiently.

This was very much the view of James Meade, head of the Economic Section in 1945–6, who in 1945 produced a classic statement of the Keynesian case in a document entitled 'Economic Planning'.[44] This document stated that 'Planning should take place in terms of the broad categories of demand upon the community's resources', and stressed that whilst (especially in the transition period) the government could not be indifferent to what was happening in specific industries, and might try and influence it, by, for example, changing relative wages, 'Such action differs widely from the rigid planning of the output of particular industries'.[45]

for fear of upsetting the consensual co-operative approach to the private sector (J. Tomlinson, 'The Iron Quadrilateral: Political Obstacles to Economic Reform under the Attlee Government', *Journal of British Studies* 34 (1995)), pp. 90–111.

[43] For this context, see also J. Tomlinson, 'Planning: Debate and Policy in the 1940s', *Twentieth Century British History* 3 (1992), pp. 154–74.

[44] PRO CAB124/890, 'Economic Planning', 10 Oct. 1945.

[45] See chapter 8.

In response to this, Mayhew wrote to the Lord President (Morrison), stressing that such a view made too many concessions to anti-planning views. He made similar points to those made in the House of Commons about the very limited impact of government planning by financial controls given the plentiful internal resources of companies. But he also argued that more could be done to guide the output structure, advocating something much more *dirigiste* than envisaged by Meade: 'A widely publicised National Plan, broken down into production targets for industrial factories, mines, etc., would be a good education in economics and an incentive to hard work.'[46]

But such views were those of an uninfluential minority in the late 1940s. Despite Meade's espial of Gosplanners elsewhere in the government and its advisers, a detailed look at the planning debates of the period shows little evidence of any such views amongst those who counted in policy-making.[47] The most important and articulate 'pro-planning' minister was Cripps, but his planning was much closer to a notion of 'tripartism' or 'corporatism', involving attempts to secure agreement on economic objectives with employers and unions via a large network of committees, than to any centralised, coercive economic planning. Centrally concerned with raising production and productivity, Cripps had little if any interest in the kinds of planning envisaged by people like Mayhew.[48]

Stephen Brooke has recently argued that 'Socialist planning was a notable, if unlikely casualty of Labour Government after the Second World War'.[49] This fate was partly conditioned by the vagueness which always attached to that concept. For a time planning came to be seen as synonymous with controls. But as the economic and political viability of these controls declined, little was found to put in their place. Whilst new planning bodies, the Economic Planning Board and Central Economic Planning Staff, were created in 1947, they did not reverse the trend towards decontrol. There was no wholesale rush to embrace Keynesianism in this period, but it seemed to offer a coherent alternative to the undoubted political problems of a more active governmental role in industry, and it formed the basis of much of the economic advice given to the government. It seemed to fulfil the promise of delivering full employment, which had been a major goal of planning, whilst largely excluding the need to find ways of determining the behaviour of private firms, many of which had in practice resisted any more than a formal

[46] PRO CAB124/890, C. Mayhew to Lord President, 13 Oct. 1945.
[47] See chapter 6.
[48] Tomlinson, 'The Iron Quadrilateral'.
[49] Brooke, 'Problems of "Socialist Planning" '.

embrace of tripartism, and maintained their hostility to the Labour government's attempts to intervene in industry.[50]

The NIB must be viewed in this context. The board was part of that enthusiasm for planning of the 1930s. It was in some respects as vague in its content. Plainly it was envisaged to control new issues, but it was explicitly excluded from any role in investment from ploughed-back profits. This was a major problem, especially in the 1940s, when such profits overwhelmingly dominated the finance of investment. This would not have mattered if borrowing controls had been combined with the physical controls to provide an overall coverage. But whilst such linkage was vaguely hinted at by Dalton when he was making a case for the continuance of the CIC, in practice this never happened.

Partly this was because Dalton wanted to keep the roles of controller of physical and financial resources separate – as the ministerial discussions already noted make clear. Rollings has argued that this desire was strongly endorsed by the Treasury, which was quite happy with physical controls, because it believed they were widely recognised to be temporary, but hostile to any overarching control of investment by any such body as the NIB. For this reason 'Treasury officials desired to show that an NIB was unnecessary and undesirable'.[51]

Against the weight of Treasury advice alternative views seem to have had little weight. For example, the Labour Party Finance Group wrote to Dalton in 1946 about the weakness of the NIC in relation to the overall control of investment, and prepared a draft Bill to allow government control of *all* investment, however financed.[52] But these efforts seemed to have had no effect, and the same must be said of similar proposals to get a single body overseeing investment from the XYZ club and its influential members like Nicholas Davenport and Lord Piercy.[53] By July 1947, with the creation of the Economic Planning Board, the NIC was writing to Dalton saying, 'we take it that the NIC can no longer pretend to any surveillance of the national investment programme', and even that implies a larger role for the NIC in the preceding periods than seems justified by the evidence.[54]

---

[50] Mercer, 'Labour Governments'.

[51] Rollings, 'Control of Inflation', pp. 231–2.

[52] British Library of Political and Economic Science, LSE, Piercy Papers, 15/91, Letter from LP Finance Group to Chancellor of Exchequer, 4 April 1946.

[53] Ibid., 15/117 XYZ Correspondence, e.g. 'Suggested Reforms in Financial Machinery', Oct. 1948.

[54] Ibid., 10/64, Letter from NIC to Dalton, 22 July 1947; a similar line was taken by Cripps, who in writing to Lord Catto, the Governor of the Bank of England, in December 1948, said: 'during the past year important changes in the organisation for the scrutiny and control of the investment programme have been made, both within the machinery of government, and in contact with industry, through the Planning Board. I

The failure of financial reform

Labour's policies on the financial system (in its external as well as its domestic areas) were remarkable for their mildness. Of course, there was the largely symbolic nationalisation of the Bank of England.[55] There was never a serious possibility of nationalising the clearing banks. New institutions in the 1940s were largely limited to the Industrial Commercial Finance Corporation and Finance Corporation for Industry. These were not creations of the Labour government, but of wartime Bank of England initiatives, spurred by the fear that the government's interest in reconstruction might lead to a direct government role in industrial finance. ICFC and FCI pre-empted this. The first aimed to fill the 'Macmillan gap' in finance for small firms. The latter had a much less clear role as a lender to 'special case' large firms.[56] Whilst the former played some part in bridging the gap at the small end of the market, neither of them addressed the broad critique of the limited links between British industry and the financial system which was articulated in the Macmillan Committee, and many other places in the inter-war period (and since).[57]

Other institutional changes were very limited. The Capital Issues Committee was continued, but its role was peripheral.[58] The broad priorities laid down for the CIC were backed by Bank of England persuasion of the clearing banks, but neither source of funds was very significant for industrial investment in this period. Banks in particular were keen to maintain their arms-length relationship from anything but a short-term role in industrial finance, and this was one reason for their support of ICFC.

The NIC, as we have seen, was never more than a talking shop, increasingly concerned with the details of new issues, and quietly faded away after a couple of years. Its role, as everyone recognised, was not even a pale reflection of that envisaged for the NIB.

think you will agree that these changes greatly reduce the field over which the NIC could effectively work' (Bank of England Archives G1/247 1396/2, 'National Investment Council'). Davenport, a member of the NIC, regarded its abolition as a 'victory for the Treasury Establishment': *Memoirs*, pp. 154–5. Dalton too 'regretted' the abolition (*High Tide*, p. 98).

[55] Durbin, *New Jerusalems*, p. 74.

[56] Fforde, *Bank of England*, pp. 704–26. The creation of ICFC and FCI was also urged on the Bank of England by the Treasury, eager to block more radical reform proposals emanating not only from the Labour Party but also the Board of Trade (e.g. Bank of England Archive G15/110 2503/1, 'Note on Discussion of Proposed Industrial Commission', 13 April 1944).

[57] (Macmillan) Committee on Finance and Industry, *Report*.

[58] Cairncross, *Years of Recovery*, pp. 444–5.

The failure to pursue a more radical reform of the City, including the creation of a NIB, cannot be accounted for by any single reason. But three factors were important: the impact of the physical controls bequeathed to Labour by the wartime coalition, the strength of Keynesianism and the nature of industrial finance. The first seemed initially to offer an alternative way of planning the economy, and by the time their long-run unsustainability – at least on the microeconomic level – had been realised, the chance of radical innovation in policy in the direction of more permanently effective mechanisms had been lost. Keynesianism, in the sense of a body of ideas which presumed that full employment could be achieved without the necessity of a *dirigisme* that would be strongly opposed by employers, the Conservative Party, and most economists, had obvious attractions. Finally, the very distance between industry and finance in the British system proved an obstacle, in the sense that it was widely recognised that the investment decisions of most companies would be little affected by changes to the financial system. In the 1930s Dalton, along with many in the Labour Party had supported the NIB idea in the context of controlling long-term credit for industry: but in the 1940s industry had little need of such credit. In addition, the concern with industrial rationalisation which had animated much of the case for reform of the financial system in the 1930s was 'resolved' by nationalisation of industries like coal, railways, and iron and steel which had been the focus of much of the rationalisation debate.

In the 1930s Labour focused its attention on institutional reforms of the financial system, whilst in the 1940s the central financial issue was monetary control.[59] The 1930s attitude had drawn support from the generally depressed economic conditions, but also from widespread criticisms of the financial system, including those by industrial firms. However, there is little evidence of such criticisms in the late 1940s. A survey of the relevant Federation of British Industries records suggests that, when they approached the government on the issue of investment finance, the only matter the FBI were interested in was the taxation of profits, emphasising, as well they might in the circumstances, the role of ploughed-back, post-tax, profits in such finance. There was no articulation of a view that financial institutions were 'failing' industry.[60]

---

[59] Howson, ' "Socialist" Monetary Policy', p. 564; Howson, *Monetary Policy*, ch. 2.
[60] Warwick University, Modern Records Centre, Federation of British Industry Archive, e.g. MSS200/F/3/E3/8, FBI to Chancellor of the Exchequer, 'Taxation and Shortage of Industrial Capital', 31 Dec. 1948; MSS200/F/3/E3/3/10, FBI Home Economic Policy Committee Report, July 1948. This notion of finance 'failing' industry was to be revived in the 1970s, leading to the creation of the National Enterprise Board which did have some success as a 'venture capital' provider, though not in its original, intended role

Ultimately, the NIB was not needed for the macroeconomic purposes originally assigned to it in the circumstances of the 1940s, and would have been ineffective for microeconomic ones. If the government really wanted to control company-level investment decisions, there would have been little choice but to have a direct role in company decision-making – a proposal made by the young Harold Wilson, President of the Board of Trade, in 1950, by then too late to have any impact on Labour's policies.[61]

Finally, Labour's failure to reform the financial system to a significant degree may be illuminated by comparison with the experience of France. Zysman has persuasively argued that the role of the financial system in attempts at economic planning in post-war Europe was crucial, and contrasts the British and French experience:

As an alternative to administrative planning, the British might have turned the financial system to the ends of planners, allocating credit as a means of distributing resources, and created a trained cadre of bureaucrats prepared to use these instruments. Indeed the French planners had turned the credit allocation precisely to avoid being trapped in existing bureaucratic commitments and trade association arrangements . . . the Labour government, then, adopted planning but eschewed one of the most powerful instruments of planning: credit planning through the financial system.[62]

Zysman ascribes this difference to Labour and civil service ignorance of finance, a belief that wartime administrative controls could be used to 'outflank' the City, and the fear of capital flight in such a precarious international economic situation.[63] All these points seem fair, though to them should definitely be added the highly liquid position of British industry, which made the control of external funds much less important in determining investment behaviour than in cash-starved French firms. Labour's political weakness in this area was thus heavily compounded by this peculiar feature of the economy it was attempting to control.

---

as an interventionist body across the breadth of manufacturing industry (Tomlinson, *Government and the Enterprise*, ch. 9).

[61] PRO PREM8/1183, 'The State and Private Industry', 4 May 1950.

[62] J. Zysman, *Governments, Markets and Growth: Financial Systems and the Politics of Industrial Change* (Ithaca, 1983), pp. 183–4.

[63] Ibid., pp. 184, 185.

8   Employment policy and the labour market

In *Let Us Face the Future* in 1945 the Labour Party accepted that full
employment was a slogan of all the political parties: 'All parties pay lip
service to the idea of jobs for all.' However, the manifesto argued, what
made Labour different was its willingness to pursue such a policy
through whatever measures might be necessary. The clear expectation
was that the new government would quickly be faced by 'slumps in
uncontrolled private industry', requiring a major extension of state
action. This extension would have four thrusts – a maintenance of
demand, to correct previous under-consumption; redistribution of
income to the lower income groups to maintain purchasing power;
planned investment under the aegis of a National Investment Board;
control of the banking system, including nationalisation of the Bank of
England.[1]

These manifesto statements make clear three things about Labour
and the employment issue in 1945. First, full employment was central
to their agenda. Second, the methods suggested for the attaining of this
objective were eclectic – a mixture of 'simple' Keynesianism, redistribution and notions of planning. Third, the threat to full employment
was seen as arising primarily on the demand side.

The importance accorded to full employment in the late 1940s was
underpinned not only by the sharp collective memory of the miseries
of 1930s mass unemployment, but also a clear recognition from wartime
debates that Labour's welfare aims depended upon the tax revenues and
limited claims on expenditure that full employment would bring.[2]

The methods of addressing the threat of unemployment, it may be
noted, as usual did not represent a tightly based programme of detailed
policy proposals. Rather they represented a combination of ideas which
had long been proposed to regulate unemployment (maintenance of
demand, control of investment) with notions which fitted with other

[1] *Let Us Face the Future*, pp. 1–2.
[2] Chapter 1.

167

Labour aspirations (income distribution, control of the financial system).

The fate of some of these various proposals is discussed elsewhere in this book. But the idea that full employment would be threatened by inadequate demand, which was always just around the corner, persisted through Labour's period in office. This persistence undercuts the idea that in this period the populace accepted the cosy assumption that full employment was 'guaranteed', and therefore required no effort on their part.[3] This perceived threat generated a number of specific proposals which deserve some attention, though of course we now know that no such threat emerged in the 1940s (indeed, not until the 1970s), so that there was a real gap between the labour market problem that Labour expected to face and the one it actually had to contend with. That expectation was of a post-war boom, as in 1919/20, followed by a slump in demand and employment.[4] The reality was persistent excess demand for labour, and labour shortages which raised quite new and unanticipated issues for policy on the labour market.

Demand and the regions

The White Paper on *Employment Policy* produced by the coalition in 1944 did, of course, symbolise the bipartisan commitment to full employment recognised by Labour in its 1945 manifesto. As is well known, this White Paper was much stronger on general principles than on policy devices.[5] These principles included that of maintaining demand, by regulation of investment, perhaps of consumption, and even more uncertainly, by use of the budget. Alongside this was a strong commitment to a 'balanced distribution of industry'.[6] In practice under Labour, whilst the fear of *future* problems of aggregate demand generated persistent debate about methods of dealing with the issue, the actuality of excess demand tended to relegate these issues to the backrooms of policy debate. On the other hand, the regional distribution of industry attracted a great deal of high-level attention and very active policy measures, especially in the early years of the Labour government.

---

[3] Crafts, 'Adjusting'; J. Tomlinson, 'No Cosy Deals: British Economic Policy in the 1940s', *Journal of European Economic History*, forthcoming.

[4] This view was clearly articulated in the manpower debate of February 1947: *Hansard* (Commons), vol. 419, cols. 1951–65, 2113–36, 27/28 Feb. 1946.

[5] G. C. Peden, 'Sir Richard Hopkins and the "Keynesian Revolution" in Employment Policy 1928–45', *Economic History Review* 36 (1983), pp. 281–96; Booth, *British Economic Policy*, ch. 7; Tomlinson, *Employment Policy*, chs. 3, 4.

[6] *Employment Policy* (1944).

Policy measures against the threat of inadequate aggregate demand focused primarily on four areas – stimulation of investment demand by local authorities, nationalised industries, and the private sector, and the stimulation of private consumption. Most of this work was pursued by the Investment Working Party, dominated by the Treasury, with little direct ministerial intervention. The working party itself, however, was primarily concerned with controlling the excess demand for investment, so the search for policy devices to stimulate investment always appeared at odds with its compelling current concerns.

The search for such devices has been discussed in detail elsewhere.[7] As far as local authorities were concerned, the picture is of periodic 'prodding' by central government to build up a 'shelf' of works against a future slump, and the local authorities regarding these efforts as an irrelevant nuisance in a context of insatiable pressures for current projects that were hampered by central government allocation of finance and, especially, materials. In 1949 the lack of response by local government was well described by the Committee on Control of Investment: 'First, the local authorities have been pre-occupied with the urgent work immediately before them; second local authorities are not interested in buying land and spending money on plans for works which will be put in hand only at an uncertain date when a slump is definitely diagnosed.'[8]

In addition to local authority lack of enthusiasm, the idea of local authorities as major instruments of investment expansion was questioned by some senior civil servants, on grounds which reflected the kind of discussions which had been conducted about inter-war public works proposals. Would, for example, local authority programmes be able to offer much beyond work for unskilled labourers, with little impact on unemployment amongst women or skilled workers?[9] Perhaps fortunately, this kind of question did not have to be tested in practice in the 1940s.

The major extension of the nationalised sector after 1945 offered, in principle, a weapon against a slump in demand not available at the time of the 1944 White Paper.[10] But, as with local authorities, such a weapon seemed to lose its potential in the late 1940s as policy-makers looked in detail at its use. The idea that nationalised industries would build up a shelf of investment projects raised the general issue of the extent of government control of these industries. As we have seen in chapter 5,

---

[7] Tomlinson, *Employment Policy*, ch. 5.
[8] PRO T229/237, *Report of the Committee on Control of Investment*, para. 31.
[9] e.g. PRO T161/1370/S53555/011/1, A. Cairncross to P. Vinter, 7 Nov. 1946.
[10] PRO T161/1297/S53555/06, Draft Report on Preparation of Investment Projects in the Public Sector, Oct. 1946.

by and large the boards of these industries effectively resisted being used as instruments of national policy, and this resistance extended to the idea of building up an unremunerative shelf of works against a future slump. The Treasury resisted the idea that such activity should be subsidised, so again the outcome of central government endeavours was very limited.

The question of stimulating private investment in a slump has to be seen against the background of the general debate about state control of investment, a background sketched in chapter 6. As argued there, the broad problem was the failure of the government to devise alternative means of controlling investment as the physical controls were eroded in the late 1940s. There was much discussion about financial mechanisms to control investment, but these ran up against the fundamental problem that effective control over company investment would require regulation of companies' use of ploughed-back profits, their main source of investment funds, and thus was deemed politically unacceptable.[11] The use of the tax system to try and achieve similar results indirectly was also mooted, but again seems to have got nowhere, partly because of the likely consequences for the revenue of such devices.[12] In fact the tax system was used to try and regulate investment in this period, by the introduction in 1945 of investment allowances. But this was not seen as part of a policy of regulating overall demand, and the effects of such policies on investment demand in this period were probably small, and likely to have been even smaller in the face of a major slump.[13]

Overall, in relation to private investment in a future slump, the government faced not only the problem that for most of its period in office it was actually discouraging investment, but also the political suspicion of the private sector about its intentions. For example, the FBI resisted Board of Trade proposals for a major survey of investment intentions, which would have provided crucial information for formulating an anti-slump policy.[14] In general, the private sector was in no mood to co-operate in measures which would expand the influence of government over their decision-making.

Finally, an idea mooted by James Meade when the White Paper of 1944 was under discussion was to use National Insurance contributions

---

[11] See also chapter 7.
[12] e.g. PRO T230/24, Economic Section Discussion Papers, 'Control of Private Investment' by J. C. R. Dow, 12 March 1947; PRO T229/169, *Committee on Control of Investment*, 18 July 1949.
[13] Dow, *Management*, pp. 204–9.
[14] PRO CAB134/438, Investment Programmes Committee, 9 Nov. 1948.

to regulate the level of consumption to smooth out the economic cycle. Such an idea was embodied in the 1946 National Insurance Act, ministerial support overcoming Treasury objections. However, the drafting of the clause was very broad, not including a specific 'sliding scale' of contributions which Meade wanted, because this would have involved the government in committing itself to a 'normal' level of unemployment. The clause was also discretionary, rather than on the automatic basis wanted by Meade, so his victory over the Treasury on this matter had something of a Pyrrhic air.[15]

In sum, the search for policy devices against a major fall in demand was not very successful in the late 1940s. No doubt this was partly because the problem hardly appeared urgent in the conditions of the time, but nevertheless it should qualify the view that the perceived consensus on full employment in the period led to a widespread agreement to co-operate with policy initiatives to achieve this objective.

Policies on the regional distribution of industry have a much more positive aspect than those intended to guard against a future slump. Politically, the prevention of a recurrence of unemployment in the depressed areas of the 1930s was central to Labour's concerns. In the war Dalton, as President of the Board of Trade, had secured the inclusion of a commitment to the 'balanced distribution of industry' in the 1944 White Paper, against strong Conservative opposition. He then pursued the enactment of a separate Distribution of Industry Act which managed to get on to the statute book in June 1945, the same day that Parliament was dissolved.[16]

Dalton and Douglas Jay, who became Attlee's economic adviser after the 1945 election, both believed that wartime experience of the use of controls over the distribution of industry illustrated the efficacy of such 'physical' planning, and made sure the policy was pursued in peacetime. Tight controls over distribution had been operated from 1941 under the Defence Regulations, basically with the aim of taking work to the workers. This had proved a successful policy in wartime, and Labour in 1945 envisaged a retention of the system to prevent a re-emergence of the old 'depressed areas' in the north and west. But in addition to the licensing system, other policy instruments were proposed, some temporary, some permanent. The existence of large numbers of Royal Ordnance Factories, superfluous to peacetime requirements, made possible the provision of factory space, much of it in the old depressed areas, when such space was in short supply. Similarly, government factories could

---

[15] PRO T230/105, J. Meade to Lord President, 5 Dec. 1945.
[16] B. Pimlott, *Hugh Dalton* (1985), pp. 400–7; Jay, *Change and Fortune*, ch. 6.

Table 8.1   *Approvals for new industrial building, 1945–51*

	Development Areas		Rest of Great Britain	
	sq. ft	%	sq. ft	%
1945–7	15.7m.	51.3	14.9m.	48.7
1948–51	8.6m.	19.4[1]	35.8m.	80.6

[1] Approx. equal to the Development Areas' share of total UK population.
Source: J. D. McCallum, 'The Development of British Regional Policy' in D. Maclennan and J. B. Parr (eds.), *Regional Policy: Past Experiences and New Directions* (Oxford, 1979), p. 8.

be made available for production in areas of unemployment, but for storage elsewhere. Longer term proposals envisaged the enlargement of the pre-war industrial estates and creation of new ones. Government lending to firms in such areas was also proposed as a way of encouraging their location there.[17]

Most of this programme, save the lending to firms, was actually carried out in the post-war years. The licensing system for new factories led to a pattern of new building heavily biased towards Development Areas in 1945–7 (table 8.1). After that date the sense of economic crisis seems to have led to a rapid reduction in the discrimination against new building in the prosperous south and east, but the spurt of building in 1945–7, coupled to the legacy of wartime building, left a longer term legacy.[18] Whilst unemployment in the Development Areas remained marginally above the national average, the rates bore no comparison to those of the 1930s.

This happy outcome was partly underpinned by the expansion of industrial estates in the late 1940s. It included a substantial programme of 'advance factories', funded by the Treasury on the basis of calculating the total working population of a region, subtracting private factory provision, and attempting to bridge the gap by subsidy. This programme was announced in 1946, before being cut back by 30 per cent in 1947 – but as with so much of building in this period, the cutback of *plans* actually enabled more completions, so that square footage provided rose from 1.1m. in 1946/7 to 3.35m. in 1947/8.[19]

[17] Jay, *Change and Fortune*, p. 112.
[18] D. W. Parsons, *The Political Economy of British Regional Policy* (1986), ch. 4.
[19] H. Loebl, *Government Factories and the Origins of British Regional Policy 1934–1948* (Aldershot, 1988), ch. 2.

Overall, regional policy can be regarded as having been a successful part of the Attlee government's economic policy. Here, it seems, economic planning could and did deliver desirable outcomes. However, a number of qualifications would have to be made to too rosy an assessment of the policy.

First, it is important to note that the success in raising the proportion of new factory building in the Development Areas in 1945–7 was highly contingent on the overall shortage of such space at the end of the war. This provided an ideal environment for a policy which relied heavily on the administration of that shortage to steer firms into locations which they otherwise might well not have chosen.

Second, the policy was not without its tensions – for example, conflicts with the trading estate companies who believed themselves to be suffering from an over-centralised and rigid bureaucracy in Whitehall in trying to pursue policies in their regions.[20] More serious and more overt were the tensions over the competing claims of the export drive and distribution policy. Following the crisis of 1947, in 1948 policy was changed to give priority in factory building to dollar earning or to saving production. This was crucial to the change in the distribution of new factories shown in table 8.1. It was soon regarded as a major threat to the policy on distribution of industry. In 1949 the Parliamentary Secretary to the Board of Trade spoke of 'distribution of industry principles being overridden in case after case because of production considerations'.[21]

This problem was taken very seriously by ministers, and new proposals were put forward for trying to steer industry to the Development Areas. However, it is apparent from the discussions surrounding the proposals that it was both difficult to co-ordinate policies in this area (e.g. on using public sector purchasing to help the Development Areas), and that by and large the desire to promote exports dominated decision-making in this and other policy debates.[22] This outcome was made more likely by the fact that when industrialists argued that a Development Area location would raise costs substantially, the Board of Trade had no experience or expertise to counter such claims.

Whilst the policy on the distribution of industry had a high political profile in the governments, its assumptions were increasingly attacked,

---

[20] Ibid., ch. 4.
[21] PRO BT177/440 'Study Group on Distribution of Industry Policy', Minutes, 26 May 1949.
[22] PRO CAB134/640, Production Committee Minutes, 20 May 1949, 19 July 1949, 4 Oct. 1949; BT177/120, 'Diversification in Relation to the Export Drive', 1948.

even by some economists sympathetic to Labour. Clearly such a policy was *dirigiste* to an extent which was increasingly challenged in the 'great planning debate' of the late 1940s. Such criticisms chimed in with the emphasis on maximising production and exports which so dominated policy, especially after the crisis of 1947.[23]

From a longer term perspective other criticisms might be made of Labour's policy in this area. Policy on the distribution of industry was very much a policy for unemployment, the key measure of its success the levels of unemployment in the Development Areas. This focus on unemployment meant that the wider aspects of regional development were *not* the prime concern. Wartime planning had envisaged comprehensive regional plans, embracing the physical, social and economic dimensions, but this emphatically was not the context of post-war regional policy. Physical planning, especially, took place largely separated from issues concerning the distribution of industry. On the narrowly economic plane, by focusing on unemployment the policy may have given too many hostages to fortune. The creation of jobs in branch plants left the areas vulnerable to future retrenchment, and the concentration of R & D in low unemployment areas may be seen as the other side of the same problem. This may be contrasted with a policy which would pay more attention to the *growth* potential of an area, though it may be somewhat anachronistic to regret the absence of such a perspective in the 1940s.[24]

Manpower planning

Distribution of industry was the most active area of policy on unemployment in the Attlee period. In the absence of a general shortage of demand, attention focused on the allocation of labour, generally in short supply. Even more important in this respect than regional distribution was the sectoral distribution, where the government was engaged in wide-ranging efforts to 'man-up' certain industries, especially those with dollar-earning or saving potential, parallel to the attempts to raise productivity in the same industry.[25]

---

[23] Parsons, *Political Economy*, pp. 112–14.

[24] Ibid., chs. 1–4.; Cairncross, 'Foreword' to D. Maclennan and J. B. Parr, *Regional Policy: Past Experience and New Directions* (Oxford, 1979), pp. ix–xiv; C. E. Heim, 'R and D, Defence, and the Spatial Division of Labour in Twentieth Century Britain', *Journal of Economic History* 47 (1987), pp. 365–78.

[25] C. A. R. Crosland, 'The Movement of Labour in 1948' *Bulletin of the Oxford University Institute of Statistics* 11 (1949), pp. 117–26 and 194–212. Note that, despite the concern with labour shortage, Labour encouraged the migration of around $\frac{3}{4}$ million people to

Policies linked to the desire to shift labour between occupations was commonly termed 'manpower planning',[26] a label with a positive resonance for many Labour people, both because of the word 'planning' and because the efficacy of such policies was widely assumed to have been proved during the war. The wartime government had certainly legislated for itself draconian powers to control the allocation of labour, which in principle gave it the ability to determine the occupation of all adult males and a significant proportion of the adult female population. In practice, these powers had been used sparingly, most labour shifting because of the usual operation of the labour market.[27]

Also the wartime coalition had certainly regarded manpower as the crucial resource for the war effort, once the entry of the US had effectively eased the foreign exchange constraint; manpower became 'the currency of wartime planning'.[28] Against this background, the idea of a 'manpower budget' had been incorporated in the 1944 *Employment Policy* White Paper, and became an important part of Labour's whole approach to economic policy in the early part of its years of government.

By this early period, with rapid demobilisation on the one hand, and strong demand for labour on the other, a concern with manpower successfully focused attention on the slow pace of demobilisation and on the high opportunity costs of the retention of such large numbers in the armed forces and military supply. Important battles were fought by the economic ministers to reduce these numbers, eventually with some success. This was part of the general battle over the economic implications of Britain's military posture.[29]

But 'manpower budgeting' faced major problems as a long-term means of managing the economy. In the first three *Economic Surveys* after the war, manpower budgets were set alongside the national income statements. As the latter were new and in some respects complex, the manpower approach seems to have had greater appeal for ministers. In broad terms the two budgets carried the same message – the economy was suffering from excess demand, or trying to do too much with the

the (white) Commonwealth in this period (K. Paul, 'British Subjects and "British Stock": Labour's Postwar Imperialism', *Journal of British Studies* 34 (1995), pp. 233–76).

[26] Only occasionally was the inappropriateness of this terminology recognised. Women's role in the labour market is discussed in chapter 9.

[27] M. Gowing, 'The Organisation of Manpower in Britain during the Second World War', *Journal of Contemporary History* 7 (1972), pp. 147–67; Robinson, *Economic Planning*, pp. 6–7. Rosenberg (*Economic Planning*) graphically demonstrates the difficulties of controlling the flow of building manpower against the tide of demand from housing repairs and maintenance.

[28] Cairncross and Watts, *Economic Section*, p. 66.

[29] See chapter 3. Part of the reason for the slow demobilisation after 1945 was the belief that it had been *too* rapid after 1918 – e.g. PRO PREM8/646, 'Production', 1947.

manpower available to it. However, the problem with manpower budgets was how they could be used not just as indicators of macro-economic problems, but as instruments of policy. How could the total supply and distribution of manpower be altered by the government? Total supply, as already noted, could be changed by the pace of demob-ilisation, but that was largely a once-and-for-all process. Once demobil-isation was completed,[30] most attention focused on the distribution of labour.

In the war manpower budgeting was crucially underpinned by govern-ment control of the demand for labour via the demand for products alongside controls of supply.[31] In the post-war period most of that demand-side control disappeared, and the primary problem was how labour was to be moved into occupations which the government regarded as crucial to economic policy, where demand for labour was strong but not directly controlled by the government. Wartime controls over labour operated largely on the supply side, by restricting workers' rights to move between occupations. A central issue for the Labour government was how far such controls could form part of 'manpower planning' in peacetime. In fact, the wartime controls were already being eroded before Labour came to power. At the end of the war in Europe the direction of labour had been replaced by Control of Engagement Orders which channelled all recruitment via labour exchanges, but which itself seems to have been widely ignored. However, this erosion did not lead to Labour's immediate acceptance that such controls should not be used in peacetime. The Lord President's Committee initially failed to agree on the issue, at least as regards the short term. The weakness of other forms of control over the economy if those relat-ing to labour disappeared was well recognised.[32]

In Cabinet the view that controls should be significantly relaxed was not unanimously accepted. Most agreed with the pragmatic case for relaxation, that the controls had become unenforceable. However, particularly because of opposition from Bevin, the discussion was deferred.[33]

Finally a proposal was made, with Bevin's support, that controls should be reduced, confining them to essential industries for men under thirty years of age. This proposal was accepted by the Cabinet.[34] The

---

[30] The main other aspect of trying to expand total labour supply related to women work-ers, discussed in detail in chapter 9.
[31] Cairncross, *Years of Recovery*, p. 311.
[32] PRO CAB129/4, 'Labour Controls', 30 Oct. 1945 by Lord President of the Council.
[33] PRO CAB128/2, 1 Nov. 1945, 20 Nov. 1945.
[34] Ibid., 3 Dec. 1945; CAB129/5, 'Labour Controls', 29 Nov. 1945.

grounds for this policy, it should be noted, were essentially pragmatic.[35] The controls were seen to be unpopular and unenforceable in the absence of wartime patriotic support.

Undoubtedly this retreat did undermine much of the conception of planning held by Labour figures at the end of the war. It exposed them to Tory jibes that planning had become a sham: 'everything is controlled except labour'.[36] Some controls were briefly extended in October 1947 to try and guide men aged 18–50 and women aged 18–40 into the key undermanned industries of coal, cotton, agriculture and woollens. However, as in wartime, the aim was to keep the power of direction as a last resort. The main impact of the change was that people who became unemployed would be strongly urged by the Labour Exchange to go into one of these industries. It was never envisaged that anyone should be forced out of their existing occupation. Overall, the impact on labour supply in the key industries seems to have been positive but small.[37]

These measures to control labour movement do not seem to have evoked a hostile response from the unions or workers involved, but they did create pressure for parallel moves to control labour in other occupations. Most especially they stimulated a widespread debate about 'spivs and drones', those deemed to be doing worthless jobs or entirely unoccupied. Particular hostility was expressed towards street traders ('barrow boys') but also those employed in clubs, football pools and other forms of gambling. More broadly, there was a concern, as the Home Secretary put it, 'that there should be no grounds for the allegation that unoccupied persons in the well to do classes were evading the liability to enter useful employment'.[38]

This kind of feeling developed to the extent of a draft Bill being proposed requiring registration of street traders and all unoccupied persons, 'with a view to their being offered, or, if necessary, directed, into useful employment'. However, because of the difficulties of picking out street traders from other occupations, this proposed Bill was rejected, but it was agreed that draft regulations to the same effect should be prepared under the Defence Regulations.[39] These came into effect in 1948, but

[35] Contrast this with the fundamental objections of some Labour thinkers, e.g. Jay and Durbin, for whom the right freely to choose an occupation was fundamental: Brooke, 'Problems of "Socialist Planning",' pp. 691–2, 695–6.

[36] *Hansard* (Commons), vol. 419, cols. 1947–8, 28 Feb. 1946.

[37] PRO CAB134/469, 'The Manpower Situation', 1 Dec. 1947; T229/32, Economic Planning Board Minutes, 18 Sept. 1947; T229/35, 'The Manning-Up of the Export and Import Saving Industries', Oct. 1947; J. Leruez, *Economic Planning and Politics in Britain* (Oxford, 1975), p. 56.

[38] PRO CAB134/509, Manpower Committee Minutes, 17 Sept. 1947.

[39] Ibid.; PREM8/606, 'Unproductive Employments', 1947.

the practical impact was certainly small; as the Ministry of Labour at least recognised: 'Little good would come to industry from 'spivs and drones', and employers did not want them anyway.'[40]

The whole episode has a slightly absurd, moralising aspect which reflects perhaps the difficulties faced by the Labour government in pursuing its 'manpower planning' ideas. Given the general rejection of controls, the other main way such planning could be pursued was by altering wage relativities between occupations in order to attract workers into the 'undermanned' industries. Hence the idea of wage planning.

Wage planning

Wage planning in this period is a controversial subject because it is seen as part of a general argument over the power of the trade unions in determining the Labour government's policies. On one side is the view that it was union resistance that scuppered the idea of wage planning, and that this reflected the economic ignorance and intransigence of the unions. The most extreme version of this line of argument was made by Roberts, when he suggested that 'of all the pressure groups to which the Labour Government might be vulnerable the trade unions were the most powerful and the most awkward to deal with', and that unions, unappreciative of the dilemmas of economic policy, wanted 'absolute full employment, cheap money, massive government expenditure, stable prices and freedom to bargain for higher wages as and when they liked, without limitation'.[41] Beer, largely basing himself on Roberts, endorses this 'trade unions versus planned economy' argument, and Pelling and Brooke have concurred.[42] The latter, in particular, has used the argument of union opposition to wage planning as central to the defeat of the whole idea of democratic planning in the late 1940s: 'Socialist planning may thus have remained ideologically vigorous after 1945, but it was untenable in practical terms given the intransigence of the unions.'[43]

Is this view justified by the evidence? Certainly advocacy of wage planning was common at the time Labour was elected in 1945, the most persuasive case being put by Barbara Wootton in her anti-Hayekian book *Freedom under Planning*. She stressed the conflict between free collective bargaining on wages and economic planning, and advocated either a wages policy administered by the unions, or compulsory arbi-

[40] PRO T229/32, Economic Planning Board Minutes, 18 Sept. 1947.
[41] B. C. Roberts, *National Wages Policy in War and Peace* (1958), pp. 62, 64.
[42] S. Beer, *Modern British Politics* (1958), pp. 200–8; Pelling, *Labour Governments*, p. 265; Brooke, 'Problems of "Socialist Planning" ', pp. 696–700.
[43] Brooke, 'Problems of "Socialist Planning" ', p. 700.

tration, whilst recognising that neither of these would be easy solutions. Other Labour intellectuals, such as Durbin, supported her arguments.[44]

At the government level a working party was set up in 1945, and reported the following year. It rejected the idea of central determination of wages on the grounds that that would destroy harmonious industrial relations and drag the government into every industrial dispute. It also rejected compulsory arbitration, partly because of the difficulties if such arbitration were imposed in situations where both sides had agreed wages deemed unacceptable. It was also stressed how such a policy would weaken the trade union leaderships *vis-à-vis* their rank-and-file members. The working party argued that there was no halfway house between a democratic and authoritarian system of industrial relations, and therefore what was needed was education and vigorous leadership. To help the former they proposed a National Industrial Conference which would provide information on the economic situation and provide confidence that full employment would be maintained, seen as a way of encouraging union flexibility.[45]

In the debate that followed the report of the working party, strong support for its rejection of a wages policy came from Morrison and most ministers. But there were also strong dissenters. Most important of these was Shinwell, the Minister of Fuel and Power. He argued for a tripartite National Wages Authority as an advisory body on wages, linked to effective price controls. Shinwell had previously backed his case by arguing that 'it would be idle for the government to claim that it was pursuing a policy of economic planning' unless wages were also planned.[46]

Advocacy of 'wages planning' generally came from those most strongly committed to the idea of physical planning, that is to say from the left of the party, despite some support from figures like Durbin. This support included figures on the trade union left, such as L. J. Gregory of the ETU, who at the 1945 TUC had unsuccessfully urged delegates to develop 'a wage strategy that corresponds to a planned economy of a Labour government'. Whilst certainly a minority view, this trade union advocacy of wage planning was quite common in the immediate postwar period.[47]

Most of the opposition to wage planning came from the right of the party and government. Both the Minister of Labour, Isaacs, and Mor-

[44] Wootton, *Freedom*, ch. 7; Durbin, *New Jerusalems*, pp. 269–70.
[45] PRO CAB132/3, 'Report of the Official Working Party on Wages Policy', 26 March 1946.
[46] PRO CAB132/5, 'A National Wages Policy' by Shinwell, 22 Oct. 1946; PRO CAB132/1, Lord President's Committee Minutes, 2 Aug. 1946.
[47] TUC Annual Congress Report 1945, pp. 342–3; L. Panitch, *Social Democracy and Industrial Militancy* (Cambridge, 1976), ch. 1.

rison vigorously attacked Shinwell's position. The objections articulated were essentially twofold. On the one hand was the belief that such a policy would undermine harmonious industrial relations. Undoubtedly this was linked to a perception of the strength of union (and party) commitment to free collective bargaining. In addition, however, there was a strong sense of the dangers of such a policy for 'statecraft' because of the politicisation of wage disputes that would result: 'It appears to be contemplated that the decisions would be definitely governmental decisions. This seems to leave no escape from a situation in which the decisions thus given could be debated in Parliament. In this way, wages might become a political issue.'[48]

Eventually most ministers supported the anti-wage planning position against Shinwell, though they tended to believe that the Ministry of Labour was too optimistic about the likely effects of education and exhortation. This scepticism led, for example, to proposals for a central arbitration tribunal, put forward by Dalton.[49] However, exhortation and education were the main staples of government policy, and these may have led to some success for efforts to raise the relative wages of coal miners, cotton and agricultural workers, changes in relativities being 'surprisingly high' according to one authority. These effects occurred despite the lack of a formal wages policy: 'the traditional attitude towards relativities has been modified, it cannot be said to have been eradicated'.[50]

The dispute over wage planning underwent a sharp change in 1947/ 8 when the issue of an incomes policy to control the general growth of wages, rather than policies aimed at changing relativities to alter the distribution of labour, came to dominate the debate. Labour, as often noted, did successfully pursue an incomes policy between 1948 and 1950.[51] In the current context the importance of this change of focus was its effect on ideological allegiances; where before the opposition to state intervention in wage bargaining had come from the right, now it predominantly came from the left. When incomes policy became the key issue, the left became defenders of free collective bargaining against the government's attempts to hold down the growth of (money) wages as part of its battle against inflation. Incomes policy had little connection

[48] PRO CAB132/5, 'National Wages Policy', Ministry of Labour, Oct. 1946.
[49] PRO CAB134/503, Lord President's Committee Minutes, 7 Jan. 1947; T229/641, 'National Wages and Prices Policy'; CAB129/4, 'Wages Policy' by Dalton.
[50] A. Flanders, 'Wages Policy and Full Employment in Britain', *Bulletin of the Oxford University Institute of Statistics* 12 (1950), pp. 225–42; T229/641, P. Proctor to H. Brittain, 28 Jan. 1948.
[51] R. Jones, *Wages and Employment Policy 1936–1985* (1987), ch. 4.

to 'planning' as understood by the left, and this facilitated the change of heart.[52]

Seen in this light the debate over wage planning in 1945–7 appears less 'government versus the trade unions' and more left versus right. This is not to dispute that the trade union leadership was strongly committed to free collective bargaining. But this attitude was common to most of the government as well, so that the battle lines on the issue went *through* both party and unions rather than between them.

This majority opinion against wage planning fitted in with the long-term commitment to free collective bargaining within the Labour movement, which, of course, long pre-dated the 1940s. The historical causes of this commitment have been much debated, but the long-standing legal hostility to trade unionism must be seen as an important element. It left a strongly entrenched view that free collective bargaining was the *raison d'être* of trade unions, and their right to engage in this practice a fundamental freedom akin to freedom of speech and assembly.[53]

The extent of the commitment to free collective bargaining is registered by the very limited legal change in the industrial relations framework in this period – largely restricted to the symbolic reversal of the much reviled post-general strike 1927 Trade Union and Trade Disputes Act. The repeal generated no general discussion about the legal framework of British industrial relations. Industrial relations is certainly one area that exemplifies Morgan's general judgement that 'the Second World War experience encouraged a somewhat complacent and very insular belief in the value of British institutions and traditions, especially when these were compared with those of other European nations'.[54]

However, to stress the extent and strength of the commitment to free collective bargaining is not the whole story of the defeat of wage planning in the 1940s. As already noted, this defeat also followed from the worries that any mechanism of state involvement in wage relativities would lead government into actions which would undermine its legitimacy by politicising areas previously outside the government's domain. This was the argument which those less attached to free collective bargaining found compelling in the debates of the 1940s, and it was not an argument urged by the trade unions so much as those ministers most sensitive to the limits of government, such as Morrison.[55]

[52] Panitch, *Social Democracy*, pp. 29–40.
[53] R. Currie, *Industrial Politics* (1979).
[54] PRO LAB10/74, 'Report on Trade Union and Trade Disputes Act' (1946); K. O. Morgan, *Labour in Power 1945–51* (Oxford, 1984), p. 136.
[55] See chapter 13.

In sum, a story of a government trying to pursue wage planning but being defeated by trade union intransigence won't do as an account of the 1940s. Although Durbin was an interesting and important figure, he was not typical of Labour Party attitudes in the period. Whilst many could see the attraction of such a policy, they were even more impressed by the threats it posed, not only to the tradition of free collective bargaining but also to Labour's statecraft.

More generally, it may be noted that the idea of a highly conflictual relation between unions and government in this period, conjured up by the wage planning debate, is misleading. Disputes and disagreements did occur, especially when the unions felt the government had been *procedurally* in error about not consulting them on major issues. But overall, Allen's conclusion on the relationship seems a fair summary: 'Trade Unions from 1945 to 1951 were loath to exert pressure on the government because they did not want to embarrass it and they made concessions to enable the Government to implement its policy'. Strikes were few and on a declining trend, and government conflict was almost entirely with *unofficial* union activity.[56] Certainly, in areas related to the government's desire to raise output and productivity this would be true, especially as far as the attitudes of union leaderships rather than the rank and file are concerned.[57] With few controls and little wage planning, the instruments available to the government to influence the supply and distribution of labour were obviously few. A list of such instruments made in 1947 contained:

- special releases from the forces
- encouragement of married women to work
- foreign workers
- encouragement via employment exchanges
- publicity

None of these was likely to make a major contribution. The numbers in the forces were stabilised from 1947/8 (until the 1950 rearmament). The encouragement of married women workers was compromised by the costs of such measures (see chapter 9). Foreign workers were employed, but faced stiff resistance from at least some unions and never came in the numbers hoped for by the government. Nevertheless,

---

[56] V. L. Allen, *Trade Unions and the Government* (1960), p. 312; H. A. Clegg, *A History of British Trade Unionism since 1889* vol. III. 1934–51 (Oxford, 1994) ch. 5.; J. Davis Smith, *The Attlee and Churchill Administrations and Industrial Unrest* (1990), chs. 1–6; J. W. Durcan, W. E. J. McCarthy and G. P. Redman, *Strikes in Postwar Britain* (1983), ch. 2.

[57] Ch. 4 and Tomlinson, 'Labour Government and the Trade Unions, 1945–51', pp. 90–105.

official additions to the workforce from this source numbered 85,000 in 1948 alone.[58]

General encouragement and exhortation may have had some effects, and such measures survived the ending of all controls in 1950. But clearly, in a fully employed economy the bargaining position favoured the worker, who was rarely denied the job slot wanted, however 'inessential' the government might consider it. In addition to these measures, the government did emphasise to employers the need to improve conditions (as well as wages) if they wanted to attract and keep labour. In this way labour shortage was used as an argument for improved welfare and other facilities at the factory level, and the Ministry of Labour was keen to impress on employers this new reality of a fully employed economy.[59]

The other broad aspects of the attempt to move labour into the 'undermanned' industries in this period should be noted. First, because these industries were mainly highly localised, occupational mobility often required geographical mobility.[60] A major obstacle was the availability of housing;[61] again, this makes the point that house-building in this period was not just about 'welfare' provision, but crucial to economic policy.

Second, the problems of moving labour to the undermanned industries underlined the desirability of raising the productivity of the existing workforce. In a naive but important sense, increasing productivity came to be regarded as a substitute for, as well as a complement to, increasing the labour force. Both would decrease the 'manpower deficit'.[62]

Conclusions

To almost everyone's surprise Labour presided over a fully employed economy, threatened briefly only by the fuel crisis of early 1947. By 1950 the government felt able to commit itself to a target of 3 per cent unemployment, a figure which would have been widely regarded as dangerously optimistic in the debates around the 1944 White Paper.[63]

[58] Cairncross, *Years of Recovery*, p. 395.
[59] PRO CAB134/509, 'Manpower Position During 1946', Ministry of Labour, 26 Jan. 1946. This line of argument was strongly pursued in cotton (see chapter 9) and coal (see chapter 11).
[60] This was certainly true for coal and agriculture. For cotton there were many workers (including large numbers of ex-cotton workers) in the Lancashire area, but many of them were in engineering, which had a priority not much below the cotton industry.
[61] PRO T229/35, 'The Manning-Up of the Export and Import-Saving Industries', Oct. 1947; CAB134/469, 'The Manpower Situation', 1 Dec. 1947.
[62] PRO CAB134/509, Manpower Committee Minutes, 2 Jan. 1946; chapter 4.
[63] Tomlinson, *Employment Policy*, pp. 122–30.

In this period full employment emerged as the seeming *sine qua non* of political success in Britain, a view to be sustained for more than a generation. Contrary to its expectations, Labour had to grapple with a general excess demand for labour rather than a shortage. This very much shaped the acceptance of fiscal instruments as the predominant form of economic management, though most Labour ministers wanted to hang on to some controls precisely because they feared that a re-emergence of full employment would not be secured purely by such instruments.[64]

On the microeconomic side policy had much less of a sense of complete success. Whilst Development Areas saw no recurrence of the unemployment rates of the 1930s, this seemed to result from the highly contingent success of the factory-building policy of 1945–7 rather than as part of a longer term strategy for these areas. Equally, attempts to 'man-up' industries such as cotton and coal achieved only limited success, reflecting the rejection of the instruments of labour controls and wage planning to achieve this end.

Whilst Brooke's account of trade union resistance as crucial to the defeat of wage planning is exaggerated, his point that failure on this front was an important contributor to the weakening of 'planning' is surely correct, though it was not the only one, as he tends to imply.[65] Nevertheless, it must be said that Labour, faced with unexpected problems in the labour market, failed to find much in the way of policy innovation to deal with them, even if, as Robinson insists, some success did crown their efforts.[66]

[64] Ibid., pp. 130–7.
[65] Brooke, 'Problems of "Socialist Planning"', p. 700. Compare chapters 6, 13.
[66] Robinson, *Economic Planning*; Robinson, 'Economic Problems', p. 180.

With its priority of expanding output and maximising labour supply in order to do so, the Labour government's policies were bound to have a major impact on women's employment. That employment had rapidly expanded in the war period (table 9.1), though the significance of the increase has been much debated. Marwick,[1] in particular, saw the war period as marking a major and positive change in women's activities and aspirations. Most recent literature has taken a much less sanguine view about the impact of the war on women. Writers such as Summerfield[2] and Smith[3] have emphasised both the limited extent of wartime changes, for example in the extent of gender segregation in employment or the absence of equal pay, and also the temporary nature of many of the changes that did occur. Smith summarises this now predominant view: 'The postwar aspirations of the vast majority of women factory workers were focused on marriage and domestic life; their wartime employment was considered a temporary response to an abnormal situation.'[4]

Whilst much of the recent argument about the limited impact of the war on women in Britain is persuasive, it commonly treats developments in the later 1940s as a minor postscript to wartime changes.[5] Yet there were major developments in the area of women's employment in this

---

[1] A. Marwick, *Britain in the Century of Total War* (1968); *War and Social Change in the Twentieth Century* (1975); *The Home Front* (1976).

[2] P. Summerfield, *Women Workers in the Second World War: Production and Patriarchy in Conflict* (1984); 'Women, Work and Warfare: A Study of Childcare and Shopping in Britain during the Second World War', *Journal of Social History* 17 (1983/4), pp. 240–69.

[3] H. L. Smith, 'The Womanpower Problem in Britain during the Second World War', *Historical Journal* 27 (1984), pp. 925–45; 'The Problem of Equal Pay for Equal Work in Great Britain during World War II', *Journal of Modern History* 53 (1981), pp. 652–72; 'Women in the Second World War' in H. L. Smith (ed.), *War and Social Change* (1986), pp. 66–89.

[4] Smith, 'Women', p. 218.

[5] Summerfield, *Women Workers*, pp. 187–91; Carruthers, 'Manning the Factories', pp. 232–56.

Table 9.1   *Women's employment, 1939–46*

(nos. of women in major sectors, 000s)

	June 1939	June 1943	June 1945	December 1946
Metal industries	433	1,635	1,257	778
Chemical industries	73	293	198	117
National government	123	471	493	385
Local government	326	458	519	485
Textiles	601	436	412	442
Clothing	449	312	301	354
Boots and shoes	57	336	343	391
Distribution	999	993	980	998
All industry (excluding forces or civil defence)	4,837	6,699	6,268	5,593

Source: Ministry of Labour and National Service. Report for 1939–46, PP 1946/7, vol. XII, pp. 230–1.

early post-war period.[6] First, some of the trends evident before the war reasserted themselves, notably the upward trend in overall female activity rates.[7] Perhaps more important, and evident by the end of the 1940s, were the shifts in the composition of women's employment. Table 9.1 suggests how much of the rise in employment in sectors like engineering was reversed in the later period of the war. But on a slightly larger view it is evident that this reversal was only partial (table 9.2).

As can be seen from this table, traditional employers of women such as the textiles, clothing and pottery industries did not recover their pre-war position, whilst others such as metal manufacture, chemicals, finance, and utilities saw significant expansions. These trends occurred despite efforts by government to retain women in some of the traditional sectors, as will be discussed below.

Accompanying the shift in the composition of women's jobs was a shift from full-time to part-time employment. Data for part-time employment before 1951 are poor, and even the census data must be used with some care – the Ministry of Labour accepted that they prob-

[6] P. Thane, 'Towards Equal Opportunities? Women in Britain since 1945' in T. Gourvish and A. O'Day (eds.), *Britain since 1945* (1991), pp. 183–208, provides an interesting overview of some of the issues in her survey of women and equal opportunities over the whole post-war period.

[7] C. Hakim, 'The Myth of Rising Female Employment', *Work, Employment and Society* 7 (1993), pp. 97–120.

Table 9.2   *Changes in number of women in selected occupations,*
1939–47/8[1]

	Index number 1948 (1939 = 100)	Total Nov. 1947 (000s)
Clothing	75	370
Textiles	69	470
Pottery	87	39
Commerce, banking, investment and finance	115	128
Chemicals, paints, oils	140	116
Food, drink and tobacco	110	247
Glass	136	16
National and local government	390	n/a
Distribution	105	927
Engineering	212	235
Metal manufacture	241	47
Gas, water and electricity supply	168	21
Communication	251	64

[1] There is a major break in the series at 1948 with the introduction of the new National Insurance system, so figures after 1948 are on a different basis.
Source: Index no.: C. Leser, 'Men and Women in Industry', *Economic Journal* 62 (1952), p. 331.
Total no.: *Ministry of Labour Gazette*, January 1948.

ably significantly underestimated the extent of part-time work in 1951. Such evidence as exists suggests a growth of part-time employment in the late 1940s, though at around 15 per cent of total women's employment, it was much less significant than it was to become in later years.[8] This trend, encouraged by the government (see below), was linked to the change in the age and marital status of working women. The long-term trend towards older and married women making up a much larger proportion of employed women is evident by the late 1940s (table 9.3).

Apart from these important underlying changes, which became apparent in the late 1940s, there was a lively political and policy debate on the question of women's employment under the Attlee government. This debate ranged across a number of aspects of it, but undoubtedly

[8] *Ministry of Labour Gazette*, March 1958, p. 97. V. Klein, *Britain's Married Women Workers* (1975), p. 25, suggests the figure in the 1950s might be an underestimate of about one-eighth. The proportion given here is calculated from PEP, 'Employment of Women', *Planning* 15 (1948), pp. 37–53; Hakim, 'Myth', p. 103 had 11 per cent for 1951, rising to 45 per cent by 1991.

Table 9.3 *Participation rates of married and unmarried women in four age groups, 1931 and 1951*

(000s)

Age	Marital status	1931			1951		
		Total	Occupied	%	Total	Occupied	%
20–24	Married	467	86	19	796	291	37
	Unmarried	1,151	969	84	897	816	91
25–29	Married	1,115	164	15	1,409	363	26
	Unmarried	815	664	82	440	385	88
30–34	Married	1,312	157	12	1,434	331	23
	Unmarried	497	380	76	310	253	82
45–54	Married	2,091	178	9	2,613	618	24
	Unmarried	832	435	52	858	576	67

Source: G. Routh, *Occupation and Pay in Britain, 1905–1960* (Cambridge, 1965), p. 46.

central was the government's concern with 'manpower' planning, which in fact focused much attention on women. Also important, and to some extent related to this central policy issue, was the issue of provision, especially of nurseries, to facilitate women working. Equal pay was also a live issue, as was the place of women in the new, post-Beveridge, structure of social security.

Given this background, the focus of this chapter is on public policy and how it impinged on women's employment in this period, concentrating mainly on the issues just outlined.[9] The central concern is with the terms within which these policy debates were conducted, what determined policy outcomes, and how far in practice policy had a significant impact on the patterns of women's employment noted above, but also how they related to wider questions about women's role in society. Whilst the focus is on central government policy-making, account is also taken of the way in which various outside groups attempted to affect government policy, and what degree of success they achieved.

[9] There exists a limited literature on some aspects of some of these questions. W. Crofts, *Coercion*, chs. 7 and 8, and Carruthers, 'Manning the Factories', focus attention on the propaganda aspect of the Attlee government's policies on women. D. Riley (*War in the Nursery* (1983), ch. 6; 'War in the Nursery', *Feminist Review* 2 (1979), pp. 82–108 and 'The Free Mothers: Pro-natalism and Working Women in Industry at the End of the Last War in Britain', *History Workshop* 11 (1981), pp. 59–118) is extremely interesting on the pro-natalist current in post-war ideology. There is surprisingly little other detailed work on issues relating to women and the labour market in this period.

A contradictory policy?

The Labour government's attitude to women's employment has commonly been seen as contradictory. Pugh[10] summarises a typical view:

The new cabinet was badly torn between a desire to boost the birth rate and an urgent need to increase industrial production and exports. As a result it pursued contradictory policies towards women. On the one hand it embarked upon a great propaganda campaign designed to encourage women to seek employment. On the other hand it closed down the wartime nurseries and withdrew funding for local authority nurseries; nor was there any pretence that the women workers were replacing men – they constituted cheap labour on a strictly temporary basis.

Carruthers'[11] discussion of propaganda and policy also suggests a contradictory message, offering women work on one hand, but also the 'worthy task of adjusting the national birth-rate on the other'.

There is no disputing that the key context of policy on women's employment in this period was the labour shortage.[12] Even before the war had ended (or the Labour government had been elected) a ministerial committee on manpower was noting the decline in women's employment, predicting that as early as the end of 1945 700,000 out of the 2m. 'extra' women recruited in wartime would have left their jobs. The aim of public policy, it was argued a little later, should be to check this loss:

At the moment many employers are tending to dismiss women and dilutees generally, on the mistaken assumption that with the coming of peace they can reasonably expect to obtain the male labour force which they normally prefer. Women workers themselves may feel that there is no longer the same need for women to remain at work. *These misconceptions ought to be removed,* and for this purpose a publicity campaign should be launched immediately to make it clear that, since manpower is going to be scarce for a considerable time to come, it will be necessary to employ more women than before the war, though the industries in which they will be most needed will not be those in which they were needed during the war [emphasis added].[13]

[10] M. Pugh, 'Domesticity and the Decline of Feminism' in H. L. Smith (ed.), *British Feminism in the Twentieth Century* (1990), pp. 144–64; *Women and the Women's Movement in Britain 1914–1959* (1992), p. 286. See also Crofts, *Coercion*, p. 91; 'Attlee', pp. 29–30.
[11] Carruthers, 'Manning the Factories', pp. 254–56; Summerfield (*Women Workers*, ch. 1) offers a similar analysis, couched in terms of 'capitalism' versus 'patriarchy'.
[12] J. Lewis, *Women in Britain since 1945* (1992), p. 153.
[13] PRO CAB92/104, Ministerial Committee on Manpower Minutes, 31 May 1945; ibid., Report on 'Manpower Positions up to 30 June 1946', 21 Dec. 1945.

Such a campaign of persuasion, aimed at both employers and women, was launched in June 1946. The parameters of that campaign as it addressed women were clearly set out in a broadcast by the Minister of Labour. Four points were emphasised. First, that he was 'not asking women to do jobs usually done by men, as had been the case during the war'. Second, he argued, the labour shortage was temporary, and 'women were being asked to take a job only for whatever length of time they could spare, whether full-time or part-time'. Third, the minister emphasised, he was not appealing to women with very young children, 'although for those who wanted to volunteer, and who had children a little older, there were in many places day nurseries and creches'. Finally, 'the appeal was not addressed to those whose domestic responsibilities were so great that they could not do an outside job'.[14]

All these aspects of the Labour government's approach deserve some comment. Labour was certainly not aiming to continue the wartime policy of 'dilution', involving widespread replacement of men by women. But the reason for this was not, as Pugh suggests, a desire to secure 'cheap labour'. Rather it was based on two features of the government's understanding of the post-war labour market – one straightforward, the other less so.

First, it was hardly sensible in a climate of trying to encourage the maximum labour supply from all sources to suggest any displacement of one group of workers by another. Women were wanted as a net addition to the labour force. Second, the Ministry of Labour anticipated that the growth of women's employment would be insufficient to match the 'gap' in labour supply, and in the medium term foresaw *men* replacing *women* rather than the other way around. This perspective arose from demographic data which suggested that in the main age group(s) providing women workers (15–59 years) there would be a decline in numbers in the post-war years flowing from the low birth-rate in the period 1912 to 1936.[15] Implicit in this view was the belief that overall female participation rates were likely to fall back towards their pre-war norms, as indeed they had been doing since about 1944. The prediction made was that the participation rate of women aged 15–59 would fall from 36.3 per cent at the end of 1946 to 34.3 per cent by 1951, partly because of a 'catch-up' in the wartime postponement of marriage. In other words, the ministry had a quite pessimistic view of the constraints under which its campaign to encourage women to work was

---

[14] *Ministry of Labour Gazette* 55 (June 1947), p. 183.
[15] PRO CAB134/510, Manpower Working Party Minutes, 28 Nov. 1945; PRO LAB8/133, Ministry of Labour, 'Manpower Trends in Great Britain 1946–51', 1947; *Ministry of Labour Gazette* 55 (May 1947), p. 142.

operating.[16] This sense of tight constraints is well summed up by a note from a senior Ministry of Labour official in February 1947:

The inescapable moral of this position seems to be that industry will have to make do with a smaller percentage of women than in the past. In other words, that industrial units which are not specially attractive to women will have to arrange for their work either to be mechanised to a considerably greater extent, or for men to do the work to a greater extent than hitherto.[17]

As shown in table 9.3, the perception that an upward shift in women's participation in the labour market would require changes in the traditional age distribution of women workers was quite accurate, though at this stage the ministry would seem to have underestimated the forces making for this shift. This pessimism extended to government's expectations of employers. Within the Ministry of Labour the conservatism of employers' attitudes to women workers was well appreciated, a point urged on the ministry by its Women's Consultative Committee,[18] but also apparent from contact with employers. For example, when Kipping of the Federation of British Industry was asked to meet the WCC to discuss women's employment opportunities as executives in British industry, he argued that women should concentrate on the 'points of least resistance', namely as private secretaries to executives with the hope of eventually advancing to PA, or from supervisor of the typing pool to a similar role in the 'methods department'.[19]

The ministerial focus on the temporary nature of women's work also derived substantially from pessimism about women's enthusiasm for paid work. A Ministry of Labour memorandum of late 1946, in discussing the nature of the appeal to be made to women, suggested it should be 'addressed to all women whose circumstances permit them to enter or return to employment, for a year at any rate. An appeal with this limited objective would, it is felt, meet with a better response than an appeal to enter employment for an indefinite period'. This approach was endorsed by members of the WCC. For example, Mrs Dorothy Elliott asked that in the campaign to recruit women 'an optimistic note should be sounded so that the women would feel they were not being expected to continue working indefinitely'.[20]

[16] PRO CAB134/509, Ministerial Committee on Manpower Minutes, 21 Jan. 1946. Bevin argued for delaying the campaign to get women back to work until the spring, partly in the hope that more consumer goods in the shops would help to attract them.
[17] PRO LAB8/133, Hitchman to Wiles, 17 Feb. 1947.
[18] PRO LAB8/1010, Women's Consultative Committee Minutes, 16 Jan. 1946. The WCC had been created by Ernest Bevin in 1941.
[19] PRO LAB8/1566, WCC Minutes, 20 July 1949.
[20] PRO LAB8/1247, WCC, Ministry of Labour, 'Possibility of Increasing the Number of Women in Industrial Employment' (n.d., but late 1946); ibid., Minutes, 2 April 1947.

Whether this argument was wise from the government's point of view may be doubted. Some women were probably put off by the notion that the jobs they might take up would be impermanent. But the point is that such impermanence was not the *aim* of policy; rather the government perceived it as raising the likelihood of women being willing to 'do their bit' before returning to their preferred domestic life. This 'temporary' emphasis was largely propaganda; in practice there was no reason why, if firms hired women, they should at a later stage discharge them.

The Ministry of Labour's perception of women's attitudes to work gains some support from survey evidence of both the war and early post-war periods. The famous Mass Observation study had found that most women workers regarded their wartime work as a test of endurance, something to give up as soon as possible. Early post-war surveys suggested that women had a fairly pragmatic attitude to work, rather than one driven by very strong notions of a 'woman's place'. The constraints on those working were considerable, but mainly related to practical issues like hours of work, the availability of time for shopping, the kinds of jobs available, and nursery provision.[21] As Riley[22] suggests, if in the late 1940s women were 'pragmatic materialists' in their attitudes to work, then, given the conditions of the period, a lack of enthusiasm to respond to government blandishments would have been perfectly rational, especially perhaps for those women who had already worked long hours over a number of years during the war.

One well-known condition of the period likely to have inhibited women's desire for work was the shortage and rationing of many commodities. There was considerable hostility to the government from women who felt that not enough priority was given to the supply of basic consumer goods, and this was famously manifested in the activities of the British Housewives' League.[23] From an economics point of view, the obvious point is that, in the absence of things to buy in the shops, increased earnings could only be used to accumulate savings at a time when the desire to save was at a low ebb. This could act as a major disincentive to work. Probably this absence of things to buy with increased earnings was a more pervasive factor (along with those already noted) than wage levels themselves. For example, in cotton, both men and women workers saw their relative wages rise in comparison with

[21] Mass Observation, *War Factory* (1943; republished 1987); G. Thomas, *Women and Industry*, Social Survey for the Ministry of Labour and National Service (1948).
[22] Riley, 'Free Mothers', pp. 82–3.
[23] P. Addison, *Now the War is Over: A Social History of Britain 1945–51* (1985), pp. 40–5; Zweiniger-Bargielowska, 'Rationing, Austerity and the Conservative Party', pp. 173–97.

competing occupations, but not enough to generate the inflow of labour desired.[24]

The Ministry of Labour also wanted to tempt women into work by encouraging the creation of part-time jobs. In September 1948 the ministry launched a campaign to encourage 'spare-time' work, by women or by anyone who felt they had time available. This campaign seems to have evinced a considerable response from women (and others) though it ran into problems because part-time work was only available in specific areas, despite the efforts of the ministry to encourage employers to make it more widely available. This expansion of part-time work seems to have been supported by trade unions and women's organisations, though both were worried about the conditions in any increase in 'outwork' or homework that might occur.[25]

The Ministry of Labour's appeal to women to return to work was not aimed at those with children below two years of age, but it suggested that those with slightly older children who wanted to work might be able to use nursery provision for their childcare. This seems to fly in the face of the common argument that Labour had a clear policy of closing down nurseries in order to discourage mothers of young children from working.

Nursery provision has played a key role in critical assessments of Labour's approach to women in this period. The fall in such provision in the late 1940s is seen as the most important sign of that ambiguity towards women and work so strongly emphasised in the literature.[26] A number of points may be made about this argument. First, as Riley has clearly shown, nursery provision *cannot* be treated as a straightforward symbol of attitudes to women and work. The perceived role of nurseries shifted notably from the 1930s to the 1950s, and by the late 1940s they were seen by many policy-makers as part of a strategy of educating women in 'motherhood' as much as facilitating entry into the labour market. As Riley suggests, there is a 'vague but handy feminist folk myth about the war nurseries; that they were done away with because the government wanted women off the labour market and back to the home'.[27]

[24] J. Singleton, *Lancashire on the Scrapheap* (Oxford, 1991), p. 61.

[25] PRO LAB 8/1283, 'Employment Policy: Part-time Employment', 1948–50. This campaign may have had some success, e.g. PEP, 'Employment', though the real boom in part-time work did not occur until the 1950s and 1960s: V. Beechey and T. Perkins, *A Matter of Hours: Women, Part-Time Work and the Labour Market* (Oxford, 1987), pp. 21–4.

[26] Carruthers, 'Manning the Factories', p. 253; Crofts, *Coercion*, pp. 91–2.

[27] Riley, *War in the Nursery*; 'War', p. 82.

Second, the provision of nursery places was always extremely marginal to the supply of women's labour. At their peak in 1944 such nurseries were providing about 72,000 places – a drop in the ocean when there were about 3.25m. children aged 0–4 in the population at that time. The bulk of childcare provision in wartime, as always, was provided by informal child-minding rather than any formal, public facility.[28]

Third, the reasons for the rundown of the nurseries had little to do with any views about 'women's place'. The rundown began in 1944, mainly because of concern about the economics of such provision. The wartime expansion of nursery places had been funded 100 per cent by the Treasury, but increasingly questions were asked (for example, by the Select Committee on National Expenditure) about this use of public money. The basic problem was that the purported aim of the nurseries, to deliver an increase in labour supply, was not very effectively achieved because of the high level of staff insisted on by the Ministry of Health. The Select Committee on National Expenditure suggested that for every 2.7 women freed for work by nurseries, one staff member was required. This assumed, rather than proved, that nursery staff could have found alternative employment. Nevertheless, primarily for this reason it was decided early in 1944 not to sanction further provision as it would not make a significant contribution to labour supply before the expected end of the European war. This position was taken explicitly in line with the policy that the wartime nursery expansion was purely an issue of facilitating war production, not part of any policy on continuing provision in this area.[29]

This rundown in provision continued in the early post-war period as the Treasury grant to local authorities was cut from 100 to 50 per cent in April 1946. This decision was highly contentious, with frequent questions in Parliament, pressure from women's groups and trade unions, and inter-ministerial discussions. The government line was, however, consistent. Continuation of the 100 per cent grant could not be justified as a policy, it was argued, because the whole basis of Health Service provision of that kind was a partnership between central and local government, where the former provided incentives, but the latter made the final decision, not least because they had to find a significant proportion of the money. For example, when challenged on the issue in the House of Commons, Aneurin Bevan, the Minister of Health,

[28] Summerfield, 'Women', pp. 250–8.

[29] PRO LAB26/133, Ministry of Labour, 'Provision for the Care of Children of Married Women in Industry Wartime Nurseries – General Policy 1943–4', 22 March 1944. PRO MH/55 1696, 'Select Committee on National Expenditure: Day Nurseries and Nursery Schools'.

Table 9.4   *State provision for pre-school children*

	1938	Summer 1944	January 1948	January 1950
Children under 5 in elementary schools	166,633[1]	140,000	179,275	169,851
Children in nursery schools	4,881	6,000	19,871	21,423
Children in day nurseries	4,291	71,805	41,736[2]	43,395[3]

[1] Under 3 and 3–5.
[2] December 1948.
[3] End of 1949.
Sources: PRO LAB26/286, 'Child Care Schemes in Great Britain during and since the War', 1 Nov. 1951; Board of Education, *Education in 1938*, PP 1938/9, vol. x; Ministry of Education, *Education in 1948*, PP 1948/9, vol. xiv.

stressed that nurseries were 'essentially a local service', that 100 per cent grants would be an 'uneconomic practice' and would be 'appallingly extravagant' and 'undermine the independence of local government'.[30]

Did this public view disguise a 'hidden agenda' to undermine the ability of women to enter or re-enter the labour force? The PRO files don't suggest so. The position of the various ministries involved in the issue differed a little in emphasis, but the basic stance seems clear.

First, by and large there was agreement that the best place for women with children under two was at home with those children rather than in paid employment. This view was perhaps more strongly held by the Ministry of Health than the Ministry of Labour, but it was not a major point of contention within the government.[31] Equally, it was accepted that it was an 'ideal' that might not always be adhered to, and that in conditions of labour shortage, if women with very young children wanted to work, they should be allowed to do so.

The dividing line at two years was linked to the encouragement of educational provision for under-5s, which did show significant expansion, especially in the form of nursery schools, in the late 1940s, though this was largely coming to a halt by about 1950 (table 9.4). This expansion was based on the permissive powers given to local authorities under the 1944 Education Act to establish such schools, which did receive initial encouragement from the Ministry of Education. However, by the

[30] *Hansard* (Commons), vol. 420, cols. 1278–9, 14 March 1946.
[31] PRO LAB26/168, 'Provision for the Care of Children of Married Women in Industry'; contrast A. Smieton (Ministry of Health) to E. A. Hitchman, 7 Sept. 1945 with the Ministry of Labour Regional Controller, who could see 'no reason why mothers of very young children should be excluded from the appeal' (Report of Conference, 12 Feb. 1947).

late 1940s the ministry was concerned that, because of the sharply rising demand for places for school-age children, resources, including staff, should be channelled to the primary school age range and away from the pre-school years.[32]

Educational provision for the under-5s also had different implications for labour supply from provision via day nurseries. Nurseries provided full-time care and were therefore fairly readily compatible with full-time jobs. Educational provision was usually for much shorter hours, and therefore fitted with the growing emphasis on women's part-time work. However, the neatness of fit of these two policies should not be exaggerated. The government tried to encourage extended hours in educational establishments and the provision of holiday care schemes to try and bridge the gap between the trend towards educational provision and the desire to encourage full-time as well as part-time women's employment.[33]

Second, although the 50 per cent grant was sacrosanct, the central government wanted local authorities to maintain nursery provision wherever possible. They argued that the major obstacle to this aim was not the level of grant support, but the return of suitable premises to their pre-war uses, and the lack of staff or buildings. Central government was also conscious of the wartime argument that, in labour supply terms, nurseries were not very effective given the high staff–children ratios.[34]

In addition, the Ministry of Health urged local authorities to give special attention to the role of married women in essential industries when they planned nursery provision. Where local authorities were seeming to fall short of their responsibilities in this area the ministries would intervene. This occurred in the case of Lancashire and the cotton industry, and the ministry, in co-operation with the cotton employers, brought considerable pressure to bear, with some success.[35]

Lancashire cotton was a key area for the campaign to mobilise more women workers, because of both its long history as a major employer of women and the enormous scope for expanding cotton exports by increasing output in the late 1940s. The government's approach to Lancashire illustrates the dominance of policy by labour supply considerations. The government did launch a campaign to mobilise women in Lancashire as a central part of its broader campaign on women's

---

[32] T. Blackstone, *A Fair Start: The Provision of Pre-School Education* (1971), pp. 61–6.
[33] PRO LAB8/1394, WCC Minutes, 5 May 1948.
[34] PRO LAB26/168, Whyte (Ministry of Labour) to Regional Controllers, 16 May 1947.
[35] Ibid., Circular 221/45, 'Nursery Provision'; ibid., G. Isaacs (Minister of Labour) to E. Bevin, 9 May 1946.

employment,[36] and, as noted above, this included pressing the local authorities to provide nurseries. But equally there was scepticism about the likely impact of this provision. The North Western Regional Board for Industry, prodded by the National Production Advisory Council for Industry, conducted an inquiry into nursery provision in Lancashire and its impact on the labour supply. Its conclusion was that whilst there was a case for such facilities, on labour supply grounds that case was limited. In September 1946 they calculated there were 161 day nurseries in Lancashire and Cheshire providing about 7,500 places, plus about 50 factory nurseries. But the government wanted to attract 60,000 married women into cotton employment, of whom perhaps 6,000 might have nursery-age children. To get that latter group into work would, it was suggested, require 150 new nurseries with 1,200 skilled staff (plus cooks and domestics). Given the contemporary shortage of buildings, the shortage of skilled nursery staff, and the overall poor ratio of women 'freed' for cotton employment in comparison with those employed to care for their children, it is not surprising that nursery provision was not regarded as likely to play a major part in increasing the supply of women to the cotton industry.[37]

Overall, there was little contradiction between letting local authorities decide on the level of nursery provision and encouraging women back to work. Although nursery provision did fall nationally in the late 1940s, the impact of that fall on labour supply was small, and where closure seemed likely to have significant labour supply implications at a local level, central government was willing to intervene to urge a change in policy. Alongside this, the government intervened in some areas to encourage employers to provide nurseries.[38]

As noted above, in this period women with children were deterred from working by the difficulties of shopping and the conditions of work. The first issue was well recognised at ministerial level, and various lines of policy were discussed. In the event the issue was dealt with by local welfare officers of the Ministry of Labour, who under wartime regulations continued to have a role, for example, in getting shops to vary opening hours where local labour conditions suggested such a course was desirable.[39]

[36] Crofts, *Coercion*, chs. 7, 8; PRO CAB134/638, Production Committee Reports of the 'Labour Textile Industries' Committee, 20 April 1948, 19 July 1948 and 31 March 1950.

[37] PRO BT190/4 NPACI, Ministries of Health and Education, 'Day Nurseries', 3 April 1947.

[38] PRO LAB8/1394, WCC, 'Report on Care of Young Children of Women in Employment', 5 May 1948.

[39] PRO LAB26/62, 'Shopping Difficulties, 1943–52'.

With regard to conditions of work, Labour in this period was strongly committed to a human relations approach to the factory, based on the idea that a 'happy worker is a productive worker'. This led to a continuation of the wartime emphasis on the provision of factory canteens, welfare provision and personnel management. Personnel officers in particular were commonly seen as especially concerned with helping women to try and combine domestic responsibilities and work.[40]

In seeking to encourage married women and mothers into work the government sometimes faced a hostile response. For example, when the ministry was trying to encourage nursery provision in Lancashire, it found some hostility from 'medical authorities in that part of the world'.[41] Similarly, a ministerial appeal to women to return to work in 1949 was attacked by the *Daily Dispatch*, the *Evening News* and the *Observer* newspapers as wrong in so far as it encouraged mothers of young children into employment.[42] However, the ministries involved generally seem to have seen their role as resisting rather than giving into such pressures against their policies.

The issue of women's employment was especially topical in policy circles in the years of severe economic crisis in 1946–8. It regained some of that importance in the face of rearmament from late 1950, with the threat that such rearmament would be inhibited by the shortage of 'manpower'. A Ministry of Labour document spelt out that 'substantial numbers of additional women will be needed as the programme develops'. It stressed the need for women to move into semi-skilled jobs in munitions-related industries, exactly as in war, and more generally for the employment of women to be encouraged by 're-arrangement of production processes, alteration of hours, the introduction of part-time and outworking schemes, etc.'.[43]

This general statement of policy had been preceded by a number of discussions in the ministry on issues relating to women's employment. There was an attempt at systematic, region-by-region survey of the potential availability of female labour. However, this seems to have taken 'availability' as given, so that the pessimistic conclusion was that the potential of recruiting women for the rearmament programme would soon run up against a 'growing shortage in most areas'.[44]

With regard to childcare, the government reiterated the view that the best place for children under two was with their mothers, but that above

[40] For the general emphasis on human relations in this period, Tiratsoo and Tomlinson, *Industrial Efficiency*, ch. 5.
[41] PRO LAB26/168, Isaacs to Bevin, 9 May 1946.
[42] PRO LAB8/1283, 'Employment Policy: Part-Time Employment'.
[43] PRO LAB10/1490, 'Manpower for the Defence Industries', 15 Jan. 1951.
[44] PRO LAB8/1760, 'Availability of Female Labour: Regional Review by Research Committee', 1950.

that age it was a matter for the mothers to decide. This view was endorsed by the WCC.[45]

The provision of state facilities for such childcare was again subject to considerable discussion. The parameters of that discussion in the Korean rearmament years were not much different from those earlier in the government's period of office. The Ministry of Labour accepted that day nurseries were an expensive (in public expenditure and womanpower) way of freeing women for work, but was unhappy with the trend for local authorities to close such provision because of restrictions on NHS expenditure, which, of course, accompanied rearmament.[46] This emphasis on the public expenditure as well as the labour aspect of childcare provision was very strong in the rearmament period. The high expenditure came to be used as an argument not only against day nurseries but also against nursery schools, which had expanded substantially in the late 1940s. Hence the emphasis tended to switch to 'cheaper' forms of provision, such as play-centres, childminders and sitter-in schemes.[47]

By the time of its departure from office in 1951 Labour's central attitude to women's employment had changed little since 1945. It was dominated by economic and financial considerations, with little evidence of any major impact from changing views about women's role; the latter were usually articulated as subordinate clauses, with little obvious effect on policy in this period. This position was well summed up by Aneurin Bevan, Minister of Health at the beginning of the rearmament programme: 'Decisions about day nurseries would have to depend on the balance of economic advantage in each particular case. Such nurseries were very expensive to run in staff and money, and he believed that mothers with young children were best employed at home looking after their families'.[48]

Equal pay

Another important aspect of women's employment, and one occasioning considerable debate in this period, was that of equal pay.

[45] PRO LAB1572, WCC Minutes, 18 Oct. 1950.
[46] PRO LAB26/286, Letter Alf Robens (Minister of Labour) to Hilary Marquand (Minister of Health), 5 Sept. 1951.
[47] PRO LAB8/1730, WCC, R. Bicknell, 'Child-Care Implications of the Defence Programme', 13 Jan. 1951. Of course there is a broader issue here, the paradox that by cutting back on 'welfare' provision to aid rearmament, one of the conditions of that rearmament, increased labour supply, was inhibited. However, this point should not be exaggerated because, as suggested above, nurseries could have had only a marginal impact on labour supply.
[48] PRO LAB10/652, National Joint Advisory Council Minutes, 31 Jan. 1951.

This issue had revived during the war and led to the wartime coalition's only substantive parliamentary defeat, when in 1944 a Commons majority voted for equal pay for teachers. This decision was reversed by a vote of confidence, but the political pressure led to the appointment of a 'fact-finding' Royal Commission, which reported in October 1946.[49]

The majority of the commission believed that unequal pay largely reflected gender-based differences in efficiency coupled to 'social conventions' which crowded women into a narrow range of occupations, and that even where the claims of justice suggested equalisation, this would threaten to bring about unacceptable inflationary pressures.[50] Three of the four women on the commission dissented from these views, arguing that differences in pay did not reflect differences in efficiency, and that removing them would lead to a rise in productivity by encouraging a more efficient allocation of man and woman power: 'We cannot agree with the majority that it is necessary to make a choice between 'exact justice' and 'oiling the wheels of economic progress'. On the contrary the claims of justice between individuals and of the development of national productivity point in the same direction.'[51]

The government's position on equal pay was commitment to the principle, but a refusal to bring it into being immediately. The first of these positions was unavoidable. The Labour Party conference of 1944 voted in favour of equal pay, and political pressure from MPs and trade unions, as well as women's organisations, made this commitment inescapable. Also important was Britain's role in the International Labour Organisation, which was committed to equal pay, though the Cabinet Committee which first looked at the issue recommended against any such acceptance even in principle.[52]

The arguments against immediate implementation were articulated by Dalton, the Chancellor of the Exchequer, in the House of Commons. The grounds were financial and economic. Equal pay in the public sector, he argued, would cost £35m. in increased public expenditure. It would lead to pressure for similar increases in private sector pay, with inflationary implications. Finally, it would lead to strong pressure for

---

[49] Smith, 'Problem'; Thane, 'Towards Equal Opportunities?' *Report of Royal Commission on Equal Pay* (1946).

[50] *Royal Commission on Equal Pay*, ch. 13. The precise argument of the Majority Report is not always clear, and there are legitimate differences in interpretation of what they said. Thane ('Towards Equal Opportunities?', pp. 190–1) sees in that report a more critical attitude to the view that women's lower pay is caused by lower efficiency than suggested here.

[51] *Royal Commission*, Memorandum of Dissent by A. Loughlin, J. Vaughan and L. F. Nettlefold, para. 32.

[52] PRO CAB128/9, 6 March 1947; CAB128/10, 3 June 1947; CAB129/19, 'Equal Pay: Memo. by Minister without Portfolio', 30 May 1947.

'occupational family allowances' to compensate married men with children in sectors where equality was achieved.[53]

This position was maintained throughout the lifetime of the Attlee government. There was considerable pressure from women's organisations, trade unions and the Labour Party for an immediate introduction of equal pay, but it was resisted. The resistance was aided by the equivocations of the TUC, which, although it had a commitment to equal pay going back to the nineteenth century, by 1948 accepted the government's case against immediate implementation.[54] This TUC change of heart was strongly resented by women trade union members, and, for example, at the 1949 conference of the unions representing women, the call was made to continue to campaign for immediate implementation despite the TUC's reversal of attitude.[55] When the change had been mooted at the 1948 TUC one woman had argued that 'In our view the treatment that we have had from Sir S. Cripps and from his predecessor in office has been quite indistinguishable from that from any Tory Chancellor for the last 25 years'.[56]

The debate over equal pay was at its height in the period following the publication of the Royal Commission's Report. During that period, and before the TUC changed its mind, it took a delegation to see senior ministers, including Attlee. A verbatim record of the meeting brings out some of the complexities of the debate and the government's position.[57] At the beginning of this meeting Dalton laid out the government's position as publicly portrayed in the House of Commons. He argued that equal pay would 'distort priorities' away from development of the NHS, social security, etc. He not only stressed the public expenditure cost of increases in public sector pay, but also maintained that such increases would not increase output. Dame Anne Loughlin, one of the dissenters on the Royal Commission, did most of the talking for the TUC. She stressed men's support for equal pay to prevent their wages being undercut, and that equal pay would provide an incentive to women to return to work, as currently they 'have no incentive to go back in comparison with what they have to pay out'.

Whilst most of the discussion focused on this pragmatic level of alleged economic effects, both Dalton and Attlee made points which

[53] *Hansard* (Commons), vol. 438, cols. 1075–81, 11 June 1947.
[54] *Report* of the 1948 TUC Congress, p. 276; *Report* of the 1949 TUC Congress, pp. 481–3.
[55] *Report* of the 19th Annual Conference of Representatives of TUs Catering for Women Workers, pp. 3–4; S. Lewenhak, *Women and Trade Unions* (1977), pp. 249–53.
[56] *Report* of 1948 TUC Congress, p. 465.
[57] PRO PREM8/1396, Equal Pay, 'Report of Discussion with TUC Delegation', 6 June 1947.

rather bring into question their support for the principle of equal pay. Dalton not only disputed the extent of men's support for such equality, but went on to argue that equal pay on the London buses had led to the displacement of women by men. This argument was in line with what many employers said in their evidence to the Royal Commission, though it was a contention disputed by the TUC. Attlee in turn conjured up a picture of resentful wives, dismayed by their husbands receiving the same pay as single women. Such questioning of the principle of equal pay received a tart response from Loughlin, who argued that the issue of principle was settled, with men and women together now both supporting it.

Ministerial opposition to the implementation of equal pay was bolstered by a Treasury Working Party Report, which, apart from the economic and financial arguments already noted, maintained that there was a 'clash of equities' between the 'argument that the same job should get the same pay whoever does it and the argument that those receiving the higher pay now are already in the main worse off (because of family responsibilities) and that it would be wrong to transfer purchasing power as an act of public policy from the more to the less needy'.[58] This point needs to be seen as linked to the fear of ministers that in the absence, as they believed, of universal support for equal pay, its implementation would lead to counter-claims by male workers, causing not only inflation, but disrupting industrial relations. This latter point had been crucial to ministerial resistance during the war.[59]

The TUC argument that equal pay would improve recruitment of women to industry was perhaps their most compelling point, given the government's priorities. But the government stressed that in the public sectors, where it directly determined pay they did not want to increase recruitment, and higher pay would not raise output. On the other hand, both the TUC and the government were agreed that in the industries which were 'undermanned' wages should be settled by free collective bargaining, without government intervention.[60]

Overall, these confidential TUC–ministerial discussions suggest that the economic and financial reasons given in public were largely those that motivated government decision-making. But they also suggest a considerably more limited degree of ministerial commitment to the principle than public statements would suggest. The issue died away, at least as far as ministers were concerned, once the TUC changed its mind on the demand for 'immediate implementation' of equal pay. It

[58] Ibid., Treasury Working Party Report on Equal Pay (n.d., but early 1947).
[59] Smith, 'Problem', p. 652.
[60] Tomlinson, 'Labour Government and the Trade Unions'.

was briefly revived in 1950/1, mainly because of publicity about International Labour Office proposals on the issue. This again led to a commitment 'in principle', but a firm refusal to move to immediate action.[61]

Social security and women

Another element of public policy in the Attlee years which affected women's role in the labour market was, of course, social security. The parameters of debate here were largely set by the Beveridge Report of 1942. Whilst this report received substantial criticism in the Labour ranks, these criticisms did not lead to the suggestion of a comprehensive alternative, and in large part the 1946 National Insurance Act followed Beveridge's design.[62]

Embodied in the new structure of social insurance was a very particular view of women – especially married women. Beveridge had argued that most married women were in fact dependent on men, and that their National Insurance position should reflect this. If they worked, they could opt in to the insurance scheme, but if they did so they would receive lower benefits than men. If they did not do so, they would receive benefits as dependants of their husbands.[63]

Not surprisingly, feminists have criticised these arrangements as embodying very limiting assumptions about the role of women, especially the assumption that most married women would be subordinate within the family and not see themselves as having a significant role in the labour market. Beveridge's view is well summarised in the report: 'the attitude of the housewife to gainful employment outside the home is not and should not be the same as that of a single woman. She has other duties.'[64]

Such criticisms of Beveridge were seldom heard in the 1940s. Under the wartime coalition Labour by no means uncritically accepted the Beveridge approach, but little of that criticism focused on his treatment of women.[65] In office, Labour's social welfare policies in this respect closely followed Beveridge. When the National Insurance Bill was debated in the Commons, a small group of women Labour MPs criticised the approach to married women, but the only concession they

[61] PRO PREM8/1396, Equal Pay, Part II, 1950/1. Also Gaitskell in *Hansard* (Commons), vol. 452, cols. 530–7, 20 June 1951.
[62] Brooke, *Labour's War* pp. 161–7, 171–7, 184–6; J. Harris, *William Beveridge: A Biography* (Oxford, 1977), pp. 448–9; Morgan, *Labour in Power*, ch. 4.
[63] Harris, *Beveridge*, pp. 402–7.
[64] *Report on Social Insurance and Allied Services* (Beveridge Report) (1942), para. 114; R. Lowe, *The Welfare State in Britain since 1945* (1992), pp. 33–4.
[65] Brooke, *Labour's War*, pp. 161–7, 171–7.

wrung from the government was that married women could opt out of contributing to the scheme rather than opting in. Griffiths, the minister piloting the legislation through the Commons, stressed that he wanted married women in the scheme, but the terms on which they were in were not a major focus of the debate. The major 'women's issue' in the whole debate was the retirement age of spinsters.[66]

How far this approach to women and social security mattered to women's participation in the labour market may be doubted – proponents of a different treatment of women in National Insurance don't seem to have suggested that the issue mattered in the supply of women's labour, and it does not figure in the reasons women gave in surveys of their views on the labour market.[67]

More directly pertinent to the labour market was the issue of family allowances. Beveridge had strongly advocated them, and Labour had become converted to them, albeit with significant resistance, during the war.[68] In 1945 they came into being, though only for the second and subsequent child and only at a meagre level. The importance of family allowances for women and the labour market was, of course, that they undercut the principle of the 'family wage' as the basis for inequalities of pay between men and women, though given their low level their practical impact must have been slight. This point of principle was urged by Loughlin on Attlee at the meeting about equal pay, when she pointed out that family allowances had been introduced 'because legislatively you accepted the fact that the man's wage was not a family wage, and the wage paid in industry was not sufficient to enable him to do certain things'.[69]

But if ministers accepted the logic of family allowances, they did not, as noted above, concede on equal pay, and the practical impact of the allowances on women's role in the labour market was probably very small, given their low value, however important they were in beginning to undercut the 'male breadwinner' ideology.

The only other change in the social security system which might have directly related to women's participation in the labour market was a small change in the Anomalies Regulations, introduced in 1931, which

---

[66] *Hansard* (Commons), vol. 418, cols. 1733–842, 6 Feb. 1946; cols. 1894–2004, 7 Feb. 1946; vol. 419, cols. 37–106, 11 Feb. 1946 (2nd Reading); vol. 423, cols. 343–476, 22 May 1946; cols. 565–698, 23 May 1946; cols. 1179–231, 29 May 1946 (Committee Stage).

[67] Thomas, *Women*; F. Zweig, *Women's Life and Labour* (Oxford, 1952).

[68] Brooke, *Labour's War*, pp. 149–60.

[69] PRO PREM8/1396, Equal Pay, 'Report of Discussion with TUC Delegates', 6 June 1947. On the 'family wage' issue generally see H. Land, 'The Family Wage', *Feminist Review* 6 (1980), pp. 55–77.

made it much more difficult for married women to receive unemployment benefit than other claimants.[70] These were amended to allow women previously employed in war work to claim benefit, but the practical impact again was very limited – the issue in the 1940s was not women's unemployment, which was usually lower than men's, but their employment.[71]

Overall, the welfare state created in the late 1940s tended to reinforce traditional views of women's role rather than subvert them. Whilst there were opponents of these views, they were small in number and also lacked an alternative approach. To put it another way, the system largely reflected the limited and subordinate role of women in the labour market rather than challenging that role: 'an insurance system based on participation in a labour market, in which women were not equally represented or rewarded, could only disadvantage women in relation to men'.[72]

Domestic employment

In some areas, such as social welfare, the Labour government's policies may be seen as having a great deal in common with proposals under the wartime coalition. In other areas aspirations, at least, had a more radical tone. One such area was what can be described as the (largely unsuccessful) attempt to reform domestic service, still one of the single largest sectors of employment for women in the 1940s.[73] This policy arose from a wartime report (commissioned by Ernest Bevin when he was Minister of Labour) on domestic service. The two women who wrote the report wanted to improve the attractiveness of domestic service. They asserted that 'domestic work, properly organised, is an entirely honourable and self-respecting occupation for any woman and an occupation which fulfils an essential service to the community'. The aim should be to provide help 'to lighten the load of the working-class mother as well as provide facilities for the woman who can afford to pay for regular service'.[74] Whilst rejecting a minimum wage as impracti-

---

[70] J. Tomlinson, 'Women as Anomalies: The Anomalies Regulations Act of 1931 and its Background and Implications', *Public Administration* 62 (1984), pp. 423–37.

[71] PRO LAB8/1236, WCC, 'Anomalies Regulations Act', 26 May 1945; *Ministry of Labour Gazette* 66 (March 1958), p. 97.

[72] Lowe, *Welfare State*, p. 134.

[73] It is notable that this approach to the area of domestic work was quite at odds with policies pursued by other social democratic governments. For example, in Sweden the focus was much more on 'socialising housework' through collective provision (I owe this point to my colleague Deborah Mabbett). This approach hardly surfaced in Britain.

[74] *Report on Post-War Organisation of Private Domestic Employment* (by Violet Markham and Florence Hancock), paras. 4, 15.

cable, the report advocated the establishment of a National Institute of Houseworkers to set minimum standards and conditions of work, provide training and to act as employment agencies for domestic workers. These recommendations were accepted and the NIH was set up in 1946.[75]

The case for such a body was accepted by Labour on two grounds:

In the first place because it provides women with an avenue of employment on a very large scale; in the second because the supply on an organised basis of qualified domestic workers to households where there are sick, aged or infirm persons, or to overworked mothers, is essential to the wellbeing of those sections of the community which our social services are designed to help.[76]

However, this endeavour was criticised from two points of view. The communist *Daily Worker* asserted that it was a case of 'taxpayers paying to train maids'.[77] This accusation is borne out by the evidence, despite the efforts of the NIH to make domestic service available to a wider range of clients. Whilst the Institute did 'take into direct employment . . . a staff of diploma holders who will be available on an hourly basis and at a charge calculated to cover the full cost, to housewives who are unable to afford the expense of full-time domestic help', the scale of this, partly because of financial constraints, was always very small.[78]

The NIH also came under criticism from the Public Accounts Committee for its use of public money 'to train housewives'. Its activities were reined back, under tight Treasury control.[79]

The NIH may be seen as a peculiarly 1940s-style body, with its desire to regulate and improve the conditions of work, whilst also trying to improve social welfare by extending domestic support down the social scale. In the event it did little to stem the tide of women away from domestic service – the numbers fell by 750,000 (70 per cent) between the census of 1931 (1.1 million) and that of 1951 (350,000). Whatever the government's intentions, women were voting with their feet against this type of employment.

Pro-natalism

The quotation from Pugh on page 189 suggested the importance to the Attlee government of the desire to increase the population. No one can

[75] *Ministry of Labour Gazette* 59 (Oct. 1951), p. 387.
[76] PRO LAB8/1226, NIH, 'Post-War Organisation of Private Domestic Employment' (no date, but 1945).
[77] *Daily Worker*, 13 Aug. 1949.
[78] NIH, *Annual Report*, 1949.
[79] PRO LAB8/1226, NIH, 'Criticism in Report of P.A.C.', 1949.

doubt this was indeed a major concern of the period, evidenced not only by the establishment of the Royal Commission on Population, but the almost obligatory reference to population issues in most major areas of public debate in the period. Riley has provided detailed accounts of the pro-natalist rhetoric of the period.[80]

Pro-natalism can, however, take many forms, and Riley emphasises that the 'official' version of the 1940s quite explicitly did *not* argue that encouraging a rise in the birth-rate should involve women in withdrawing from paid employment. The Royal Commission strongly repudiated attempts to 'bring women back into the home. Such a policy not only runs against the democratic conception of individual freedom, but in Great Britain it would be a rebuking of the tide.' The aim should be to 'devise adjustments that would render it easier for women to combine motherhood and the care of a home with outside activities'.[81] This was a common position under the Attlee government, a kind of 'social democratic pro-natalism' which gained widespread support.[82] The view that pro-natalism led to policies inhibiting women from working is oversimplified, at least for the 1940s.

Pro-natalism does not seem to have played a significant role in any of the policies which might be deemed to have limited the success of Labour's efforts to get women into employment – such as the decline of day nurseries, or the failure to implement equal pay. Family allowances might be portrayed as pro-natalist, but they also undercut 'male breadwinner' ideas against equal pay. In any event the main reasons for their introduction were concerns about wage inflation under conditions of full employment and maintaining incentives among the low paid with large families,[83] not the birth-rate, and at the level paid in the 1940s they could hardly have been a major incentive for childbirth.

Rather, the picture of the 1940s is generally one of a government rhetorically committed to a 'progressive pro-natalism', aimed at encouraging women to combine work with care of children. This has rightly been portrayed as a serious attempt to 'reconstruct the family'.[84] Government failure was not in giving pro-natalism priority over women's conditions of work, but in not providing adequate resources to make such a combination an attractive option for large numbers of women.[85]

---

[80] Riley, *War in the Nursery*, ch. 6; 'Free Mothers', pp. 89–109.
[81] *Report of R.C. on Population*, para. 429.
[82] Riley, *War in the Nursery*, pp. 167–75.
[83] J. MacNicol, *The Movement for Family Allowances 1918–45: A Study in Social Policy Development* (1980), Conclusion.
[84] Lewis, *Women in Britain*, pp. 16–26.
[85] Riley, *War in the Nursery*, p. 188.

Feminism and labour

Feminism does not appear to have been a powerful political force in the late 1940s, despite some wartime revival.[86] Labour women on the whole explicitly distanced themselves from such a classification. For example, when all twenty-one of the newly elected women Labour MPs contributed to an issue of *Labour Woman* in September 1945 several went out of their way to stress they were elected as 'socialists not women'. Only Jennie Lee, with her talk of the 'new woman', suggested much sympathy with views challenging the traditional roles of women.[87] When Anne Loughlin addressed cabinet ministers on the issue of equal pay she prefaced her remarks with 'no one could accuse me of being a feminist'.[88]

Of course, the term 'feminism' covers many varieties of opinion, and often the point of Labour women distancing themselves from the term was a concern to prevent themselves from being closely associated with the interests of single working women, especially middle-class and professional women. Progressive women in the Labour Party in the 1940s therefore tended to focus their attention on improving conditions for working-class women within the home and in their roles as mothers.[89] Hence their approach tended to encourage the prevalence of 'progressive pro-natalism', as noted above.

Feminism of a kind prevalent from the 1970s onwards, in the sense of a politics of pressing for the rights of women as workers, and seeing that role as primary, was not something that significantly constrained the Labour government's policies. Contemporary feminism generally had other concerns, and there is little evidence to suggest that the mass of women dissented from this approach. Government policies, as suggested above, were largely determined by economic and financial priorities. These priorities dictated policies aimed at maximising women's employment but minimising the costs of it. Policies such as abolishing the marriage bar in the civil service and teaching, or increasing the married women's tax allowance (in 1948), cost little or nothing. Policies which would have been expensive – equal pay, a big expansion of day nurseries – were resisted.

---

[86] Smith, 'Problem', pp. 654–5; Pugh, *Women*, ch. 10. However, research on this complex topic is in its infancy, and generalisations need considerable qualification.

[87] *Labour Woman* 33 (Sept. 1945). For Labour women's views see also Standing Joint Committee of Working Women's Organisations, 'Working Women Discuss Population, Equal Pay and Domestic Work', 1946.

[88] PRO LAB8/1396, Equal Pay, 'Report Discussions with TUC Delegation', 6 June 1947.

[89] Riley, *War in the Nursery*, p. 182.

How much impact did Labour's policies have? It is difficult to be definite about this, but the impression certainly is that the impact was relatively slight. For example, the attempt to expand part-time work seems to have been resisted quite strongly by many employers. PEP suggested that 'Employers seem, on the whole, inclined to employ part-time workers only if they are desperately short of labour, and sometimes not even then'.[90] Their view that the demand for part-time work amongst women far exceeded the supply of such work is borne out by the Ministry of Labour material.[91]

The attempt to attract women to jobs in cotton, woollens and pottery also achieved only limited success. In cotton, for example, as has often been noted, the numbers recruited fell significantly short of early hopes.[92] The wider aim of shifting women out of metal, engineering, chemicals distribution, catering, entertainment and sport remained little more than a pious hope, especially given the rejection of any form of direction of women workers.[93] As table 9.2 suggests, the pattern of women's employment was tending in broadly the opposite direction.

Undoubtedly the dominant factors in the changes in the volume and character of women's employment in this period were probably not public policy, but shifting patterns of demand and supply of women's labour. On the demand side women gained from the fact that both areas where they had long had a role (e.g. clerical work, teaching, nursing) expanded fast in the post-war years, as did areas where they had gained at least a toe-hold in the war (e.g. engineering, transport). On the supply side, the constraints on working for married women remained the heavy 'double burden' involved, little ameliorated in the late 1940s, and not to be significantly lightened until the rapid growth of part-time work in the years after 1951. Whilst a growing number of older married women were working in this period, and this heralded a major shift in women's lives, people like Dalton unsurprisingly felt 'the flow of women back to industry is extraordinarily slow in relation to the national requirements'.[94]

However, to conclude that 'manpower' policy was totally ineffective against the pressure of the labour market is too simplistic. For example,

---

[90] PEP, 'Employment', p. 50.
[91] PRO LAB8/1283, 'Employment Policy: Part-Time Employment', 1948–50.
[92] Crofts, *Coercion*, pp. 119–21, 132–4; Carruthers, 'Manning the Factories', p. 252; Singleton, *Lancashire*, ch. 3.
[93] PRO PREM8/646, Memo to PM on Employment of Women, 29 Jan. 1947. Direction of women was proposed by Cripps, but rejected by the Cabinet (see PRO CAB128/9, 30 Jan. 1947).
[94] PRO LAB8/1396, Equal Pay, 'Report of Discussions with TUC Delegation', 6 June 1947.

to return to the crucial example of cotton, whilst it is often noted that the rise in the labour force fell far short of restoring the pre-war levels of employment, attempts to recruit workers, especially women, for this industry may be seen as showing considerable success, measured by less extreme standards.

The Working Party Report of 1946 thought 250,000 a *maximum* for the likely workforce of the industry in the foreseeable future, and thought a decline to around 200,000 'probable . . . over the next few years'. But in fact the labour force grew quickly in the post-war period to a peak of 296,000 in 1952, the biggest increase being amongst women workers[95] (and therefore providing no evidence that the replacement of women by men, as suggested by the Ministry of Labour, was needed to increase the industry's workforce).

Overall, whilst there were, then, strong underlying forces on both demand and supply side limiting women's participation, where the effort of encouragement – by improved amenities as well as propaganda – was large enough, some impact could be made. However, that effect was extremely contingent on a sense of immediate crisis, and once that passed the underlying forces reasserted themselves.

That immediate economic crisis, rather than any strong pressure to change women's role, largely motivated Labour's policies in the Attlee period. The application of stringent financial and economic tests to any policy to encourage the expansion of women's employment role was not seriously resisted by any major faction in the Labour movement. In relation to women, Labour's overall stance was not as regressive as often suggested (for example, in relation to nurseries), but equally it would be quite inappropriate to see Labour guided strongly by 'feminist' motives in encouraging women's employment. In this, as in so many policy areas, the needs of production dominated all other considerations.[96]

[95] Working Party, *Cotton*, p. 61; Duprée, 'Cotton Industry', p. 157. This total includes 15,000 European voluntary workers.
[96] Tiratsoo and Tomlinson, *Industrial Efficiency*, ch. 8

10   Towards a Keynesian policy?

The fiscal policy of the Attlee government has often been seen as having significance well beyond the immediate conduct of economic policy. On the one hand, there has been much dispute about how far 'Keynesianism' was evident in that policy, and whether the late 1940s can be seen as crucial in the (alleged) Keynesian revolution in economic policy in Britain. On the other hand, the character of fiscal policy in this period has been seen as a key to Labour's approach to policy-making. In particular, the extent to which fiscal policy displaced controls and 'planning' in Labour's policy repertoire has often been seen as indicative of the strength or weakness of its socialist commitment.

On the first issue, particular attention has focused on the second budget of 1947. Cairncross called this budget 'a turning point in postwar fiscal policy', whilst Booth saw it as 'a major milestone, when the Treasury finally turned in peacetime and out of choice to Keynesian analysis to help control inflation'.[1] In contrast to this view, Rollings has brought out the distinction between the views of Treasury officials and the actual conduct of policy, and suggested that from either perspective the extent of Keynesianism in the 1947 budget can easily be exaggerated.[2] Also critical of the view of 1947 as a key turning point is Howson who nevertheless acknowledges the extent of the Keynesian advice being pressed upon the Labour government from its earliest days.[3]

Alongside this debate has been a closely argued but passionate dispute about how far the Attlee government ran down controls in favour of the use of the budget to control the economy, and in doing so flagged its movement away from traditional socialist approaches to the economy. Howell, for example, takes such a change in policy as self-evident, and

---

[1] Cairncross, *Years of Recovery*, pp. 419–20; A. Booth, 'The "Keynesian Revolution" in Economic Policy-Making', *Economic History Review* 36 (1983), p. 123. But see also Booth, *Economic Policy*, chs. 9–11.

[2] N. Rollings, 'British Budgetary Policy 1945–54: A "Keynesian Revolution?" ' *Economic History Review* 41 (1988), pp. 283–98.

[3] Howson, *Monetary Policy*, pp. 332–4.

suggests that this Keynesian approach from the November 1947 budget 'marked in practice an abandonment of any claim to be constructing a new economic order'.[4] By contrast, Cairncross, who also regards this change in policy as clear-cut, considers it as a move to be applauded.[5]

This dispute is plainly a very broad one between competing political philosophies. However, it is a dispute usually grounded on very little evidence about the extent to which, in fact, Labour moved from reliance on controls and planning to reliance on fiscal forms of management. On this empirical point recent work has questioned the idea of a straightforward rise of fiscal policy at the expense of controls.[6]

Given this background of controversy, this chapter surveys fiscal policy in the Attlee years. It attempts to assess the nature and development of that policy in this period and to throw light both on the impact of Keynesianism and the extent to which fiscal policy displaced planning and controls in Labour's policy agenda. In doing so it recognises two points which to some extent have bedevilled the literature so far: first, that Keynesianism cannot sensibly be reduced solely to fiscal policy, but involves other policy instruments as well; second, that the theoretical allegiance of some policy advisers is not necessarily a good guide to the actual determinants of the conduct of policy.

The legacy of war

Two important legacies for post-war fiscal policy were bequeathed by the wartime coalition. First, the *combined* use of controls and fiscal policy to contain inflation: the 1941 budget, 'the first Keynesian budget',[7] had famously embodied the idea of using budgetary policy together with national income forecasting to regulate aggregate demand, the primary purpose being to contain inflationary pressure. But fiscal policy had never been expected to take the full weight of such pressure, and price controls, subsidies and rationing had been widely used as accompaniments to budgetary policy, though with additional egalitarian aims of their own.

Alongside this dual regime of controls and fiscal policy was a strong prejudice against another policy instrument – monetary policy. Britain, of course, had had a low interest rate, 'cheap money' policy in the 1930s, and this had been continued in wartime largely to minimise the cost of

[4] D. Howell, *British Social Democracy* (1976), pp. 158–60.
[5] Cairncross, *Years of Recovery*, ch. 15.
[6] Rollings, 'Reichstag Method of Governing?'.
[7] Sayers, *British Financial Policy*, p. 69.

servicing the debt which was an unavoidable consequence of the war. Near the end of the war the issue of post-war monetary policy had been addressed by the National Debt enquiry. Dominated by Keynes, this enquiry had come out strongly in favour of maintaining low interest rates as a way of containing the costs of the national debt. It was also expected that physical controls over the economy would continue into the post-war period, so that the traditional role of monetary policy in respect of the level of investment would be irrelevant.[8]

The dismissive attitude to monetary policy fitted in with most Labour thinking. Many in the Labour ranks were suspicious of both bankers themselves and their use of monetary policy, a view especially reflecting the hostility evoked by the Bank of England's role in defending the pound in the late 1920s and in the debacle of 1931. In addition, Dalton, a key figure in Labour's economic policy debates from the 1930s onwards, and the Chancellor of the Exchequer in 1945–7, had long expressed worries about the distributive consequences of public borrowing, and low interest rates were one obvious way of trying to reduce that burden.[9] As Howson points out, given the other instruments of economic policy available to him, Dalton tended to regard monetary policy and low interest rates as primarily instruments of income redistribution, rather than tools in the pursuit of macroeconomic objectives.[10]

This is an interesting example of how a particular policy approach can have quite variable intellectual and political underlying assumptions. Dalton's 'socialist' monetary policy of cheap money (though not his attempt at *cheaper* money) had the support of Keynes and other Keynesians, not so much for distributional reasons as from a belief that in this way the potential disincentive effects of high taxes to pay interest on the national debt would be minimised, and also that, in current circumstances especially, interest rates were not an effective way of managing the economy. In this slightly curious sense Dalton was perhaps more of a 'Keynesian' in monetary policy than he was in fiscal policy.[11]

Overall, the legacy of the war on the place of budgetary policy was its already established use as an anti-inflationary weapon, though in combination with a variety of other policy instruments. On the other hand, and for a range of reasons, low interest rates and an inactive mon-

---

[8] Howson, *Monetary Policy*, pp. 60–1; Dow, *Management*, p. 21.
[9] H. Dalton, *Principles of Public Finance* (1923), ch. 22. This theme was enlarged upon, and used to justify the policies of 1945–7, in the 1954 edition of this book, chs. 27 and 28.
[10] Howson, *Monetary Policy*, pp. 327–8.
[11] Ibid., pp. 149, 326–7.

etary policy were widely regarded as desirable. One implication, though not one drawn by Keynes, was that fiscal policy would therefore have to be tight to contain inflation.[12]

Politically, Labour seemed to have embraced the Keynesian creed in the key wartime policy statement *Full Employment and Financial Policy*. This asserted that 'the central point in our financial policy for the maintenance of full employment is the maintenance of the total purchasing power of the community'. If deflation threatens after the initial post-war boom, 'we need not aim at balancing the Budget year by year . . . The time for a Budget surplus is a year of really good trade; if trade is bad or even showing signs of turning bad, then is the time for a Budget deficit, for the State to spend beyond its income and borrow the difference.'[13]

However, it should be noted that this was a document produced by Labour's economists, and is notably more Keynesian in tone than the more widely debated election manifesto, *Let Us Face the Future*, of 1945. This document went little beyond generalities about the need for 'keeping up the national purchasing power and controlling changes in the national expenditure through government action'. It was notably silent on the role of the budget.[14]

The policy mix 1945–7

The immediate budgetary inheritance of the Labour government was a budget deficit running at over £2 billion. This would 'naturally' change as government spending on the war effort was reduced. A central question for Labour's first budget of October 1945 was to weigh the tax cuts made possible by this fall in expenditure against the overall pressure of demand which would be exacerbated by such cuts. Tax cuts, mainly in income tax, were probably inescapable, both as an incentive to production and as a recognition that some relief from the burdens of war must be given. The result was tax cuts of around £400m. and the reduction of the deficit as traditionally defined to around £700m.[15]

The dominant immediate concern of the 1945 budget was the minimisation of inflation. This was emphasised by the Chancellor in his budget speech and by his advisers. Meade, head of the Economic Section, especially claimed that too rapid a reduction in taxation would throw

[12] Booth, *Economic Policy*, p. 155.
[13] Labour Party, *Full Employment*, pp. 3, 4.
[14] On *Full Employment and Financial Policy* see Brooke, *Labour's War*, pp. 258–67.
[15] Cairncross, *Years of Recovery*, p. 421.

an unsustainable burden for preventing inflation on to physical controls. But for Dalton, presenting his budget to the Cabinet, the argument was rather different – for him the inflation pressure urged the need to restrain excess demand but to maintain price controls, alongside subsidies to the cost of living and encouragement of savings.[16] This last element played a strikingly large part in budgetary rhetoric in 1945 and right through the Attlee government. In his Commons statement Dalton argued that 'by far the best defence against inflation in present conditions is large and continuous saving by all sections of our people . . . it remains an imperative duty on each of us, whatever the size of our income, whatever our occupation, to save all that we can and lend it to the Government'.[17] However, such exhortation was largely ineffective, as people sought to restock after the wartime depletion of their consumption goods, so in the Attlee period budgetary policy had to be framed on the assumption that private, especially household, saving would be very low indeed.

Dalton's commitment to Keynesian policies has been much disputed. The specific reasons for his support of Keynesian cheap money have already been noted. His own writings also reflect something of the difficulties of making a judgement about his approach to budgetary policy. The 1954 edition of his textbook on public finance had an additional chapter devoted to 'new ideas' in budgetary policy. Following Keynes, he argued: 'we may now free ourselves from the old and narrow conception of balancing the budget, no matter over what period, and more towards the new and wider conception of the budget balancing the whole economy'.[18]

Yet in 1945 the extent to which Dalton had freed himself from these 'old and narrow' conceptions was far from clear. The vision of fiscal policy he proposed in that year was akin to that in the 1944 White Paper on Employment Policy, one of balancing the budget over the trade cycle. It meant moving to surpluses once the immediate transition was over, and building them up against the expected future decline in demand, when deficits would be needed. This line was reiterated in 1946.[19] It was, of course, not the same as 'functional finance', in which the budgetary position would simply reflect the perceived need to restrain or stimulate aggregate demand.[20]

---

[16] PRO T171/371, Meade to Brittan, 24 Sept. 1945; Cabinet Summary of Budget 22 Oct. 1945.
[17] *Hansard* (Commons), vol. 414, 23 Oct. 1945.
[18] *Principles*, 4th edn, p. 221.
[19] *Hansard* (Commons), vol. 414, col. 1886, 23 Oct. 1945; cols. 1817–19, 9 Apr. 1946.
[20] The term 'functional finance' comes from A. Lerner, *The Economics of Control* (1945).

The ambiguity of Dalton's position is reflected in the parliamentary response. Whilst John Anderson for the Tories endorsed the 'balance over the cycle' approach, some of his fellow Conservatives saw Dalton as still preoccupied 'with the more old-fashioned view of examining the matter entirely from the narrow outlook of Treasury receipts and expenditure'.[21]

Such a confused picture partly resulted from two features of the budget presentation. First, the budget figures themselves were presented wholly in the traditional form, with the surplus or deficit being calculated 'above the line'. This definition reflected parliamentary procedure, 'above the line' basically meaning expenditure and revenue not requiring specific legislation to finance Exchequer borrowing. Hence it bore little relation to national income notions of the budget, and could not readily be integrated with any overall judgement on the pressure of demand in the economy. This latter point relates to the second feature of the presentation of the second 1945 budget – the absence with this budget and its successor of a published *Economic Survey* which would place the budget in the broad context of the economy's development. Perhaps in this period of rapid transition and demobilisation it was not surprising that calculations of the 'inflationary gap' were regarded as highly problematic, but the absence of published attempts at such calculations raised question marks about how exactly budgetary policy was being integrated into management of the economy as a whole.[22]

Under Dalton budgetary policy was not clearly integrated with other parts of the economic policy-making apparatus. As discussed in chapter 8, the government in 1945 was strongly committed to the idea of 'manpower planning', and this approach is reflected in the early *Economic Surveys*, where Keynesian analysis of the inflationary gap was accompanied by tables outlining the economic problem in terms of manpower and its allocation.[23]

Whatever Dalton's precise views, this enthusiasm for 'manpower planning' certainly reflected a lack of general acceptance and enthusiasm for Keynesianism and the role of budgetary policy in the Cabinet and wider Labour movement. This lukewarm attitude was reflected, down to 1947, in the role of Herbert Morrison as the co-ordinator of economic policy, leaving the Chancellor of the Exchequer, nominally and to a significant degree in practice as simply one amongst several economic ministers, rather than having the dominant role usual before 1939 and revived from 1947.

---

[21] *Hansard* (Commons), vol. 414, cols. 2017, 2045, 24 Oct. 1945.
[22] Cairncross, *Years of Recovery*, pp. 80–6, 386–92, 410–18.
[23] Booth, *Economic Policy*, p. 160.

The problems of integration of fiscal with other facets of policy was illustrated by the failure to get the early *Economic Surveys* on a financial year as opposed to a calendar year basis. Thus the budget was presented separately from the economic 'Plan' analysed in the *Surveys*, and the budget statements of late 1945 and early 1946 made no attempt to bring the two together.[24]

Until at least early 1947 it is clear that budgetary policy cannot be seen as unambiguously Keynesian. Dalton was concerned to contain inflation, even though he regarded unemployment as the more important threat in the medium term. He regarded financial controls as playing only a minor role in containing that inflation, with most of the weight falling upon physical controls.[25] In this he was probably at one with most Labour opinion and most official opinion – with the exception of the Economic Section, whose position is returned to below.

Dalton's non-Keynesianism can nevertheless be exaggerated.[26] Certainly his first three budgets were not presented in terms of the overall pressures of demand in the economy. Rather, he focused on a rapid return to budgetary balance, explicitly trying to restore that balance faster than had been achieved after the First World War.[27] Tax cuts were fitted in both as a way of cutting the burden on the low-paid and of encouraging an increase in output, which for Dalton and many on the Labour side was the prime way of dealing with 'excess demand'. But insofar as Dalton and Labour had taken on board Keynesian fiscal policy arguments it was in the context of preventing unemployment, and this was plainly not the problem in 1945–7. Development Area policy appeared the relevant instrument for unemployment in this period, not an increase in demand. In short, prior to the crises of 1947 Keynesianism appeared somewhat irrelevant to the issues at hand.[28]

This was not, however, how it was seen in the Economic Section, the main source of professional economic advice to the government. In a very strong sense the Economic Section owed its existence to wartime Keynesianism, and was the main conduit for that ideology into Whitehall.[29] James Meade, who was head of the section from 1945 to 1947, was probably the most important Keynesian economist after Keynes, and very consciously saw his mission in these years to proselytise his

[24] Cairncross, *Years of Recovery*, p. 322; Meade, *Cabinet Office Diary*, pp. 240–1.
[25] Howson, *Monetary Policy*, p. 150.
[26] e.g. Pimlott, *Dalton*, pp. 486–94.
[27] PRO T171/371, Budget Papers Autumn 1945, vol. 1; *Hansard* (Commons), vol. 421, cols. 1917–1819, 9 April 1946.
[28] Rollings, 'Budgetary Policy', p. 285. On Development Area policy see chapter 8.
[29] Cairncross and Watts, *Economic Section*; I. M. D. Little, 'The Economist in Whitehall', *Lloyds Bank Review* 44 (1957), p. 35.

version of 'liberal-socialism' against the alleged Gosplanners active in the Labour Party.[30] Both the content and tone of Meade's position is well summarised by his diary entry for 23 February 1946, in which he refers to 'the great campaign which we must open sooner or later to persuade Whitehall that monetary policy (rate of interest), fiscal policy (rates of taxation and subsidy) and wages policy (rates of rewards to factors) must be the liberal socialist instruments for economic planning'.[31] In the summer of 1946 he saw the opportunity to clarify these views in writing a major paper on the 'Control of Inflation'.[32]

This paper, after demonstrating the build-up of inflationary pressure from the build-up of liquidity in the war, coupled to the major supply constraints, focused its argument on why 'in present conditions there is much to be said for a shift in emphasis in our anti-inflationary policy away from too great a reliance on such direct controls as price control, rationing etc., and rather more on to a policy designed to restore the essential balance between available supplies and spendable funds'.

Direct controls were attacked as generating black markets, harming incentives to produce, rigidifying *relative* prices, and leading to not only administrative but political costs arising from the 'petty annoyance of innumerable and extensive particular controls over every form of economic activity'. This position logically led to an emphasis on achieving a quick movement to a fiscal surplus, coupled to preparation for fiscal deficits if and when excess demand was succeeded by excess supply.

One particularly contentious part of Meade's proposals was the call to reduce demand by big cuts in food subsidies. These subsidies had originally been brought in during the war to control the cost of living and so contain wage inflation. Meade argued that inflation largely reflected the impact of excess demand on the labour market rather than changes in the cost of living. He saw subsidies not only as inflationary, but also as distorting, by exaggerating excess demand for the subsidised products and not allowing relative prices to perform their allocatory role. He coupled proposals for a big cut in these subsidies with the idea of using a proportion of the revenue saved to finance an increase in social security benefits, including family allowances.

This emphasis on cutting subsidies became symbolic of the Keynesian approach to policy in this period. Keynes himself, in his last two written submissions to the Budget Committee, urged cuts in subsidies even if

---

[30] The existence of these Gosplanners has been discussed in chapter 6.
[31] Meade, *Cabinet Office Diary*, p. 222.
[32] Ibid., entry for 7 June 1946, p. 272. This paper is in PRO T171/389, Budget Papers April 1947, vol. I.

this meant a rise in the cost of living. Subsidies, he argued shortly before his death in April 1946, were 'in danger of becoming the biggest item in the whole Budget and seriously overwhelming efforts towards equilibrium'.[33] In consequence, 'During 1947 the cost of living should be allowed to rise gradually to 150, first of all by withdrawing as many individual subsidies as possible and concentrating on a few articles and then by reducing it on the remaining articles'.[34]

Meade expressed his alliance with Keynes on the subsidies issue, and its symbolic significance as a Keynesian policy proposal can be readily understood.[35] It combined using the budget as the primary economic regulator with a marked hostility to *micro*economic policy measures, which could be seen to distort the market and undermine incentives.

On the other hand, such a proposal was bound to raise hostility within Labour. Subsidies, primarily on food, were seen as a direct means of aiding the lower paid and poor. They were also seen as integral to the attempt to contain wage inflation.[36]

The battle over subsidies was to continue throughout the life of the Labour government. But at least until the crises of the summer of 1947, Dalton and the government gave little ground to the Keynesian pressure. Despite support from the Treasury, the most that could be extracted from Dalton was not the large cuts in subsidies proposed by Meade and Keynes, but a ceiling of £392m. agreed early in 1947.[37]

If the Keynesians could see relatively little progress in cuts in subsidies before the crises of 1947, what of the role of controls which they so strongly wished to see reduced in scope? At the end of the war both Labour and the other parties had seen a continuing role for controls in the immediate post-war period of demobilisation. This view seems to have been all but universally accepted; there seems to have been no one who advocated the kind of speedy abolition of controls practised after the First World War.[38] But beyond that immediate period there was much less agreement. Very soon the Conservatives made the controls central to their attack on the 'socialist meddling and bureaucracy' of the government. Whilst the rhetoric was different, advisers like Meade

[33] PRO T171/386, J. M. Keynes to Chancellor of the Exchequer, 1 April 1946.
[34] PRO T171/389 vol. 1, Lord Keynes, 'Post Budget Reflections' (n.d., but April 1946). Policy at the time was to hold the official Cost of Living Index at 31 per cent above its pre-war level.
[35] Meade, *Cabinet Office Diary*, p. 259.
[36] e.g. PRO T171/391, D. Jay to Dalton, 10 Oct. 1947.
[37] Rollings, 'Budgetary Policy', pp. 287–8.
[38] The speed of that previous abolition was eloquently denounced by Tawney in 'The Abolition of Economic Controls'.

urged a reduction of controls, to be replaced as far as possible by fiscal policy.[39]

Labour's position on controls underwent no sharp change in their period in office. The message of *Let Us Face the Future* was that controls would be used as necessary, particularly in ensuring full employment. But post-war employment was not, of course, the problem; the issue was how far controls could be used for 'planning', in the sense of being used to allocate resources. In the labour market, as discussed in chapter 8, controls were almost immediately removed, with a few minor exceptions. The problem then was that most of the controls were designed to deal with shortages – with situations where demand exceeded supply, including the case of foreign exchange. This gave many of the controls an inherently short-term character – their logic was undermined as and when supply expanded. (Meade, of course, wanted to speed this process of undermining by checking the strength of demand by fiscal means.)

Controls also required the active co-operation of companies if they were to be effective. Many of the controls had been administered by people closely connected with the industries concerned. This was therefore an area of policy where consent was both vital and politically problematic, given the high level of politicisation of many employers and their organisations.[40]

From this context emerged a process of decontrol almost from the government's accession to office. As early as December 1945 the Lord President's Committee set up an official committee 'to carry out urgently a review of the possibilities of reducing the number, diminishing the irksomeness and streamlining the operation of existing economic controls'.[41] The result of this initiative, which reflects Labour's early political sensitiveness on the issue, led to some unqualified but probably small reductions in controls. But it also highlighted the uncertainty of policy in this area. Whilst some specific controls could readily be abolished as shortages receded, the whole issue could not be resolved until ministers made up their mind as to the long-term role of controls in allocating resources. Apart, again, from labour controls, it is difficult to find evidence of ministers or senior policy advisers (outside the Economic Section) mapping out these long-term views of controls. Some controls, for example machinery licensing, were given up very quickly but this seems to have been an entirely negative decision, made on administrative grounds, rather than based on a clear assessment of the

[39] e.g. *Cabinet Office Diary*, p. 294, 29 April 1946.
[40] Mercer, 'The Labour Governments of 1945–51 and Private Industry' in Tiratsoo, *The Attlee Years*, esp. pp. 77–8.
[41] PRO CAB132/58, Official Committee on Controls, 10 Dec. 1945.

long-run place of controls. Certainly in the investment field, a continuing commitment to controls was not accompanied by a clear policy line on how it was to be achieved.[42]

Indeed, in the crucial case of investment it would be right to say that the control system was extremely weak. The machinery for control via finance was never established, but in any event most companies were constrained far more by physical shortages, including labour, than finance in this period.[43] Down to 1947 far more investment was licensed than there were materials to complete, so that too many projects were allowed to start than was justifiable by the resource position. Control over resource allocation was therefore very poor in this period – the antithesis of planning.[44]

This particular point about investment leads on to a general point about the relation between controls and fiscal policy, which will be returned to in the next section. Excess demand in the late 1940s gave a rationale for controls, as it had done in wartime. But it also provided a strong incentive for firms and others to avoid the controls – there was a ready market for the controlled commodity. In that sense regulating the economy by fiscal control of aggregate demand and by physical controls are not necessarily alternatives, but may be complements. Effective regulation of aggregate demand may be a precondition for effective controls of resource allocation.

1947

The year 1947, as is well known, was one of crises for the Attlee government, dominated by the coal crisis at the beginning of the year, and the convertibility crisis in the summer. Partly as a consequence of these crises, both the terms of debate and the machinery of economic policy were subject to major pressures during this year. There were two budgets (the second presented by Dalton) and it is that one which is commonly seen as marking a decisive shift in the overall thrust of economic policy on to a Keynesian basis. This section will offer an assessment of such a view of policy development in that year.

The first budget of 1947 aimed at a substantial budget surplus in the context of particular emphasis on the dangers of inflation. In the early preparation of this budget, the Budget Committee had asked Meade for the paper on the 'Control of Inflation' previously discussed. This was followed up by a further Budget Committee paper on 'The Economic

[42] PRO CAB134/63, 'Report of Committee on Control of Investment', 23 July 1949.
[43] As discussed at length in chapter 7.
[44] Cairncross, *Years of Recovery*, pp. 448–52.

Survey for 1947 and the Budget for 1947/8' which reiterated many of the same points about the desirability of controlling inflation primarily by fiscal means.[45] These papers, in so far as they focused on fighting inflation and cutting subsidies seem to have found considerable support in the Treasury, though opposition was strong to Meade's proposals to present the budget accounts in a national income framework most appropriate to his Keynesian approach.[46] Dalton, on the other hand, seems to have been increasingly won over by the anti-inflationary stance of his advisers, whilst remaining resistant to their views on focusing expenditure cuts on subsidies.[47]

This April budget was followed by another in November 1947. The possibility of a supplementary budget was first suggested by Dalton in August 1947, though the prospect of the government coming back to the Commons with 'stronger and more drastic measures' had been suggested in the April budget speech.[48]

This proposal came right in the middle of the convertibility crisis, only six days before convertibility was suspended. According to Dalton, the budget's 'sole purpose, if it were decided to have one, would be to lessen inflationary pressure by "mopping up" some purchasing power, and at the same time to illustrate the Government's intention that there shall be "equality of sacrifice" as between different sectors of the community'.[49]

Bridges put a slightly different gloss on the proposal: 'The purpose is, not the old-fashioned one of extra taxation to balance the Budget, but a reduction of the inflationary pressure which threatens to prevent the emergency measures from achieving their objective . . . a Budget so presented would maintain confidence in the value of the pound, not only in this country but also abroad, and particularly in America.'[50]

Both the timing and content of the proposal for another budget support Cairncross' argument that the intention was 'a public acknowledgement of danger', in a way parallel to the previous use of the Bank Rate, now ruled out by the commitment to cheap money.[51] Danger was very apparent at that time, not only in the run on the pound, but also in the concurrent discussions in the American Congress on Marshall Aid,

[45] PRO T171/389, J. Meade, 'The Economic Survey for 1947 and the Budget for 1947/8' (n.d., but Nov. 1947).
[46] Ibid., note by B. Trend, 27 July 1946; B. Gilbert to E. Bridges, 14 March 1947.
[47] Howson, *Monetary Policy*, pp. 163–5.
[48] PRO T171/392, Dalton to Bridges, 11 Aug. 1947; *Hansard* (Commons), vol. 436, col. 90, 15 April 1947.
[49] PRO T171/392, Dalton to Bridges.
[50] PRO T171/391, E. Bridges, 'Autumn Budget', 23 Sept. 1947.
[51] Cairncross, *Years of Recovery*, p. 424.

which at that time were by no means clearly going to favour the granting of aid to Britain.

This was an opportunity not to be lost by the advocates of a tough budgetary stance. In September Robert Hall, James Meade's less articulate but equally Keynesian successor as head of the Economic Section, was circulating to the Budget Committee a paper on 'The Inflationary Pressure' which reiterated many of Meade's previous points on the dangers of inflation.[52]

Whilst Dalton played a key role in initiating the autumn budget, he remained distinctly lukewarm about the idea urged by his advisers, and summarised by Bridges, that cutting the cost-of-living subsidies was 'the pivot of the whole Autumn Budget, and indeed its one absolutely essential feature'.[53] On his copy of this memorandum Dalton scrawled: 'I don't accept a lot of this.' This comment has been interpreted as a sign of Dalton's resistance to Keynesianism,[54] but the comment seems to have been aimed not at the general framework of the approach suggested by Bridges but at its focus on subsidies as the key component. Dalton questioned this idea, offering the alternative option of cuts in defence spending, both for equity reasons, and because the movement of manpower from the armed forces to a civilian role would increase supply in the economy, unlike cuts in transfer payments such as the cost-of-living subsidies. He also pointed out the political difficulties of combining cuts in subsidies with a wages step.[55]

Dalton came under sustained pressure on this issue. His official advisers seem to have been unanimous in wanting subsidy cuts to be the centrepiece of the budget. Bridges, for example, argued that unless the budget dealt 'openly and resolutely' with the subsidies it would have a 'serious effect on national credit, both internal and external'.[56]

However, Dalton refused to be bounced into taking this line. As Rollings notes: 'Given Dalton's physical and mental exhaustion by this time and the degree of pressure put on him by Treasury Officials, he showed considerable resolve.'[57] He was strengthened in this resolve by the support of Douglas Jay, Economic Secretary to the Treasury. Jay argued that 'Quite apart from its social and political unwisdom such a policy would be economic folly for two reasons' – it would have most impact

---

[52] PRO T171/392, 1 Sept. 1947. Hall's Keynesianism was arguably more simplistic than that of Meade, for example in not trying to integrate wages policy with the budgetary stance (Booth, *Economic Policy*, pp. 167–8). See also *Robert Hall Diaries* (1989).

[53] PRO T171/391, E. Bridges, 'Autumn Budget', 23 Sept. 1947.

[54] A. Booth, 'The "Keynesian Revolution" ', p. 122.

[55] PRO T171/391, ' Chancellor of the Exchequer Discussion with Advisers', 30 Sept. 1947.

[56] PRO T171/391, E. Bridges, 'Autumn Budget', 22 Oct. 1947.

[57] Rollings, 'Budgetary Policy', p. 289.

on the non-working poor, whose benefit levels would have to be raised, and it would stimulate wage claims. Given that one of the emergency measures of the summer of 1947 had been an agreement on wage restraint with the trade unions, this latter point was especially important, politically and economically.[58] In the event subsidies were maintained at the £392m. level agreed in the April budget, rather than being cut to the £300m. Bridges had regarded as the highest acceptable level.

What does all this say about the Keynesian content of the November 1947 budget? It is important here to distinguish official from ministerial views. On the official side Hall's replacement of Meade at the Economic Section made no difference to the Keynesian stance. This stance, it should be noted, involved cuts in subsidies not only for their anti-inflationary effects on demand, but perhaps as much because of their distortionary microeconomic effects. On the Treasury side, enthusiasm for subsidy cuts grew through the crises of 1947 – previously the Treasury too had seen the dangers of the impact of such cuts on wages. But in that summer they seem to have realised the possibility that the crisis situation offered them to reassert their control over public expenditure; subsidies, as a large and growing part of that expenditure, offered an ideal target.[59]

With regard to the more general issue of the budget surplus, the Treasury seem to have perceived well prior to 1947 that this kind of arithmetic provided an instrument to pursue their long-standing objectives. In March 1945, Gilbert, a most unenthusiastic Keynesian, had noted of such arithmetic: 'For some years, it is likely that the policy will involve keeping the brake on with varying degrees of pressure, on both capital and consumer expenditure. I see no difficulty about that, it is in harmony with all our past training and experience, and the contribution of the machinery of government is well-fitted for the exercise of negative controls.'[60]

Keeping the brakes on both public expenditure and inflation could be helped by Keynesian arguments. In the summer of 1947 it was inflation which dominated Treasury thinking, and the Economic Section was a firm ally in that battle, however sceptical Treasury officials remained of other aspects of the Keynesian package.

As Alan Booth has rightly pointed out, there is no evidence of a major inflationary problem in 1947.[61] Rather, the crisis of the balance of pay-

[58] PRO T171/39, Jay to Dalton, 10 Oct. 1947.
[59] Rollings, 'Budgetary Policy', pp. 287–8.
[60] PRO T161/1297/S531555/3, Gilbert to Bridges, 20 March 1945.
[61] Booth, *Economic Policy*, p. 166; the chart in Cairncross (*Years of Recovery*, p. 40) suggests rising import prices were having surprisingly little impact on domestic prices or wages.

ments and the need to secure the American loan, focused attention on the need to maintain 'confidence', and anxieties about inflation acted as a kind of summary of that perceived need. The Treasury also, it should be noted, strongly supported the idea of cheap money (if not the excesses of Dalton's *cheaper* money) in order to minimise the cost of the debt service, and inflation threatened that policy. If the bank rate, logically, could not be used to maintain 'confidence', then fiscal policy became much more important.

At the ministerial level Dalton was clearly subject to a number of strong pressures. As already noted, he was being very strongly urged by both the Economic Section and the Treasury to take a tough budget stance. To an extent he accepted their arguments, most importantly in raising taxation against the clear policy of previous budgets. On the other hand, he not only resisted cuts in subsidies, but also did not find other expenditure cuts to bridge the inflationary gap.[62]

In so far as Dalton accepted the anti-inflationary rhetoric of his advisers, this reflected the problems of the external balance, which became so manifestly the problem in the summer of 1947. More generally it is clear that the government, and the Chancellor in particular, was suffering from a lack of confidence by the financial markets and financial press. Dalton, in fact, had always had a hostile press in his period as Chancellor, most notably in the *Financial Times*. This was exacerbated by his cheaper money policy, which was clearly failing by the summer of 1947.[63] Not surprisingly, therefore, some ground had to be given to the pressure for more anti-inflationary policies, though, as noted above, the attempt to turn cuts in subsidies into the symbol of financial responsibility (rather like unemployment benefit in 1931) was resisted. Politically, subsidies combined an egalitarian and a pro-wage restraint attraction which made any substantial cuts highly problematic.

In summary, the view of 1947 as pivotal in moving Britain towards a Keynesian policy regime appears exaggerated. A budgetary surplus was pursued by, for example, unwelcome tax increases, to try and restrain inflation and maintain confidence. But this strategy, after all, had been followed after the First World War in similar 'crisis' circumstances (though with more serious inflation) without anyone having seen it as a pro-Keynesian policy. The language of inflationary gaps and the arithmetic of national income were new in the 1940s, but in other respects the policy owed more to the outcome of a battle between traditional

---

[62] Rollings, 'Budgetary Policy', pp. 289–90.
[63] D. Kynaston, *The Financial Times: A Centenary History* (1988), pp. 272–80; Howson, *Monetary Policy*, pp. 166–74.

Treasury priorities and politicians' views of political realities than a major change in analytical allegiance amongst either group.

Parallel to the changes in budgetary policy in 1947 were major changes in the whole organisation of policy-making. In the early post-war years the Treasury did not immediately regain its pre-war status as by far the most important body in economic policy-making, a role ceded in wartime when finance lost its crucial role in determining economic activity. From 1945 to 1947 the machinery of economic policy-making broadly reflected the uncertainty about how policy was to be conducted. In this period the *de facto* centre of policy-making was the Ministerial Committee on Economic Planning, chaired by Morrison and consisting of Cripps, the President of the Board of Trade, Dalton and Isaacs, the Minister of Labour. But this body did not effectively integrate the various aspects – financial, labour, foreign trade – of economic policy. Neither did it build up an economic planning staff, so the Economic Section remained the main source of economic expertise in the government machine.[64]

In response to the crisis of 1947 this machinery underwent a number of major changes. Edwin Plowden was appointed Chief Planning Officer early in the year and a small Central Economic Planning Staff was established, and a tripartite Economic Planning Board was set up. This series of moves culminated in Cripps becoming Minister of Economic Affairs in September, and for a while it looked as though economic policy was to be dominated by a ministry other than the Treasury. But after Dalton's resignation in November, Cripps became Chancellor and the Ministry of Economic Affairs was merged with the Treasury.

In practice this series of changes returned the Treasury to dominance of economic policy-making, and effected a much better co-ordination between budgetary and other aspects of policy. At one level this meant that Keynesian views of the dominance of budgetary policy in overall economic management won out against those who would have had 'planning' by physical controls at the centre of policy. But in fact a coherent planning philosophy in strong opposition to the new role of the budget never emerged. As suggested in chapter 6, Gosplanners were extremely thin on the ground, even in the Central Economic Planning Staff, where Meade tried to conjure them up. On the other hand, if Cripps was no Gosplanner, he was equally not an adherent of Meade-style Keynesianism. Above all, he strongly believed in 'planning' via tripartite co-operation in a way quite at variance with any current *economic* doctrine. Neither he, nor the policies pursued under his Chan-

---

[64] Cairncross, *Years of Recovery*, pp. 50–2.

cellorship, can sensibly be placed on the economists' simple 'central planning versus management of aggregate demand' spectrum.

The Treasury under Cripps

Under Cripps, between 1948 and 1950, budgetary policy broadly followed the pattern set in November 1947. Calculations of the 'inflationary gap' in the *Economic Survey* were given greater prominence, and led to a policy of persistent budget surpluses. These gaps were calculated around an assessment of the extent to which expected private savings fell short of expected total investment, with the budget designed to cover this shortfall in savings.[65]

However, the use of the budget as a Keynesian instrument was still bedevilled by the lack of proper integration of the budget with the national income accounts. In the 1948 budget, following criticism of the way the budget was presented in 1947, an 'alternative classification' was appended to the normal accounts to try and link the budget surplus to the level of demand in the economy as a whole. But this change was less than might have first appeared because the new figures basically involved just a reshuffling of the existing Exchequer accounts, not a wholesale reclassification.[66] Such a reclassification was urged by the Economic Section, but without support from the Treasury. The Treasury's main concerns were to reduce expenditure and to maintain confidence by giving the appearance of a budget surplus, and for these purposes a 'conventional' surplus was adequate. For example, in 1949 Trend argued for an overall (conventional) surplus as being 'mainly required for purposes of the preservation of our credit at home and abroad' and as the figure 'most easily understood by the general public and the foreigner'.[67]

On the ministerial side Cripps found growing doubts about the case for large budget surpluses. In March 1950 Attlee wrote to him suggesting that the high taxation used to finance the surpluses discouraged saving and encouraged the rich to consume out of previous savings, with the result that the wealthy were consuming at the expense of the less well-off.[68] Others in the Cabinet seemed to agree with this analysis, and Cripps had to make a major presentation to the Cabinet to convince

---

[65] PRO T171/396, 'Draft Budget Speech', March 1948; T171/397, 'Roffey Park Discussions' 5–6 Feb. 1949.

[66] Dow, *Management*, p. 183.

[67] PRO T171/397, Trend to Chancellor of the Exchequer, 24 Feb. 1949; 'Chancellor's Brief for Cabinet', 10 March 1949.

[68] PRO T171/400, Attlee to Cripps, 11 March 1950.

them of the appropriateness of the budget surplus in current economic
circumstances. He argued that any tax cuts to try and increase savings
would have to be highly regressive if they were to be effective, and therefore quite at odds with Labour's redistributional policies.[69]

In fact, the general point made by Attlee, that the level of taxation
to finance budget surpluses was having a counter-productive effect on
the level of savings, was pursued strongly by Cripps' advisers in this
period. The tone was set by a memorandum by Hall in 1948 in a survey
of budgetary prospects over the next four years, which argued that tax
reductions could be combined with a budgetary surplus only if those
tax cuts were concentrated on higher incomes in order to boost private
savings. His way out of this dilemma was to cut expenditure, especially
on subsidies.[70] This general line on the disincentive effects of the current
level of taxation and the need to cut expenditure was supported by the
Treasury, and became the most persistent theme in budgetary advice
for the rest of Cripps' period in office. It also gained support from ministerial figures like Douglas Jay, who wanted to ease the budgetary pressure by combining 'a mild credit disinflation with a slightly less savage
Budget'. This was the basis of Jay's strong interest in trying to revive
the use of monetary policy, albeit without higher interest rates.[71]

Whilst this perception of the new contradictions of very large budget
surpluses was widespread in official circles, and led, for example, to the
pressure for a royal commission on taxation,[72] it was by no means so
widely agreed that subsidies should be the key area for cuts on the
expenditure side. In 1948 and 1949 at least, the Treasury did not put
as much emphasis on this aspect of budgetary tightening as Hall did,
though their respective roles seem to have changed from 1950. Attitudes
to subsidies at the official level seem to have varied according to current
calculations of the importance of trying to reduce wage inflation by sub-
sidising the cost of living.[73]

At the ministerial level there was a more unwavering resistance to any
cuts. Although Dalton alleged that Cripps had at one stage proposed the
complete elimination of subsidies, there is no evidence for this beyond
Dalton's diary.[74] The Budget Papers suggest Cripps had a clear view
that subsidies should be maintained, though subject to a ceiling. In early
1948 he suggested a ceiling of £400m., but this was overtaken by the

[69] PRO T171/400, Cripps, 'Budget Policy', 15 March 1950.
[70] PROT171/397, Hall, 'Budgetary Prospects and Policies 1948–52', 17 July 1948.
[71] PRO T171/397, Jay to Cripps, 3 Feb. 1949; Howson, *Monetary Policy*, pp. 225–30, 284.
[72] See chapter 12 below, where the issue of taxation is discussed.
[73] Rollings, 'Budgetary Policy', pp. 290–1.
[74] Cited in ibid., p. 290.

incomes policy agreement in February 1948, which committed the government to tight control of the rise in the cost of living.[75]

A ceiling of £465m. was put forward in the 1949 budget, but following the devaluation of September that year this figure was reduced to £410m. However, in the context of the continuing attempt to restrain wage inflation, this figure became a floor as well as a ceiling. Further cuts were proposed but resisted in 1951, so that, as Rollings rightly says, 'until the change of government in November 1951, food subsidies continued to be a crucial element of anti-inflationary policy'.[76]

The previous paragraphs have suggested some qualifications that need to be entered against any view that post-1947 Labour adopted a full-blooded Keynesian approach to budgetary policy. The other half of the story is what happened to controls – how far were they given up under Cripps? One of the paradoxes of 1947 was that the shift to a tighter budgetary policy was coupled to more effective 'planning' of investment by tightened use of controls rather than financial mechanisms. This was the basis of Dalton's oft-quoted remark in response to the Investment Programmes Committee Report that it marked 'a real start to central planning'.[77] Dalton, as so often, was hyperbolic, but there was an important grain of truth in his remark, especially as far as intentions rather than outcomes were concerned. Less pressure on aggregate demand plus a reformed administrative machinery should have made it easier to control the level and composition of investment. In practice this happened to only a limited extent, and mainly in the area of investment in building rather than plant and machinery. The latter was mainly controlled by informal pressure on producers of machinery to maximise their exports.[78]

Curiously, these attempts to control investment were accompanied by 1949 by an increase in the investment tax allowance, first introduced in 1945. This was despite Douglas Jay's cogent criticism that this measure would increase company cash flow but do nothing to affect the level of investment, which was determined largely by the availability of physical resources.[79] It would be idle, therefore, to suggest that in this period budgetary policy and physical planning together generated a close control of investment. One reason was the schizophrenia about investment evident in many discussions. On the one hand investment was a major

---

[75] PRO T171/394, 'Subsidies and Prices' by Chancellor of the Exchequer, 13 Jan. 1948; Treasury, *Statement on Personal Incomes, Costs and Prices* (1947).

[76] Rollings, 'Budgetary Policy', p. 291.

[77] PRO T229/66, 'Investment Programmes Committee: White Paper on Investment Programme, 1948', 10 Dec.1947.

[78] Dow, *Management*, pp. 150–3.

[79] PRO T171/397, Jay to Cripps, 3 Feb. 1949.

component of demand, and therefore needed to be restrained in the name of disinflation. On the other hand, it was a source of increased production and productivity, and should be encouraged. Schumpeter argued that, in this area at least, British economists tended to be too Keynesian, in regarding investment too much as a source of short-run demand, rather than long-run supply expansion.[80] The government too seems to have oscillated between these two views.

In the current context, the important point to emphasise is that budgetary policy after 1947 was not accompanied by a lessening of controls as they affected investment. In the case of foreign transactions tight exchange control also remained in place throughout the Attlee period, except for the unfortunate interlude in the summer of 1947. Direct controls on imports were almost comprehensive down to 1949/50, but were then slowly eased before being tightened again during the Korean War.[81]

Much the most contentious area of controls politically was consumer rationing. Its scope was increased in 1946 and 1947 when bread and potatoes, previously free of control, were included. Food was the main focus and at the peak in 1947/8 about 50 per cent of consumer expenditure on food was rationed, many of these goods being subject to subsidy and price control as well. But from 1948 a process of derationing began, including all clothes and furniture but also progressively many foodstuffs. After the loosening, consumer rationing accounted for only about 12 per cent of total consumer expenditure.[82] These figures put some perspective on this highly contentious area. There seems little doubt that it was the perception of the political sensitivity of consumer rationing, coupled to industrialists' pressure for fewer controls, especially of materials, that led to the highly publicised 'bonfire of controls' announced by Harold Wilson at the Board of Trade in 1948.

However, as already noted, the desire to reduce controls where possible had been there from almost the beginning of the government, and machinery had been set up to pursue this aim. This machinery had been notably expanded in 1947/8. In 1947 a wide-ranging review of controls was undertaken with three purposes. One was to respond to the 'widespread view that controls hamper and delay'. The second aim was to save civil service manpower, and the final one to look at the legislative problems involved, because most controls operated under the Wartime Defence Regulations, which were for a limited period only.[83]

[80] J. Schumpeter, 'English Economists and the State-Managed Economy', *Journal of Political Economy* 57 (1949), pp. 371–82.

[81] Dow, *Management*, pp. 153–8.

[82] Ibid., pp. 147–9.

[83] PRO T222/214, J. H. Woods, 'Review of Controls', 9 Dec. 1947.

As a result of this review the Board of Trade established its own Special Examiner of Controls, whilst an interdepartmental Controls and Efficiency Committee was set up with a more general remit. The report of the examiner argued that the main problem was the control of the allocation of materials, because this froze the industrial structure, made it almost impossible for new firms to enter an industry, and so encouraged inefficiency. The examiner further argued that the logical way to move on controls was to start at the consumer end, then to reduce controls on manufactures, and finally on material allocations.[84] This broad view was largely endorsed by the Controls and Efficiency Committee. However, it is important to note that this committee did not envisage a complete abolition of controls as the aim; rather it was to review their operation to minimise their ill effects on efficiency, especially in blocking changes in the industrial structure.[85]

These arguments lay behind Wilson's announcement in November 1948 that decontrol would be pursued 'as the balance of payments allows' but subject to any requirements to retain control for reasons of 'economic recovery for industrial efficiency or for full employment'.[86] There was probably plenty of scope for a 'bonfire of controls' without very much loss of effective regulation of the economy. For example, the bonfire seems to have led to the loss of only 30–40 civil service jobs in the Board of Trade. When this was questioned, it was found that, of the 200,000 licences abolished by the bonfire, 125,000 had been for the production of thermos flasks, involving 25 civil servants in what must have been a highly routine procedure whose ending was unlikely to have had a major economic impact.[87]

This example may illustrate a broader truth. The controls in existence in early post-war Britain were immensely complex and elaborate, and many could be abolished with little implication for general policy. There was a great deal of scope for what was called a 'preliminary clearing of the ground' before starting on any 'far-reaching change in the structure of controls operated through the present allocation system'.[88]

Alongside the 'rationalisation' of especially material and consumption controls there was undoubtedly a broad trend towards their reduction, notably in 1948 to 1950. Again, the political aspect of this needs highlighting. If the reduction of shortages provided an economic rationale for this easing, it was important politically for the government to

---

[84] PRO T222/214, 'Interim Report' by Examiner of Controls, 8 Sept. 1948.
[85] PRO T222/214, 'Interim Report' by Controls and Efficiency Committee, 3 Aug. 1948.
[86] H. Wilson, Hansard (Commons), vol. 457, cols. 113–14, 4 Nov. 1948.
[87] PRO T222/215, J. H. Woods to E. Bridges, 2 Dec. 1948.
[88] PRO T222/215, Co-ordinating Committee on Controls, 'Progress Report No. 2', 1949.

respond. Exactly how the public felt on controls is difficult to judge. Some authors have rightly noted the virulence of attacks on controls, such as in John Jewkes' 1948 book.[89] How far this was translated into popular discontent and loss of support for the government remains a matter of dispute. A significant proportion of the population, at least, accepted the government case that controls were an acceptable price to pay for a policy of 'fair shares for all'.[90]

In sum, controls were reduced in Cripps' period at the Treasury, and this does not seem to have been a matter of great controversy in the government, partly because many of the controls fulfilled no useful purpose, or their purpose was lost as supply expanded. But there is no evidence that amongst ministers (as opposed to officials) there was a view developing that there should be a general movement to replace such controls by budgetary management. This was true, as argued in the next section, even amongst those on the right of the party who might be expected to be most hostile to such 'planning'.

The final phase

In 1950 Cripps was replaced by Gaitskell as the Chancellor of the Exchequer. Gaitskell's short period in office was dominated by the attempt greatly to speed up the pace of rearmament in response to the Korean War. This led to a famous clash with Bevan over spending on the NHS and Bevan's resignation. Budgetary policy was thus at the centre of Labour's concerns in this period, though it was a clash over spending priorities rather than the general use of the budget to manage the economy which excited the controversy.

The 1951 budget discussions began before the Korean emergency led to proposals for a major expansion in defence spending. In the summer of 1950 the Budget Committee was given an optimistic 'steady as she goes' assessment, with evidence of the need for continuing disinflation counterbalanced by evidence that in a number of consumer markets competitive conditions were returning – in other words demand was slackening. But once the defence expansion was proposed demand conditions were seen to 'present us with a formidable problem on the budgets of the next two years. It is clear that drastic measures will be necessary to maintain our present policy of avoiding inflation.'[91]

[89] Booth, *Economic Policy*, p. 166; Jewkes, *Ordeal by Planning*.
[90] Zweiniger-Bargielowska, 'Rationing, Austerity and the Conservative Party Revival'.
[91] PRO T171/403, 'Budget Prospects for 1951/2 and 1952/3'.

This was the continuing theme of budget discussion up to April 1951. Already in the discussions of the 1950 budget some of the 'formidable difficulties' on the expenditure side had been highlighted. Three areas of expenditure were noted as large and rapidly rising – defence, subsidies and the NHS. But with current defence policy ruling out the first, wage policy ruling out major changes on subsidies, the focus was on NHS expenditure.[92] But while in 1950 the budget position was stable enough to rule out significant tax increases, in 1951 both sides of the budget had to be adjusted to achieve the government's aims.

As always, however, the budget decision was not just a matter of getting the arithmetic right. For example, the Treasury resisted the conclusions of the rather optimistic view taken by Hall of the budgetary prospects, that taxes should be increased and expenditure cut 'to take advantage of public expectations of tightening'. In addition, it was argued that because of the 'impact of the budget on opinion at home and abroad it should have an approximate above the line balance'.[93]

Eventually it was agreed that the surplus in 1951 could be smaller than in 1950 because of the rise in company saving and the reduction in demand arising from the deterioration in the balance of payments. But the surplus generated automatically was cut by the sharp rise in expenditure, especially on defence but also to a much smaller extent on civilian expenditure. Overall the need was to reduce expenditure/raise taxes by £100–200m. Gaitskell summarised the position:

In this situation, the task of the Budget is to ensure the smooth and swift transfer of resources from production for home consumption to production for defence and exports and to provide appropriate conditions for the working of the necessary physical controls by securing that the money spent at home is enough, but not more than enough, to buy – at prices which cover their costs – the goods and services which will be available after the needs of defence, exports and home investment have been met.[94]

Alongside tax increases, including raising the standard rate of income tax back to 9s 6d (47½p), the result of these calculations was an insistence on expenditure cuts, which fell most famously on the NHS. The actual amount involved in this was small – about £13m. out of a total expenditure of around £400m., a point emphasised by Bevan in his resignation speech.[95] However, it is clear that for the Treasury, and for Gaitskell, the size of the cut was not the crucial issue; rather, what mat-

---

[92] PRO T171/400, Budget Committee, 'The Budget Position 1950/51' (n.d., but March 1950). The debate over NHS expenditure is looked at in more detail in chapter 12.
[93] PRO T171/403, E. Bridges, 'Budgetary Problem, 1951', 6 Feb. 1951.
[94] PRO T171/403, Gaitskell, 'Summary of Budget Proposals', 9 April 1951.
[95] M. Foot, *Aneurin Bevan 1945–60* (1975), pp. 333–5.

tered was the symbolic subordination of social service expenditure to the budgetary arithmetic and ultimately to the claims of the defence programme.

In retrospect Bevan proved correct that this programme was unworkable. As Samuel Brittan noted:

The most extraordinary episode in the Labour Government's history was the cavalier way in which it embarked upon an enormous rearmament programme at the time of Korea . . . The Treasury, which is habitually pessimistic about the capacity of the economy to bear civilian programmes which are quite tiny by comparison, took the view that the nation would just *have* to afford the extra arms bill. Mr. Gaitskell and his official advisers, who shared his devotion to the cause of Western defence, made the mistake of assuming that sufficiently strict budgetary planning, together with the reimposition of physical controls, would produce raw materials, machine tools, and components required for an enormously enlarged defence programme.[96]

This verdict has not seriously been challenged, and if it is noted that defence expenditure, already 7 per cent of GNP in 1950, was going to be doubled under the 1950 plan, it is hardly surprising that the effort failed, only remarkable that it was ever thought it could work. Whether this effort, by diverting resources from exports and investment, damaged Britain's economic performance in the long run remains disputed.[97] What seems clearer is that the fundamental reason for such a reckless gamble was the desire to maintain a role as a world power by proving to the US that Britain could still deliver a major defence effort.[98]

Whilst the 1951 budget was extremely important for both the British economy and the Labour government, it cannot readily be used to summarise the long-run evolution of Labour's budgetary policies. It was an aberration not only in the sense of being a response to an emergency – the Korean War – but also in the extent to which political considerations so blatantly dominated over issues of economic management.

In that context the budget of 1950 in some ways provides a better pointer to the trend of budgetary policy. The budget of that year 'sounded sweeter in the ears of taxpayer and tax gatherer alike than the previous few 'austerity' ones. At least the postwar era of economic crisis was closing and a new more plentiful one beginning.'[99]

But did the closing of the age of austerity imply the end of controls and the movement towards an entirely fiscally managed economy? This

---

[96] S. Brittan, *Steering the Economy* (1969), pp. 110–11. See also J. Mitchell, *Crisis in Britain 1951* (1951), p. 276.
[97] Dow, *Management*, p. 64; Cairncross, *Years of Recovery*, p. 231–2.
[98] Cairncross, *Years of Recovery*, pp. 232–3.
[99] Mitchell, *Crisis*, p. 15.

does not seem to have been a prospectus accepted by any major Labour figure in 1950. As Rollings has shown, in the debate over the future of controls from 1948 onwards, opinion across the major cabinet ministers concerned with economic issues was united in seeing a continuing role for controls for the foreseeable future. The failure to embody this in legislation resulted not from a lack of political will, but the overtaking of events by the Korean War.[100]

However, as Rollings has noted, this continuation of controls was seen as largely for macroeconomic purposes:

Although some still saw a microeconomic role for direct controls, the increasing focus was on the macroeconomic objective of full employment. Those who did have a conscious image of their purpose were not recommending permanent economic controls with the aim of restructuring industry. The objective was not to determine the long-term development of industry, but rather to achieve short-term management of the economy.[101]

This point is important for the general thesis of this chapter, that the debate over the role of budgetary policy under the Attlee government should not be seen in terms of Gosplanners versus Keynesians as Meade suggested. Rather, budgetary policy (up to 1950) evolved in the context of what may be simplified as a three-way battle. This was between a Keynesian Economic Section, strongly committed to the ultimate triumph of budgetary policy as the key weapon of economic management, in significant part because of their (classically Keynesian) belief that in a context of adequate aggregate demand government should play a very limited microeconomic role. Second was the Treasury, largely concerned to limit public expenditure, contain inflation and maintain both internal and external 'confidence'. For them Keynesian budgetary arithmetic was a convenient new bottle for some pretty old wine. Third was the ministers, differing in their style and attitudes, but all highly political animals, committed to full employment, but finding that this was not after all to be the issue they had to face. With problems of inflation and the balance of payments deficit to the fore, Keynesian approaches appeared to offer a politically congenial *complement* to retaining broad-brush controls on trade, investment and consumption whilst aiding the running down of many of the politically irksome controls which no one believed formed the basis of a 'planned economy' in the sense of a Soviet-style five-year plan.

By 1950, to reiterate, budgetary policy and the remaining controls seemed to have delivered a non-inflationary economy, with full employ-

[100] Rollings, 'Reichstag Method of Governing?'; 'Poor Mr. Butskell', pp. 183–205.
[101] Rollings, 'Reichstag Method of Governing?', p. 28.

ment and without serious balance-of-payments problems. Ministers were generally convinced that this combination of instruments should be sufficient to face any threats which might appear on the horizon. Unsurprisingly, they didn't see that the threat would come from a war in Korea and the intensely political economic policies which would flow from this.

11 The economics of the welfare state

The creation of the welfare state remains at the centre of most accounts of the 1945 Labour government.[1] It would indeed be hard to deny that the setting up of a comprehensive National Health Service, a major extension of social insurance and the extension of free secondary education to all children marked major changes in British society. Accounts of British social policy give full weight to these changes, especially to their long-run implications.[2] On the other hand, accounts of British economic policy deal rather cursorily with this aspect of the Attlee government's activities.[3] To a large extent accounts of social policy and economic policy have gone along separate channels.[4] A partial exception to this separation has been the work of those, such as Barnett, who have analysed social welfare policy as imposing a 'burden' on the economy. However, this approach, whatever its popularity, rests not only on a very vague understanding of the nature of the welfare state in the 1940s, but more particularly on a simplistic view of the economic impact of social welfare.[5]

The main purpose of this chapter is to combine the analysis of social policy and that of the economy in this period by looking at the economic impact of the welfare state. Within that broad purpose one aim is to explore the complexity of the relationship between social policy and the economy. But, more substantively, it will be argued that the literature which emphasises the 'burden' of the welfare state is not only conceptually confused but even in its own terms exaggerates the size of that 'burden'.

Discussion of the welfare state from any perspective raises enormous problems of definition. Most generally, the key underpinning of any

---

[1] Morgan, *Labour in Power*, ch. 4; Hennessy, *Never Again*, ch. 4.

[2] Lowe, *Welfare State*, Part II.

[3] Cairncross, *Years of Recovery*, pp. 17–18.

[4] This follows the pattern of sharp separation of the 'economic' from the 'social' in much twentieth-century historiography.

[5] Barnett, *Audit of War*; J. Harris, 'Enterprise and the Welfare State: A Comparative Perspective' in Gourvish and O'Day (eds.), *Britain since 1945*, pp. 39–58.

welfare state is full employment, not only because for most people in a capitalist economy 'welfare' depends on access to the labour market, but also because an economy with buoyant employment provides the fiscal resources for state welfare expenditure.[6] More specifically, Titmuss long ago pointed out that the traditional identification of a 'welfare state for the working classes' with the social policy measures of the late 1940s ignored the transfers of income embodied in tax reliefs, and the complex of occupational benefits which also represented a disguised welfare state. Titmuss lamented not only the inegalitarian impact of these last two facets of 'welfare' provision, but also the failure of analysts to consider them together.[7]

Unfortunately, overall accounts of fiscal and occupational welfare to put alongside those of the traditional 'welfare state' remain notably absent from the literature. Whilst much work has been done of late on the scale and impact of tax allowances, this has been limited to recent decades. We have much more historical information on occupational or company welfare, but this is mainly fragmentary, and does not allow an overall picture to be drawn.[8] Hence, despite the clear shortcomings of such an approach, the attention here is on the 'welfare state' as narrowly conceived. Even this narrow definition is to a degree arbitrary, as the boundaries of 'welfare' are not easily drawn – as Titmuss has again pointed out.[9] The approach adopted here is to follow the definitions actually used in the 1940s, whilst recognising their arbitrary nature. Attention is therefore focused on social insurance, health care, education and housing as defining what most people meant (and probably still mean) by the 'welfare state'.

Approaching the welfare state from an economic aspect raises its own peculiar problems. There is the general problem of seeing welfare provision as a 'burden' on the economy, a problem returned to in the con-

---

[6] Rodney Lowe rightly has a substantial chapter on employment policy in his *Welfare State*.

[7] R. Titmuss, *Essays on the Welfare State* (1958), ch. 2. The failure of social policy analysts to use this distinction is lamented by A. Sinfield, 'Analyses of the Social Divisions of Welfare', *Journal of Social Policy* 7 (1978), pp. 129–56.

[8] D. Heald, *Public Expenditure: Its Defence and Reform* (Oxford, 1983), pp. 20–2. Details of the revenue costs of tax allowances were not published in any detail until *The Government's Expenditure Plans 1979/80 to 1982/83* (1979). For a discussion of the issues see C. Pond, 'Tax Expenditures and Fiscal Welfare' in C. Sandford, C. Pond and R. Walker (eds.), *Taxation and Social Policy* (1980), pp. 47–63. On pensions and occupational welfare see L. Hannah, *Inventing Retirement: The Development of Occupational Pensions in Britain* (Cambridge, 1986); A. Russell, *The Growth of Occupational Welfare in Great Britain* (Basingstoke, 1991).

[9] Titmuss, *Essays*, pp. 40–2.

cluding section below. More specifically, there is the need to distinguish between welfare provision which consumes real resources (labour and physical inputs) and that which involves only a transfer of income between taxpayers and recipients of provision. The latter matters for the level of public expenditure and hence taxation. It needs to be looked at in the context of the impact of that taxation on incentives to produce and save, which is returned to below. But such transfers do not have a direct opportunity cost in terms of alternative uses for resources.

Plainly 'exhaustive' (non-transfer) expenditures need to be looked at separately because they do involve a diversion of resources from other uses. Such a diversion was particularly an issue in the 1940s, when the economy was constrained largely by physical shortages of such inputs as steel and timber, and by labour shortages.[10] Hence it is especially important for this period to assess the scale and nature of real resource use resulting from the creation of the welfare state.

The first part of the chapter focuses on this real resource issue in relation to education, housing, health and social insurance. The second looks at the public expenditure and the third at the taxation aspect. The final section offers a summary of the economic impact of the early welfare state, and links this to broader issues of assessment of the economics of welfare provision.

Education

Consideration of the Labour government's education policies usually begins with the coalition government's 1944 Education Act. Undoubtedly this was symbolically highly important, especially in its guarantee of free secondary education for all. Yet in terms of resources involved in the expansion of the education system after 1945 the focus on the 1944 Act is rather inappropriate. The 1944 Act suggested a major improvement in educational provision, with its call for the school leaving age to be raised to 16, the compulsory attendance of 15–18-year-olds at county (further education) colleges, an increase in teacher training from two to three years, a major reduction in class sizes, and the provision of separate schools for secondary-age children. In the event, only a limited part of this was achieved in the 1945–51 period. The school leaving age was raised, but only to 15, in 1947. Further education did grow, but only from a very low base. (Numbers in part-time technical education rose from 40,000 in 1938/9 to 200,000 by 1948/9.) Teacher

---

[10] Chapters 4 and 8 above.

Table 11.1   *Size of classes in state schools, 1945–50*

(000s)

	1945	1950
Primary schools (no. of pupils per class)		
1–30	16.8	23.8
31–40	22.3	32.2
41–50	26.0	27.4
51+	3.1	1.4
Total	68.1	84.7
Total no. of pupils	2,527.6	3,009.6
All-age schools (no. of pupils per class)		
1–30	18.9	14.3
31–40	13.2	11.9
41–50	6.7	4.3
51+	0.6	0.2
Total	39.4	30.7
Total no. of pupils	1,208.1	945.9
Secondary schools (no. of pupils per class)		
1–30	20.1	26.8
31–40	18.1	25.3
41–50	0.1	0.06
Total	41.8	56.1
Total no. of pupils	1,268.5	1,695.7

Source: Annual Abstract of Statistics 1952, table 91.

training was not lengthened.[11] Class sizes fell only slightly, with only the very largest classes showing a fall in numbers (table 11.1). As would be expected, pupil–teacher ratios showed little change (table 11.2). There was very limited school building in the secondary sector, so that the numbers in 'all-age' schools fell relatively slowly (table 11.1), and much of this amounted to little more than changing the school sign from 'elementary' to 'secondary modern'.[12] The major achievement of the period was to raise the number of secondary-age children at school by a third, at a time when the total number in that age group was flat.

The failure to implement most of the 1944 agenda in the late 1940s was conditioned by the fact that the education system had to cope with

[11] PEP, *Technological Education*, pp. 61–80. In fact, many of the new teachers went through a shortened, emergency training scheme of one year. W. A. C. Stewart, *Higher Education in Postwar Britain* (1989), p. 68; B. Vernon, *Ellen Wilkinson 1891–1947* (Beckenham, 1982), pp. 206–9.
[12] Roy Lowe, *Education in the Postwar Years* (1988), p. 40.

Table 11.2   *Pupils and teachers in state schools, 1946–50*

	1946	1950
Primary[1]		
Pupils (millions)	3.7	4.0
Teachers (thousands)	116.8	130.0
Ratio	32/1	30.4/1
Secondary		
Pupils (millions)	1.3	1.7
Teachers (thousands)	58.5	80.5
Ratio	21.7/1	21.1/1

[1] Includes 'all-age' schools.
Source: Department of Education and Science, *Statistics of Education* (1970), vol. I, *Historical Tables*, table 1.

the consequences of demographic change. From 1942 the birth-rate began to rise, leading to a growth in the number of primary-age children of over 300,000 between 1946 and 1950 (table 11.2). Most of the expansion in numbers in secondary schools in this period came from the raising of the school leaving age in 1947, the wave of wartime births not hitting these schools until 1952 and after.[13]

Throughout the late 1940s the Ministry of Education was battling for the resources to meet its programmes. The focus of those battles was physical resources for investment, with public spending a secondary consideration.[14] Whilst labour markets were tight in this period, there was seemingly little concern with the labour market aspects of increased teacher recruitment.[15] This reflected the fact that the perceived shortages of labour in this period were primarily in a range of manual jobs – coal miners, textile and agricultural workers, building workers – rather than the kind of jobs where teachers might be regarded as a potential source of labour. Though it is an area about which little is known, the war also seems to have expanded the pool of those who aspired to white-collar jobs such as teaching rather than manual jobs. The main way the

[13] Lowe, *Welfare State*, p. 71, p. 204. ROSLA took place only after a considerable Cabinet battle: Vernon, *Ellen Wilkinson*, pp. 209–11.
[14] For example, PRO T227/150, Education – Investment Programmes, 1947–53; T229/492, 493, Investment Programmes Committee, Ministry of Education, 1948/9, 1950/2; PREM8/1415, Government Expenditure, 1949.
[15] The withdrawal of 400,000 14-year-olds from the labour market via ROSLA in 1947 was agonised over by the government largely because of its labour market implications (PRO CAB129/16, 'Proposed Postponement of the Raising of the School Leaving Age', 14 Jan. 1947).

Table 11.3   *Distribution of gross fixed investment by value, 1948*

(%)

Fuel and power	10.1
Transport and communications	15.2
Agriculture	4.1
Industry	25.3
Defence and administration	3.5
Other (including housing maintenance)	23.0
Social services	18.8
of which:	
New housing	15.5
Health, water and sewerage	1.9
BBC	0.1
Education	1.3
Home departments	0.2

Source: PRO CAB134/448 Investment Programmes Committee Working Party, 'Capital Investment 1948–52', 8 Sept. 1948.

labour shortage impinged on educational provision was therefore via the shortage of construction workers, which contributed, along with problems of steel and timber, to the limitations on investment. As tables 11.3, 11.4, 11.5 and 11.6 make clear, education's share of investment resources, however measured, was quite small.

At the most general level this limited share of investment resources reflects the fact that education is a labour- rather than capital-intensive activity. But in particular it reflects the fact that education investment in the 1940s was squeezed hard, so that, whilst expanding in the late

Table 11.4   *Allocation of building workers, June 1947*

	Total	Percentage
Fuel and power	31,000	3.2
Transport and communications	18,500	1.9
Agriculture	22,000	2.3
Industry	120,000	12.4
Education	34,000	3.5
Health	27,000	2.8
Housing (including maintenance)	582,000	60.0
Others	136,500	13.9
Total	971,000	100.0

Source: PRO CAB134/447, Investment Programmes Committee Report, 8 Oct. 1947.

Table 11.5 *Timber allocations, 1947*

(%)

	Education	Housing	Health
Softwood	0.4	22.7	25.7
Hardwood	0.2	2.2	2.7
Plywood	0.25	9.2	18.6

Source: PRO CAB134/478, Material Allocations Committee, 'Timber Allocations in 1947', 17 March 1947.

Table 11.6 *Distribution of steel in 1948*

	Total (000 tons)	Percentage
Housing	106	0.9
Education	25[1] } 115	0.2
Health	90[1] }	0.7
Total investment	6,314	
Home, non-investment users	5,013	
Total	11,327	

[1] Estimated on basis of 1 ton of steel per £1,000 of investment in education as given in PRO T227/150 Ministry of Education: Educational Building Programme 1947–52.
Source: PRO CAB134/191, Investment Programmes Committee, 'Capital Investment in 1949', 16 July 1949.

1940s from the exceptionally low wartime levels, such investment only exceeded the pre-war level in 1950, and then by only 2 per cent.[16]

The pattern of this investment is given in table 11.7. A precise quantitative breakdown of the distribution of new places between age groups is not available, but all the discussion suggests that the great bulk of the expansion was in new primary places – perhaps to the extent of 75 per cent.[17] By the time it became evident in 1947, that investment would have to be reined back, given the shortages of materials and the general problem of excess demand in the economy, the Ministry of Education accepted that the bulk of its investment programme would have to be spent on simply keeping up with expanding pupil numbers, rather than

[16] J. Vaizey, *The Costs of Education* (1958), p. 86. The figures (at 100 = 1948) are: 1935 = 183, 1940 = 196, 1950 = 203.
[17] Ministry of Education, *Education 1900–1950* (1951), p. 99.

Table 11.7   *Distribution of educational investment, 1947–50*

(£m. current prices)

	1947	1948	1949	1950
New places	5.5	12.0	22.0	37.0
School meals	2.0	3.0	3.5	0.5
Technical education	0.2	0.7	4.0	4.25
Other	1.0	3.7	7.5	6.0
Maintenance	3.0	3.0	3.0	3.0
Total	11.7	22.4	40.0	50.75

Sources: 1947–9: PRO T229/492, Investment Programmes Committee: Ministry of Education 1948/9, 5 Jan. 1949.
1950: PRO T229/493 Investment Programmes Committee: Ministry of Education 1950–52, 10 Jan. 1950.

any major improvement in the quality of facilities.[18] In accepting the proposed labour ceiling for educational investment in August 1947, the ministry stressed that in doing so it would focus its attention on provision for new places to accommodate the rise in the birth-rate, the creation of new housing developments and for the raising of the school leaving age. In addition, resources would go into the 'expansion and improvement of technical education as a contribution towards increased productivity in industry'.[19]

As table 11.7 suggests, technical education provision did rise more rapidly than any other sector of educational investment in the late 1940s, though from a very low base. This certainly took priority over, for example, nursery schools, which again had been heralded as a major area of expansion by the 1944 Act, but which grew relatively slowly in this period, from 6,000 places in 1944 to 21,000 by the end of 1949, most of the growth coming in the first couple of years of the Labour government.[20] By the end of the decade expansion in this area was restricted solely to areas of perceived economic needs: 'Fifteen new nursery schools were completed and 23 were under construction at the end

[18] In fact, the quality of school building was reduced by tight controls on the unit cost of provision, including the provision of emergency hutted accommodation on a large scale, e.g. Ministry of Education, *Education 1900–1950*, pp. 96–9.
[19] PRO T227/150, Education: Investment Programmes 1947–53, A. Part to F. Vinter, 21, Aug. 1947. See also PRO CAB134/447, Investment Programmes Committee, 27 Aug. 1947.
[20] PRO LAB26/286, 'Child Care Schemes in Great Britain during and since the War', 1 Nov. 1951.

of the year in areas where exporting industries need the services of working mothers.'[21]

This attempt to present educational provision as a contributor to economic performance, by provision of buildings for both technical education and nursery classes, does not seem to have cut much ice with the Treasury in its programme of investment control. Within the general strategy which developed from 1947, of giving priority to fuel, transport and industry, education was treated as a 'social service' whose demands had to be minimised.[22] A paradoxical consequence was that the expansion of technical education in this period was significantly constrained by the supply of premises.[23]

There was no New Jerusalem in education in the late 1940s. Provision, especially in the sense of buildings, did not keep pace with demand. In 1950 George Tomlinson, the Minister of Education, conceded that many of the hopes entertained in 1945, for example on nursery schools, had not been realised and that of the 2,827 school buildings blacklisted as unfit in 1925, 636 were still in use.[24]

Housing

It is in the case of housing that the strongest suggestions have been made of excessive 'welfare' provision putting an unreasonable burden on the economy in this period.[25]

Politically, there is no doubt that housing was a high priority for the Labour government, a priority endorsed by public opinion.[26] Housing's impact on the economy was largely through its use of materials and labour. The key materials shortage of the late 1940s was steel. Given the way British houses were then built, it is not surprising, as Table 11.6 shows, that housing consumed a trivial amount of this material. In the allocation of steel the competition for resources was essentially one between domestic non-social service investment and exports.[27] In no sense did housing crowd out industrial investment by its use of steel.

In the cases of timber and labour, by contrast, housing was a significant consumer (tables 11.4 and 11.5). Housing used 20–25 per cent of

[21] Ministry of Education, *Education in 1951* (1952), p. 7.
[22] PRO T229/492, Investment Programmes Committee, Ministry of Education, esp. F. Vinter to W. Strath, 20 Oct. 1949.
[23] Lowe, *Education*, pp. 62–3.
[24] *Times Educational Supplement*, 24 March 1950, cited Lowe, *Education*, p. 27.
[25] Barnett, *Audit of War*, pp. 242–7.
[26] Fielding, 'What Did "the People" Want?', p. 635.
[27] Cairncross, *Years of Recovery*, pp. 34–5.

softwood consumption, and 500,000–600,000 workers out of an employed population of almost 19 million in the late 1940s. These resource uses had a clear opportunity cost. On the other hand, how far they constrained industrial investment, as alleged by Barnett, remains unclear.

The reason why timber was in short supply was that most of it was imported, a significant proportion from dollar countries, when the shortage of dollars was at the centre of the economic policy agenda. In 1949, prior to devaluation, for example, of a total timber supply of 702,000 standards, all but 4,000 were imported, 175,000 from the dollar area (at approximately £40 per standard). So it was as a dollar-saving policy that restrictions were put on the use of timber in houses, leading to a significant fall (20–25 per cent), largely because of the installation of concrete ground floors.[28]

On the labour front, approximately half of all the workers in housing were engaged in building new houses, most of the rest restoring war damage and doing repairs and maintenance. The key question for this labour and the timber used in house building is how far the resources used could have been diverted. The transferability of resources is always a contentious matter, but it seems hard to dispute that in principle this labour and timber could have been employed in building new factories. However, in practice such a transfer was inhibited not just by the political commitment to housing but also by the shortage of steel, which was the binding constraint – both steel to go into the actual construction of the factories, and also steel to make the machines to go into those factories. Of course, there could also have been some transfer of dollars from imports of timber to imports of steel, but even if no softwood had been used for housing at all, this would have financed only approximately 250,000 tons of 'average' steel, significantly less of any of the more sophisticated imports.[29]

Discussions in the late 1940s nearly always assumed that housing was a social service which reduced resources available to expanding output. As with education, resources for housing were generally treated as a burden (perhaps a desirable burden) on the economy. Yet it was apparent to some participants in the resource allocation procedure that housing was also important in facilitating economic expansion, especially in the sectors given priority by the government: 'It is still true that we do not have enough factory space for all our workers. One of the problems is that workers are in the wrong places. This is because the housing

---

[28] PRO T229/214, 'Timber: Requirements for Housing', 1949.
[29] PRO CAB134/447, Investment Programmes Committee, 28 Aug. 1947. Trade values calculated from *Accounts Relating to Trade and Navigation of the UK*, 1948.

shortage means a considerable immobility of labour. So it can be argued with some truth that more houses will ease our industrial problems appreciably in 1948.'[30]

Overall, whether we should regard the resource used by housing in this period as 'excessive' depends on the benchmark employed. First, whilst housing investment as a share of GNP in Britain was higher than in neighbouring European countries, it was no higher than in 1925–37, and the relative costs of building had risen sharply since that period.[31] Indeed, the authorities eventually decided to use the inter-war level of building as a ceiling for the post-war years.[32] Second, the trend in housing investment, both in absolute terms and relative to other investment, was clearly downwards from 1947.[33]

As suggested above, the degree of direct crowding out of industrial investment in this period was quite limited. And in so far as these sectors did compete for resources it would be difficult to say that housing triumphed. Shonfield, for example, in his well-known book at the end of the 1950s denouncing post-war governments for allowing too low levels of investment, nevertheless congratulated Labour's efforts in the industrial investment field, asserting that 'the achievement lay essentially in holding back house-building'.[34] The real house-building bonanza in Britain had to await the Conservative governments in the 1950s.[35]

The National Health Service

The National Health Service, created in 1948, was at once the most prominent symbol of the welfare state of the 1940s, and the one that came most rapidly under attack for its cost. From 1948 there was a growing 'crisis of expenditure' which was to lead to major political disputes in the Labour government. This crisis was focused almost entirely on the public expenditure aspects of the NHS, rather than the real resource implications.[36] This public expenditure issue will be returned

[30] PRO T229/66, Plowden to Cripps, 10 Dec. 1947. Plowden was the head of the Central Economic Planning staff created in 1947.

[31] Milward, *Reconstruction*, pp. 479–80; Matthews et al., *British Economic Growth*, pp. 332, 413–14.

[32] PRO CAB134/642, Production Committee, 'Capital Investment in Housing', 24 May 1949.

[33] Cairncross, *Years of Recovery*, p. 456.

[34] Shonfield, *British Economic Policy*, p. 176.

[35] J. Stevenson, ' "The Jerusalem that Failed?": The Rebuilding of Post-War Britain' in Gourvish and O'Day (eds.), *Britain since 1945*, pp. 98–100.

[36] C. Webster, *The Health Services since the War*, vol. I, *Problems of Health Care. The National Health Service before 1957* (1988), ch. 5.

to in the next section, but there are a number of points to be made about how far the NHS in its early days drew real resources away from other sectors.

As demonstrated in tables 11.4, 11.5 and 11.6, health drew very little on supplies of steel or supplies of building workers. It did consume substantial amounts of timber, though here the same arguments as suggested for housing would apply: timber was an issue in the 1940s because of its foreign exchange, especially dollar cost, but it was not a major issue in relation to industrial investment, where steel was the key constraint.

As with education, the tight constraints imposed on building work in the NHS opened up a huge gap between the hopes of the reform programmes and the achievements in place by 1951. For example, one of the key ideas of the NHS was to 'rationalise' hospital provision, by concentrating provision on the district general hospital. But no such hospital was even begun in the late 1940s – in fact the first new hospital for almost twenty years did not open until almost at the end of the 1950s.[37] Even such low-cost items as local authority health centres (another central proposal of the Health Service legislation) were tightly regulated by the investment control system. For example, in 1950 West Ham had to fight hard for approval for a health centre costing £10,000.[38]

Less than 5 per cent of the spending on the NHS in its early years was on capital assets, including stocks.[39] In the hospital sector, by far the biggest slice of health expenditure, the proportion of capital to total expenditure fell from almost 20 per cent in 1938/9 to little more than 4 per cent by 1952/3, and the absolute value of capital expenditure by two-thirds in constant prices. Abel-Smith and Townsend calculated that, on plausible assumptions, this level of capital provision was only about 50 per cent of the replacement level – i.e. depreciation of the assets was faster than the improvements in this period.[40]

Interestingly, a similar view of the implication of the early NHS was presented from a quite different ideological perspective by John Jewkes. Whilst Abel-Smith and Townsend had stressed the low cost of the early

---

[37] Ibid. This is not to say that total bed availability was stagnant. In particular, the wartime Emergency Medical Service provision for casualties led to some rationalisation and expansion of provision, usually in the form of hutted extensions to existing hospitals (R. Titmuss, *Problems of Social Policy* (1950), pp. 459–66).

[38] PRO T227/955, NHS Hospital Accommodation 1949–54, F. Turnbull to E. Compton, 14 Sept. 1950.

[39] B. Abel-Smith and P. Townsend, *The Cost of the NHS in England and Wales* (Cambridge, 1956), pp. 25–6. A similar breakdown of costs for Scotland is given in the (Guillebaud) *Report of the Commission of Enquiry into the Cost of the NHS* (1956), Appendix 2.

[40] Abel-Smith and Townsend, *Cost*, pp. 52–3.

NHS, with evidence that underpinned the conclusion of the Guillebaud Report, Jewkes argued that the NHS had restricted the supply of medical services excessively. After pointing out the low levels of capital expenditure in the early NHS he argued that:

Between 1949 and 1959 the total number of available beds in the hospital service of England and Wales increased by about 6 per cent; the main increase was in mental hospital beds and the increase of general hospitals only about 2 per cent. When allowance is made for the increase in population and for the decline in the number of beds in nursing homes it is doubtful whether, in proportion to the population, there were more general hospital beds in 1959 than in 1948 or, indeed, than in 1939.[41]

With so much attention focused on the public expenditure aspect, the Ministry of Health seems to have offered little resistance to the tight controls over its investment programme. (How far this was due to its realisation that the housing programme, which it was also responsible for, was a major contestant – with health – for resources, especially timber, remains obscure.) From the beginning of the social service investment cuts in 1947 the ministry rather fatalistically accepted that:

owing to the prior claim of other services almost no new work had been authorised on building new hospitals. A limited amount was being done in the way of small extensions, but in spite of the unsuitable accommodation of many of the hospitals in old Poor Law buildings, the Ministry recognised that the new health service would have to make do for the time being with existing accommodation.[42]

Successive rounds of investment cuts fell heavily on health after 1947, and the ministry soon postponed the hopes of any new hospitals to the indefinite future, aiming only to restore capital expenditure to pre-war levels 'as soon as possible'.[43]

Like education, the National Health Service was a highly labour-intensive field. In this period wages and salaries accounted for between 60 and 65 per cent of NHS expenditure.[44] Numbers employed in hospitals increased, as shown in table 11.8. (There were in addition about 30,000 GPs, the main labour force outside the hospitals.)[45]

The main claim for real resources made by the NHS in its early years was for labour. But in assessing the impact of this, it is important to

[41] J. Jewkes, The Genesis of the British NHS, 2nd edn (Oxford, 1962), p. 9.
[42] PRO CAB134/447, Investment Programmes Committee, 28 Aug. 1947.
[43] PRO CAB134/448, Investment Programmes Committee Working Party, 'Draft Report – Appendix on Health Services', 17 June 1948; CAB134/642, Production Committee 24 May 1949, 'Capital Investment in 1950–52', paras. 257–68.
[44] Abel-Smith and Townsend, Cost, p. 32.
[45] Jewkes, Genesis, appendix 1.

Table 11.8 *Hospital staff, 1949 and 1951*

| | December 1949 | | December 1951 | |
	Full-time	Part-time	Full-time	Part-time
Medical and dentistry	8,954	20,280	10,245	23,281
Nursing	125,752	23,060	136,210	25,756
Domestic	101,206	27,148	105,416	33,630

Source: Report of the Ministry of Health Covering the Period 1/4/50 to 31/12/51, CMD. 8655 PP 1951/2 xv.

note, as Abel-Smith and Townsend did for the period 1949 to 1953, that most of this growth in employment was for women, a significant proportion of them part-time workers.[46] The direct impact on the national economy was therefore likely to have been slight, as the main problem of labour supply in this period was a shortage of male workers in traditional 'heavy' industries like agriculture, building and mining where, according to the norms of the time, women, especially women part-time workers, were unlikely to have been a possible labour force (the one significant exception to this being cotton spinning).

Finally, the really striking increase in demand in the NHS in its earliest phase was in the supply of dentures and other dental treatment and spectacles. The large increase in supply of these goods did not involve any great use of physical resources, but was registered predominantly in the earnings of dentists and opticians.[47]

Social security

The fourth component of the welfare state considered in this chapter, the social security system, was overwhelmingly a mechanism for transferring resources between households, with very little direct resource use. The administration of this system did of course employ labour. Precise figures are difficult to obtain, but the numbers employed in the Ministry of Pensions and National Insurance rose from 8,000 at the end of 1945 to a peak of 39,650 in September 1948.[48] National Assistance, being more discretionary, was more labour-intensive, though precise numbers are not available. Detailed breakdowns of numbers employed in government service are only available for central government, which

[46] Abel-Smith and Townsend, *Cost*, p. 33.
[47] Webster, *Health Services*, pp. 359–63, 369–71.
[48] G. S. King, *The Ministry of Pensions and National Insurance* (Oxford, 1958), pp. 116–17.

Table 11.9 *Public employment in 'welfare' services, 1951*

(ooos)

Education	618
Health	492
Personal social services	116
Social security	58
Employment services	28
	1,312

Source: R. Parry, 'Britain: Stable Aggregates, Changing Composition' in R. Rose (ed.), *Public Employment in Western Nations* (Cambridge, 1985), p. 63.

gives a highly misleading picture given the decentralised nature of much provision.[49]

Taking all the parts of the welfare state together, the above discussion has suggested that the early years of expanded provision did not involve a major shift of real resources away from other uses, especially those resources (notably steel) which really constrained industrial growth and expansion in this period. The housing and health services did absorb significant amounts of timber, which had a significant foreign exchange cost – but precisely because of this, major efforts were made both to economise on this material and to hold down the total investment programmes of these activities.

Probably the most important impact of this expansion on real resources was on the labour market. Total employment did expand, and by 1951 the total in 'welfare services' very broadly defined was over 1.3 million (table 11.9), and to these would have to be added construction workers building for these sectors (table 11.4). The impact of this labour use on the national economy was considerably affected by the fact that much of the expansion was in the employment of women, including part-time women, so that 'crowding out' of other forms of economic activity by labour shortage was minimised. In an important sense, the new welfare state created a new labour supply, which in significant part matched the new demand.

Social services expenditure

The precise scale of public expenditure on the social services is far more difficult to ascertain than might be thought, because of both conceptual

[49] M. Abramowitz and V. F. Eliasberg, *The Growth of Public Employment in Great Britain* (Princeton, 1957); PRO T227/401, Social Service Economy Exercises: General Questions 1949–54, 'Administrative Cost of the Social Services', 1 April 1949.

Table 11.10   *Central government public expenditure on social services, 1949–50 and 1950/1*

(£m.)

	1949/50	1950/1
Exchequer contribution to National Insurance Fund (including industrial injuries)	141.7[1]	146.8[1]
Unemployment benefit (paid outside NI Fund)	5.5	5.2
Family allowances	62.6	63.6
War pensions	81.8	79.1
Non-contributory pensions	27.0	25.0
National assistance	62.9	75.5
Central government expenditure on industrial rehabilitation and training	1.7	2.8
Nutrition services (school meals, milk, etc.)	60.6	59.6
Education	267.5	280.7
Child care	14.0	16.7
NHS	411.1[2]	439.5[2]
Housing	67.0	71.5
Total	1,203.4	1,265.0
Of which:		
Grants to persons (transfer payments)	420.8	437.3
Exhaustive expenditure	782.6	828.7

[1] i.e. excluding employer and employee contributions.
[2] This appears to be the gross cost, before deduction of charges.
Source: Annual Abstract of Statistics, vol. 89, 1952.

and administrative complexities. Most books begin their detailed accounts from 1950 or 1951, partly because of the problems of availability of statistics before that date.[50] Comprehensive, disaggregated figures are not available before 1949/50, though figures for individual components of expenditure are available.[51] For all these complexities, the broad picture seems clear enough (table 11.10). As we are interested here in the impact of social welfare on total public spending and taxation, these figures include transfer payments. Strictly speaking transfer payments should be netted out of any comparison with GDP, because they are not derived as factor incomes, and therefore do not form part of the measure of total product. (In principle this means public expenditure could be more than 100 per cent of GDP.)[52]

[50] e.g. Lowe, *Welfare State*, appendix tables A3 to A5.
[51] C. Gordon, 'The Welfare State: Sources of Data on Government Expenditure', LSE Welfare State Programme WSP/RN/14 (1988). I am grateful to Paul Johnson for bringing this publication to my attention.
[52] Heald, *Public Expenditure*, pp. 12–18.

The published figures in table 11.10 broadly accord with contemporary confidential assessments of social welfare expenditure. The 1951 Budget Committee discussions used a figure of £1,167m. for 'social services', though in his budget speech the Chancellor expanded the scope of this term and included food subsidies under this heading.[53] Food subsidies represent a good example of the difficulties of categorising welfare expenditure. Originally introduced to hold down the costs of food to the working class and so reduce wartime inflationary pressure, these subsidies had been retained largely as a means of reducing wage claims under the Labour government. Because of their concentration on items bought particularly by wage earners, food subsidies were redistributive in impact, but they are probably best seen as an instrument of macroeconomic policy rather than of the welfare state in any strict sense. By 1950 they were costing as much as the NHS and had become a considerable bone of contention in the government.[54]

It is also worth noting the other major items in expenditure. In 1950/1 these included payments of interest on the national debt of £535m. and defence expenditure of £780m. (increased to £1,114m. for 1951/2 in the wake of the Korean invasion). Hence, overall, social service expenditure bulked less large in total public spending than in later years, especially in the 1980s and 1990s.[55]

Over Labour's period in office total public spending first fell by over 20 per cent in the fiscal years 1945/6 to 1949/50, as defence expenditure was cut back, but then rose again from 1950/1 as defence again expanded. Within the total, social services grew from perhaps £900m. in 1945/6 to £1,265m. in 1950/1 in current prices, from approximately 10 to 14 per cent of GDP (including transfer payments). This, it may be noted, is only half the scale of expansion suggested by Minford in a recent essay on the welfare state in post-war Britain. He does not give the detailed basis for the figures on which he bases his claim for an 'explosion in civil state spending', largely welfare-related, between 1945 and 1951.[56]

---

[53] PRO T171/403, Budget Committee 1951, Memo by Chancellor of the Exchequer (n.d.). The revenue from NHS charges has been netted out from the NHS figure, to give a total of £398m. (T171/407, Budget Committee, Draft Budget Speech, 6 April 1951).

[54] On the debate on food subsidies, see Rollings, 'Budgetary Policy', pp. 283–98.

[55] Lowe, *Welfare State*, table A1.

[56] GDP at factor cost was £8787m. in 1945, £11,366m. in 1950 (Feinstein, *National Income*, Table T.6). The figure for social service spending in 1945/6 is a 'guesstimate' based on the figures in the *Annual Abstract of Statistics*, no. 91, 1954; P. Minford, 'Reconstruction and the UK Postwar Welfare State: False Start and New Beginning' in R. Dornbusch, W. Nolling and R. Layard (eds.), *Postwar Economic Reconstruction and the Lessons for the East Today* (Cambridge, Mass., 1993), pp. 115–38.

Growth in expenditure on health, education and housing was held back in part by the real resource constraints discussed in the previous section. Expenditure on transfer payments through the National Insurance system was substantially less than had been anticipated before the system came into operation. In 1946 calculations were made of the future costs of National Insurance, and hence of the Exchequer's contribution on the tripartite contribution system, on the basis of a projected average unemployment rate of $8\frac{1}{2}$ per cent. In the event unemployment averaged around 2 per cent and claims on the fund were much fewer than expected. This related not only to unemployment benefit, but also sickness benefit, where claims fell by 15–20 per cent rather than rising the 20–25 per cent anticipated.[57]

The result of this buoyancy in the labour market was to generate a surplus in the National Insurance Fund, which was partially offset by cuts in the Exchequer contribution from 1950 onwards. Between 1948 and 1954 Exchequer costs were in total £136m.[58] less than expected in 1946. In this period at least, the National Insurance Fund remained rather more than actuarially sound.

Both contemporary and historical opinion has focused a great deal on the NHS in discussing the public expenditure costs of the welfare state. Why this should be so is not immediately obvious given the figures cited above, though part of the answer would seem to lie in the internal politics of the Labour government. The Minister of Health, Bevan, was the key figure of the Labour left, and his department's 'extravagance' was attacked most vigorously by Herbert Morrison, a rival on the right of the party, but also the man who had been most obviously defeated over the structure of the NHS.[59]

Popular perceptions of this issue are difficult to gauge. The NHS was undoubtedly popular, yet it did have a high visibility as an item of public expenditure, and as the most favoured item when survey respondents were asked on what area they thought the government should spend less money. A November 1948 social survey showed 26 per cent mentioning the NHS as something on which government spent money, with

---

[57] *National Insurance Act 1946. Report by the Government Actuary on the First Quinquennial Review* (1954); Titmuss, *Essays*, pp. 57–8. The fall in claims for sickness benefit reflects the fact that such claims are closely linked to the pressure of demand in the labour market. For the inter-war period this has been analysed by N. Whiteside, 'Counting the Cost: Sickness and Disability among Working People in an Era of Industrial Recession, 1920–30', *Economic History Review* 40 (1987), pp. 228–46. Presumably this relationship underlies the recent well-publicised rise in claims for disablement benefits.

[58] *Report by the Government Actuary*, paras. 24–8.

[59] Webster, *Health Services*, pp. 85–8, 134; R. Klein, *The Politics of the National Health Service* (1989), pp. 18–20.

10 per cent saying they spent too much on it (the same proportion mentioned the 'civil service').[60] A later survey found that 17 per cent of respondents thought the NHS was the item on which government spent most, though in fact at that time it ranked behind food subsidies, pensions, and interest on the national debt, let alone defence. As the survey commented: 'Thus there exists among a substantial proportion of the population an exaggerated idea of the cost of the Health Service in relation to other items which tends to be associated with belief that the Government is spending more than it should be on the service.'[61]

It remains unclear how far politicians were responding to this mood, and how far they created it. In any event a climate of crisis surrounded the public expenditure costs of the NHS almost from its inception.[62] Partly this was due to the gross underestimates of the cost of the service, both in the planning period and in the period immediately following its creation. This underestimation does not seem to have arisen from any attempt to fudge the issue by the Ministry of Health. In reply to allegations in 1950 that Bevan had dodged the issue of costs, Norman Brook, the Cabinet Secretary, pointed out to Attlee that this was not the case, that the original estimates had been consensual, and that Bevan had reported the higher than expected costs to the Cabinet as soon as they emerged. However, Bevan did suggest in 1950 that even prior to its establishment he thought it might cost £225m. p.a. *excluding* opticians, hearing aids and artificial limbs, which would have been significantly more realistic than the £170m. total projected at the service's foundation in 1948.[63]

In retrospect, as Klein observes, 'the political furore may seem disproportionate to the cause: a battle fought over paper figures and symbols, rather than real issues'.[64] The problem was not so much that spending was accelerating out of control, but that its base level was much higher than expected. The underestimate seems to have resulted from the failure to anticipate (i) a 20 per cent increase in the average frequency with which people consulted doctors; (ii) a very large increase in consultation rates amongst very old men and young women under thirty-five, and (iii) a big increase in rates of consultation for all those aged over sixty-five, as well as from the famous increase in demand for dentures, spec-

---

[60] PRO RG23/103, Survey of Knowledge and Opinion on the Economic Situation, Nov. 1948.
[61] Ibid., July 1949.
[62] Webster, *Health Services*, ch. 5.
[63] PRO PREM8/1486, Part I, National Health Service Norman Brook to PM, 29 March 1950; Klein, *Politics*, pp. 34–5; Webster, *Health Services*, pp. 133–43.
[64] Klein, *Politics*, p. 34.

tacles and medicines.[65] In fact, expenditure on the service over the period from its foundation until the early 1950s was only just keeping up with the expansion of the population, once allowance is made for the rise in the number of births and children, with their disproportionate demands on health care.[66] As a share of GNP, expenditure was actually falling after 1950, and indeed showed no tendency to rise until the mid-1960s.[67] The Guillebaud Committee of 1956 was able, on the basis of Abel-Smith and Townsend's figures, to argue that the cost of the NHS was not rising inexorably under Labour, as many seemed to have supposed.[68]

Taxation

The public expenditure cost of welfare in this period had to be financed entirely from taxation, as from 1947 onwards the government was running a budget surplus and repaying debt. The question that must be asked is how far this level of public expenditure imposed a cost on the economy by its effects on incentives to produce and save. This is especially important given that the British welfare state of the late 1940s, though no larger in scale of expenditure than, say, that in Germany, was characterised by a higher level of dependence on direct taxation than insurance contributions from employers and employees.[69]

The Labour government was extremely sensitive to the possible impact of high taxation on the level of economic activity.[70] It was an issue raised in every budget discussion in the late 1940s, and the standard rate of income tax was reduced to 9s (45p) in the pound in 1945, and the bands of lower rate tax and allowances were raised to reduce the impact of this rate at the lower end of the income tax range. There was also some switching of the tax burden from direct to indirect tax, especially on to the tobacco tax, which also had the benefit of marginally reducing demand for a dollar import. The government's economic advisers were sufficiently exercised on this incentive issue to press successfully for the setting up of a royal commission. The explicit purpose of this was to give an 'impartial and authoritative statement, to which

---

[65] Jewkes, *Genesis*, pp. 19–20.
[66] Abel-Smith and Townsend, *Cost*, p. 72.
[67] Ibid., p. 60; *Royal Commission on the NHS* (1978), table E6.
[68] Guillebaud, *Report*, para. 21.
[69] Harris, 'Enterprise and the Welfare State'.
[70] R. C. Whiting, 'Taxation Policy', pp. 117–34. Whiting focuses upon the impact of tax on business. Generally taxation in this period has been little explored, but see B. E. V. Sabine, *A History of Income Tax* (1966), ch. 13 and more generally J. E. Cronin, *The Politics of State Expansion: War, State and Society in Twentieth Century Britain* (1991), pp. 172–5.

everyone in the country would have to pay attention, to the effect that there are features in our present tax system which in the long run are very likely to damage our industrial efficiency'.[71]

On the business side, Labour introduced a differentiation between a high rate of tax on distributed profits and a lower one on those retained. The aim was to encourage investment, and to encourage wage earners to accept that shareholders were not gaining unreasonably from the high level of profits.[72] The overall level of taxation of profits was ritually denounced by the FBI and other employer bodies, but these protests were quite muted. This was partly because of support for the government's policies of budget surpluses, partly because of the recognition of this form of taxation as a quid pro quo for wage restraint, but also because of a belief that the rates might well have been higher.[73]

It would be difficult to point to any evidence that in this period high taxation inhibited business investment. Financially business was in a very strong position, with liquid resources unspent from the war period and added to by post-war profits. Control of investment was by physical controls rather than financial constraint, and from 1947 such controls were tightened significantly. However, these controls fell particularly heavily on the public sector, and investment in industrial plant and machinery rose sharply throughout the period.[74] It is in fact hard to find evidence (e.g. from business histories relating to the period) of substantial industrial investment projects being desired by the private sector and blocked by government action.

As far as individual taxation goes it was an article of faith on the Labour right that the level of this was damaging to the economy as well as to Labour's political support. For example, in 1949 Herbert Morrison wrote that: 'The incentive to effort for workers as well as professional and technical people and employers is seriously affected by this burden, which, in turn, reacts on our costs, and on our capacity to earn dollars. Sooner rather than later the taxpayer will rebel verbally and at the ballot box.'[75]

However, the evidence for this view is extremely unclear. First, there is the general problem of conflicting *a priori* assumptions in this area, the conflict between the 'income effect', which suggests people will work

---

[71] PRO T171/394, Budget Committee 1948, 'Note on Income Tax and Incentive', 6 Dec. 1947; T171/400, Budget Committee 1950, 'The Budget Position 1950/51', 22 Feb. 1950; T171/427, R. Hall to E. Plowden, 'Taxation Enquiry', 18 May 1950. Hall was the government's chief economic adviser.
[72] Whiting, 'Taxation Policy', pp. 123–5.
[73] Ibid., p. 125.
[74] Cairncross, *Years of Recovery*, pp. 34–5, 446–62; Tomlinson, 'Mr. Attlee's Supply-Side Socialism', *Economic History Review* 46 (1993), pp. 6–16.
[75] PRO PREM8/1415, Government Expenditure, 'The Economic Situation', 21 July 1949.

harder and/or longer to maintain their post-tax income in the face of a tax rise, and the 'substitution effect', which suggests that people will substitute leisure/lower effort in such circumstances. Second, there are always serious problems of evidence directly linking taxation to work effort and hours.[76]

For the 1940s there are no extant academic studies of this issue, but there are social surveys which can be used at least to give some idea of the impact of contemporary tax levels. In the late 1940s the government conducted a number of social surveys which attempted to gauge public perceptions of the economic situation. Some raised the tax issue only in an indirect form, such as asking respondents to list their 'personal problems'. Such a question in late 1947 yielded food shortages/rations 46 per cent, high prices 26 per cent, general shortages 15 per cent, clothes and cloth rationing 12 per cent, housing 7 per cent, with income tax/low wages at the bottom of the list with 2 per cent.[77]

The following year respondents were asked a more directly relevant question about how to increase production. When asked this as a *general* question 30 per cent mentioned income tax, 17 per cent high prices/low wages, 13 per cent food shortages. When asked how they *personally* would be encouraged to increase output, the largest proportion (unspecified) said 'more food/better food'.[78] A similar question the following year yielded parallel results with 8 per cent saying income tax cuts would increase their productivity. This survey also suggested that the impact of income tax, on which most attention in this period focused, may have been exaggerated: asked which tax they disliked most personally, 27 per cent said income tax, 24 per cent purchase tax and 23 per cent tobacco duty.[79]

None of these surveys yielded very decisive results, partly because their methodologies were rather crude. Significantly more sophisticated was a study carried out for the Royal Commission on the Taxation of Profits and Incomes in February/March 1952, when tax levels were still as high as during the Labour government's period in office.[80]

A stratified sample of people were asked a range of questions on attitudes to taxation, but the questions were also linked to behaviour via measures such as hours worked. Perhaps the most striking single result was a good empirical demonstration of the income versus the substi-

---

[76] C. Brown, *Taxation: The Incentive to Work* (Oxford, 1980), ch. 1.
[77] PRO RG23/92, Survey of Knowledge and Opinion about the Economic Situation, Dec. 1947.
[78] PRO RG23/103, Survey, Nov. 1948.
[79] PRO RG23/107, Survey, July 1949.
[80] *Royal Commission on the Taxation of Profits and Income 2nd Report* (1953), Appendix I: 'PAYE and Incentives'.

tution effect. Whilst 30 per cent of men and 25 per cent of women said higher taxes reduced their productive effort, 27 and 22 per cent respectively said it acted as an incentive to increased effort. Taken together with its studies of hours worked, the Survey concluded that:

Perhaps fewer than 5 per cent of the sample believed that their personal actions and behaviour had been materially affected by income tax. It seems then that whilst workers consider tax to be a deterrent and nearly all grumble about it in general discussion, it is not regarded as the most important deterrent and few carry the grumbling to the point of letting it affect their productive behaviour.[81]

One of the groups to whom the idea of tax disincentives had been particularly applied under Labour was coal miners. However, the Main Report of the Royal Commission reported an NCB study which showed that the tax level explained only one-third of 1 per cent of absences from the pit. As with the general survey, a major reason for such results was simply that very few people knew with any degree of accuracy what level of taxes they were subject to.[82]

Overall, it is difficult not to conclude that Labour probably had an exaggerated view of the effects of the level of tax on economic behaviour, though that does not of course necessarily mean that high taxation did not undermine Labour's political popularity.[83] One unintended consequence of the higher levels of taxation of the 1940s was to encourage the expansion of occupational welfare subsidised by tax concessions. In the case of pensions such concessions had long existed, but the higher levels of tax plus the big expansion in the numbers paying direct tax fuelled a major expansion of occupational pensions at the same time as Labour was seeking to improve state provision.[84] Labour was not enthusiastic about occupational pensions, but eventually seems to have accepted that they were popular. In 1950 they set up the Millard-Tucker Committee to look into tax concessions in this area.[85]

Welfare versus industry

The idea that resources devoted to social welfare place a burden upon 'industry' and the expansion of the economy is not just a retrospective

---

[81] Ibid., para. 6.
[82] *Royal Commission Report*, paras. 38–41; Appendix, 'Tax', para. 4.
[83] Zweiniger-Bargielowska, 'Rationing, Austerity and the Conservative Party'.
[84] Hannah, *Inventing Retirement*, pp. 44–5.
[85] Ibid., pp. 41, 47–9. Hannah describes the fiscal system in this area as a 'fundamentally rotten edifice of conflicting tax privileges' (p. 47). The Report, which didn't appear until 1954, had little to say on the Exchequer cost of occupational pensions (*Report of the Committee on the Taxation Treatment of Provision for Retirement* (1953)).

criticism, but a perspective largely, though not entirely, shared by the Labour government itself. Whilst committed to the creation of a 'welfare state', its members generally perceived that such a state could only be built on the basis of a strong economy. The idea that such expenditure of resources might have a positive effect on economic performance, whilst occasionally present in the rhetoric of the period, rarely affected policy decisions. As Bevan pointed out, in responding to calls for cuts in expenditure on health care, the budgetary calculations which under-pinned such calls 'took no account of national benefits to be secured by the health service, through improved health and the consequent increases in industrial production, since these effects were not precisely calculable'.[86]

This ideological posture of the welfare state is something of a puzzle. After all, there was a long-standing if thin tradition of seeing 'welfare' as a route to efficiency, most obviously embodied in the 'Efficients' pro-gramme at the turn of the century, and which had drawn support from prominent Fabians such as the Webbs.[87] Yet in general this strand of thinking was weak in Labour ideology in the 1940s. It is also worth noting that Beveridge himself, whilst often emphasising the causal link between a strong economy and welfare, on occasions brought out the potential contribution of improved welfare for economic efficiency.[88]

Occasionally the argument that social service programmes could ben-efit economic performance did surface, but it usually related to only a very small and specific part of the programmes – for example, technical education, as we have seen, or nursery classes in areas such as Lanca-shire. A similar point was made in debates about health service expendi-ture in so far as it related to nursery provision; such nurseries 'play an important part in the campaign to bring married women back into employment, and so there is a special drive to increase accommodation in the textile areas'.[89]

One reason for this approach was the lack of techniques for assessing the benefits of social programmes. The human-capital approach to edu-cation, for example, with its assessment of rates of return on investment, had not yet been invented. Similarly, the effects of health care of the type coming under the umbrella of the NHS on health states, mortality, etc. was something hardly discussed except in the vaguest possible

---

[86] PRO CAB134/220, Economic Policy Committee, 10 Oct. 1949.
[87] Searle, *National Efficiency*.
[88] I owe this point to Rodney Lowe. However, whilst difficult to summarise, Beveridge's views seem to have been dominated by the desire to build 'social cohesion' rather than a direct concern with efficiency (Harris, *Beveridge*, p. 418).
[89] PRO CAB134/448, Investment Programmes Working Party, 'Draft Report – Appendix on Health Services', 17 June 1946.

terms. The costs of provision were carefully calculated, but the benefits remained strikingly vague.[90] It was also commonly assumed that expenditure on health and education was highly redistributive, though the evidence on this was very thin.[91]

In the context of the way the debate was structured in the 1940s it seemed quite clear that social service provision should be subordinated to other considerations. This was most apparent in the allocation of investment resources, where from the beginning of investment controls it was emphasised that industry and infrastructure would have priority.[92] This view was spelt out in some detail in the 'Long-Term Programme' provided for the OEEC in 1948. This listed investment priorities in order of importance. Eighth and last on the list was 'the provision of essential services, such as housing, and of basic social services, such as water, health services and education [particularly on the technical side] which contribute to the nation's economic strength'.[93] The stress on contributing to economic strength seemingly did not raise the priority level of such expenditure.

In debates on public expenditure a similar approach was apparent: social service expenditure was largely seen as a burden on production via its alleged ill-effects on tax levels, though, as already suggested, the basis for such a view was extremely fragile. The one exception to this priority for economic objectives was defence, where, despite the absence of detailed analysis of benefits beyond a few slogans about Britain's role in the world, expenditure remained very high even before the disastrous attempt to expand during the Korean War.[94]

Overall, it is clear that in many respects the 'welfare state' of the 1940s was an austerity product of an age of austerity. Of course this was not commonly how it was seen by many enthusiasts during the war or

---

[90] On the basis of current literature the case for educational spending would have been greatly strengthened by such studies, but for health a much more ambiguous conclusion appears. On education see e.g. M. Blaug, *The Economics of Education* (1966); on health, from an enormous literature, T. McKeown, *The Role of Medicine: Dream, Mirage or Nemesis?* (Oxford, 1979).

[91] e.g. PRO T171/399, Budget Committee 1949 vol. III, 'Draft Speech', 1 April 1949. The fact that so much of the system was financed from central taxation may have made it more redistributive than those systems based more fully on 'Beveridge' principles of high levels of employer and employee contributions. Of course, later analysts were to stress the benefits to the middle classes of welfare provision: J. Le Grand, *The Strategy of Equality* (1982).

[92] *Capital Investment in 1948* (1947); F. A. Burchardt, 'Cuts in Capital Expenditure', *Bulletin of the Oxford Institute of Statistics* 10 (1948), pp. 1–8.

[93] *European Co-operation. Memoranda submitted to the OEEC Relating to Economic Affairs in the Period 1949–53: Long Term Programme* (1948), para. 157.

[94] PRO PREM8/1415, Government Expenditure 1945 Part II: Norman Brook to PM, 13 Oct. 1949. On the rearmament programme, see Cairncross, *Years of Recovery*, ch. 8.

immediately after Labour's victory in 1945, though social insurance according to the Beveridge model was always a minimal programme, and Labour's policies did not implement the key Beveridge proposal of radically reducing the role of means-tested benefits.[95] But after 1945 the economic priorities, narrowly conceived, of raising output and correcting the balance of payments quickly asserted themselves. The welfare state was created, but in a context where it consumed a quite limited level of resources, and where it was continuously vulnerable to a resource allocation system which gave priority to exports and industry, and restrained both private and collective consumption.

[95] Harris, 'Enterprise and the Welfare State', pp. 49–51; A. Deacon, 'An End to the Means Test? Social Security and the Attlee Government', *Journal of Social Policy* 11 (1982), pp. 289–306. Beveridge was, of course, based on the idea of a subsistence income upon which base 'voluntary action' would build. In the event what was built was not by friendly societies, as he envisaged, but largely by employers, with state subsidy (Russell, *Growth*, p. 106).

12   Equality versus efficiency?

The policy objectives of the 1945 Labour government were, perhaps like all governments, complex and potentially contradictory. This chapter is concerned with the place of equality within that set of objectives, and its relation to the efficiency concerns which, as earlier chapters have emphasised, came to be seen as so important. Lessening inequality was certainly a long-standing general aim of Labour policy. The case for equality had been powerfully argued with both practical trenchancy and ethical force in Tawney's *Equality*, first published in 1931. This became a standard reference point for much later Labour discussion, including the key works of Dalton and Durbin.[1] But even those who didn't acknowledge Tawney's work saw inequality as central to the socialist project, and with a similar ethical stress: 'economic inequality is in itself bad. It is bad because it propagates a false scale of values: a false servility on the one hand, and a false compliance on the other. It is impossible to deny that inequality destroys freedom, independence, self-respect and integrity . . . But besides all this inequality is evil because it is unjust.'[2]

A general predisposition to reduce inequality doesn't go very far in making a practical political programme. But Tawney and those who followed him had a clear, if broad, view about how greater equality was to be achieved. Tawney's 'strategy of equality' can be summarised as involving 'social policies to extend collective provision and equalise opportunities in education, health and housing, of taxation policies to strengthen the position of the worker, and of economic policies to bring the power of private capital under public direction'.[3] This quotation brings out some of the complexities of discussing equality. First, inequality is multi-dimensional, and Tawney himself especially empha-

[1] R. H. Tawney, *Equality* (4th edn 1952); Dalton, *Practical Socialism*, pp. 320–2; E. Durbin, *The Politics of Democratic Socialism* (1940), p. 13. For discussion of Tawney's arguments see A. W. Wright, *R. H. Tawney* (Manchester, 1987), ch. 5.

[2] Jay, *The Socialist Case*, p. 3. For parallel views from Gaitskell see Durbin, *New Jerusalems*, pp. 127–8.

[3] Wright, *Tawney*, p. 67; Tawney, *Equality*, pt. IV, 'The Strategy of Equality'.

sised two dimensions – inequalities in access to health and education provision on the one hand, and inequalities in economic power on the other. In addition, inequality can be measured in a variety of ways – inequality of opportunity and inequality of outcome being only the most obvious examples of the possibilities.[4]

This complexity means that almost any policy area can be discussed in terms of egalitarian criteria, but at the same time none of these criteria is likely to be definitive – a policy which reduces inequality in one direction may be neutral or even inegalitarian in another. One example of these complexities is nationalisation of industry, which many Labour theorists and supporters saw as reducing the economic power of the capitalist class, whilst regarding its impact on the distribution of income as minor, given a policy of full compensation of the previous owners.[5] Another rather different case is the NHS, where the principle of equality on a 'horizontal' or geographic basis was used to argue against local control of hospitals, leading to a centralisation which, both at the time and subsequently, has been seen as a significant undermining of local democracy in the welfare state.[6]

It would be impossible within the scope of one chapter to deal with all these ramifications on the pursuit of greater equality under the Attlee government. Here the focus is rather a narrower one – the pursuit of greater 'vertical' equality of income and wealth by means of increased provision of social services and their financing by taxation. The (alleged) conflict focused upon is that between the pursuit of such egalitarian ends and economic efficiency.

The emphasis on vertical redistribution by social service expenditure and higher taxes was crucial to, though by no means exhausted, Tawney's 'strategy of equality'. He argued that the means of achieving equality were 'no mystery, and the measures embodying it are the most familiar of commonplaces'. The first of these measures was 'the extension of social services and progressive taxation, which mitigate disparities of opportunity and circumstance, by securing that wealth which would otherwise be spent by a minority is applied to purposes of common advantage'.[7]

---

[4] Le Grand, *Strategy of Equality*, ch. 7.
[5] Dalton, *Practical Socialism*, pp. 176–7.
[6] Klein, *Politics*, pp. 18–19; Webster, *Health Services* (1988). In this period Labour tended to extend the duties of local government generally, but to make it more dependent on central finance. On the latter aspect see D. N. Chester, 'Local Finance', *Lloyds Bank Review* 21 (1951), pp. 33–47.
[7] Tawney, *Equality*, p. 119.

The focus on 'equality versus efficiency' derives both from the frequency with which that conflict is discussed in a wide range of literature,[8] and also from the specific suggestion that under Labour this conflict was resolved in favour of equality. In his *Audit of War*, as discussed in chapter 4, Barnett argued that the 'New Jerusalem' of welfare provision deprived the industrial economy of resources, and undermined any possibility of an effective 'national industrial strategy' in the late 1940s. The specifics of this argument will not be rehearsed again; rather, the focus will be on the extent to which the 'New Jerusalem' in the sense of welfare provision and progressive taxation did generate greater equality, and whether in turn that programme created inefficiencies.

A strategy of equality?

To talk of equality versus efficiency under the Attlee government is to prejudge a major issue – to what extent did the policy of creating a welfare state (and other policies) involve a clear and explicit attempt to achieve equality?

Certainly some authors have seen in Labour's policy in this period such a 'strategy of equality', which was embodied in the institutions of the welfare state, both those which involved a direct transfer of income and those, like education and health, which provided services in kind.[9] However, this strategy is difficult to find in the 1940s. The centrepiece of the social security system, the National Insurance system, provided for flat-rate benefits from flat-rate contributions, as Beveridge had proposed, which meant a substantial part of the system was financed by a regressive poll-tax, with any progressivity coming only through the employers' and Exchequer contributions. This was in conflict with proposals to make the contributions income-related, which would have brought a much greater degree of redistribution. But it reflected the fact that Labour had developed its own social insurance plan prior to Beveridge which also embodied a flat-rate system.[10]

The NHS was the result of many conflicting aims, but on the government side the predominant one seems to have been to provide a good, minimum standard of health care for everyone. In education a similar summary of objectives seems appropriate. The central aim was to make secondary education available free to all, whilst sustaining the equality

---

[8] On the broad intellectual background to these arguments, see E. H. Phelps Brown, *Egalitarianism and the Generation of Inequality* (Oxford, 1988).
[9] Le Grand, *Strategy of Equality*, pp. 6–12.
[10] Harris, *Beveridge*, p. 416; Brooke, *Labour's War*, pp. 145–65.

of *opportunity* allegedly provided by the grammar school system. In the cases of both health and education nothing was done to undermine the private systems, and in particular the public schools remained as one of Tawney's 'massive pillars of indefensible disparities of income and opportunity'.[11]

Overall, to talk about the welfare state as part of a 'strategy of equality' is seriously to misunderstand the approach taken by Labour in the 1940s. This is not to say that Labour did not believe in some general sense in greater equality, but they expected this to come as a by-product of provision created with different primary ends.[12] Central to those ends in the 1940s was a reduction of insecurity. This is one of the key themes of the 1945 general election manifesto, *Let Us Face the Future*. Nowhere in this document is equality mentioned, but a key general aim of Labour policy is said to be to provide 'security for all against a rainy day', and this metaphor recurs in the more specific discussion of the case for social insurance. This emphasis on security is reflected in some analyses of the British welfare state, which see its expansion in the 1940s as driven by a heightened perception of risk and insecurity brought about by the war.[13]

Conditioned by this fear of insecurity, the strategy of Labour – rather than one of equality – might be better summarised as that of the universal minimum – a slogan coined by the Webbs before the First World War (see chapter 1). This focus on 'minimum universalism' in practice had contradictory effects on equality of outcome. On the one hand, in so far as everyone was given access to minimum levels of income, education and health care, the gap between the position of the poor and that of higher income groups was reduced. On the other hand, for those who had previously paid for health and education, and found the standards of the new free services acceptable, major benefits accrued from no longer having to pay, and inequality increased.

What these examples point up again is, of course, the great complexity of both conceptualising and measuring equality even within a particular policy area. This issue will be returned to. But the point to be emphasised

[11] Klein, *Politics*; Tawney, *Equality*, p. 223.

[12] Crosland, whom Le Grand treats as key exponent of the strategy of equality wrote 'social security cannot be held to be the ultimate purpose of the social services. This must surely be the relief of social distress handling and the correction of social need; though naturally measures directed to this end will often also enhance social equality, which in any case remains an important subsidiary objective' (*The Future of Socialism* (1956), p. 148).

[13] Labour Party, *Let Us Face the Future*, pp. 2, 8; R. E. Goodin and J. Dryzek, 'Risk-Sharing and Social Justice: The Motivational Foundations of the Post-War Welfare State' in Goodin and Le Grand (eds.), *Not Only the Poor* (1987), ch. 3. For contemporary emphasis on insecurity see Jay, *The Socialist Case*, pp. 3–6; Durbin, *Politics*, pp. 101–2; J. Griffiths, *Pages from Memory* (1969), pp. 88–9.

here is that such complexities rarely arose in the contemporary political and administrative debates about the design of the welfare system, because equality was not the prime concern. As Rodney Lowe has pointed out, 'greater equality of outcome was not an initial objective of the welfare state'. Rather, the Labour Party's objective 'was the establishment of a national minimum of subsistence, below which no one would fall, whether through ill health, unemployment, poverty, or old age'.[14]

If Le Grand exaggerates Labour's commitment to a 'strategy of equality' in the 1940s, his argument that the provision of free services like health and education benefits the well-off disproportionately was not one widely accepted by ministers and administrators in the 1940s. The distributive consequences of the welfare state not being a primary concern, they were little investigated, at least by officials. The whole question of the impact of spending in such areas remained largely unexamined. As a high-ranking official expressed it in 1950: 'We have made, so far as I know, no serious enquiries into the economics of health and education. Is increased expenditure in these sectors remunerative or not? I do not know: and the economists' conventional complaints about the burden of social services do not seem to me the answer either.'[15]

But outside ministerial and official circles Labour's policies and their impact on income distribution stimulated a considerable literature. As regards the social services, one analyst of the late 1940s argued, as Le Grand was to do over thirty years later, that:

A strong case could be made out that the postwar extension of social security benefited mainly the middle classes. Those in the higher income brackets who came to make use of the health service enjoyed the biggest saving when it was introduced; food subsidies are increasingly becoming a social service to the rich as rationing is abandoned; and educational expenditure especially benefits the middle class both because their children have a start in the scramble for scholarships and because much of it is a direct subsidy to higher education.

Such a perception was not limited to academics. For example, James Callaghan MP argued in 1948 that there was little inter-class transfer via the social security system as 'most working class benefits are paid for by the working class'.[16]

Neither of these authors, however, provided quantitative evidence on this issue. As already noted, such analysis was not provided by govern-

[14] Lowe, *Welfare State*, p. 292 (see also pp. 11–12); Brooke, *Labour's War*, pp. 147–8.
[15] PRO T230/328, D. Bensusan-Butt to R. Hall, 'The Presentation of Economic Policies', 15 Nov. 1950.
[16] D. Seers, *The Levelling of Incomes since 1938* (Oxford, 1951), p. 4; J. Callaghan, 'The Approach to Social Equality' in D. Munro (ed.), *Socialism: The British Way* (1948), pp. 139–40.

ment and its officials. One reason for this was perhaps not just naivety or lack of resources, but an implicit understanding that the assumption of the redistributive consequences of the expansion of social welfare provision was necessary both generally to sustain working-class support for the government, and more explicitly to sustain the relationship with the trade unions, in a period when the 'social wage' played a key role in the government's relationship with the unions.[17]

In trying to restrain wage inflation in this period Labour ministers would directly emphasise the benefits accruing to the workers from welfare expenditure, and the superiority of this social wage to increases in money wages. For example, in 1947 Bevin told a delegation of trade unionists that the current food subsidies were equal to 12s 6d ($72\frac{1}{2}$p) per head of population, and that 'It took us a very long time to win that after a very long strike at the end of the last war'.[18] In fact, as the quote from Seers above suggests, food subsidies were not just a subsidy to wages, but significantly aided salary earners and all who consumed food. Whilst the lower income groups spent *proportionately* more on food, the better-off spent *absolutely* more, so it would be difficult to pronounce on the overall distributive effects of the subsidies, as would be true of other social services. The *Economist*, keen to analyse the scale of redistribution, published an index in 1950 purporting to show that the cost of living of those on £500 p.a. had risen by 10 per cent more than those on a working-class income between 1938 and 1949, but as they themselves conceded, these were 'very rough estimates'.[19]

The argument so far has stressed that in constructing the 'welfare state', Labour in the 1940s was not primarily concerned with equality (however measured), that it usually hoped and assumed that the results would be egalitarian but did not seriously examine this assumption, even though some commentators questioned it. The central point is to focus on the historical context of the creation of the welfare state, and to correct common notions about a 'strategy of equality'. The aim has not been to disparage Labour's 'universal minimum' approach, however much it might be accurate to note its conservative implications in some areas, notably education.[20]

---

[17] N. Whiteside, 'Aiming at Consensus: Social Welfare and Industrial Relations 1939–79' in C. Wrigley (ed.), *A History of British Industrial Relations*, forthcoming.

[18] PRO T171/394, Budget Papers, Meeting of Ministers with TUC, 17 Nov. 1947.

[19] *Economist*, 158, 21 Jan. 1951, pp. 121–2.

[20] For example, Morgan, *Labour in Power*, p. 177 castigates the Attlee government in this area: 'education was an area where the Labour Government failed to provide any new ideas or inspiration', and the support of grammar schools 'enshrined inequality'. For a persuasive case for seeing the commitment to grammar schools as compatible with Labour's general ideology at this time, see M. Francis, 'A Socialist Policy for Edu-

The strategy of a universal minimum meant above all that the aim of the welfare state was to defeat poverty. The evidence suggests that this strategy met with considerable success, though not perhaps with quite as much as was commonly believed at the time. The classic piece of evidence, which received a lot of attention when it was published, was Rowntree and Lavers' Survey of York in 1950, following up Rowntree's famous poverty studies of 1898 and 1936. In this book Rowntree and Lavers directly compared the level of poverty of 1936 and 1950, and suggested that, whereas in the earlier year 31.1 per cent of the working class and 17.7 per cent of the total population lived in poverty, by 1950 the comparable figures were 2.77 and 1.66 per cent.[21] Not surprisingly, these figures were used in the 1951 general election as a vindication of Labour's policies.

However, Townsend shortly after, and Atkinson much later, suggested that these figures were unduly optimistic.[22] Because of problems in the sampling techniques used, the quality of the data obtained, the use of the 'household' rather than the 'family' as the unit of assessment, and the fact that York was not typical of the rest of Britain because of the relative absence of low-paid jobs, Rowntree's estimates need some upward adjustment. Using the National Assistance Standard, Atkinson suggests that Rowntree's figure for the proportion of families in poverty might be put at 5.8 per cent rather than 1.66, which would bring it closer into line with other post-war estimates. This was still, on any calculation, a substantial improvement on the 1930s, though, as Rowntree himself pointed out, a substantial part of it was not due to welfare spending but to full employment and higher wages. According to the survey, where unemployment was the cause of poverty in 28.6 per cent of all cases in 1936, and low wages in 32.8 per cent, by 1950 the comparable figures were zero and 1 per cent. Poverty had become overwhelmingly a problem of sickness and especially old age. Rowntree and Lavers made a separate calculation that if welfare legislation had remained unaltered between 1936 and 1950, the fall in the level of poverty in poor working-class households would have been from 31.1 per cent to 22.2 per cent rather than the actual figure of 2.8 per cent.[23] None of these figures suggest that the 1940s welfare state was ineffective in raising minimum standards, though they do caution against contem-

cation?: Labour and the Secondary School 1945–51', *History of Education* 24 (1995), pp. 319–35.

[21] S. B. Rowntree and G. Lavers, *Poverty and the Welfare State* (1951), pp. 30–1.
[22] P. Townsend, 'Poverty: Ten Years after Beveridge', *Planning* 19 (1952), pp. 21–40; A. B. Atkinson, 'Poverty in York: A Re-Analysis of Rowntree's 1950 Survey' in Atkinson, *Poverty and Social Security* (1989); Lowe, *Welfare State*, pp. 139–41.
[23] Rowntree and Lavers, *Poverty*, chs. 3, 4.

Table 12.1   *Public expenditure, 1949/50*

Main components	£m.
Defence	740.7
Interest on national debt	470.6
Foreign and imperial	63.9
Home departments	51.6
Trade, industry and transport	150.6
'Welfare' (including Exchequer contribution to National Insurance)	1,203.4
Of which:	
Transfer payments	(420.8)
Food subsidies	410.0
Total	3,375.3

Source: Annual Abstract of Statistics, vol. 89, 1952.

porary euphoria, and bring out the key role of the change in the labour market in underpinning those standards.

The impact of taxation

The effects of the Labour government's policies on equality in Britain cannot just be viewed in relation to spending on the social services. These services were financed by taxation, and that taxation had, at least potentially, major redistributive effects. In addition, the scale and character of taxation is usually seen as an important determinant of efficiency and growth. This section will therefore look at both the 'equality' and 'efficiency' aspects of taxation in this period.

A prior consideration is the overall pattern of expenditure, in particular how much was spent on social welfare. Table 12.1 gives a broad picture of public expenditure for 1949/50, though the serious problems of definition in this area should be noted. For example, how far food subsidies should be treated as 'welfare' and how far as part of macroeconomic (anti-inflationary) policy is contentious, an important issue because of both the large amounts spent under this heading in the late 1940s and the big dispute that arose over it at the time (a point returned to below).

As can be seen from table 12.1, social welfare expenditure according to the broadest definition made up somewhat less than half of total government expenditure.[24] In addition it should be noted that taxation was greater than expenditure in 1949/50 (as it was in the two preceding

[24] In his 1951 budget speech the Chancellor stressed that 'nearly half' of government spending was on defence and debt interest, three-eighths on food subsidies and social services.

budgetary years) so that the tax system was financing a significant amount of public sector saving, calculated at £757m. for 1949/50 by Cairncross.[25]

If we include financing the surplus, central taxation under Labour was equivalent to 35–38 per cent of national income if National Insurance contributions are also included. Prior to the Korean War the trend in this figure was (gradually) downwards, from 37.7 per cent in 1946 to 34.9 per cent in 1951.[26] The starting point for Labour in raising this money was, of course, the tax structure bequeathed by the wartime policy of expanding the income tax down the income scale to embrace a significant proportion of manual workers, whilst increasing indirect taxes on a large number of consumption items, but with some exceptions aimed at stabilising the cost of living as far as possible. The wartime budgets had therefore been used not only to balance the overall economy, notably from Kingsley Wood's 'first Keynesian budget' of 1941,[27] but as far as possible to make the much higher tax impositions socially acceptable. Keynes' wartime call for a 'social policy budget' may not have got very far,[28] but there was a new recognition in wartime of the distributive impact of taxation. However, the scale of the redistribution of income via tax was not closely assessed, and in the post-war period serious discussion of this issue was largely confined to outside academics, rather than the Treasury or Inland Revenue.[29]

Table 12.2 gives some idea of the pattern of taxation in the late 1940s. Just more than half of total taxation was from direct taxation, with the great bulk of that coming from income tax. On the indirect side, perhaps the most striking feature is the weight of taxation on alcohol and tobacco, the latter encouraged by the desire to save dollar imports.

Changes in the pattern of taxation under Attlee were quite small, falling expenditure on the military as demobilisation proceeded (and until reversed by the Korean War) being largely offset by rises in spending on civil programmes, coupled to the desire to raise revenue to hold domestic demand in check. Tax reductions were largely focused on raising the income tax threshold and reducing the rates in the lower bands. The standard rate was reduced from 10s to 9s in 1945, before being raised to 9s 6d in 1951 to help finance Korean War expenditure. This fall in direct tax revenue was partly offset by rises in indirect taxation, especially in the two budgets of 1947 and that of 1948.[30]

The focus of tax cuts on the threshold for paying income tax seems

[25] Cairncross, *Years of Recovery*, p. 420.
[26] Dow, *Management*, p. 188.
[27] Sayers, *Financial Policy*.
[28] PRO T171/360, J. M. Keynes, 'Notes on the Budget', 3 Nov. 1941.
[29] Lowe, *Welfare State*, p. 283.
[30] Dow, *Management*, pp. 198–200.

Table 12.2   *Tax receipts, 1948/9*

(£m.)

Direct		
Income tax	1,410	
Surtax	90	
Profits tax	200	
Total	1,700	
Capital		
Death duties	160	
Special contribution	105	
Total	265	1,965
Indirect		
Stamp duties	55	
Alcohol	440	
Tobacco	580	
Entertainment	50	
Purchase tax	275	
Oil	55	
Other	90[1]	
		1,545
Other receipts		135
Total tax liabilities		3,645

[1] Original has 145 here, in error.

Source: PRO T171/397, R. Hall, 'Budgetary Prospects and Policies, 1948–1952', 17 July 1948.

to have been largely stimulated by incentive arguments. In his 1945 budget, for example, Dalton argued that, in relation to its impact on low incomes, 'there is plenty of evidence that it has reduced incentive and discouraged effort, and thus diminished production'. The effect of the 1945 budget was to take perhaps 2 million people out of tax entirely, and to reduce the tax on a man earning £5 a week (a good manual wage in 1945) from 19s 3d (97p) to 11s 5d (56p).[31] A similar theme is common in budget discussions in the late 1940s, and with the action that followed, large numbers of low-paid workers were eliminated from the income tax system. By 1949 a married man with two children would have had to reach 103 per cent of average earnings before paying any income tax, and 187 per cent before paying at the standard rate. Whilst income tax was no longer the middle-class tax it had been before 1939, it remained the case that indirect taxes were the main tax burden for the

[31] PRO T171/37, 'Draft Budget Speech', 22 Oct. 1945; T171/386, 'Draft Budget Speech', 6 April 1946.

bulk of the working class, plus of course the highly regressive employees' flat-rate National Insurance contributions, which amounted to about 1.9 per cent of national income in 1951.[32]

The adjustments to income tax thresholds and bands reflected a broader concern with incentives amongst the working class which informed a lot of policy discussion in the late 1940s. There were proposals, for example, for exempting all overtime from income tax, or at least doing so for coal miners, whose output was deemed so important for the whole economic situation.[33] Ministers rejected this particular proposal, though most continued to be convinced that significant disincentives existed. Evidence on this aspect of the tax system is imperfect, though surveys done at the time suggest that *indirect* tax was often more disliked by the working class (perhaps not surprisingly, given the discussion above) and that the impact of income tax on workers' effort was probably exaggerated in ministers' minds.

For example, in an official survey in late 1947, only 2 per cent of respondents cited income tax as a personal economic problem, the majority citing rationing and food shortages, high prices and queuing as the major issues. In February 1948 a more explicit question was asked: 'Which of these taxes do you dislike most personally?' and the answer was 36 per cent purchase tax, 30 per cent income tax and 17 per cent tobacco tax. Hostility to income tax increased with income, whilst 'the tobacco tax is the most unpopular in the middle group which includes the majority of manual workers'. The Survey of July 1949 asked: 'Which tax do you dislike most, personally?' and the replies were income tax 27 per cent, purchase tax 24 per cent, tobacco 23 per cent. (It is noticeable that apparently no one cited the highly regressive National Insurance contribution when asked about taxation.)[34]

This focus on incentives did not mean that Labour Chancellors ignored the impact of the tax system on equality. In his budget of 1945 Dalton declared the need to maintain a high level of surtax in pursuit of equality, and his 1946 budget speech argued for tax as part of the strategy in which 'this Government, and the Parliamentary majority behind it, intend to press steadily forward towards the goal of greater social equality, for which, through six long years of war, our soldiers fought and died'.[35]

---

[32] PRO T171/394 Inland Revenue, 'Note on Income Tax and Incentive', 6 Dec. 1947; Lowe, *Welfare State*, p. 285; Dow, *Management*, p. 188.

[33] P. M. Williams (ed.), *The Diary of Hugh Gaitskell 1945-56* (1983), p. 39.

[34] PRO RG23/92, 23/94, 23/103, 23/107, Survey of Knowledge and Opinion about the Economic Situation, Dec. 1947, Feb. 1948, Nov. 1948, July 1949.

[35] PRO T171/371, 'Draft Budget Speech', 22 Oct. 1945; T171/386, *Budget 1946*, Draft of BBC Speech, 9 April 1946. See also Dalton, *High Tide*, pp. 26-7, 113-14.

This rhetoric notably shifted in the later 1940s. Cripps' budget speech of 1949, after establishing the unavoidable nature of continued high taxation to pay for the current level of defence and social service expenditure, went on to argue that there was little future scope for further income redistribution, and that attention should concentrate on increasing total wealth. In fact, Cripps' speech embodied two contradictory views about redistribution which were increasingly heard in Labour circles in this period. On the one hand, he argued that redistribution resulted 'to a large extent from the provision of these extended social services for the less well to do at the expense of the well to do'. On the other hand, he suggested that with the total tax burden 'now more than 40 per cent', the recipients of social services were largely paid for by the same group.[36] This confusing message about redistribution was to become quite widely prevalent in the late 1940s and early 1950s, and will be returned to below.

One example of the limits of redistribution via the tax system was the issue of capital taxation. Dalton, the Chancellor in 1945–7, had long been an advocate of capital taxation, and indeed was widely cited for his advocacy of a reformed version of the Rignano system of inheritance tax.[37] Dalton's advocacy reflected both a socialist belief in the need to redistribute wealth and an economist's belief that capital taxation represented a way of raising revenue with minimum disincentive effects. There was much debate in Treasury circles on this issue, culminating in the preparation of the 1948 budget. At that time the main form of capital taxation was the death duties, which Dalton had made substantially more progressive in the budget of 1947. In 1948 the argument focused on the issue of a capital levy. It had been much debated, though never implemented, after the First World War, as a means of trying to pay off the national debt. This approach had been rejected in 1945, partly because low interest rates made the idea of the burden of the debt less compelling. Opposition to the levy was reiterated by the Inland Revenue in late 1947, coupled to questioning of the administrative feasibility and the scale of the net revenue likely to be raised by such an impost.[38]

This traditional Inland Revenue posture was backed up by the head of the Economic Section, Robert Hall, who foresaw an 'all round shock

---

[36] PRO T171/399, 'Draft Budget Speech', 1 April 1949; see also Cronin, *Politics of State*, p. 173.

[37] The Rignano system, broadly speaking, imposed a higher tax on an inheritance as it passed from generation to generation (Dalton, *The Inequality of Incomes* (1920), ch. 9; see also Jay, *The Socialist Case*, pp. 226–31).

[38] Dalton, *High Tide*, pp. 115–17; PRO T171/395, *Budget 1948* vol. 2. Inland Revenue, 'Note on Capital Levy', 30 Dec. 1947. On the long-run debate on such a levy, see R. C. Whiting, 'The Boundaries of Taxation' in S. J. D. Green and R. C. Whiting (eds.), *The Boundaries of the State in Modern Britain* (Cambridge, forthcoming).

to business confidence' from such a measure.[39] This was the general tenor of official advice, and it was successful – up to a point. In the event Cripps imposed a 'Special Contribution', which was effectively a capital tax, but which avoided some of the administrative difficulties of such taxes by being levied on surtax payers. The reason for Cripps' insistence on going ahead with this measure seems to have been a combination of the belief that other sources of revenue, especially from direct tax, were reaching their limit and that wealth should be taxed as part of the process of holding demand in check.[40] However, in going against the advice of most officials, Cripps responded to their criticism by pointing out that the Special Contribution was once and for all, and reduced the originally proposed top rate of the tax from 15s to 10s.[41]

This sensitivity to issues of 'confidence' may be seen as part of the move in budgetary rhetoric and policy away from the egalitarian aims and achievements of the fiscal system and towards a greater regard for the interests of higher income groups. Perhaps Cripps was particularly susceptible to such pressures because of the priority he gave to economic modernisation, which he hoped could be achieved in alliance with business as well as trade unions. Hence his advisers aimed well when they told him: 'During the last 6 months you have done what no other man in the country could have done, and that is to secure the general support of industry and commerce for a Labour government. This is a priceless asset, and one without which there is no hope of our surmounting our economic problems.'[42]

Certainly, some of the officials by this time were explicitly saying that efficiency was being sacrificed to equality by the fiscal system. For example, in 1950 Hall argued that 'the real trouble comes in the effect of taxation on enterprise and the supply of capital'. There was, he argued, a clear need to reduce the higher tax rates 'if we could only get over the political difficulties of doing anything at all for the capitalist'. His solution was to press for a royal commission to try and persuade the public of what, for him, was an obvious truth.[43] This view of incentives was widely stated at this time by politicians and industrialists, and the latter of course determined the level of 'confidence' in the government. Typical of the

---

[39] Inland Revenue, 'A Capital Levy and Deflation', Dec. 1947.

[40] This macroeconomic aspect of capital taxation had been examined in a widely cited article by J. R. Hicks ('The Empty Economy', *Lloyds Bank Review* 5 (1947), pp. 1–13), who concentrated on the anti-inflationary rather than the revenue-raising aspect of such a tax.

[41] PRO T171/395, E. Plowden to Cripps, 31 March 1948.

[42] Ibid.

[43] PRO T171/427, Hall to Plowden, 18 May 1950. This was eventually done, in the form of the Royal Commission on the Taxation of Income and Profits, which reported in 1953/4.

views expressed by industrialists was the argument that Britain had 'heavier taxation than that imposed upon industry in any other country in the world' and to couple this directly with Britain's low productivity, so touching directly on the government's most sensitive spot.[44]

In addressing the issue of taxation of the well-off, Labour was faced with what might be called a classic social democratic dilemma. On the one hand, faced with the need to finance higher levels of public spending on a 'fair' basis, stiff taxes on high incomes were unavoidable; on the other hand, the government wanted to encourage savings and investment. The government tried in part to square this circle by combining fiscal incentives for investment with taxation that discriminated against distributed and in favour of retained profits. Thus, alongside the investment allowances introduced in 1945 and doubled in 1949, Labour imposed differential taxes on distributed and undistributed profits. At one level this latter measure met the political need to contain the growth of non-wage incomes, especially at a time when the government put so much emphasis on limiting wage inflation. On the other hand, its distributive effects were of course offset by the fact that retained profits lead to capital gains, which in Britain remained lightly taxed, so the egalitarian effect of such measures was largely illusory.[45]

The effect of high taxation on savings and investment in this period, as always, presents a complex picture. Investment is in some respects more straightforward. Investment rose sharply in post-war Britain, and indeed continually threatened the economy's capacity to cope with either the consequences for aggregate demand or the balance of payments. The restraint on investment was the availability not of finance but of physical resources, most notably steel.[46] Hence it cannot be argued that the company sector had any difficulty in obtaining investment finance either through ploughed-back profits or borrowing at low interest rates. Company savings seem to have been buoyant in the face of the tax pressure on distributed profits (table 12.3). As Cairncross remarks: 'these figures suggest that what has been taken by the Exchequer in higher taxation of profits has been at the expense of the shareholder rather than of the consumer on the one side or the self-financing of industrial expansion on the other'.[47]

[44] S. P. Chambers, 'Taxation and the Supply of Capital for Industry', Lloyds Bank Review 11 (1949), pp. 1–20; this view was strongly contested by G. Walker, 'Some Economic Aspects of the Taxation of Companies', Manchester School 22 (1954), pp. 1–36.

[45] Seers, Levelling, pp. 34–5.

[46] Tomlinson, 'Mr. Attlee's Supply-Side Socialism', pp. 1–22.

[47] A. Cairncross, 'Saving and Investment since the War', Westminster Bank Review (Feb. 1955), pp. 4–8; see also A. R. Ilersic, Government Finance and Fiscal Policy in Postwar Britain (1955), pp. 114, 122–3.

Table 12.3 *Income and outgoings as a percentage of turnover, 1936–8 and 1948–9*

	Annual average	
	1936–8	1948–9
Gross income	11.84	11.14
Taxation	1.34	3.56
Dividends	6.68	3.14
Undistributed profits and depreciation	3.83	4.41

Source: D. Walker, 'Some Economic Aspects of Taxation of Companies', *Manchester School* 22 (1954), p. 18.

Given that Britain was a large capital exporter through most of the Attlee period, it must be the case that savings exceeded domestic investment by a substantial margin. In that sense savings were not a problem, and the tax levels of the period would appear to have had little effect. But this would be somewhat misleading, in that a significant part of total savings after 1947 were from the budget surplus. For 1948–50 this source of savings was around 30 per cent of all gross domestic investment.[48] Household saving, as opposed to corporate saving, was low in the early post-war years, and this is where the level of taxation had some impact, though it would seem likely that it was also affected by understandable desire of people to rebuild their stocks and improve their consumption after the privations of war. On the other hand, the greater propensity to buy houses and purchase life insurance partly offset this desire.[49] Some fall in saving would be the inevitable result of any egalitarian shift in the distribution of income, however caused, because the propensity to save tends to rise with income levels.

How much equality?

How much redistribution was achieved by the combination of Labour's spending and taxation policies? This was a subject on which there was little official investigation in the early post-war period, but that did not prevent strong statements on the issue being made by politicians, often of a contradictory nature. Labour increasingly wanted to satisfy different political ends – it wanted to tell its working-class supporters that they were getting a good deal because of the redistribution brought about by

[48] Data from Cairncross, *Years of Recovery*, pp. 421, 456.
[49] Ilersic, *Finance*, pp. 82–4.

Table 12.4   *Distribution of original income, 1938 and 1947*

(Gini coefficients[1])

	1938	1947
Distributed private income	0.43	0.35
Distributed and undistributed profits	0.44	0.42
All private incomes	0.42	0.39

[1] A Gini coefficient is a measure of inequality, such that if all units received equal income its value would be zero, and if one unit received all income, its value would be one.
Source: D. Seers, *The Levelling of Incomes since 1938* (Oxford, 1951), p. 38.

its policies. On the other hand, by the late 1940s it wanted to argue that this process had inherent limits, that too much redistribution would kill the golden goose. Thirdly, it became concerned that redistribution was alienating potential middle-class support.[50]

The change in the distribution of income between the 1930s and the late 1940s was not solely the effect of government spending and taxation. The tight labour market of the war and post-war years, coupled perhaps to price and rent controls, produced some shift in original, pre-tax money incomes (table 12.4), and this shift undoubtedly began in the war years rather than being initiated under Attlee.

As the figures in table 12.4 suggest, the exclusion of undistributed profits makes the shift appear much greater than would otherwise be the case. A further stage of analysis would be just to take into account taxation, and if this is done a greater shift in distribution is apparent, basically towards wages and salaries at the expense of property incomes but also of wage earners gaining relative to those on salaries (table 12.5).[51]

Plainly the figures in table 12.5, whilst instructive, leave out a large part of the story because they ignore the role of government expenditure, which is the most difficult and controversial part of the redistribution issue. One major study of this issue argued, like Cripps in 1948, that the expanded spending on social services after the war had been entirely paid for by increased taxation of the working class, especially taxes on alcohol and tobacco. In this view redistribution was largely horizontal: 'Those who do not smoke or drink, but who live in a govern-

[50] PRO T171/400, 'Taxation of the Middle Classes', 12 Jan. 1950.
[51] For scepticism on the extent of this redistribution, see J. A. Brittain, 'Some Neglected Features of Britain's Income Levelling', *American Economic Review* 50 (1960), pp. 593–603.

Table 12.5 *Shares of post-tax income, 1938 and 1949*

(%)

	1938	1949
Undistributed corporate profits	4.6	5.5
Distributed corporate profits and mixed income	30.3	21.6
Total property and mixed income	34.9	27.1
Wages	35.5	42.0
Salaries	22.2	20.7
Forces pay	1.6	2.4
Total work incomes	59.3	65.1
Social income	5.7	7.8
Total	100.0	100.0

Source: Seers, *Levelling*, p. 52.

ment-owned house, wear utility clothing, use utility furniture, and have a large family enjoy the maximum of benefits and pay the minimum of taxes. This advantageous position is related more to their consumption habits than their income.'[52]

Whilst this analysis pointed to some important aspects of post-war redistribution, its conclusions on the absence of vertical redistribution appear exaggerated. The problem is that Weaver allocates all expenditure on the social services to the working class whilst all other expenditure is deemed to accrue to other income groups. This is plainly not satisfactory, as the middle classes also benefited from 'universal' welfare provision.[53] The most systematic attempt to go beyond this crude method was made by Carter.[54] He divided public expenditure into three types – transfer payments, divisible services such as housing, education and health, and indivisible (law and order, military, debt interest, etc.). He then attempted to apportion each of these to income groups, for the last category making three different calculations based on assumption of benefit accordance with (i) equal division per capita, (ii) division proportional to private income level, (iii) division according to taxes paid. As would be expected, these give progressively declining levels of benefit to the lowest income groups.

[52] F. Weaver, 'Taxation and Redistribution in the UK', *Review of Economics and Statistics* 32 (1950), p. 213.
[53] A. T. Peacock and P. R. Browning, 'The Social Services in Great Britain and the Redistribution of Income' in Peacock (ed.), *Income Distribution and Social Policy* (1954), pp. 156–9.
[54] A. M. Carter, *The Redistribution of Income in Postwar Britain* (New Haven, 1955), chs. 5, 6.

Whichever of the latter assumptions is used, clear gains are made by those with incomes below the taxable £500 income per annum in 1948/9, and losses above that figure. The middle assumption would have those on £135 per annum or less having their incomes raised by 57 per cent, those on £135–250 by 29 per cent, and those with £250–500 by 13 per cent.

The major question mark over Carter's study is probably the allocation of expenditure in areas such as health and education. On health, for example, he adjusts for the fact that registration with the NHS was more or less universal in the lowest income groups, and then fell broadly as income rose. But beyond that he links expenditure solely to age, thus not dealing with the issue of the differential level of expenditure on the better-off, as analysed by Le Grand. Similarly, he does not allow for the greater benefits accruing to the higher income groups *among* those participating in the state sector.[55] Possibly, because of these latter points, Carter exaggerates the vertical income redistribution brought about by Labour's policies. Nevertheless, it seems likely that his broad conclusion, that those policies did have a significant impact on those earning less than £500 per annum, is correct, and provides the best guide to the overall egalitarian impact of Labour's policies.

Equality versus efficiency?

What relationship did members of the Attlee government see between equality and efficiency? Two lines of thought are evident. On the one hand there was the view that efficiency required social solidarity, a solidarity only to be secured by a 'feeling' of equality. The alternative view was that too much equality threatened the goal of increased efficiency. The first of these arguments is a well-known theme of Crosland's *Future of Socialism*, but it can be found in earlier writings, such as those by Callaghan, who urged the need for people in Britain to 'feel unity and kinship' and considered that the existence of this feeling depended on an erosion of class distinctions.[56] This kind of approach may be seen as parallel to all the emphasis on 'human relations' in discussions of productivity in this period, where the key to productivity was seen to be the feelings of workers about how they were treated and how they were involved in factory life.[57]

---

[55] Ibid., pp. 221–4; Le Grand, *Strategy of Equality*, chs. 3, 4.
[56] B. Hindess, *Freedom, Equality and the Market* (1987), p. 18; Callaghan, 'Approach', p. 128.
[57] Tiratsoo and Tomlinson, *Industrial Efficiency*, ch. 5.

However realistic such an emphasis on *perceptions* of equality might be, the danger is that perceptions may easily be manipulated, and arguably this was done in this period to some extent, with the imposition of restrictions on distributed profits, whilst the resulting capital gains were ignored. But more generally it can be argued that this argument at least tries to question the equality *versus* efficiency assumption that so often dominates public discussion.

This idea of a conflict between equality and efficiency is one generally accepted, of course, by economists. In the late 1940s it was they especially who urged on the Attlee government the idea that current measures of redistribution threatened efficiency. As noted above, this became a consistent argument made by Robert Hall, the government's chief economic adviser. The argument seems to have had some influence, because the idea that the 'limits' of redistribution had been reached emerges as quite a common theme of Labour discussion by the late 1940s.[58]

Yet, as we have seen, contemporary evidence on this issue was extremely limited. Its public acceptance by many Labour figures reflected a combination of strong advice from many officials, anxiety about 'confidence' plus perhaps a general drift towards 'consolidation' rather than much in the way of hard evidence. It also fitted with a 'productionist'/growth orientation – if people's income could not rise by means of further redistribution, then growth was the only solution. Indeed, one could perhaps go further and say that, having determined to set higher productivity as a policy goal, Labour leaders then found it congenial to link this with the argument that redistribution no longer provided a viable route to higher incomes.

The view that redistribution had reached its limits was largely confined to the discussion of income. Almost every Labour figure agreed that more should, in principle at least, be done to redistribute wealth. The evidence certainly suggests that the inequality in that distribution had not been shifted very much by Labour's period in office. Even the figures in table 12.6 may exaggerate the amount of redistribution, because they measure only individual wealth-holding, and so ignore the process (encouraged by the increase in death duties) whereby the very

---

[58] Callaghan, 'Approach', p. 145; R. Jenkins, 'Equality' in R. H. S. Crossman (ed.), *New Fabian Essays* (1952), pp. 75–6; PRO T171/399, 'Draft Budget speech' 1 April 1949. It seems to have been accepted even by figures on the left of the party. For example, in 1950 Michael Foot accepted that 'We had probably gone as far as we could in obtaining equality of income through governmental action, but we couldn't be satisfied whilst the existing gross disparity of wealth was maintained' (Labour Party Archives, Dorking Conference, May 1950). For a contrary view, see the Fabian Society evidence to the Royal Commission on the Taxation of Income and Wealth, *Evidence*, vol. 2, Document no. 140, 1952.

Table 12.6 *Proportions of wealth-holding sections of the population, 1936 and 1951–6*

	1936	1951–6
Top 1 per cent of holders	56	42
Top 5 per cent	81	67.5
Top 10 per cent	88	79
Top 20 per cent	94	89

Source: H. F. Lydall and D. G. Tipping, 'The Distribution of Personal Wealth in Britain', *Bulletin of Oxford University Institute of Statistics* 23 (1961), p. 83.

wealthy spread their assets amongst their families. There is also good evidence that most of this pattern of wealth-holding was just as much the result of inheritance in the 1950s as it had been before 1939.[59]

The case for doing something about this distribution was strongly urged throughout the late 1940s, but apart from the increase in death duties little was attempted. This gap between widely perceived inequities in wealth distribution and designing policy instruments to change that distribution was not peculiar to the 1940s. The evidence suggests how hard it is to find effective means of redistributing wealth when so many avenues of evasion and avoidance can be deployed, more easily for wealth than for income.[60] On the other hand, it is perhaps particularly striking that a government such as Attlee's, with such a strong 'productionist' rhetoric, was not able to find the political energy to address the distribution of wealth more seriously, as this would seem to have raised many fewer issues of 'efficiency versus equality' than other forms of taxation.

In its summary of Labour's record just prior to the 1950 general election the *Economist* said:

The pursuit of equality is the most firmly rooted of all the policies of the Labour Party. There can be little doubt that the wage-earning class has been better off under the Labour Government than ever before – certainly in relative terms and probably in absolute terms as well. The great redistribution of incomes, however, was a product of the war; Labour had taken it over and pursued it rather than initiated it.[61]

[59] C. Harbury, 'Inheritance and the Distribution of Personal Wealth in Britain', *Economic Journal* 72 (1962), pp. 845–68. On wealth distribution more generally, see Phelps Brown, *Egalitarianism*, ch. 14.

[60] Whiting, 'Boundaries'.

[61] *Economist*, 158, 4 Feb. 1950, p. 244. This article was typical of a 1950s literature which based itelf on comparisons of pre- and post-war income distribution whose statistical foundations were masterfully undermined by R. Titmuss, *Income Distribution and Social Change* (1962), esp. pp. 195–9.

All three of these conclusions, characteristically for the *Economist*, were glib rather than wholly accurate. First, Labour did pursue 'equality' in this period, but it also pursued other policies which often conflicted with this goal – even including, paradoxically enough, the policy of the universal minimum, which for many Labour people was the instrument of equality. Second, whilst there were certainly large working-class gains under Labour, these were pre-eminently in the area of collective rather than individual consumption, and significant benefits from that type of consumption accrued to all classes. Finally, whilst it was undoubtedly true that the full employment, social service expansion and increased taxation of the war had a major impact, Labour did build on this and not just preserve it. For example, when Tawney noted in 1951 that 'the two most massive pillars of indefensible disparities of income and opportunity consist, as before the war, of inherited wealth and the education system', he nevertheless went on to note that with regard to the former: 'The state, which from 1930 to 1938 took 20 per cent from an estate of £100,000 and 50 per cent from one of £1,000,000, now takes 50 per cent from the first and 80 per cent from the second.'[62] And, as noted above, capital taxation was regarded by many as one of the weakest aspects of Labour's redistributive policies – yet the change noted by Tawney was almost wholly a post-war phenomenon. Coupled to the raising of the income tax threshold and the high tax on distributed profits, parts at least of the tax system had become much more progressive than they had been in the war.

It is important not to exaggerate the coherence and single-mindedness of Labour's 'strategy of equality', and to bring out the severe limits of both the conceptualisation and evidence on the issues invoked in the 1940s. Nevertheless, to a significant degree Labour did shift the income distribution in an egalitarian direction in this period, and without evidently paying a very high price in terms of efficiency.

[62] Tawney, *Equality*, p. 223.

13 Conclusions: political obstacles to economic reform

That the Attlee government faced severe economic constraints in the pursuit of its policies is well known and those constraints have been explored in detail in this book. The wearing out and destruction of capital during the war, the extraordinarily high degree of war mobilisation, the sale of foreign assets and the retreat from overseas markets during the conflict left an economic situation worse than any government has had to deal with in modern times. Economic recovery, above all the rebuilding of the international accounts and the expansion of exports and investment deemed necessary to secure this end, dominated the economic agenda. In the name of economic recovery other aims – colonial development, gender equality most obviously – were substantially compromised, and whilst the welfare state was established, by the end of the 1940s its improvement was subject to severe scrutiny in the belief that there existed a conflict between welfare and further economic expansion.

Economic policy is never without a political context, and economic policy objectives are usually best seen in the light of the political strategy they support. This point has already been made in the discussion of the balance of payments, where it is clear that this problem was dominated by the political desire to rebuild the British capacity to play its role as a major military and diplomatic power in the world, underpinned by capital exports and the maintenance of the sterling area.

In this conclusion the dominance of the political is looked at on a broader front, showing how certain political assumptions underpinned and constrained Labour's economic aims. The first section discusses the argument frequently made that Labour's primary aim was to maintain or return to the status of a 'great power' alongside the USA and USSR. The following sections deal with Labour's broad assumptions about domestic politics: the ideas which, it will be argued, restricted the range of options available in pursuing its reformist programme.

A great power?

For Morgan[1] Britain in 1945 was 'manifestly still a great power . . . the British government, like its successors perhaps down to that of Harold Wilson in 1964–70, accepted this as axiomatic'. As a broad point of departure this assertion seems indisputable. The arguments within Labour in the Attlee period were not about whether Britain was and should aspire to be a great power, but how this power was to be maintained/restored and how it was to be exercised. Thus the left of the party never seem to have attacked this aim, however much they might have differed with Bevin and others about Britain's policies. When, in 1947, Denis Healey attacked many of the cherished assumptions of the left about foreign policy in his *Cards on the Table*, he nevertheless suggested that 'the maintenance of Britain as a world power is the precondition of a socialist foreign policy', in which he was at one with his critics. The objections of the critics were to Healey's views on what constituted a socialist foreign policy, not to the assumption he made about the desirability of Britain playing a world role.[2]

The one area where Britain may be seen as retreating from this global aspiration is in the beginnings of decolonisation, most notably in South Asia. Yet it seems evident that this process was one widely seen as requiring a reshaping of Britain's aspirations rather than their reduction. As John Kent, for example, argues, the replacement of colonial rule was expected to preserve influence through informal means, so that the ending of direct rule by Britain was seen not 'as part of managing Britain's imperial decline in the sense of projecting less power and influence in the world, but as part of the attempts to rebuild the British Empire as a global system on somewhat different lines'.[3] Again, the left did not differ seriously from this view; they too saw a commonwealth of (eventually) self-governing states as a way of projecting a benign British power through the world. Whilst many on the left had a proud history of protest against colonial oppression, they maintained a belief that a reformed relationship between Britain and its overseas possessions could be mutually beneficial.[4]

What was the relation between this near-universal assumption of great power status and the widespread recognition of economic weakness? Predominantly the view taken was that the economic problems *con-*

[1] Morgan, *Labour in Power*, p. 233.
[2] D. Healey, *Cards on the Table* (1947); *LPACR* 1947, p. 106.
[3] Kent, *British Imperial Strategy*, p. x.
[4] P. S. Gupta, *Imperialism and the British Labour Movement 1914–1964* (1975), chs. 9, 10; Gupta, 'Imperialism', pp. 98–120

strained Britain's role in the world, but that this was a temporary problem. A Foreign Office paper of March 1945 defined a position that was to remain widely prevalent under the Attlee government: 'It must, however, be stressed that, given skill and good fortune our financial difficulties will be acute only during the immediate post-war years. There are sound reasons for hoping that they will be a temporary phenomenon, for this country possesses all the skill and resources required to recover a dominating place in the economic world.'[5]

The important point here is that no one in the 1940s thought of Britain in terms of long-run 'economic decline', a term which became popular only at the end of the 1950s.[6] Thus even in the battles over resources devoted to overseas military expenditure in 1946 and 1947, when the great power versus economic recovery arguments emerged most strongly, the arguments were largely short-run. The cuts in overseas military expenditure pressed by Dalton and Cripps were seen as necessary to deal with the immediate crisis, not as part of a long-term rundown of global ambition. If, as Adamthwaite argues, the Foreign Office was beginning by 1946 to regard the economic weakness as long-term, this does not seem to have been the view which mainly informed policy.[7]

Of course, there is not necessarily a conflict between aspirations to world power and national economic performance. As has been noted in chapter 3, Britain's tight control over the trade of parts of its colonial empire in the late 1940s was undoubtedly beneficial to the foreign exchange position, as dollar imports into these areas were squeezed and dollar exports maximised. Equally, the sterling area provided a zone for maximizing trade in a dollar-starved world, even if the price of this was a large capital outflow that could ill be afforded. Great Power pretensions did impose some costs, most obviously in the scale of overseas expenditure. In the immediate post-war period this was well recognised in governmental circles, as summed up in the Keynes memorandum quoted in chapter 3. Defenders of the government's policies on this issue have tended to accept the economic damage caused, but argue there was no alternative. Thus Bullock asserts this argument in relation to Britain's presence in Asia, because, he suggests, of the 'slowness with which people adjust to new situations, and the strong pressure on the British as the only power with forces available to restore some sort of

[5] PRO FO371/45694, 'The Effect of our External Financial Position on our Foreign Policy', 30 March 1945.
[6] I. Clark and N. I. Wheeler, *The British Origins of Nuclear Strategy 1945–55* (Oxford, 1989), pp. 2–5; Bullock, *Ernest Bevin*, p. 51.
[7] Adamthwaite, 'Britain and the World', pp. 223–35.

order and avert famine'.[8] This seems a plausible if rather vague defence of Bevin and the government's policies, certainly stronger than the suggestion that Britain's status as a world power was of economic benefit, because it secured Marshall Aid and help under the Military Assistance Programme.[9] Other recipients of these benefits did not have to aspire to be a 'world power' to get their share of the cake.

Perhaps most interesting, though inescapably speculative, is the question of the impact of Britain's world power ambitions in this period on the longer term performance of the British economy. A view put forward by Douglas Jay is that Britain's long-term post-war performance was derailed by the Korean War:

Had it not been for the Korean War (one can now see) the immediate post-1945 economic difficulties would have been overcome, and relaxation at home would have been combined – in an easier world context – with an assault on the long-term aim of faster economic growth in the British economy. Into this brightening picture burst the North Korean forces in the summer of 1950'.[10]

This view is relevant to the current theme because it is difficult to see the scale of Britain's commitment to the Korean conflict as anything other than part of an attempt to demonstrate, especially to the US, that Britain was still a world power. The risks taken by the rearmament were enormous, and the economic arguments seem to have been overborne by what can only be called an emotional desire to impress the Americans on the part of Gaitskell and the majority of the Cabinet.[11]

Jay's view that this over-commitment to defence in 1950–2 had long-run consequences gains plausibility from the fact that this was the period when many world markets were becoming more competitive, and when markets in engineering and metal goods, the type of products diverted into rearmament, were growing particularly rapidly. However, this case can be overstated. Hennessy's view that 'there are powerful reasons for supposing our best hopes for the kind of postwar economic miracle enjoyed by so many western European countries were scattered in fragments in the committee rooms of Whitehall, on the hills above Imjin in Korea and along the Rhine in Germany as British occupation forces were rearmed in readiness for a Stalinist assault'[12] seems exaggerated.

---

[8] Bullock, *Ernest Bevin*, p. 33.

[9] Ibid., pp. 845–6.

[10] D. Jay, 'Civil Servant and Minister' in W. Rodgers (ed.), *Hugh Gaitskell 1906–1963* (1964), p. 97.

[11] Morgan, *Labour in Power*, p. 434, cf. P. Williams, *Hugh Gaitskell* (Oxford, 1982), pp. 166–71, 190–5; on the scale of rearmament Cairncross, *Years of Recovery*, ch. 8.

[12] Hennessy, *Never Again*, p. 415.

The British economy, whilst undoubtedly recovering before Korea, and despite the government's best endeavours, still had too many weaknesses for the suggestion that a simple absence of the diversion of resources because of Korea would have brought an economic miracle to be plausible.[13] Additionally, the focus on the Korean rearmament has tended to obscure the other important ways in which the Attlee government's attempts to secure 'world power' status had long-term deleterious economic consequences.

British overseas military expenditure remained high by international standards down to the 1960s, a pattern set by the Attlee government.[14] Alongside the overseas investment, this spending put an excessive burden on the British balance of payments and, to put the argument at a minimum, encouraged too much policy attention to the payments position at the expense of domestic economic issues.

The domestic economy was affected by Britain's great power aspirations in at least four direct ways. Manpower was clearly one of these, one of the paradoxes of the period being the way in which empire sentiment encouraged the migration to the white commonwealth of up to three-quarters of a million people in this period. Coupled to this was the diversion of manpower into the services on a scale requiring the politically traumatic imposition of peacetime conscription.[15] Second was simply the scale of British military expenditure (both at home and overseas). As table 13.1 shows, as a share of GDP this was significantly higher than other major industrial countries, except the USA, at least until the late 1950s.

In a fully employed economy high military spending necessarily diverts resources from other uses. Whether overall those resources would have been more productively used in other sectors of the economy is impossible to say. But there is at least a *prima facie* case that economic growth would have been faster if some of the resources devoted to military expenditure had been deployed in the civilian sector.

Related to military expenditure (though not all coming under that budget category) was expenditure on nuclear research and production. In the nuclear industry the British programme, launched under Attlee, was dominated by military and political concerns, rather than economic.

---

[13] This argument raises the very broad issue about how far Britain's relatively slow growth was reversible by any policy stance. For one approach to this, M. Abramowitz, 'Catching Up, Forging Ahead and Falling Behind', *Journal of Economic History* 66 (1986), pp. 385–406.

[14] W. A. P. Manser, *Britain in Balance: The Myth of Failure* (1971), ch. 4.

[15] Paul, 'British Subjects'; L. V. Scott, *Conscription and the Attlee Governments: The Politics and Policy of National Service, 1945–51* (Oxford, 1993).

Table 13.1   *Military expenditure as a percentage of GDP, 1950–60*

	1950	1955	1960
USA	5.1	10.2	9.2
UK	6.6	8.2	6.5
France	5.5	6.4	6.5
Germany	4.4	4.1	4.0
Italy	4.3	3.7	3.3
Japan	—	1.8	1.1

Source: M. Chalmers, *Paying for Defence: Military Spending and British Decline* (1985), p. 113.

Morgan rightly sees the atomic programme as a result of 'Britain's awareness of itself as a great power'.[16] The economics ministers, Dalton and Cripps, were excluded from the (secret) discussion of this issue and economic considerations seem to have been little in evidence. It was only in the 1950s that the argument was heard that nuclear weapons were a 'cheap' form of defence.[17] The development of this programme, military and civil, absorbed large financial and real resources (especially of skilled labour) which on any economic assessment must appear immensely wasteful. Britain never in practice had an 'independent' nuclear deterrent for all the money spent in this area, and the civilian nuclear electricity programme has been one of the great white elephants of post-war Britain.

Finally, the political and military posture of Britain, in a manner less well explored than the nuclear policy, biased government-financed Research and Development towards non-commercial areas. In addition to the nuclear industry, this included aircraft and military electronics, areas with little commercial potential, especially in a small country like Britain. This damaging pattern, again using significant amounts of scarce resources, especially of skilled labour, was initiated under the Attlee government.[18]

If the idea of being a 'great power' was crucial in shaping the Attlee government's economic policies, so too were certain assumptions about domestic politics. Four of these assumptions, concerning the desirability

[16] Morgan, *Labour in Power*, p. 281; D. Keohane, *Labour Party Defence Policy since 1945* (Leicester, 1993), p. 21.

[17] Hennessy, *Never Again*, pp. 267–71; Clark and Wheeler, *British Origins*, pp. 27–30.

[18] M. Peck, 'Science and Technology' in R. Caves (ed.), *Britain's Economic Prospects* (Washington, 1968), pp. 448–84.

of parliamentary sovereignty, tripartism, free collective bargaining, and the Morrisonian form of public corporation are explored in more detail in the remainder of this chapter.

Parliamentary sovereignty

The Labour Party from its foundation was committed to the parliamentary road to socialism – its *raison d'être* was to get parliamentary representation for the working class. As has often been noted, it resisted the anti-parliamentary strategies of syndicalism and guild-socialism around the First World War, and its parliamentarism was reaffirmed by the experience of the general strike.[19]

Politically, such a posture was to be expected. It fitted with Labour's claim to political respectability and responsibility. In the 1920s and 1930s it enabled clear lines to be drawn separating Labour from communism and of course fascism. The rise of these anti-parliamentary ideologies reinforced the commitment to parliamentary norms. The Labour leadership's hostile response to talk in the 1930s of the need for socialists to have emergency powers and enabling bills in order to get their legislation in place showed the strength of commitment to existing forms of parliamentary procedure.[20]

But whilst the political force of the 'parliamentary democracy versus dictatorship' argument in the 1920s and 1930s can hardly be denied, its effects were to narrow immensely the scope of political debate. Defence of democracy tended to mean no more than the defence of existing forms of parliamentary democracy. This point should not be pressed too far. Labour in the 1930s was committed to such measures as abolition of the House of Lords, reform of the franchise, changes in parliamentary procedure and Cabinet reform.[21] Such positions reflected a fundamental faith in Parliament as the sovereign body which could, by rather limited reforms, be made the instrument of the people's will.

This posture needs to be contrasted with the wide-ranging debate, largely but not entirely on the left, about the limits of parliamentary sovereignty as a doctrine in the first two decades of the twentieth century. As Hirst has argued, in those decades theorists of a particular kind of political pluralism, opposed to the basic concept of Parliament as capable of representing the 'will' of the populace, had made the running

---

[19] B. Jones and M. Keating, *Labour and the British State* (Oxford, 1985), ch. 3.
[20] Ibid., pp. 58–9.
[21] K. Theakston, *The Labour Party and Whitehall* (1992), chs. 1, 2; J. H. Brookshire, 'Clement Attlee and Cabinet Reform, 1930–45', *Historical Journal* 24 (1981), pp. 175–88.

in much of the political debate. Such figures as Laski, G. D. H. Cole and Figgis had in their different ways stressed the autonomy of voluntary associations, the principle of functional as opposed to a geographic basis for representation and the need to put limits on the scope of state power.[22]

Whilst much of this work was highly theoretical, it did have an impact on practical politics – both Laski and Cole were highly active politically as well as being prolific authors. Guild socialism, in which Cole was a key figure, was never a simple assertion of workers' power at the workplace, but based on a complex (if problematic) political theory centred on proper forms of representation.[23]

The debate between such positions and the Labour leadership can be too easily represented as a 'left versus right' argument, whereas to a degree it even encompassed such pillars of the Labour establishment as the Webbs, who in their 1920 *Constitution for a Socialist Commonwealth of Great Britain* called for a 'social parliament' alongside the political parliament to deal with economic affairs, an idea which owed a lot to pluralist arguments.[24]

But this tradition proved unavailing in the face of the narrowing of political debate in the 1930s. Even such critics of the leadership line as Cripps and Laski, for all their rhetoric, 'did not in practice seem to envisage sweeping away the existing institutional landscape of British government'.[25] One of the many political prices paid by democratic socialism for the rise of communism was this understandable but debilitating narrowing of what 'democracy' might mean.

The commitment to the norms of parliamentary democracy and the rhetoric of parliamentary sovereignty was massively reinforced by Labour's experiences of the Second World War. Most of its senior Cabinet figures after 1945 were ministers during the war, and emerged with their rosy view of the working of the system enhanced. The war was commonly seen as a vindication of the parliamentary system. This view was not confined to the centre and right of the party. The 1930s Marxist intellectual, John Strachey, a Labour minister in the 1940s, symbolised the acceptance by almost everyone in the Labour movement in the 1940s of the power of Parliament. In his New Fabian Essay of 1952 he recanted his previous views on the inability of British capitalism to solve

---

[22] P. Q. Hirst, (ed.), *The Pluralist Theory of the State: Selected Writings of G. D. H. Cole, J. N. Figgis and H. J. Laski* (1989), Introduction.
[23] A. W. Wright, *G. D. H. Cole and Socialist Democracy* (Oxford, 1979).
[24] S. Webb and B. Webb, *Constitution*.
[25] Jones and Keating, *Labour*, p. 55. The Bill, of course, did not abolish the House of Lords, but further reduced its delaying powers.

its economic ills, arguing that the 1945–51 government had shown that, by shifting the distribution of income and wealth, Parliament could fundamentally change economic behaviour and performance.[26]

Most even of those who remained Marxists did not advocate anti-parliamentary positions. A 'fellow-traveller' like D. N. Pritt, who wrote a long critical book about the 1945–51 government, focused his criticism on the *misuse* of Labour's parliamentary majority for unsocialist ends, not on the incapacity of that majority to (potentially) deliver socialism.[27]

Pritt was not typical of the Labour left, his servile pro-Soviet position being anathema to most of those on that wing of the party. But they were even less likely to criticise the assumptions of the power of Parliament, precisely because such views were likely to be portrayed as putting them in the pro-Soviet camp. In fact a feature of the left in this period is its overall weakness in the party, and this was especially striking on domestic as opposed to foreign policy.[28] There was little internecine warfare about Labour's domestic programme in this period, in part because Labour was so obviously delivering on the manifesto commitments of 1945 in this area.

The weakness of the left was partially related to the strength of the government in relation to the party outside Parliament, symbolised above all by the quiescence of the annual conference. At the 1948 conference Bevan, leader of the left, proclaimed his independence from conference resolutions, in a manner, as Kenneth Morgan remarks, 'inconceivable in the 1930s – or the 1970s'.[29] The contrast with this latter decade is perhaps most instructive in the current context, because it was in part because of the perceived weakness of Parliament to deal especially with big private companies that the idea of concentrating power in the parliamentary party and the Cabinet came in for so much criticism from the left.[30]

Labour's attitude after 1945 to changing the political system was minimalist. Even those rather limited changes advocated in the 1930s were watered down. The major legislation, the Parliament Act of 1949, 'can hardly be interpreted as part of a long-term strategy of institutional

---

[26] J. Strachey, 'Tasks and Achievements of British Labour' in R. H. S. Crossman (ed.), *New Fabian Essays* (1952), pp. 188–9.

[27] D. N. Pritt, *The Labour Government 1945–51* (1963), *passim*.

[28] R. Miliband, *Parliamentary Socialism* (1972), pp. 295–8, 305–7; A. Warde, *Consensus and Beyond: The Development of Labour Party Strategy since the Second World War* (Manchester, 1982), pp. 77–8.

[29] K. O. Morgan, 'The High and Low Politics of Labour' in Bentley and Stevenson (eds.), *High and Low Politics in Britain* (Oxford, 1983), p. 303; also Howell, *Social Democracy*, pp. 137–42.

[30] D. Coates, *Labour in Power: A Study of the Labour Government, 1974–9* (1980), esp. ch. 4.

reform. It was a pragmatic response to the problems posed by the passage of the Iron and Steel bill'.[31] Even within the framework of the 1930s' ideas about the institutions of British politics, the period after 1945 has been called a 'missed opportunity', though this was not how Labour ministers saw it. For them, the post-war government, like that of the war period, had vindicated the system.[32]

Why did this commitment to parliamentary sovereignty and the associated doctrine of ministerial responsibility inhibit economic reform under the Attlee government? The answer especially relates to the issue of 'planning'. This word had no simple meaning for the Attlee government, though it was crucial to the government's rhetoric.[33] In the context of economic policy, a crucial question was how planning was to be formulated and implemented. Was it to be like any other policy area, decided ultimately at Cabinet level in the context of whatever current political conditions dictated? Or was it to achieve a degree of autonomy by being outside this structure? Under Labour the answer is plain. Planning was done by the traditional means of interdepartmental official and ministerial committees. In the early years a non-departmental minister, the Lord President, was responsible for 'co-ordinating' planning but this seems to have worked badly, largely because Morrison, who filled this post was grossly overloaded. In 1947 a new minister, Cripps, combined being Minister of Economic Affairs and Chancellor of the Exchequer with being essentially Minister for Planning. In that same year a Central Economic Planning Staff was created, but as its name suggests, it was designed to provide support for the planning minister, not to function with any autonomy. Not surprisingly perhaps, its 'planning' quickly became subordinated to short-term macroeconomic issues not only because of the seriousness of the short-term economic problems, but also because of the lack of institutional 'distance' from those problems.[34]

[31] Ibid. The internal government debate on reform of the House of Lords seems to have been very narrow – whether the Lords' delaying powers should be reduced to one year or whether legislation which passed the Commons should pass the Lords in the same session. The former path was chosen as leaving the Lords with some effective revising powers (PRO CAB134/504, Machinery of Government Committee Minutes, 16 Oct. 1947).

[32] P. Hennessy, *Whitehall* (1989), ch. 4; H. Morrison, *Government and Parliament* (Oxford, 1959); C. Attlee, 'Civil Servants, Ministers, Parliament and the Public', *Political Quarterly* 25 (1954), pp. 308–15. Contributions by wartime Labour ministers to the Machinery of Government Committee focused on relatively narrow issues, such as the distribution of responsibilities between ministries, and reform of the training and organisation of the civil service. For example, PRO CAB87/72, H. Dalton, 'Post-war Functions of the Board of Trade', 4 Aug. 1943; CAB87/74, C. Attlee, 'Note by Deputy Prime Minister', 31 Dec. 1942.

[33] e.g. Labour Party, *Let Us Face the Future*.

[34] Cairncross, *Years of Recovery*, pp. 50–5.

The fate of planning under the Labour government cannot be reduced to the effect of any single factor. It was an ambiguous notion, the subject of wide dispute and substantial change in its aims and mechanisms.[35] But its subordination to parliamentary sovereignty and ministerial responsibility was an important element in its restricted and transient character. This is brought out quite neatly by the discussion of contemporary French planning, which may be seen as the obvious model of successful planning in a democratic framework. An outline of French planning was supplied to Whitehall by James Meade, head of the Economic Section, early in 1947. He noted its different objectives from British planning – above all, its focus on growth and industrial development rather than employment as the primary goals. But he also noted the fact that French planning took place 'outside the normal administrative machinery', and pointed out the benefits that stemmed from this.[36] The document carries a strong sense that 'they do things differently abroad', above all that it would be inconceivable that such a system would be allowed in Britain with its different political assumptions about ministerial responsibility. Thus the French style of planning was regarded as interesting, but a curiosity rather than a model to be followed.[37]

Discussions of economic planning in the 1940s often recognised the difficulties of such planning in Britain, but usually saw these difficulties in terms of the absence of effective mechanisms and conflicting economic pressures. For example, Edward Bridges, the chairman of the major civil service committee on economic policy, wrote in 1946: 'We are trying to work a planned economy without labour controls and in conditions of general inflationary pressure in which financial incentives alone cannot be strong enough to take their place. Moreover, some of the controls have now been appreciably weakened.'[38] Whilst these points are valid in themselves, and some will be returned to below, they ignored the problems arising from trying to organise planning within the assumption that it could be effectively done without taking powers away from the executive. Meade had noted in his report that the autonomy of the Commissariat Générale du Plan allowed a much better relationship with employers and workers than was possible in Britain because they had a real say in its deliberations. In Britain the doctrine of parliamentary sovereignty precisely ruled out such a say. But wasn't

---

[35] Ibid., ch. 11; Tomlinson, 'Planning', pp. 154–74.

[36] PRO CAB134/190, 'Monnet Plan: Anglo-French Discussions in Paris, January 1947', 26 Feb. 1947.

[37] Ibid.

[38] PRO T230/323, 'Means of Implementing Planning Decisions', Oct. 1946.

Labour strongly committed to tripartism, and the creation of institutions for meeting employers and union representatives on all major issues, including those of economic policy?[39] This leads on to the next section of this chapter, the meaning and effects of Labour's tripartism.

Tripartism

There is no doubt about the sincerity and depth of Labour's commitment to creating forums for discussion between the peak associations of Labour and capital and government. The TUC, FBI and the BEC participated in vast range of such bodies, in the economic field the main examples being the National Joint Advisory Council (for industrial relations), the National Production Advisory Council for Industry, and, from 1947, the Economic Planning Board.[40] The first two were extensions of similar wartime bodies created as part of the attempt to build a wartime consensus.[41]

It seems clear that for major Labour figures a large part of what was meant by planning was fundamentally this form of tripartism. In the section on Economic Planning in the 1947 *Economic Survey* Cripps spelt out his notion of the 'essential difference between totalitarian and democratic planning'. Above all, 'the execution of the economic plan must be much more a matter of co-operation between Government, industry and the people, than of rigid application by the State of controls and compulsions'.[42]

In his first job, as President of the Board of Trade, this view was very much to the fore. In setting out his goals, Cripps argued for investigations into major private sector industries by bodies representing unions and employers, with the addition of experts, 'with the primary object of getting from both sides of the industry an agreed and considered statement of what the industry needs in order to make it as efficient as possible in the national interest'.[43] Thus Cripps' advocacy of what came to be called working parties was not just a continuation of wartime and pre-war ideas for industrial boards, but was explicitly based on involving both sides of industry in the discussion. Tripartism

---

[39] This of course is a major theme of the work of Middlemas, and his emphasis on 'corporate bias'. For this period see his *Power*, chs. 4–6.

[40] The records of these bodies can be found, respectively, at PRO LAB10/652, 655–8; BT190/2–7; T229/28–42 and CAB124/210–214.

[41] Middlemas, *Power* chs. 1, 2.

[42] *Economic Survey for 1947* (1946).

[43] PRO CAB72/21, 'The Government Plan for Encouraging Industrial Organisation and Efficiency', 27 Aug. 1945. Discussed at CAB71/19, Lord President's Committee, 31 Aug. 1945.

was to extend down to the industry level, not just be confined to the 'peak associations'.[44] Tripartism was not then just a rhetorical flourish. It was instituted widely. It was defended against encroachment, e.g. by bodies claiming to speak for 'management' as separate from employers.[45] It was taken seriously by the participants – perhaps especially by the TUC, which came to put almost more importance on being properly consulted than on the substance of government decisions.[46]

The employers played a willing role on NJAC, NPACI and the EPB but resisted the extension of tripartism or joint consultation to industry or factory levels. They successfully resisted the establishment of Development Councils in most industries, and blocked a tripartite body in engineering. They also largely neutered the role of Joint Production Committees at factory level, especially resisting any attempt to link them to any industry-wide or regional bodies.[47]

If we look at the deliberations of the peak tripartite bodies – NJAC, NPACI, EPB – what becomes apparent is the extent to which they were consultative bodies only in a very particular sense. By and large the government used them for two purposes – on the one hand to disseminate information about the economy and about their policies and intentions; and on the other hand, to get feedback on certain proposals which had been tentatively arrived at. It seems clear from the minutes that it was these two functions – information provision and sounding-boards – which largely defined the meaning of tripartism.[48] It did not mean the sharing of decisions by government, but was basically a mechanism of trying to secure consent for decisions made by ministers. When such consent was deemed unlikely to be forthcoming, then the tripartite

---

[44] Compare Mercer, 'Labour Governments', p. 79. In one of his first meetings as President of the Board of Trade Cripps declared: 'It is essential that in all our dealings with industry we will give equal weight to the views of employers and employees, they are to be regarded as equal partners in the job of production' (PRO BT13/220, President's Morning Meeting, 29 Aug. 1945).

[45] PRO BT64/2360, 'Committee on Industrial Productivity', Daken to Nowell, 16 April 1948, 6 May 1948 on opposition to any role for the British Institute of Management on the major tripartite bodies.

[46] e.g. its response to the government White Paper on wage inflation (Jones, *Wages*, ch. 3) . See also PRO T172/2033, 'Note on Meeting of TUC with PM and Senior Ministers', 11 Feb. 1948.

[47] Mercer 'Labour Governments'; Tomlinson, 'Mr. Attlee's Supply-Side Socialism'; Tomlinson, 'Productivity Policy' in Mercer et al. (eds.), *Labour and Private Industry*, pp. 37–54; Hinton, *Shop Floor Citizens*, chs. 8, 9.

[48] For example, PRO LAB10/652 NJAC Minutes, 31 July 1946. Morrison saw the council as giving 'an opportunity of discussing the government's economic planning programme with the representatives of industry', planning which could only succeed 'with the ready participation and co-operation of all concerned'.

boards were ignored – as in the case of wages policy. (Equally, some major economic decisions were entirely outside this framework of tripartism – most obviously budgetary policy, which the Treasury continued to keep very much to itself.)

The limitations of peak-level tripartism are reflected in the views of the FBI. When the government proposed the creation of the Economic Planning Board in 1947, the FBI responded quite favourably. This was because it perceived the existing bodies, the NPACI and NJAC, as 'too big' to give policy advice, and said that 'they had not been used for that purpose'. But in later years, when the EPB had been running for a few years, complaints were levelled in turn at its functioning. The FBI saw it as having been ignored in key economic policy areas (e.g. the devaluation of 1949), of having minutes which didn't reveal the policy criticisms voiced, and generally having much less input into policy than the original claims made about its importance had implied.[49]

It is not unreasonable to compare 1940s tripartism with 1920s- and 1930s-style 'industrial diplomacy'. Though tripartism was more formalised and involved a much more equal role for unions and employers, a primary aim remained to maintain the (alleged) dominance of Parliament in decisions whilst trying to persuade the private sector to change its behaviour. It may equally be said that in neither case did the strategy generate much in the way of obvious success.[50]

Tripartism faced little opposition in the late 1940s. This is curious, in the light of what might appear the obvious ideological difficulties of a socialist government so strongly seeking co-operation with the owners of private property, and also because of the pre-war and wartime record of Labour criticism of the cosy relationship between private industry and government.[51]

Brady has offered the most detailed attempt to answer the question of how Labour became so strongly wedded to its form of industrial diplomacy, and why it was so little resisted. He addresses this issue by focusing on the Development Councils, tripartite bodies which Labour saw as the model for relationships with the private sector.[52] He saw the

---

[49] Warwick University, Modern Records Centre MSS200/F/3/03/9/7, 'Economic Planning Board FBI Representations', 1947–9.

[50] R. Roberts, 'The Administrative Origins of Industrial Diplomacy: An Aspect of Government–Industry Relations, 1929–35' in J. Turner (ed.), *Businessmen and Politics* (1984), pp. 93–104. The failures of this policy should not be overstated. The government did enjoy a measure of success in such industries as cotton (Tomlinson, 'Labour Government and the Trade Unions', pp. 90–105).

[51] e.g. E. Davies, *National Capitalism* (1940).

[52] R. Brady, *Crisis in Britain: Plans and Achievements of the Labour Government* (1950), pp. 560–1. On the failure of Development Councils see A. A. Rogow and P. Shore,

basis of this position in large part as 'the decline within British Labour circles of the syndicalist programme and the rise, in its place, of Burnham's thesis of the managerial state'.[53] Tripartism was in this way linked to a rejection of any notion of workers' control, and a belief that expertise could displace private interest in the management of enterprises. As with the other elements of the iron quadrilateral, the ideological fragility of Labour's position was not exposed by coherent criticism from the left of the party. Insofar as the Labour left had a clear position on industry it was a general case for more (and more democratic) nationalisation, more planning, but little on how these terms could be translated into practicable policies, given, not least, the absence of a large cadre of potential industrial managers sympathetic to any form of socialism.[54]

The argument here has not been intended to belittle tripartism as a component of Labour's democratic socialism. It was integral to that doctrine, and to the consensual, co-operative style of politics practised by the government. But it was clearly limited in its impact by the clear perception by ministers and civil servants that policy decisions should not be delegated to outside bodies. On the other hand, the desire to achieve consensus meant the government made little use of the leverage it did have over the private sector. In particular, it made little use of its powers to control the distribution of output between firms by means of its controls over raw materials. To discriminate between firms would be to undercut a crucial part of that consensus. Hence most of the controls were effectively 'subcontracted' to industry-based associations, which operated them on a non-discriminatory basis. The one documented and significant exception was to use the allocation of steel supplies to favour car manufacturers who achieved target levels of exports. This policy fits in with the fact that cars came under the Ministry of Supply rather than the Board of Trade. The former was notably less committed to tripartism, and perhaps partly as a consequence, more willing to pursue discriminatory, interventionist policies.[55]

The doctrines of parliamentary sovereignty and ministerial responsibility on the one hand, and tripartism on the other, therefore drew the major peak associations into government deliberations, whilst granting them no substantial clout in those deliberations. Consensus was

   The Labour Government and British Industry 1945–51 (Oxford, 1955), pp. 86–92; H. Mercer, 'Labour Governments', pp. 78–83.

[53]   J. Burnham's *The Managerial Revolution* was first published in Britain in 1942.

[54]   R. H. S. Crossman, M. Foot and I. Mikardo, *Keep Left* (1947), pp. 14–25; Schneer, *Labour's Conscience*, ch. 4.

[55]   Tiratsoo, 'The Motor Car Industry' in Mercer et al. (eds.), *Labour Governments*, pp. 162–85; D. Edgerton, 'Whatever Happened', pp. 91–116.

achieved to a significant degree, but the extent of reform was limited by the incapacity of the normal mechanisms of Cabinet government to deliver a vigorous break with the economic past. Planning in a micro-economic sense could not be successfully conducted by a political system still essentially geared to the days of *laissez-faire*.

Free collective bargaining

The limit put on the possibility of planning the British economy in the late 1940s by the absence of control over the labour market has long been a theme of the literature, and has recently been reiterated. Stephen Brooke, for example, argues that 'As the history of the Attlee Government shows, the refusal of the unions to accept some compromise over their powers of free collective bargaining was to be the major obstacle to the development of socialist planning.'[56] Certainly the Labour government soon came to recognise that with the political impossibility of directing labour on any large scale, but the desire to 'man-up' certain industries, 'wage planning' was the obvious alternative. The failure of demobilised workers to return in sufficient numbers to industries like coal mining, textiles and agriculture led to the argument that the way to get them into those industries was to change wage relativities to make such occupations more attractive. This fitted in with the belief that Britain should have a 'manpower budget' alongside the national income budget if the economy were to be properly planned.[57]

Wages planning was of great symbolic importance. If it were successfully implemented, it would mean that a planned economy could be made compatible with individual liberty in the crucial area of choice of occupation. For Labour thinkers like Durbin it therefore had a central place in their whole approach to politics, and this was echoed by other thinkers.[58] But, as shown in chapter 8, the idea of such planning was at odds with the commitment to free collective bargaining so strongly held in the government, unions and Labour Party.

The failure of the Attlee government to adopt wage planning was not, then, a consequence of defeat by the unions. A majority of both trade unionists and government members shared the long-standing commitment to voluntarism and free collective bargaining, which has indeed

[56] Brooke, *Labour's War*, p. 256; see also Beer, *Modern British Politics*, ch. 7, which draws on B. Roberts, *National Wages*; Brooke, 'Problems of "Socialist Planning" '.

[57] *Economic Survey 1947*, paras. 15–16, 28.

[58] For Durbin see Brooke, 'Problems of "Socialist Planning" '. Pigou argued, against Hayek's *Road to Serfdom*, that planning was compatible with individual freedom if individuals moved occupations in response to government-inspired changes in wage relativities (Review of Hayek, *Economic Journal* 54 (1944), pp. 217–19).

been one of the most continuous features of Labour's history in Britain. This commitment can be seen from two sides – from that of the proper role of government and that of the proper role of unions. From the former, the major danger of wage planning was seen as the politicisation of wage bargaining. In responding to proposals for such a policy, Isaacs, the Minister of Labour, argued: 'The most difficult element in the proposals of the Minister of Fuel and Power was the suggestion that the Government should assume direct responsibility for fixing wage rates. This would mean that one or other of the parties to any industrial dispute would come into direct conflict with the Government.' On another occasion in the debate he argued that such a policy would inevitably lead Parliament to become involved in wage issues: 'In this way, wages might become a political issue. This to my mind is an insuperable objection to the proposal'.[59]

This politicisation of wage issues would in turn undermine the industrial relations system: 'We think that it is vitally important that nothing should be done to weaken the sense of responsibility of the leaders of both sides of industry. We are impressed by the argument that any intervention by the state would turn wage disputes from conflicts with employers into conflict with the Government, with disastrous consequences to industrial peace.'[60]

On the other side, wage planning would cut across long-standing views about the role of trade unions. Partly this tradition reflected the well-known peculiarities of the development of unions as 'extra-legal' bodies in Britain – having no positive rights, but only surviving on the basis of precarious immunities from common law actions. In concert with this legal context, the unions developed free collective bargaining as their *raison d'être*, and came to regard the right to such bargaining as on a par with the other basic freedoms of thought, speech and assembly.[61]

To a striking extent this tradition reasserted itself post-war, despite all the legal infringements on free collective bargaining and voluntarism that developed in wartime. Labour's period in office marked no sharp

---

[59] PRO CAB132/1, Lord President's Committee Minutes, 2 Aug. 1946; CAB132/5, Ministry of Labour, 'National Wages Policy', 29 Oct. 1946.
[60] PRO CAB134/189, 'Report of Steering Committee on Wages and Prices Policy', 21 Dec. 1946.
[61] W. Wedderburn, 'Freedom of Association and Philosophies of Labour Law', *Industrial Law Journal* 18 (1989), pp. 1–38; H. Phelps-Brown, *The Origins of Trade Union Power* (Oxford, 1986); TUC, *Annual Congress Report* 1946, p. 230; the most extensive official defence of this position is in 'Trade Unionism: The Evidence of the TUC to the Royal Commission on TUs and Employers' Associations' (1967).

break in this tradition. As Morgan[62] notes: 'The government and the TUC made no effort to alter the adversarial character of relations between labour and management – even while, ironically enough, Britain was encouraging moves towards *Mitbestimmung* in Western Germany at precisely this period.'

With the direction of labour more or less ruled out on general liberal grounds, and wage planning stymied by the commitment to depoliticised wage-setting free collective bargaining, the Labour government's capacity to control the economy was obviously gravely weakened. The allocation of labour was then largely left to propaganda and exhortation (as in the campaign to recruit workers back into coal and cotton), or the forces of free collective bargaining on wage relativities, which, given the social norms embedded in that bargaining, mirrored the pattern of shortages very slowly, if at all.[63]

The public corporation

The nationalised industries represent an odd, perhaps paradoxical, feature of Labour's policies seen from the aspect of their effects on the government's capacity to control the economy. On the one hand, part of the basis for nationalisation was the idea that in this manner the government would gain control of the basic industries (later called the 'commanding heights'), by means of which overall control and planning of the economy would be greatly facilitated. On the other hand, the form of nationalisation, the Morrisonian-style public corporation, made the capacity of government to direct the activities of these industries at best unsure and ambiguous. Hence the Morrisonian public corporation represents the fourth feature of Labour's political views which functioned as an obstacle to at least some kinds of economic reform in the Attlee period.

The Morrisonian corporation was driven by both economic and political ideas. Economically, it was driven by the belief that large-scale enterprises could achieve economies of scale not available to fragmented, private entities, as long as they were run by experts and people with a 'business' approach. Politically, this form of organisation was based on the idea that the claims of parliamentary sovereignty meant that such enterprises should not be run by any interest group, but by

[62] Morgan, *Labour in Power*, p. 136.
[63] On the campaign in cotton see Crofts, *Coercion* and Carruthers, 'Manning the Factories', pp. 232–56. On the pattern of wages under free collective bargaining, see the classic work of B. Wootton, *The Social Foundations of Wages Policy* (1962).

bodies appointed by ministers solely on the grounds of competence. The need for management by experts, for a flexible 'businesslike' approach, meant that once these appointments were made, the ministerial role should be restricted to general issues, and should not involve interference in the day-to-day management of the enterprise.[64]

From the debates of the 1930s, as outlined in chapter 5, emerged a wide but not unanimous agreement on this form of public ownership, and so all the nationalisations after 1945, with small variations, embodied the idea of a public corporation managed by experts and subject to parliamentary control only on general issues. In the 1930s the Labour leadership had made the very limited concession to the advocates of workers' control of a statutory right of unions to be consulted on some board-level appointments, but even this was not embodied in the legislation of the 1940s.[65]

Labour's nationalisation of the 1940s aimed both to run the industries more efficiently and to use them as a basis for running the economy, without effectively reconciling these two objectives. The Fabian veneration for the 'expert' led to the emphasis on keeping the industries free from day-to-day interference by ministries.[66] Equally, the idea that the nationalisation programme was the basis for a planned economy is clearly seen in the crucial area of investment planning, where it was argued that Labour's proposed National Investment Board was unnecessary, because so much of the nation's investment was subject to government planning by control of the nationalised industries.[67]

The Labour government increasingly discussed the issue of how much control ministers should have over the decisions of the nationalised industries. Wartime debate had tended to push towards a greater role for ministers than previously envisaged, but in the post-war years ministers were divided. For example, in discussing the nationalisation of steel, the responsible minister, the Minister of Supply, wanted to give detailed instructions to the industry on such matters as the pattern of production, the overall capacity of the industry and the location of new plant, but the majority of ministers regarded this as impinging too much on the board's decision-making.[68]

But the precise boundaries between ministers' and boards' powers was a cause of rumbling discontent, as shown in chapter 5. This discontent arose around a range of issues. The question of the role of workers

[64] On the general background to the Morrisonian corporation see chapter 5.
[65] Dahl, 'Workers' Control', pp. 893–5.
[66] Chester, Nationalisation, pp. 1034–5.
[67] Davenport, Memoirs.
[68] Chester, Nationalisation, pp. 906–12.

was one such. Though the lack of a direct union/worker role in the management of the industries was now uncontested at least in ministerial circles, there was still the issue of the scale and character of worker consultation. Partly because of its enthusiasm for such consultation as a route to higher productivity, ministers often felt that the nationalised industries were doing too little to encourage it.[69] As was typical in this period, ministerial enthusiasm to 'do something' was not matched by the boards of the nationalised industries, where, for example, there was resistance to any enquiry into 'human relations' in the industries. Ministers remained concerned about this issue right up to the end of the Labour government, especially because of evidence of worker discontent with the outcome of nationalisation.[70]

Most important of all was the issue of the degree of ministerial control over investment decisions by the nationalised industries. Given that investment by the industries amounted to around one-half of all domestic investment at this time, this issue was central to the government's ability to plan the national economy. But whilst the government had a general power to sanction investment expenditure, the precise degree of control it could exert was unclear. Partly the problem was the industries' remit to balance their books over a number of years, which provided a basis on which they could resist what they regarded as investments which did not fulfil proper commercial criteria. For example, the Minister of Fuel and Power came into a degree of conflict with the National Coal Board over the level of investment in coke ovens, because the board felt that demand for the output of such ovens might not match the ministry's expectation, and hence the investment might not pay its way.[71]

It would be wrong to give the impression of an unremitting conflict between the ministries and the boards of nationalised industries on the issue of investment or any of the other issues discussed above in the period 1945–51.[72] This was not the situation. In many cases the two sides found their way to amicable settlement of issues rather than engaging in continuous dispute. Nevertheless, it is evident that the idea of

[69] On the general emphasis on 'human relations' as a route to greater efficiency in this period, Tiratsoo and Tomlinson, *Industrial Efficiency*, ch. 7.

[70] PRO CAB134/690, 'Management–Worker Relationships in the Socialised Industries', 7 April 1949; CAB134/691, 'Workers' Attitudes in the Socialised Industries', 6 Dec. 1950; CAB134/691, 'Report of Sub-committee on Relationships with Workers in the Socialised Industries', 10 May 1951. See also generally PRO BT64/2416, 'Socialisation of Industries: Workers' Assistance in Management', 1946–51.

[71] Chester, *Nationalisation*, pp. 981–90.

[72] On the issue of investment in the major nationalised industries in this period, see Hannah, *Engineers, Managers and Politicians*, chs. 3, 4, 8; Gourvish, *British Railways*, ch. 3; Ashworth, *Coal*, chs. 3, 5.

the industries as subordinate agents of a national economic strategy or plan would be quite inappropriate to describe the relationship that emerged in this period. The precise status of the boards *vis-à-vis* ministers was never settled in these years (or indeed at any later date), but it became apparent that the Morrisonian board gave a degree of autonomy to the nationalised industries which made them independent of the government's will.

Perhaps it is most appropriate to quote Morrison's own view of this relationship (in 1949):

We ought to take a fairly early opportunity to review the powers of the government to control socialised industries. It is of great advantage to have brought the public utility services and certain basic industries under the control of public boards which can administer those services and industries in the public interest; but the government has a wider viewpoint of the public interest than the boards, and I am far from happy that we are in a position to exercise the control on wide issues of policy which the national economy requires.[73]

Thus the transfer of ownership of the industries from private to public hands marked not an unambiguous extension of state power but the creation of new centres of power with considerable capacity, legal and practical, to resist government wishes.

Conclusions

The obstacles to more radical economic reform under the Attlee government were not just ones of political doctrine and assumptions. As argued elsewhere in this book, the compelling macroeconomic problems forced attention onto short-run issues rather than long-run reform. The opposition of the private sector to much of government policy was well organised and powerful. Popular enthusiasm for economic reconstruction was less than overwhelming; indeed, the extent of popular radicalism at this time has been frequently exaggerated. The advice given to the government by economists was largely of a 'liberal-socialist' kind which focused attention on macroeconomic policy issues and devices. Nevertheless, as this chapter has tried to suggest, Labour's approach was necessarily conditioned by the political assumptions it brought to bear on day-to-day policy issues.

Most of those assumptions, it should be clear from the above discussion, were already well entrenched before 1945. Belief that Britain should be a world power was part of the mental world of Labour from its foundations. The almost unchallenged faith in parliamentary sover-

[73] PRO CAB134/690, 'Government Control over Socialised Industries', 26 April 1949.

eignty was in large part a reaction to the anti-parliamentary doctrines of the 1920s and 1930s, but greatly strengthened by the seeming capacity of Labour's parliamentary majority to 'deliver the goods'. Similarly, the commitments to free collective bargaining and to the 'Morrisonian' form of nationalisation pre-dated the war and, whilst subject to challenge after 1945, emerged triumphant.

Tripartism is a rather different case. This was not a position clearly articulated before the war, and emerged only as Labour grappled with the problems of power after 1945. It emerged partly as a pragmatic response to the realities of the entrenchment of organised business and labour and the political process in the war. But beyond that its strength reflected what Harold Wilson (President of the Board of Trade 1947–51) was to call the 'vacuum in socialist thought' regarding the relations between Labour governments and private industry.[74] Politics, like nature, abhors a vacuum and tripartism emerged to fill this one.

The argument of this chapter, and of the book as a whole, has not been the normative one that the government *should* have done more in the way of economic reconstruction. Rather, the argument has been that in understanding why that reconstruction, radical in some regards, was so limited in others, leaving many institutions and practices unreformed, we must look to the hitherto relatively unexplored area of Labour's political assumptions and how they provided a constraining framework within which the more pragmatic level of economic policy operated.

[74] PRO PREM8/1183, 'The State and Private Industry', 4 May 1950.

Bibliography

ARCHIVES

PUBLIC RECORD OFFICE

BT13	Board of Trade, Establishments
BT64	Board of Trade, Industries and Manufactures
BT177	Board of Trade, Distribution of Industry
BT190	Board of Trade, National Production Advisory Council for Industry
BT195	Board of Trade, Economic Affairs
CAB21	Cabinet Papers
CAB71	Lord President's Committee
CAB87	Reconstruction Committees
CAB124	Lord President's Secretariat
CAB128	Cabinet Minutes
CAB129	Cabinet Papers
CAB131	Defence Committee
CAB132	Lord President's Committee
CAB134	Cabinet Committees
COAL26	National Coal Board
FO371	Foreign Office
LAB8	Ministry of Labour, Employment
LAB10	Ministry of Labour, Industrial Relations
LAB26	Ministry of Labour, Welfare
POWE20	Ministry of Power, Coal Division
POWE37	Ministry of Power, Coal Division
PREM8	Prime Minister's Papers
RG23	Central Office of Information
SUPP14	Ministry of Supply
T161	Treasury, Supply
T171	Treasury, Budget Papers
T172	Treasury, Chancellor of the Exchequer's Office
T222	Treasury, Organisation and Methods
T227	Treasury, Social Services
T228	Treasury, Trade and Industry
T229	Treasury, Central Economic Planning Staff
T230	Treasury, Economic Section

T232   Treasury, European Economic Co-operation
T233   Treasury, Home Finance
T236   Treasury, Overseas Finance
T237   Treasury, Overseas Finance (Marshall Aid)
T269   Treasury, Permanent Secretary's Papers

BRITISH LIBRARY OF POLITICAL AND ECONOMIC SCIENCE

Piercy Papers
MISC196 Infancy of the Labour Party

BANK OF ENGLAND

G1   Governor's Files
G14   Committee of Treasury Files
G15   Secretary's Files

LABOUR PARTY ARCHIVES

Morgan Phillips Papers
Research Department Papers

MODERN RECORDS CENTRE

MSS44   Amalgamated Engineering Union
MSS200   Federation of British Industries
MSS292   Trades Union Congress

GOVERNMENT PUBLICATIONS

PERIODICALS

Board of Trade Gazette
Hansard
Ministry of Labour Gazette

PARLIAMENTARY PUBLICATIONS

Report of Committee on Finance and Industry (1930/1, vol. XIII)
Report of Social Insurance and Allied Services (1941/2, vol. VII)
Employment Policy (1943/4, vol. VIII)
Coal Mining: Report of the Technical Advisory Committee (1944/5, vol. IV)
Report of Committee on Scientific Manpower (1946, vol. XIV)
Report of Royal Commission on Equal Pay (1945/6, vol. XI)
Economic Survey for 1947 (1946/7, vol. XIX)
Capital Investment in 1948 (1947/8, vol. XXII)

Statement on Personal Incomes, Costs and Prices (1947/8, vol. XXII)
European Co-operation. Memorandum Submitted to the OEEC (1948/9, vol. XXXIV)
Education 1900–50 (1950/1, vol. XI)
Ministry of Labour Report for 1950 (1950/1, vol. XVI)
Education in 1951 (1951/2, vol. X)
Report of Royal Commission on the Taxation of Profits and Incomes (1953/4, vol. XIX)
NI Act. Report by the Government Actuary on the 1st Quinquennial Review (1954/5, vol. VI)
Commission of Enquiry into the Cost of the NHS (1955/6, vol. XX)
The Government's Expenditure Plans 1979/80 to 1982/3 (1978/9, vol. XVIII)
Report of Royal Commission on the NHS (1978/9, vol. XIX)

NON-PARLIAMENTARY

Report of Committee on Higher Technical Education, 1945
Working Party, Report on Cotton, 1946
National Institute of Houseworkers, Annual Report, 1949
Committee on the Working of the Monetary System, Minutes of Evidence, 1958/9

SECONDARY SOURCES

BOOKS (place of publication London unless otherwise noted)

Abel-Smith, B. and Townsend, P., *The Cost of the NHS in England and Wales* (Cambridge, 1956).
Abramowitz, M. and Eliasberg, V. F., *The Growth of Public Employment in Great Britain* (Princeton, 1957).
Acton Society Trust, *Accountability to Parliament* (1950).
    The Men on the Board (1951).
    Problems of Promotions Policy (1951).
    Training and Promotion in Nationalised Industry (1951).
    The Extent of Centralisation (1951).
    The Framework of Joint Consultation (1952).
    The Workers' Point of View (1952).
Addison, P., *The Road to 1945* (1975).
    Now the War Is Over: A Social History of Britain, 1945–51 (1985).
Allen, V., *Trade Unions and the Government* (1960).
Armstrong, P., *The Abandonment of Productive Intervention in Management Teaching Syllabi: An Historical Analysis* (Coventry, 1987).
Ashworth, W. A., *The History of the British Coal Industry*, vol. V: *The Nationalized Industry* (Oxford, 1986).
    The State in Business, 1945 to the Mid-1980s (1991).
Atkinson, A. B., *Poverty and Social Security* (1989).
Balogh, T., *The Dollar Crisis: Causes and Cure* (Oxford, 1949).
    Unequal Partners, vol. II: Historical Episodes (Oxford, 1963).

Barker, E., *The British between the Superpowers* (1984).

Barker, R., *Education and Politics* (Oxford, 1972).

Barnett, C., *The Audit of War* (1986).

The Lost Victory (1995).

Barry, E. E., *Nationalization in British Politics* (1965).

Bartlett, C. J., *British Foreign Policy in the Twentieth Century* (1989).

Bauer, P. T., *West African Trade* (1963).

Beechey, V. and Perkins, T., *A Matter of Hours: Women, Part-Time Work and the Labour Market* (Oxford, 1987).

Beer, S., *Modern British Politics* (1958).

Bell, P. W., *The Sterling Area in the Post-War World* (Oxford, 1956).

Benney, M., *Charity Main* (1948).

Bentley, M. and Stevenson, J., eds., *The Working Class in Modern British History* (Oxford, 1983).

Blackstone, T., *A Fair Start: The Provision of Pre-School Education* (1971).

Blank, S., *Government and Industry in Britain: The F.B.I. in Politics, 1945–65* (Farnborough, 1973).

Blaug, M., *The Economics of Education* (1966).

Booth, A., *British Economic Policy, 1931–49: A Keynesian Revolution?* (1989).

Booth, A. and Pack, M., *Employment, Capital and Economic Policy: Great Britain 1918–31* (Oxford, 1985).

Boyce, D., *British Capitalism at the Crossroads* (Cambridge, 1987).

Brady, R., *Crisis in Britain: Plans and Achievements of the Labour Government* (1950).

Brailsford, H. N., Hobson, J. A., Creech Jones, A. and Wise, E. F., *The Living Wage* (1926).

Brittan, S., *Steering the Economy* (1969).

Brooke, S., *Labour's War* (Oxford, 1992).

Brown, C., *Taxation: The Incentive to Work* (Oxford, 1980).

Brown, K. D., *Labour and Unemployment, 1900–1914* (Newton Abbott, 1971).

Brown, K. D., ed., *The First Labour Party, 1906–14* (1985).

Brown, W. A. and Howell-Everson, N., *Industrial Democracy at Work* (1950).

Bullock, A., *Ernest Bevin, Foreign Secretary* (Oxford, 1985).

Burn, D., *The Steel Industry 1939–1959* (Cambridge, 1961).

Burnham, J., *The Managerial Revolution* (1942).

Burnham, P., *The Political Economy of Postwar Reconstruction* (1990).

Burridge, T., *Clement Attlee: A Political Biography* (1985).

Cain, P. and Hopkins, W. G., *British Imperialism: Crisis and Deconstruction* (1993).

Callaghan, J., *Socialism in Britain since 1884* (Oxford, 1990).

Cairncross, A., *Years of Recovery: British Economic Policy 1945–51* (1986).

Cairncross, A. and Watts, N., *The Economic Section 1939–61: A Study in Economic Advising* (1989).

Carew, A., *Labour under the Marshall Plan* (Manchester, 1987).

Carter, A. M., *The Redistribution of Income in Postwar Britain* (New Haven, 1955).

Caves, R., ed., *Britain's Economic Prospects* (Washington, D.C., 1968).

Chalmers, M., *Paying for Defence: Military Spending and British Decline* (1985).

Chester, D. N., *The Nationalisation of British Industry, 1945–51* (1975).

Chick, M., ed., *Governments, Industries and Markets* (Aldershot, 1991).

Child, J., *British Management Thought* (1969).

Clark, I. and Wheeler, N. I., *The British Origins of Nuclear Strategy, 1945–55* (Oxford, 1989).

Clarke, R. W. B., *Anglo-American Co-operation in War and Peace, 1942–49*, ed. A. Cairncross (Oxford, 1982).

Clegg, H. A., *A History of British Trade Unionism since 1889*, vol. III: *1934–51* (Oxford, 1994).

Coates, D., *Labour in Power: A Study of the Labour Government, 1974–9* (1980).

Cole, G. D. H., *The Machinery of Socialist Planning* (1938).

Cole, G. D. H., ed., *What Everybody Wants to Know about Money* (1936).

Cole, M., *Miners and the Board* (1949).

Coleman, D. C., *Courtaulds: An Economic and Social History* (Oxford, 1980).

Conan, A. R., *The Sterling Area* (Oxford, 1952).

Court, W. H. B., *Coal* (1951).

Craig, F. W. S., ed., *British General Election Manifestos, 1900–74* (1970).

Crofts, W., *Coercion or Persuasion? Economic Propaganda 1945–51* (1989).

Cronin, J. E., *The Politics of State Expansion: War, State and Society in Twentieth Century Britain* (1991).

Crosland, C. A. R., *Britain's Economic Problem* (1953).

The Future of Socialism (1956).

Crossman, R. H. S., ed., *New Fabian Essays* (1952).

Crossman, R. H. S., Foot, M. and Mikardo, M., *Keep Left* (1947).

Currie, R., *Industrial Politics* (1979).

Cutler, T., Williams, J. and Williams, K., *Keynes, Beveridge and Beyond* (1986).

Dalton, H., *The Inequality of Incomes* (1920).

Principles of Public Finance (1923).

Practical Socialism for Britain (1935).

Memoirs, vol. I: *The Fateful Years* (1957).

Memoirs, vol. II: *High Tide and After* (1962).

Danchev, A., *Oliver Franks, Founding Father* (Oxford, 1993).

Davenport, N., *Memoirs of a City Radical* (1974).

Davies, E., *National Capitalism* (1940).

Davis Smith, J., *The Attlee and Churchill Governments and Industrial Unrest* (1990).

Deighton, A., ed., *Britain and the First Cold War* (1990).

Dell, E., *The Schuman Plan and the Abdication of British Leadership in Europe* (Oxford, 1995).

Devons, E., *Planning in Practice* (Cambridge, 1950).

Essays in Economics (1961).

Dickinson, H., *Economics of Socialism* (Oxford, 1939).

Dockrill, M. and Young, J. W., eds., *British Foreign Policy, 1945–56* (1989).

Dornbusch, R., Nolling, W. and Layand, R., eds., *Postwar Economic Reconstruction and the Lessons for the East Today* (Cambridge, Mass., 1993).

Dow, J. C. R., *The Management of the British Economy, 1945–60* (Cambridge, 1965).

Dowse, R. E., *Left in the Centre: The I.L.P. 1893–1940* (1966).

Drummond, I., *Imperial Economic Policy 1917–39* (1974).

Durbin, Evan, *The Politics of Democratic Socialism* (1940).

Problems of Socialist Planning (1949).

Durbin, Elizabeth, *New Jerusalems: The Labour Party and the Economics of Democratic Socialism* (1985).

Durcan, J. W., McCarthy, W. E. J. and Redman, G. P., *Strikes in Postwar Britain* (1983).

Eichengreen, B. and Cairncross, A., *Sterling in Decline* (Oxford, 1983).

Elbaum, B. and Lazonick, W., eds., *The Decline of the British Economy* (Oxford, 1987).

Feinstein, C. H., *National Income, Expenditure and Output of the UK, 1855–1965* (Cambridge, 1972).

Fforde, J., *The Bank of England and Public Policy, 1941–1958* (1992).

Fielding, S., Thompson, P. and Tiratsoo, N., *England Arise!: The Labour Party and Popular Politics in the 1940s* (Manchester, 1995).

Flanders, A. and Clegg, H., *The System of Industrial Relations in Great Britain* (Oxford, 1964).

Foot, M., *Aneurin Bevan 1945–60* (1975).

Foote, G., *The Labour Party's Political Thought: A History* (Beckenham, 1985).

Franks, O., *Central Planning and Control in War and Peace* (1947).

Friedberg, A. L., *The Weary Titan: Britain and the Experience of Relative Decline, 1895–1905* (Princeton, 1988).

Gardner, R. N., *Sterling–Dollar Diplomacy* (Oxford, 1956).

Goodin, R. E. and Le Grand, J., *Not Only the Poor* (1987).

Gourvish, T., *British Railways 1948–1973: A Business History* (Cambridge, 1986).

Gourvish, T. and O'Day, A. eds., *Britain since 1945* (1991).

Griffiths, J., *Pages from Memory* (1969).

Gummett, P., *Scientists in Whitehall* (Manchester, 1980).

Gupta, P. S., *Imperialism and the British Labour Movement* (1975).

Hague, D. C. and Wilkinson, G., *The I.R.C.* (1983).

Hall, R., *The Economic System in a Socialist State* (1937).

The Robert Hall Diaries, ed. A. Cairncross (1989).

Hannah, L., *Electricity before Nationalisation* (1979).

Engineers, Managers and Politicians: The First Fifteen Years of Nationalised Electricity Supply in Britain (1982).

Inventing Retirement (Cambridge, 1986).

Harris, J., *Unemployment and Politics: A Study in English Social Policy, 1886–1914* (Oxford, 1972).

William Beveridge: A Biography (Oxford, 1977).

Hayek, F., ed., *Collectivist Economic Planning* (1935).

The Road to Serfdom (1944).

Individualism and Economic Order (1948).

Heald, D., *Public Expenditure: Its Defence and Reform* (Oxford, 1983).

Healey, D., *Cards on the Table* (1947).

Heinemann, M., *Coal Must Come First* (1948).

Hennessy, P., *Whitehall* (1989).

Never Again: Britain 1945–51 (1992).

Hindess, B., *Freedom, Equality and the Market* (1987).

Hinton, J., *Shop Floor Citizens: Engineering Democracy in 1940s Britain* (1995).

Hirst, P. Q., ed., *The Pluralist Theory of the State: Selected Writings of G. D. H. Cole, J. N. Figgis and H. J. Laski* (1989).

Hobson, J. A., *The Evolution of Modern Capitalism* (1894).

Hoff, T. J. B., *Economic Calculation in a Socialist State* (1949, reprinted Chicago, 1981).

Holderness, B., *British Agriculture since 1945* (1985).

Horsefield, J. K., *The International Monetary Fund 1946–1965*, 3 vols. (Washington, 1969).

Howell, D., *British Social Democracy* (1976).

   British Workers and the Independent Labour Party 1885–1906 (Manchester, 1983).

Howson, S., *British Monetary Policy 1945–51* (Oxford, 1993).

Hutchison, T. W., *Economics and Economic Policy in Britain, 1946–66* (1968).

Ilersic, A. R., *Government Finance and Fiscal Policy in Postwar Britain* (1955).

Jaques, E., *The Changing Culture of a Factory* (1951).

Jay, D., *The Socialist Case* (1937).

   Change and Fortune (1980).

Jay, D., ed., *The Road to Recovery* (1948).

Jewkes, J., *Ordeal by Planning* (1948).

   The Genesis of the British N.H.S. (Oxford, 1962).

Jones, B. and Keating, M., *Labour and the British State* (Oxford, 1985).

Jones, G. and Kirby, M. W., eds., *Competitiveness and the State* (Manchester, 1991).

Jones, R., *Wages and Employment Policy, 1936–1985* (1987).

Kent, J., *British Imperial Strategy and the Origins of the Cold War* (Leicester, 1994).

Keohane, D., *Labour Party Defence Policy since 1945* (Leicester, 1993).

Keynes, J. M., *Collected Writings*, vol. XXI: *Activities 1931–39: World Crises and Policies in Britain and America* (1982).

   vol. XXIII: *Activities 1940–3: Internal War Finance* (1979).

   vol. XXIV: *Activities 1944–6: The Transition to Peace* (1979).

   vol. XXV: *Activities 1940–4: Shaping the Postwar World: the Clearing Union* (1979).

   vol. XXVI: *Activities 1941–6: Shaping the Postwar World: Bretton Woods and Reparations* (1981).

   vol. XXVII: *Activities 1941–6: Shaping the Postwar World: Employment and Commodities* (1980).

Kindleberger, C. P., *Marshall Plan Days* (Boston, 1987).

King, G. S., *The Ministry of Pensions and National Insurance* (1958).

Kirby, M. W., *The British Coal-mining Industry 1870–1946* (1977).

Klein, R., *The Politics of the National Health Service* (1989).

Klein, V., *Britain's Married Women Workers* (1975).

Kuniholm, B. R., *The Origins of the Cold War in the Near East* (1980).

Kynaston, D., *The Financial Times: A Centenary History* (1988).

Labour Party, *Labour and the New Social Order* (1918).

   Labour and the Nation (1928).

   Labour's Reply to Lloyd George: How to Conquer Unemployment (1929).

Currency, Banking and Finance (1932).
For Socialism and Peace (1934).
Labour's Immediate Programme (1937).
Full Employment and Financial Policy (1944).
Let Us Face the Future (1945).
Production: the Bridge to Socialism (1948).
Labour Believes in Britain (1949).
Labour and the New Society (1950).
Let Us Win Through Together (1950).
Research Department RD33, *Criteria for Nationalisation* (1946).
Research Department RD38, *Public Ownership: The Next Step* (1947).
Research Department RD161, *Future Nationalisation Policy* (1948).
Research Department RD300, *Competitive Public Enterprise* (1949).
Lange, O. and Taylor, F. M., *On the Economic Theory of Socialism*, ed. B. Lippincott (New York, 1938).
Lavoie, D., *The Calculation Debate Reconsidered* (Cambridge, 1985).
Le Grand, J., *The Strategy of Equality* (1982).
Lerner, A. P., *The Economics of Control* (1945).
Leruez, J., *Economic Planning and Politics in Britain* (Oxford, 1975).
Lewenhak, S., *Women and Trade Unions* (1977).
Lewis, J., *Women in Britain since 1945* (1992).
Liberal Party, *Industrial Inquiry* (1928).
Locke, R., *Management and Higher Education since 1940* (Cambridge, 1989).
Loebl, H., *Government Factories and the Origins of British Regional Policy 1934–1948* (1988).
Lowe, Rodney, *The Welfare State in Britain since 1945* (1992).
Lowe, Roy, *Education in the Postwar Years* (1988).
Lowndes, G., *The Silent Social Revolution* (2nd edn, 1969).
McBriar, A. M., *Fabian Socialism and English Politics 1884–1918* (Cambridge, 1962).
McKeown, T., *The Role of Medicine: Dream, Mirage or Nemesis?* (Oxford, 1979).
McKibbin, R., *The Evolution of the Labour Party 1910–1924* (Oxford, 1974).
McKinlay, A. and Melling, J., eds., *Management, Labour and Production in Twentieth Century Europe* (1996).
Maclennan, G., and Parr, J. B., eds., *Regional Policy: Past Experience and New Directions* (Oxford, 1979).
Macmillan, H. *The Middle Way* (1938).
MacNicol, J., *The Movement for Family Allowances 1918–45: A Study in Social Policy Development* (1980).
Macrosty, H. W., *Trusts and the State* (1901).
The Trust Movement in Great Britain (1907).
Manser, W. A. P., *Britain in Balance: The Myth of Failure* (1971).
Marris, R., *The Machinery of Economic Policy* (1954).
Martin, D. E. and Rubinstein, D., eds., *Ideology and the Labour Movement* (1990).
Marwick, A., *Britain in the Century of Total War* (1968).
War and Social Change in the Twentieth Century (1975).
The Home Front (1976).

314   Bibliography

Mass Observation, *War Factory* (1943; republished 1987).
Matthews, R. C. O., Feinstein, C. H. and Odling-Smee, J., *British Economic Growth 1856–1973* (Oxford, 1982).
Mayhew, C., *Planned Investment*, Fabian Research Series no. 45 (1939).
Meade, J. E., *An Introduction to Economic Analysis and Policy* (Oxford, 1936).
    Planning and the Price Mechanism (1948).
    The Intelligent Radical's Guide to Economic Policy (1975).
    Collected Papers, vol. I: *Employment and Inflation* (1989).
    Collected Papers, vol. IV: *The Cabinet Office Diary 1944–46* (1990).
Mercer, H., *Constructing a Competitive Order: The Hidden History of British Anti-Trust* (Cambridge, 1995).
Mercer, H., Rollings, N., Tomlinson, J., eds., *Labour Governments and Private Industry: The Experience of 1945–51* (Edinburgh, 1992).
Middlemas, K., *Power, Competition and the State*, vol. I: *1940–61: Britain in Search of Balance* (1986).
Miliband, R., *Parliamentary Socialism*, 2nd. edn (1972).
Millward, R. and Singleton, J., eds., *The Political Economy of Nationalisation in Britain 1920–50* (Cambridge, 1994).
Milward, A. S., *The Reconstruction of Western Europe 1945–51* (1984).
Ministry of Education, *Education 1900–1950* (1951).
    Education in 1951 (1952).
Mitchell, J., *Crisis in Britain, 1951* (1951).
Moggridge, D. E., *Maynard Keynes: An Economist's Biography* (1992).
Montgomery, B., *Memoirs* (1956).
Morgan, D. J., *Official History of Colonial Development*, vol. II: *Developing Colonial Resources 1945–51* (1980).
Morgan, K. O., *Keir Hardie: Radical and Socialist* (1975).
    Labour in Power 1945–51 (Oxford, 1984).
Morrison, H., *Socialisation and Transport* (1933).
    Government and Parliament (Oxford, 1959).
Munro, D., ed., *Socialism: The British Way* (1948).
Nicholas, H. G., *The British General Election of 1950* (Oxford, 1951).
Ovendale, R., ed., *The Foreign Policy of the British Labour Governments 1945–51* (Leicester, 1984).
National Coal Board, *Annual Report* (1947).
    Annual Report (1948).
    Annual Report (1949).
    Plan for Coal (1950).
    Advisory Committee on Organization, [Fleck] *Report* (1955).
    National Consultative Committee, *Joint Consultation in Coal* (1948).
National Institute of Industrial Psychology, *Joint Consultation* (1952).
Panitch, L., *Social Democracy and Industrial Militancy* (Cambridge, 1976).
Parsons, D. W., *The Political Economy of British Regional Policy* (1986).
Payne, P., *Colvilles and the Scottish Steel Industry* (Oxford, 1979).
Peacock, A. T., ed., *Income Distribution and Social Policy* (1954).
Pelling, H., *The Labour Governments 1945–51* (1984).
Phelps Brown, E. H., *The Origins of Trade Union Power* (Oxford, 1986).
    Egalitarianism and the Generation of Inequality (Oxford, 1988).

Pimlott, B., *Hugh Dalton* (1985).

Plowden, E., *An Industrialist in the Treasury* (1989).

Political and Economic Planning, *Manpower* (1951).
Technological Education (1952).

Porter, A. N. and Stockwell, A. J., *British Imperial Policy and Decolonisation 1938–64*, vol. I: *1938–51* (1987).

Pressnell, L., *External Economic Policy since the War*, vol. III: *The Post-war Financial Settlement* (1986).

Pritt, D. N., *The Labour Government, 1945–51* (1963).

Pugh, M., *Women and the Women's Movement in Britain 1914–1959* (1992).

Reader, W. J., *I.C.I.: A History* (1975).

Riley, D., *War in the Nursery* (1983).

Robbins, L., *Economic Planning in Peace and War* (1947).

Roberts, B. C., *National Wages Policy in War and Peace* (1958).

Robinson, E. A. G., *Economic Planning in the UK: Some Lessons* (Cambridge, 1967).

Robson, W. A., ed., *Social Security* (1937).

Rogow, A. A. and Shore, P., *The Labour Government and British Industry, 1945–51* (Oxford, 1955).

Rose, R., ed., *Public Employment in Western Nations* (Cambridge, 1985).

Rosenberg, N., *Economic Planning in the British Building Industry, 1945–49* (Philadelphia, 1960).

Rosencrance, R. N., *Defence of the Realm: British Strategy in a Nuclear Epoch* (1968).

Routh, G., *Occupation and Pay in Britain, 1905–1960* (Cambridge, 1965).

Rowntree, S. and Lavers, G., *Poverty and the Welfare State* (1951).

Russell, A., *The Growth of Occupational Welfare in Great Britain* (1991).

Sabine, B. E. V., *A History of Income Tax* (1966).

Sanderson, M., *The Universities and British Industry, 1850–1970* (1972).

Sandford, C., Pond, C. and Walker, R., eds., *Taxation and Social Policy* (1980).

Saville, J., *The Politics of Continuity* (1993).

Sayers, R. S., *British Financial Policy 1939–45* (1956).
The Bank of England (Cambridge, 1976).

Schenk, C., *Britain and the Sterling Area: From Devaluation to Convertibility in the 1950s* (1994).

Schneer, J., *Labour's Conscience: The Labour Left 1945–51* (1988).

Scott, J. D., *Vickers: A History* (1962).

Scott, L. V., *Conscription and the Attlee Governments: The Politics and Policy of National Service, 1945–51* (Oxford, 1993).

Scott, W. H., *Industrial Leadership and Joint Consultation* (Liverpool, 1952).

Searle, G. R., *The Quest for National Efficiency* (Oxford, 1971).

Seers, D., *The Levelling of Incomes since 1938* (Oxford, 1951).

Shanks, M., ed., *The Lessons of Public Enterprise* (1963).

Sharp, T., *The Wartime Alliance and the Zonal Division of Germany* (1975).

Shaw, B., *Fabian Essays in Socialism 1889* (1948 edn).

Shonfield, A., *British Economic Policy since the War* (1959).

Singleton, J., *Lancashire on the Scrapheap* (Oxford, 1991).

Skidelsky, R., *Politicians and the Slump: The Labour Government of 1929–31* (1970).
  Oswald Mosley (1975).
Smith, H. L. (ed.) *War and Social Change* (1986).
  British Feminism in the Twentieth Century (1990).
Smith, T., *The Politics of the Corporate Economy* (1979).
Snowden, P., *A Few Hints to Lloyd George: Where Is the Money to Come From?* (1909).
  Labour and National Finance (1920).
Stewart, W. A. C., *Higher Education in Postwar Britain* (1989).
Strachey, J., *Revolution by Reason* (1924).
Strange, S., *Sterling and British Policy* (Oxford, 1971).
Streat, R., *Lancashire and Whitehall: The Diary of Sir Raymond Streat*, ed. M. Duprée (1987).
Summerfield, P., *Women Workers in the Second World War: Production and Patriarchy in Conflict* (1984).
Supple, B., *The History of the British Coal Industry*, vol. IV: *The Political Economy of Decline* (Oxford, 1987).
Tanner, D., *Political Change and the Labour Party 1900–18* (Cambridge, 1990).
Tawney, R. H., *Equality* (1952).
Tew, B. and Henderson, P. D., *Studies in Company Finance* (Cambridge, 1959).
Theakston, K., *The Labour Party and Whitehall* (1992).
Thomas, G., *Women and Industry*, Social Survey for the Ministry of Labour and National Service (1948).
Thorpe, A., *The British General Election of 1931* (Oxford, 1991).
Tiratsoo, N., *Reconstruction, Affluence, and Labour Politics: Coventry 1945–60* (1990).
Tiratsoo, N., ed., *The Attlee Years* (1991).
Tiratsoo, N. and Tomlinson, J., *Industrial Efficiency and State Intervention: Labour 1939–51* (1993).
Titmuss, R., *Problems of Social Policy* (1950).
  Essays on the Welfare State (1958).
  Income Distribution and Social Change (1962).
Tomlinson, J., *Problems of British Economic Policy 1870–1945* (1981).
  The Unequal Struggle?: British Socialism and the Capitalist Enterprise (1982).
  Employment Policy: The Crucial Years 1939–55 (Oxford, 1987).
  Hayek and the Market (1990).
  Government and the Enterprise since 1900: The Changing Problem of Efficiency (Oxford, 1994).
Trade Union Congress, *Interim Report on Postwar Reconstruction* (1944).
Turner, H. A., *Trade Union Growth, Structure and Policy: A Comparative Study of the Cotton Unions* (1962).
Turner, J., ed., *Businessmen and Politics* (1984).
Vaizey, J., *The Costs of Education* (1958).
van Dormel, A., *Bretton Woods: Birth of a Monetary System* (1978).
Vernon, B., *Ellen Wilkinson, 1891–1947* (Beckenham, 1982).
Vig, N. J., *Science and Technology in British Politics* (Oxford, 1968).

Warde, A. *Consensus and Beyond: The Development of Labour Party Strategy since the Second World War* (Manchester, 1982).

Webb, S., *Twentieth Century Politics: A Policy of National Efficiency*, Fabian Tract 108 (1901).

The Works Manager Today (1917).

Webb, S. and Webb, B., *Problems of Modern Industry* (1902).

Constitution for a Socialist Commonwealth of Great Britain (1920).

The Decay of Capitalist Civilisation (1923).

Webster, C., *The Health Services since the War*, vol. 1: *Problems of Health Care. The National Health Service before 1957* (1988).

Williams, P., *Hugh Gaitskell* (1982).

Williams, P., ed., *The Diary of Hugh Gaitskell, 1945–56* (1983).

Williamson, P., *National Crisis and National Government: British Politics, the Economy and Empire, 1926–32* (Cambridge, 1992).

Wilson, T. and Andrews, P. W. S., eds., *Oxford Studies in the Price Mechanism* (Oxford, 1951).

Winch, D., *Economics and Policy* (1972).

Winter, J., *Socialism and the Challenge of War* (1974).

The Working Class in Modern British History (Cambridge, 1983).

Wootton, B., *Freedom under Planning* (1945).

The Social Foundations of Wages Policy (1962).

Worswick, G. D. N. and Ady, P. H., eds., *The British Economy 1945–50* (Oxford, 1952).

Wright, A. W., *G. D. H. Cole and Socialist Democracy* (Oxford, 1979).

R. H. Tawney (Manchester, 1987).

Zweig, F., *Productivity and the Trade Unions* (Oxford, 1952).

Women's Life and Labour (Oxford, 1952).

Zysman, J., *Governments, Markets and Growth: Financial Systems and the Politics of Industrial Change* (Ithaca, 1983).

ARTICLES AND THESES

Abramowitz, M., 'Catching Up, Forging Ahead and Falling Behind', *Journal of Economic History* 66 (1986), pp. 385–406.

Adamthwaite, A., 'Britain and the World 1945–9: The View from the Foreign Office', *International Affairs* 61 (1985), pp. 223–35.

Albu, A., 'Ministerial and Parliamentary Control' in M. Shanks, ed., *The Lessons of Public Enterprise* (1963), pp. 90–113.

Atkinson, A. B., 'Poverty in York: A Re-analysis of Rowntree's 1950 Survey' in A. B. Atkinson, ed., *Poverty and Social Security* (1989), pp. 62–76.

Attlee, C. R., 'Civil Servants, Ministers, Parliament and the Public', *Political Quarterly* 25 (1954), pp. 308–15.

Balogh, T., 'Britain's Foreign Trade Problem', *Economic Journal* 58 (1948), pp. 74–85.

'Britain's Economic Problem', *Quarterly Journal of Economics* 43 (1949), pp. 32–76.

Barna, T., 'Those "Frightfully High" Profits', *Oxford University Bulletin of Statistics* 11 (1949), pp. 213–26.

Bauer, P., 'Statistics of Statutory Marketing in West Africa, 1939–51', *Journal of the Royal Statistical Society* 117 (1954) pp. 1–20.

Blank, S., 'Britain: The Politics of Foreign Economic Policy, the Domestic Economy, and the Problem of Pluralistic Stagnation', *International Organization* 31 (1977), pp. 673–721.

Booth, A., 'The "Keynesian Revolution" in Economic Policy-Making', *Economic History Review* 36 (1983), pp. 103–23.

'Britain in the 1930s: A Managed Economy?' *Economic History Review* 40 (1987), pp. 499–522.

Brittain, J. A., 'Some Neglected Features of Britain's Income Levelling', *American Economic Review* 50 (1960), pp. 593–603.

Broadbery, S. and Crafts, N., 'Explaining Anglo-American Productivity Differences in the Mid-Twentieth Century', *Bulletin of the Oxford University Institute of Statistics* 52 (1990), pp. 375–402.

Brooke, S., 'Revisionists and Fundamentalists: The Labour Party and Economic Policy during the Second World War', *Historical Journal* 32 (1989), pp. 157–75.

'Problems of "Socialist Planning": Evan Durbin and the Labour Government of 1945', *Historical Journal* 34 (1991), pp. 678–702.

Brookshire, J. H., 'Clement Attlee and Cabinet Reform 1930–45', *Historical Journal* 24 (1981), pp. 175–88.

Burchardt, F. A., 'Cuts in Capital Expenditure', *Bulletin of the Oxford Institute of Statistics* 10 (1948), pp. 1–8.

Burgess, S., 'The Attlee Governments in Perspective: Commitment and Detachment in the Writing of Contemporary History', Ph.D. thesis, London School of Economics, 1994.

Burn, D., 'The National Coal Board', *Lloyds Bank Review* 19 (1951), pp. 33–48.

Cairncross, A., 'Saving and Investment since the War', *Westminster Bank Review* (1955), pp. 4–8.

Callaghan, James, 'The Approach to Social Equality' in D. Munro, ed., *Socialism: The British Way* (1948), pp. 127–52.

Callaghan, John, 'In Search of Eldorado: Labour's Colonial Economic Policy' in J. Fyrth, ed., *Labour's High Noon: The Government and the Economy 1945–51* (1993), pp. 115–34.

Carr, F., 'Cold War: The Economy and Foreign Policy' in J. Fyrth, ed., *Labour's High Noon* (1993), pp. 135–47.

Carruthers, S., 'Manning the Factories: Propaganda and Policy on the Employment of Women', *History* 75 (1990), pp. 232–56.

Chambers, S. P., 'Taxation and the Supply of Capital for Industry', *Lloyds Bank Review* 11 (1949), pp. 1–20.

Chester, D. N., 'Local Finance', *Lloyds Bank Review* 21 (1951), pp. 33–47.

Chick, M., 'Economic Planning, Managerial Decision-Making and the Role of Fixed Capital Investment in the Economic Recovery of the U.K. 1945–55', Ph.D. thesis, London School of Economics, 1986.

'Competition, Competitiveness and Nationalisation, 1945–51' in G. Jones and M. Kirby, eds., *Competitiveness and the State* (Manchester, 1991), pp. 60–77.

'Marginal Cost Pricing and the Post-war Demand for Electricity' in M. Chick, ed., *Governments, Industries and Markets* (1991), pp. 110–26.

Clegg, H. A. and Chester, T. E., 'Joint Consultation' in A. Flanders and H. A. Clegg, eds., *The System of Industrial Relations in Great Britain* (Oxford, 1964), pp. 338–46.

Cole, G. D. H., 'Labour and Staff Problems under Nationalisation', *Political Quarterly* 21 (1950), pp. 160–70.

Crafts, N., 'Adjusting from War to Peace in 1940s' Britain', *The Economic and Social Review* 25 (1993), pp. 1–20.

Crofts, S. W., 'The Attlee Governments' Pursuit of Women', *History Today* 36 (1986), pp. 29–35.

Crosland, C. A. R., 'The Movement of Labour in 1948', *Bulletin of the Oxford University Institute of Statistics* parts I and II, 11 (1949), pp. 117–26 and 194–212.

Dahl, R., 'Workers' Control of Industry and the British Labour Party', *American Political Science Review* 41 (1947), pp. 875–900.

Deacon, A., 'An End to the Means Test?: Social Security and the Attlee Government', *Journal of Social Policy* 11 (1982), pp. 289–306.

Dennison, S. R., 'The Price Policy of the NCB', *Lloyds Bank Review* 26 (1952), pp. 17–34.

Duprée, M., 'The Cotton Industry: A Middle Way between Nationalisation and Self-Government?' in H. Mercer, N. Rollings and J. Tomlinson, eds., *Labour Governments and Private Industry: The Experience of 1945–51*, (Edinburgh, 1991), pp. 137–61.

Edgerton, D., 'Whatever Happened to the Warfare State?: The Ministry of Supply, 1945–51' in H. Mercer, N. Rollings and J. Tomlinson, eds., *Labour Governments and Private Industry: The Experience of 1945–51* (Edinburgh, 1991), pp. 91–116.

Fieldhouse, K., 'The Labour Governments and the Empire-Commonwealth' in R. Ovendale, ed., *The Foreign Policy of the Labour Governments 1945–51* (Leicester, 1984), pp. 83–120.

Fielding, S., 'What Did "the People" Want?: The Meaning of the 1945 General Election', *Historical Journal* 35 (1992), pp. 623–39.

Flanders, A., 'Wages Policy and Full Employment in Britain', *Bulletin of the Oxford University Institute of Statistics* 12 (1950), pp. 225–42.

Florence, S. and Walker, G., 'Efficiency under Nationalisation and its Measurement', *Political Quarterly* 21 (1950), pp. 197–208.

Francis, M., 'Economics and Ethics: The Nature of Labour's Socialism, 1945–51', *Twentieth Century British History* 6 (1995), pp. 220–43.

'A Socialist Policy for Education?: Labour and the Secondary School 1945–51' *History of Education* 24 (1995), pp. 319–35.

Franklin, N. N., 'South Africa's Balance of Payments and the Sterling Area', *Economic Journal* 61 (1951), pp. 290–309.

Gaitskell, H., 'The Sterling Area', *International Affairs* 28 (1952), pp. 170–6.

Gilliatt, S., 'The Management of Reconstruction with Special Reference to the Housebuilding Programme', Ph.D. thesis, Sussex University, 1982.

Goodin, R. and Dryzek, J., 'Risk-Sharing and Social Justice: The Motivational Foundations of the Post-War Welfare State' in Goodin and Le Grand, eds., *Not Only the Poor* (1987), pp. 37–63.

Gordon, C., 'The Welfare State: Sources of Data on Government Expenditure', LSE Welfare State Programme WSP/RN/14 (1988).

Gourvish, T., 'The Rise (and Fall?) of State-Owned Enterprise' in T. Gourvish and A. O'Day, eds., *Britain since 1945* (1991), pp. 111–33.

Gowing, M., 'The Organisation of Manpower in Britain during the Second World War', *Journal of Contemporary History* 7 (1972), pp. 147–67.

Greasley, D., 'The Coal Industry: Images and Reality on the Road to Nationalisation' in R. Millward and J. Singleton, eds., *Political Economy of Nationalisation* (Cambridge, 1994), pp. 37–64.

Gupta, P. S., 'Imperialism and the Labour Governments, 1945–51' in J. M. Winter, ed., *The Working Class in Modern British History* (Cambridge, 1983), pp. 98–120.

Hakim, C., 'The Myth of Rising Female Employment', *Work, Employment and Society* 7 (1993), pp. 97–120.

Hall, R. and Hitch, C. J., 'Price Theory and Business Behaviour' in T. Wilson and P. W. S. Andrews, eds., *Oxford Studies in the Price Mechanism* (Oxford, 1951), pp. 107–38.

Harbury, C., 'Inheritance and the Distribution of Personal Wealth in Britain', *Economic Journal* 72 (1962), pp. 845–68.

Harris, J., 'Enterprise and the Welfare State: A Comparative Perspective' in T. Gourvish and A. O'Day, eds., *Britain since 1945* (1991), pp. 39–58.

Harrod, R., Review of Jewkes, *Ordeal by Planning, Economica* 15 (1948), p. 223.

Heim, C. E., 'Limits to Intervention: The Bank of England and Industrial Diversification in the Depressed Areas', *Economic History Review* 37 (1984), pp. 533–50.

'R and D, Defence, and the Spatial Division of Labour in Twentieth Century Britain', *Journal of Economic History* 47 (1987), pp. 365–78.

Henderson, H., 'A Criticism of the Havana Charter', *American Economic Review* 39 (1939), pp. 605–17.

Hicks, J. R., 'The Empty Economy', *Lloyds Bank Review* 5 (1947), pp. 1–13.

Hinds, A., 'Sterling and Imperial Policy, 1945–51', *Journal of Imperial and Commonwealth Policy* 15 (1987), pp. 148–69.

'Imperial Policy and the Colonial Sterling Balances, 1943–56', *Journal of Imperial and Commonwealth History* 19 (1991), pp. 24–44.

Holland, R. F., 'The Imperial Factor in British Strategies from Attlee to Macmillan', *Journal of Imperial and Commonwealth History* 12 (1984), pp. 165–86.

Howson, S., ' "Socialist" Monetary Policy: Monetary Thought in the Labour Party in the 1940s', *History of Political Economy* 20 (1988), pp. 433–52.

Hyam, R., 'Africa and the Labour Government, 1945–51', *Journal of Imperial and Commonwealth History* 16 (1988), pp. 148–72.

Jay, D., 'Civil Servant and Minister' in W. Rodgers, ed., *Hugh Gaitskell 1906–1963* (1964), pp. 77–103.

Jefferys, K., 'British Politics and Social Policy during the Second World War', *Historical Journal* 30 (1987), pp. 123–44.

Jenkins, R., 'Equality' in R. H. S. Crossman, ed., *New Fabian Essays* (1952), pp. 69–90.

Kent, J., 'Bevin's Imperialism and the Idea of Euro-Africa, 1945–49' in M. Dockrill and J. W. Young, eds., *British Foreign Policy 1945–56* (1989), pp. 47–75.

'The British Empire and the Origins of the Cold War, 1944–49' in A. Deighton, ed., *Britain and the First Cold War* (1990), pp. 165–83.

Kenworthy, L., 'Are Industrial Policy and Corporatism Compatible?', *Journal of Public Policy* 10 (1990), pp. 233–65.

Land, H., 'The Family Wage', *Feminist Review* 6 (1980), pp. 55–77.

L'Estrange Fawcett, L., 'Invitation to the Cold War: British Policy in Iran, 1941–47' in A. Deighton, ed., *Britain and the First Cold War* (1990), pp. 184–200.

Little, I. M. D., 'The Economist in Whitehall', *Lloyds Bank Review* 44 (1957), pp. 29–40.

Lowe, R., 'The Second World War, Consensus, and the Foundations of the Welfare State', *Twentieth Century British History* 1 (1990), pp. 152–182.

Lydall, H. F. and Tipping, D. G., 'The Distribution of Personal Wealth in Britain', *Bulletin of Oxford University Institute of Statistics* 23 (1961), pp. 83–104.

McCallum, J. D., 'The Development of British Regional Policy' in D. Maclennan and J. B. Parr, eds., *Regional Policy: Past Experiences and New Directions* (Oxford, 1979).

MacDougall, G. D. A., 'Britain's Foreign Trade Problem: A Reply', *Economic Journal* 58 (1948), pp. 86–98.

McKibbin, R., 'The Economic Policy of the Second Labour Government 1929–31', *Past and Present* 68 (1975), pp. 95–123.

Marwick, A., 'Middle Opinion in the Thirties: Planning, Progress and Political "Agreement" ', *English Historical Review* 79 (1964), pp. 285–98.

Meade, J., 'Bretton Woods, Havana, and the UK Balance of Payments', *Lloyds Bank Review* 7 (1948), pp. 1–18.

'Planning without Prices', *Economica* 15 (1948), pp. 28–35.

Mercer, H., 'The Labour Governments of 1945–51 and Private Industry' in N. Tiratsoo, ed., *The Attlee Years* (1991), pp. 71–89.

'Anti-monopoly Policy' in H. Mercer *et al.*, eds., *Labour Governments* (1992), pp. 55–73.

Minford, P., 'Reconstruction and the UK Postwar Welfare State: False Start and New Beginning' in R. Dornbusch, W. Nolling and R. Layard, eds., *Postwar Economic Reconstruction and the Lessons for the East Today* (Cambridge, Mass. 1993), pp. 115–38.

Morgan, K. O., 'The High and Low Politics of Labour' in M. Bentley and J. Stevenson, eds., *The Working Class in Modern British History* (Oxford, 1983), pp. 285–312.

Newton, C., 'The Sterling Crisis of 1947 and the British Response to the Marshall Plan', *Economic History Review* 37 (1984), pp. 391–408.

'Britain, the Sterling Area, and European Integration', *Journal of Imperial and Commonwealth History* 13 (1985), pp. 163–82.

Nicholson, R. J. and Gupta, S., 'Output and Productivity Changes in British Manufacturing, 1948–52', *Journal of the Royal Statistical Society* 23 (1960), pp. 427–59.

Oldfield, A., 'The Labour Party and Planning – 1934 or 1918?', *Bulletin of the Society for the Study of Social History* 25 (1972), pp. 41–55.

Ostergaard, G. N., 'Labour and the Development of the Public Corporation', *Manchester School* 22 (1954), pp. 192–216.

Parry, R., 'Britain: Stable Aggregates, Changing Composition' in R. Rose, ed., *Public Employment in Western Nations* (Cambridge, 1985), pp. 54–96.

Paul, K., ' "British Subjects" and "British Stock": Labour's Postwar Imperialism', *Journal of British Studies* 34 (1995), pp. 233–76.

Peacock, A. T. and Browning, P. R., 'The Social Services in Great Britain and the Redistribution of Income' in A. T. Peacock, ed., *Income Distribution and Social Policy* (1954), pp. 139–77.

Peck, M., 'Science and Technology' in R. Caves, ed., *Britain's Economic Prospects* (Washington, 1968), pp. 448–84.

Peden, G. C., 'Sir Richard Hopkins and the "Keynesian Revolution" in Employment Policy, 1928–45', *Economic History Review* 36 (1983), pp. 281–96.

Pigou, A. C., Review of *The Road to Serfdom*, *Economic Journal* 54 (1944), pp. 217–19.

 'Central Planning and Professor Robbins', *Economica* 15 (1948), pp. 17–27.

Political and Economic Planning, 'Employment of Women', *Planning* 15 (1948), pp. 37–53.

Pollard, S., 'The Nationalisation of the Banks: The Chequered History of a Socialist Proposal' in D. E. Martin and D. Rubinstein, eds., *Ideology and the Labour Movement* (1990), pp. 167–90.

Pond, C., 'Tax Expenditures and Fiscal Welfare' in C. Sandford, C. Pond and R. Walker, eds., *Taxation and Social Policy* (1980), pp. 47–63.

Pugh, M., 'Domesticity and the Decline of Feminism' in H. L. Smith, ed., *British Feminism in the Twentieth Century* (1990), pp. 144–64.

Radice, E. A., 'Commercial Banks and Credit' in G. D. H. Cole, ed., *What Everybody Wants to Know about Money* (1937), pp. 162–225.

Reddaway, W. B. and Smith, A. B., 'Progress in British Manufacturing Industries, 1948–50', *Economic Journal* 70 (1960), pp. 17–31.

Riley, D., 'War in the Nursery', *Feminist Review* 2 (1979), pp. 82–108.

 'The Free Mothers: Pro-natalism and Working Women in Industry at the End of the Last War in Britain', *History Workshop* 11 (1981), pp. 58–118.

Ritschel, D., 'A Corporatist Economy in Britain? Capitalist Planning for Industrial Self-Government in the 1930s', *English Historical Review* 106 (1991), pp. 57–64.

Roberts, R., 'The Administrative Origins of Industrial Diplomacy: An Aspect of Government–Industry Relations, 1929–35' in J. Turner, ed., *Businessmen and Politics* (1984), pp. 93–104.

Robertson, D. H., 'The Economic Outlook', *Economic Journal* 57 (1947), pp. 421–437.

Robinson, A., 'The Economic Problems of the Transition from War to Peace, 1945–9', *Cambridge Journal of Economics* 10 (1986), pp. 165–85.

Rollings, N., 'British Budgetary Policy 1945–54: A "Keynesian Revolution?" ', *Economic History Review* 41 (1988), pp. 283–98.

'The Control of Inflation in the Managed Economy: Britain 1945–53', Ph.D. thesis, Bristol University, 1990.

'The Reichstag Method of Governing? The Attlee Government and Economic Controls' in H. Mercer et al., eds., *Labour Governments* (1992), pp. 15–36.

'Poor Mr. Butskell: A Short Life Wrecked by Schizophrenia?', *Twentieth Century British History* 5 (1994), pp. 183–205.

Rosenhead, J., 'Operational Research at the Crossroads: Cecil Gordon and the Development of Postwar OR', *Journal of the Operational Research Society* 40 (1989), pp. 9–15.

Rostas, L., 'Changes in the Productivity of British Industry, 1945–50', *Economic Journal* 62 (1952), pp. 15–24.

Schumpeter, J., 'English Economists and the State-Managed Economy', *Journal of Political Economy*, 57 (1949), pp. 371–82.

Shannon, H., 'The Sterling Balances of the Sterling Area', *Economic Journal* 60 (1950), pp. 531–51.

Sinfield, A., 'Analyses of the Social Division of Welfare', *Journal of Social Policy* 7 (1978), pp. 129–56.

Singleton, J., 'Planning for Cotton 1945–51', *Economic History Review* 43 (1990), pp. 62–78.

'Showing the White Flag: The Lancashire Cotton Industry 1945–65', *Business History* 32 (1990), pp. 129–49.

'Planning for Cotton: A Reply', *Economic History Review* 44 (1991), pp. 526–30.

Smith, H. L., 'The Problem of Equal Pay for Equal Work in Great Britain during World War II', *Journal of Modern History* 53 (1981), pp. 652–72.

'The Womanpower Problem in Britain during the Second World War', *Historical Journal* 27 (1984), pp. 925–45.

'Women in the Second World War' in H. L. Smith, ed., *War and Social Change* (1986), pp. 66–89.

Smith, R. and Zametica, J., 'The Cold Warrior: Clement Attlee Reconsidered', *International Affairs* 61 (1985), pp. 237–52.

Stevenson, J. ' "The Jerusalem that Failed?": The Rebuilding of Post-War Britain' in T. Gourvish and A. O'Day, eds., *Britain since 1945* (1991), pp. 89–110

Strachey, J., 'Tasks and Achievements of British Labour' in R. H. S. Crossman, ed., *New Fabian Essays* (1952), pp. 181–215.

Summerfield, P., 'Women, Work and Warfare: A Study of Childcare and Shopping in Britain during the Second World War', *Journal of Social History* 17 (1983/4), pp. 240–69.

Tawney, R. H., 'The Abolition of Economic Controls 1918–21', *Economic History Review* 13 (1943), pp. 1–13.

Thane, P., 'The Working Class and State "Welfare" in Britain, 1880–1914', *Historical Journal* 27 (1984), pp. 877–900.

'Towards Equal Opportunities' in T. Gourvish and A. O'Day, eds., *Britain since 1945* (1991), pp. 183–208.

Tiratsoo, N., 'The Motor Car Industry' in H. Mercer et al., eds., *Labour Governments* (1992), pp. 162–85.

Tomlinson, B. R., 'Indo-British Relations in the Post-Colonial Era: The Sterling Balances Negotiations, 1947–49', *Journal of Imperial and Commonwealth History* 13 (1985), pp. 142–62.

Tomlinson, J., 'Women as Anomalies: The Anomalies Regulations Act of 1931 and its Background and Implications', *Public Administration* 62 (1984), pp. 423–37.

'Planning for Cotton: A Comment', *Economic History Review* 44 (1991), pp. 522–5.

'The 1945 Labour Government and the Trade Unions' in N. Tiratsoo, ed., *Attlee Years* (1991), pp. 90–105.

'The Failure of the Anglo-American Council on Productivity', *Business History* 33 (1991), pp. 82–92.

'Planning: Debate and Policy in the 1940s', *Twentieth Century British History* 3 (1992), pp. 154–74.

'Mr. Attlee's Supply-Side Socialism', *Economic History Review* 46 (1993), pp. 1–22.

'The Iron Quadrilateral: Political Obstacles to Economic Reform under the Attlee Government', *Journal of British Studies* 34 (1995), pp. 90–111.

'Productivity, Joint Consultation and Human Relations: The Attlee Government and the Workplace' in A. McKinlay and J. Melling, eds., *Management, Labour and Production in Twentieth Century Europe* (1996), pp. 25–43.

'No Cosy Deals: British Economic Policy in the 1940s', *Journal of European Economic History*, forthcoming.

Townsend, P., 'Poverty: Ten Years after Beveridge', *Planning* 19 (1952), pp. 21–40.

von Mises, L., 'Economic Calculation in a Socialist Community' in F. Hayek, ed., *Collectivist Economic Planning* (1935), pp. 87–130.

Walker, G., 'Some Economic Aspects of the Taxation of Companies', *Manchester School* 22 (1954), pp. 1–36.

Weaver, F., 'Taxation and Redistribution in the UK', *Review of Economics and Statistics* 32 (1950), pp. 201–13.

Wedderburn, W., 'Freedom of Association and Philosophies of Labour Law', *Industrial Law Journal* 18 (1989), pp. 1–38.

Whiteside, N., 'Counting the Cost: Sickness and Disability among Working People in an Era of Industrial Recession, 1920–30', *Economic History Review* 40 (1987), pp. 228–46.

'Aiming at Consensus: Social Welfare and Industrial Relations 1939–79' in C. Wrigley, ed., *A History of British Industrial Relations*, forthcoming.

Whiting, R. C., 'Taxation Policy' in H. Mercer *et al.*, eds., *Labour Governments* (1992), pp. 117–34.

'The Boundaries of Taxation' in S. J. D. Green and R. C. Whiting, eds., *The Boundaries of the State in Modern Britain* , forthcoming.

Williamson, P., ' "Safety First": Baldwin, the Conservative Party, and the 1929 General Election', *Historical Journal* 25 (1982), pp. 385–409.

Wilson, T., 'Price and Outlay of State Enterprise', *Economic Journal* 55 (1945), pp. 454–61.

Winter, J., 'Arthur Henderson, the Russian Revolution, and the Reconstruction of the Labour Party', *Historical Journal* 15 (1973), pp. 753–73.

Zweiniger-Bargielowska, I., 'Industrial Relationships and Nationalisation in the South Wales Coal Mining Industry', Ph.D. thesis, Cambridge University, 1990.

'Colliery Managers and Nationalisation', *Business History* 34 (1992), pp. 59–78.

'Miners' Militancy: A Study of Four South Wales Collieries during the Middle of the Twentieth Century', *Welsh History Review* 16 (1993), pp. 356–89.

'Rationing, Austerity and the Conservative Party Recovery after 1945', *Historical Journal* 37 (1994), pp. 173–97.

Index